1979

A New America?

Essays by

Elizabeth Hardwick
Sydney E. Ahlstrom
Steven Muller
Rosabeth Moss Kanter
John T. Dunlop
Nancy Needham Wardell
Edward K. Hamilton
Louise Weinberg
Marvin E. Wolfgang
Adam Yarmolinsky
Paul Starr
Anthony Smith
Thomas Sowell
Elliot Zashin
Daniel Yergin
McGeorge Bundy
Ronald I. McKinnion
Pierre Nora

A New America?

Edited by STEPHEN R. GRAUBARD

 W · W · NORTON & COMPANY · INC · New York

Library of Congress Cataloging in Publication Date
Main entry under title:
A New America?
    Originally published as the winter 1978 issue of Dædalus.
    1. United States—Civilization—1970-   —Addresses, essays,
lectures.   I. Graubard, Stephen Richards.   II. Dædalus.
E169.12.N43   1978   973.92   78–12423
ISBN 0-393-01197-6
ISBN 0-393-095019-0 pbk.

1 2 3 4 5 6 7 8 9 0

Contents

Preface to the Issue
"A New America?"

FROM SOME TIME early in the 1960s, perhaps even before the assassination of John F. Kennedy, it was common to believe that the times were exceptional, that events were moving with unaccustomed speed, and that the United States would never again resemble what it had once been. That sentiment became even more pronounced as the decade proceeded; in the late 1960s and early 1970s, when new violence erupted, public confidence and trust were shaken. A host of established institutions, conventions, and opinions seemed suddenly threatened, and there was talk of "revolutionary" change touching much that had once seemed permanent and inviolable. No innovation seemed impossible. Why not believe, as many did, that we were witnessing the beginnings of a "new" politics, the creation of a "new" generation animated by "new" ideals and values, and responsive to "new" social demands? There was talk of a "new" morality; indeed, of a "new" liberty. The mass media, intentionally or unwittingly, abetted all such expectations; their foreshortened time horizons contributed to the illusion that institutions were malleable, indeed vulnerable, and that they would necessarily collapse before the violence and passion that were being reported.

War, riot, assassination, civil disorder, public protest—the eye of the camera recorded it all, for two-minute presentations interrupted only by the more insistent demands of the advertiser. Whatever pleasure or pain such fleeting images inflicted on their mass audiences, they communicated a public distress and anger that could not be ignored. The storms came on suddenly, indeed, almost without warning; curiously, they have ended almost as abruptly. Not surprisingly, questions are raised today about the meaning of all this. How is one to interpret the events of these long, difficult, and agitated years? Why, in the end, do they matter? What, in fact, is their residue? Where is it to be searched for? How is the country different today from what it was when Eisenhower was President? Is it fundamentally transformed or only superficially altered? May the greatest change not be in the collective memory of the American people? Are not Vietnam and Watergate, for example, shorthand expressions for what many millions today regard as a time of national shame and dishonor? Are these the sorts of changes that we ought to dwell on? Or, are there others, more substantial, more subtle, more concealed? Have we been so preoccupied with watching a drama (indeed, more recently, a cheap melodrama) that more significant events, occurring offstage (off camera) have largely escaped us?

This issue of *Daedalus* presumes that such may indeed be the situation today. Without explicitly instructing any author to avoid ruminating on what may legitimately be called "television's version" of the history of the 1960s and 1970s, which is now rapidly finding its way into print—a telling commentary on certain aspects of contemporary American culture—we posed questions intended to bring into focus a more complex America, of greater variety and more bewildering contradictions. The spirit of the *Daedalus* inquiry may be suggested by quoting selectively from very long letters of invitation issued to most of the prospective authors in June 1976. I wrote at that time:

Our purposes can be simply stated; they are essentially four: to ascertain whether certain major institutional changes and changes in the population, widely assumed to have occurred, have in fact taken place; to establish, if we can, criteria for judging the import of such changes and, if possible, to account for them; to ascertain whether and how far such changes as may have taken place in the population, or a significant segment of it, may have affected habits, tastes, mores, perceptions, values, and beliefs; to consider how America's intrusion into the world, and the world's intrusion into the consciousness of this country have affected both institutions and the population, producing consequences both unintended and unanticipated.

Whether the individual articles deal with public or private institutions—business corporations, churches, trade unions, health systems, political parties, the judiciary, the press, television, science and technology, professions, schools, or universities—subtlety is imperative. The failures are impressive; so, also, in some instances, are the successes. How can we render both without seeming sanguine? The effects of economic growth and, more recently, of unprecedented inflation, have created wholly new patterns of privilege and discrimination. Are we capable of looking objectively at both, considering their implications both for institutions and individuals? Ours is not an age given to "celebration," least of all, to a celebration of institutions, but it ought to be possible for a critical examination to be made of major institutions and of how they have fared in recent years.

When such institutional studies are combined in a volume with essays that deal with specific intellectual, moral, aesthetic, and attitudinal changes, thought to be significant for substantial parts of the population, the turmoil of recent years may appear in a wholly new perspective. It would be useful to know whether values are indeed as mutable as is sometimes argued. Do habits change as rapidly as some say? Have recent "cultural revolutions" been media events, or have they in fact taken place? How are we to treat themes like legality, racism, equality, intellectuality, sexuality? What are we to make of the supposed decline of belief in the "work ethic"? Who is prepared to write about how recognition is secured in American society today, and how it relates to fame or celebrity? Is anyone disposed to write about power, and how it is perceived? The perceptions, attitudes, and beliefs of significant numbers of Americans are said to have changed. Do we know this to be true? How do we know? Why has the change occurred now? What does it suggest about the authority of traditional institutions? What may it portend for the future? Facile explanations for attitudinal and value changes conceal much of the complexity of contemporary American industrial society; they generally induce a vague nostalgia for an allegedly more stable past, largely mythical, fabricated principally to provide a contrast with the disorder and violence of our own day. Is our age, in fact, as violent as some say?

The links between foreign policy and domestic policy are constantly mentioned, and almost never studied. Each is isolated in its own compartment with its own band of experts; neither is thought to be an inseparable partner of the other. Arms control agreements, détente, and trade policies are represented as the inspired (or mistaken) accomplishments of individuals in high places. Much of foreign policy is personalized, and when it is not, it is represented as arcane. The ways in which domestic policy (and politics) influence foreign policy, and the reciprocal impact of events abroad on American policy and politics are all too rarely considered. Because foreign and domestic economic policies have become interlaced, perhaps inextricably, and because both depend for their inception and execution on many institutions, and not only on those that are governmental, the belief that a reform within government will significantly alter policy may be a dubious proposition. Many today see the problems of foreign policy largely in moral or political terms, insisting always on the need for new leaders and new candor; they claim to know why so many recent appeals to the public have fallen on deaf ears, gaining neither a sympathetic hearing nor a politically useful response. Foreign policy is in fact Janus-faced, both here and in all other democratic societies; it looks both outside and within, and is as much affected by resources, of a very great variety and complexity, by traditions and habits of mind, as by a volatile and changing public opinion. And all this—inevitably—is affected by events and opinion abroad, over which Americans may have little if any control.

A great debt is owed the Carnegie Corporation for making this inquiry possible. Our intention, from the beginning, was to bring together men and women of disparate political and ideological views to consult together on America's recent past and on certain of its more pressing contemporary problems. We hoped that this would lead also to some consideration of the future, but our purpose was never to set ourselves up as forecasters. We assumed that the preponderant number of our company would be American, but we hoped that we might involve a number of Europeans as well. Finally, and most importantly, at a time when generational differences were thought significant, we agreed to ignore them; we intended from the outset to recruit authors whose only resemblance was their commitment to study contemporary America.

Our common effort has worked remarkably well. Differences have been aired; they have not been papered over. The essays printed in this issue do not express a single orthodoxy; they have, in most instances, been greatly altered from their original presentations to take account of the criticism of others. Indeed, nothing has been more encouraging in this enterprise than the civility shown by so many in responding to the views of their colleagues. In large meetings and in small, we have experimented with encouraging a dialogue that might once have been dismissed as unlikely or impossible. Our gratitude to the Carnegie Corporation for this *Daedalus* issue is very real.

Thanks are due also the Woodrow Wilson International Center for Scholars, and to its Director, Dr. James Billington, for their cordial welcome to the group last January when we met in Washington, D.C., to discuss early drafts of these papers.

S.R.G.

ELIZABETH HARDWICK

Domestic Manners

How ARE WE living today? Of course, there is no "we" except for those who address us, advise us, praise us in the round, as "the American people." The phrase is a signal for the wary, doing as it so often does more honor to the exhorter and his plans than to those millions gathered in under the grant title.

Only the forgetful can easily ignore the duplicity practiced upon the defining imagination by the sudden obsolescence of attitudes and styles just past, styles that collapsed or scattered into fragments just as one had felt free to identify them as facts, changes, alterations of consciousness, shiftings of power or threats to power. These elements, at least at the moment of identification, had the shape of reality, of historical presence, of genuine displacements; and even though they could not be asserted as eternal they still could not be experienced as mere historical moments soon, very soon, to be reversed or simply erased. It is with some perturbation that one has to learn again and again that the power of external forces is greater than style, stronger than fleeting attitude.

"Confidence in the future" is a peculiar phrase, although in frequent use. It is not meant to signify the mere expectation of continuing existence, but rather to signify hope—perhaps for the stock market, for relations with recalcitrant and truculent foreign countries, for our own life as a whole, or for small groups, rich or poor, protected or beleaguered, who are in need of reassurance. It seems to mean that it is reasonable to assume the future will not diminish rewards in some cases or that the future will augment rewards in others. Most seriously it imagines that the future will, with all its attendant inequities and surprises, remain open to the understanding and the efforts of those leaders and advisers we have grown accustomed to and from whom, given the nature of things, we have generously not asked very much. These assumptions about the future are in grave disorder and "confidence" is merely a sentiment.

There is always the question of the will to understand first and then the greater will of society to undertake even the most reasonable alleviations, for alleviations on the one hand are the cue for disgruntlements elsewhere. Lacking the will, society waits for events to which it must respond, often in a final condition of fear and crisis and anger; or, in long, drawn-out, hopelessly tangled injustices and dangerous defaults it simply waits not to respond at all. Things reveal themselves in an atmosphere of grotesque folly. The persons exploiting oil in Arab countries are the same persons theatrically throwing pound notes on

1

the ground in London rather than on the ground of the poor of their own regions. The waste of Western capitalism is not always different, but America at least is used to the waste and looks upon reduction with alarm.

To speak of persons as the "product" of their decade, or half-decade in some cases, is a severe reduction of history, and yet it has an obvious descriptive usefulness, a conversational meaning that is measured by the clear recognition others give to the terms, a recognition coming out of the very grossness of the designations.

Certain persons and certain aspects of our society appear to be a product of the 1960s. The legacy of the period is intractable morally and socially in the manner of all history and it bears the peculiar opacity of its closeness to the present—that is, the period is *experience*, and its transformation into history is somewhat a work of the subjective imagination, a work close to autobiography in the way it reenters the memory.

There is sadness and regret in the memory of the sixties. For those who reached the age of 18 in the last years of the decade the temptations to self-destruction were everywhere, bursting forth from what was called the "counter-culture." The hallucinations of LSD, deformations by drugs that lingered on in apathy, addiction, aborted education, restlessness, the deprivations and fantasies of numerous torpid "communes," the beginnings of hysterical youth cults—this still lies there behind us, for it seems that historical rubble is no more easily disposed of than the stone and steel and concrete of misbegotten highways, shopping centers, overweening towers for habitation. For those who in the sixties were "revolutionaries," it meant hiding, police records, death, exile, the delusions of youthful power that took little account of the brutal rebukes the genuine power of society can command. It meant disillusionment with "infantile leftism," with postures that time and the sluggishness of history outmoded.

For the youth of the sixties who remained outside the general reaches of a vibrating, rebellious youth culture, the decade meant death in Vietnam, mutilation, bad dreams, drug addiction, the bad faith of corrupted authority, and, at the least, a weird and agitating confusion of values. President Carter's campaign made an effort to give voice to the youth who accommodated the sixties, those who agreed as it were and suffered, but it was disheartening to realize how little he could find to say, how vague and unreal were the consolations, the approbations. If sacrifice is not to be praised as a value based upon its objectives, the gratitude of authority is therefore bound to be mixed with shame and to come forth merely as rhetoric.

Casualties of every spiritual and personal nature lay about as the legacy of the sixties. Authorities experienced much of the decade as a form of insult and fell into a state of paranoia. It was only by accident that the paranoids were removed from the domination of the state and from the determination to corrupt all of its institutions.

On the other side, the agitated scrutiny directed in the sixties to the arrangements of society discovered many pieties and hypocrisies which had claimed the aspect of eternity but which were, in fact, merely prejudices and matters of unexamined convenience. Deeply benign and practical refusals and reversals marked the period—the questioning of unnecessary, self-serving authority in the home and in institutions, the pure hopes of the civil rights movement. Informalities of all sorts, trivial and important, could, it turned out, be more or less painlessly accepted and removed from the domain of social oppression. Tolerance of deviation, acceptance of a pluralism long ago established by ocular evidence, concern for the integrity and endurance of nature, ridicule of the endless consumption of redundant goods, personal relations, masculine presumption, the old and the young—the mere listing of customs and tyrannies challenged in the sixties is, as Chaucer said, like "trying to catch the wind in a net."

The children of the sixties had been brought up in the fifties and no doubt this earlier, seemingly plausible and hopeful, period floated about parent and child like an ectoplasmic memory. The fifties—they seem to have taken place on a sunny afternoon that asked nothing of you except a drifting belief in the moment and its power to satisfy: a handsome young couple, with two or three children, a station wagon, a large dog, a house and a summer house, a great deal of picnicking and camping together.

For the middle class the fifties passed in a dream, a dream in which benevolent wishes for oneself were not thought of as always hostile to the enlarging possibilities of others. The treasured child would do well in school and the psychiatrist could be summoned for the troubled. The suburbs offered the space and grass that would bless family existence. The cars and the second cars were symbols of power over one's life, as anyone can see who looks at the gleaming chariots that decorate the filthy, blasted streets of the ghettos.

The sixties seemed to grow, nationally and personally, upon the beguiling confidence of the decade just past. Wars to establish credibility are for the prosperous. Time was not slow, however, but speeded up, unreal, very much like time in the air; by the late sixties the happy child was scarcely to be distinguished as he went into his teens from the quarrelsome one. Complacent parents had, after all, expected more than they realized, more of their children and more of each other. And so a decade was only ten years. And a new year could be more like a tornado uprooting the grass than another period of growth.

But how *real* the sixties were, how dreadfully memorable the horrors, how haunting the alterations, everywhere, in feeling, in belief. Already the receding years have character, violently ambivalent, and beyond repeal. And how American, one is tempted to insist. In what way? Perhaps in the way destruction was created out of the pleasures of plenitude, assassinations out of the riveting excitements of leadership, diminishment out of a manic sense of expansiveness. What went down were people here, whole countries far away, and a few of the unnecessary follies that had been sitting in our lives, like memorial plaques on the mantlepiece.

A strange decade indeed. How is one to set a value upon the sensible pleasures of "informality" and the limited liberation of maligned groups against the slaughter of people? And what is the historical connection, finally? The connection between the rights of personal style in dress and living arrangements, the right to homosexuality, to marihuana, and the present nightmare in Cambodia? It was a terrifying decade, anarchic, brutal—and fortunately for all of us, the absolutely saving energy of a profound protest, sustained by youth and a few older allies, a protest against dehumanization, military control, political lying, and power madness. To look back on the sixties is to look straight into the scarred eye of life.

The 1970s have passed their zenith. Did they take place—this handful of years—somewhere else, in another land, inside the house, the head? Fatigue and recession, cold winters and expensive heat, resignations and disgrace. Quietism, inner peace, having their turn, as if history were a concert program, some long and some short selections, a few modern and the steady traditional. For young people, it is common to say that things have settled down. *Down* is the key: accommodation, docility, depression of spirit.

Many people are going to law school, searching, one supposes, for the little opening, the ray of sun at the mouth of the cave. It does not seem possible that what our world needs is a generation of new young lawyers. In certain respects what is being honored, at least by the approving adults, is not always the actual profession so much as the sign of a willingness to begin and to persevere to the end for a practical purpose, to memorize, to master a process without the demands for the gratifications of supreme interest at each moment along the way. Yet, out there at the end are the litigious anxieties of the corporate world to which whole young lives are to be prosperously dedicated and consumed.

Advanced studies in the humanities are another matter. They are felt to be impractical—and that means that society does not find them necessary. There are not only enough of you, it says, there are too many. To go on in the study of literature, philosophy, or history can be a personal passion, but as a profession it depends upon someone out there to teach and a supply of teachers in reasonable relation to the waiting learners. At the present time, the Ph.D.s remind one of the fervish, superfluous clerks in Russian literature, anxious persons floating in a menacing void, waving their supererogatory diplomas. It is not quite clear that to come to the end of one's college years is to have arrived anywhere.

The seventies have not been free of definition; even drift has its direction. Intimacy, the validation of the self in a narrow, intense relation with a few others, or one other, is seen by many thinkers as a definition of our period. Very few of those who do the naming are pleased with the turn of the wheel. It is not the activism of the sixties that is mourned by conventional commentators but rather a wish for a more aggressive, outward-looking intrusion of the individual ego into the realities of power, into concern for a material grasp of self-interest rather than the vaporous transcendence of self-absorption.

The past reclaimed as an image, the opacity of life lightened by dichotomies, the fall and the rise. Our own time: "It is the localizing of human experience, so that what is close to the immediate circumstances of life is paramount." The quotation is from Richard Sennett's ambitious book called *The Fall of the Public Man*,[1] a fall which led naturally to the elevation of private man, ourselves, and "The Tyrannies of Intimacy."

The public life, as Sennett somewhat vaguely reconstructs its lost shape, was lived out of a rich variety of experiences and acceptances largely impersonal. The life of the city was possible then; intimacy, however, lives out of a fear of the unknown and the different and allows the self to retreat, nervously, into absorption in the private. Finally, one cannot in present history know others unless he knows them in a fearful closeness, accepts them as part of the returning reassurance of looking into a mirror. It is the nature of intimacy to be unattainable, a mood trembling with anxieties and insecurities because the self is insatiable. The city, along with many other things, dies, frozen by the retreat from the public domain.

Sennett's book is an abstruse effort in cultural history, designed to reach its destination—contemporary "narcissism." Narcissism, awareness, intimacy, new consciousness—these terms appear again and again in theoretical and auto-biographical descriptions of the seventies. The works are strikingly varied in quality and seriousness—the least "serious" usually being revelations and tran-scendencies achieved in the autobiographies, the very process of "success" pro-viding the despairing material of the more distant and critical theoreticians.

The self's unanchored demand for security and relief from psychological unease dominates the inhabitants of Christopher Lasch's brilliant essays on the "narcissist society." (It is part of the puzzle of current writing on the elusive present that Sennett's *reign* of private man is in many respects another way of describing Lasch's "The *Waning* of Private Life."[2] "Private life" in Lasch's work appears to represent roughly what has been called "family life.") About the ubiquitous drift to narcissism, Lasch writes, "Having no hope of improving their lives in any of the ways that matter, people have convinced themselves that what matters is psychic self-improvement: getting in touch with their feelings, eating health food, taking lessons in ballet or belly dancing, immersing them-selves in the wisdom of the East, jogging, learning how to 'relate,' overcoming the 'fear of pleasure.' "

The cultural analyst, Philip Rieff, has assumed the present under the notion of the "triumph of the therapeutic"[3]—the hunger for personal satisfaction that imposes upon the will the privilege or the burden of escaping painful feelings. The "therapeutic" (strangely, at times Rieff speaks of it, or to it, as "him") in the writings of the often-hectoring Rieff, means many things, among them that ideas, emotions, experiences take their moral and social value from how they make you feel. The contemporary soul escapes from anxiety, duty, orderly thought by means of therapy and by therapeutic assaults upon intellectual and social authority. All of these writers, naming the not-quite-measurable sense of the present, are different in tone and in the atmosphere of recommendation, warning, regret that is the surrounding mist of the intellectual, political, and temperamental inclination of the individual writer at his desk. There is no doubt that they all prefigure (in Rieff's case) and describe one phenomenon of the seventies—the demonic acceleration of investments in gurus, encounters, magical healings, diets, transcendences, and transformations that compete, like varieties of aspirin, for the remission of aches of the mind and psyche.

Life at home, domestic drama, sexual warfare are part of history, and, with-out exegesis, the matter of fiction. Divorce statistics are little figures of decline that reveal more than mere legal possibility and fact. The numbers are rich in attitudes, assumptions, hopes and lost hopes. It is not necessary to seek a di-vorce in order to live out personally the deepest skepticisms about the future of marriage. Irony about romantic love is the inescapable soil of existence upon which both marriage and divorce grow simultaneously, shooting up in the same season like plants in the garden.

Irony represents the recognition of the shortened life of the feelings. It says that the attachment to a particular person, even the legal attachment, defines the moment or the year but is far from being the key to the future. Disruption may represent failure, but it also represents the dearest boundaries of new hopes. If we can trust fiction and film, our period is, like that of Restoration drama, *comic*.

An abundance of cynical wit and coarseness are the necessary conditions for verisimilitude about prevailing manners. In speaking of the cynical and coarse one is not investing the words with moral outrage; they are instead descriptive. With the appearance of a large number of licentious works by women, even the cuckold has returned as a familiar figure in literature. Certain types return and certain are lost forever, figures such as the awkward, trusting ingenue or country girl of the Restoration period. Don Giovanni's *mille e tre*, the once singular arithmetic of the frenzied aristocrat, appears as a natural accumulation of the normal sexual exuberance of men and women freed, instructed, and determined.

The comic destinations of romantic love are shown in Saul Bellow's last novel. In *Humboldt's Gift*, the most engaging of the novel's female characters, Renata, leaves the intellectual, Citrine, to marry a mortician. In Joseph Heller's *Something Happened*, the hero sighs and says it sometimes occurs to him that he got married so that he could then be divorced.

Ennui is an attendant of irony. Andy Warhol, the painter, said about his decision to abandon his emotional and sexual life: "I was happy to see it go." Love, with its ancient distresses, cannot be removed from the landscape by fashion. It cannot be separated from power, for one thing. Nevertheless, the pains of rejection and loss, representing as they do interferences encountered by the individual will, are not sympathetically understood as sufferings to be endured. And in no way does such suffering take on any of the sweetness of fidelity injured, loyalty degraded.

Improvisation, moving on, substitution, defiance, inner healing—characteristics of the strategies by which a sexually relaxed society copes with regret and denial—have a moral dominance in matters of painful love. A broken heart, caressed too long, is a dishonor often seen as a weapon of revenge, manipulation. "Anger" is the word psychiatrists give to assertions of the anguish of love.

Sex, sex—what good does it do anyone to "study" more and better orgasms, to open forbidden orifices, to experiment, to put himself into the satisfaction laboratory, the intensive care ward of fulfillment? The body is a poor vessel for transcendence. The Marquis de Sade spent his whole life, and his enormous powers of imagination, on positions, tortures, combinations, dream-like prowess and endurance. But it was a dream indeed, and most of the far reaches his imagination sent him toward are physically impossible. Satiety, in life, is quick and inevitable. The return of anxiety, debts, bad luck, age, work, thought, interest in the passing scene, ambition, anger cannot be deferred by lovemaking. The consolations of sex are fixed and just what they have always been.

In the seventies sex has become information, about yourself, about others, about yourself in relation to others. The practices of "polling"—one technique invading or pretending to invade the public mind—works here in the interest of sexual technique and attitude, giving a quasi-consensus, often to nothing more than the mere practice of polling itself. Questionnaires, reports, new studies, "probing surveys" (*sic*), the "real" truth about women, homosexuality, premarital and postmarital intercourse, about changing views and changing positions. These dubious statistics are an industry, and like the manufacture of other products there is little worry about repetition, need, accuracy, or significance. The title of each new book is very much like a new brand name for an old offering.

The most depressing part of the sexual information business is that, in the way of commerce, it is offered for our health and reassurance. Pessimism, naturally, does not sell, nor does skepticism—that, one assumes, the poor consumer can provide for himself, from his own experience. In the books and articles conclusions never fail to liberate, and if there is nothing new, whatever exists takes value from its mere occurrence, that is, if one believes the surveys give any true picture of contemporary sexual life. Piety, exploitation, complacency, triviality, and spurious objectivity deface these scrofulous enterprises.

Sexual Behavior in the 1970's[4] is a study exposed to the public by Morton Hunt on behalf of the Playboy Foundation. The pastoral note on which the study ends is typical of this kind of work. "The changes that are taking place are none the less important and profound for taking place within the culture rather than breaking away from it; indeed, they may be more valuable than total sexual radicalism would be. For while they are bringing so much that is pleasurable, healthful and enriching into American life, they are doing so without destroying emotional values we have rightly prized, and without demolishing institutions necessary to the stability of society itself." More valuable, pleasurable, healthful, emotional values, stability of society. The sadness, the corruption, the meaningless of all this is one aspect of the 1970s.

To think of the family today is bewildering because the classes are so far apart in the scenery in which daily life takes place. For those in the light the uncertainties have to do with hanging on, imagining the future, imagining if possible the meaning of the generations, of youth and old age, money, and the menace of reduction. In the darkness below, within the family there are joblessness, crime, madness, cruelty, and despair. It is not easy to remember that these scenes are part of the same play.

When the politicians, the candidates, speak of the "poor" and the unemployed, of those on welfare, they are being no more empty than the rest of us in being unable to convey any sense of the experience of the condition, the misery and horror. There is still an inclination to see the poor in previous images, perhaps the more consoling ones of the 1930s: a wrinkled face, battered but benign; a worn body in which Christian doctrine still circulates in the veins; young families in decaying bungalows with an unpaid-for car in the drive. The sharecropper, the Okie, the miner, the laid-off factory force, memories from one's own family. Television, magical as it is for certain events in real life, cannot fully picture on its small frame the slums of the city, the menacing breakdown, the insanity, the brutality, the leprous isolation. What has become unimaginable exists in images of fear, hatred, and withdrawal. Fear is sanctioned just now because there is much to be afraid of.

One thing that distorts our comprehension of the life of the poor is that on the street, in the supermarket, the marvelous disguise of the mass-produced American clothes gives a plausible surface, almost a shine, to what is really implausible and dark. On the evening news, the young thief or killer in his sneakers, his jacket, his jeans; his family in turtlenecks, jerseys. Together they appear in a state of health, often beautiful, well provided for, their clear and startling contemporariness like a miraculous mask.

In the city slums it is the houses, the rooms, the halls, the very walls that define the actual life. It is here that everything necessary and hospitable to a decent life is lacking. This is home and family and relationship. It is here, inside, that deformations are so pervasive and inescapable, here that the devastations of character and purpose grow. Society is never asked to experience directly the misery and its attendant, hidden rages and abusive idleness.

In New York City the old, the very old have become victims of the very young. Poor, crippled people, 82 years old or even in one case 103 years old, are beaten, killed for two dollars, ninety-five cents, for nothing. The age of the victims, the paltriness of the "take," the youth of the criminals, the bizarre equality of poverty between the robbed and the robber, outrages every sense of reason, even criminal reason, and makes one look beyond the act. Part of the choice of victim is that his weakness is immediately evident and is itself a sort of affront. An old and enfeebled, poverty-worn person is, apparently, to the battered children of the slums an object that is contemptible and finally not quite real, for to imagine old age one has to imagine life as a long flow, something protected by nature and therefore meaningful in its orderly progress from one stage to another.

Part of the preying upon each other comes from the familiarity of neighborhood, the known turf, known for its vulnerability, its exposure to every injury and insult. Middle-class neighborhoods in the city are places of warm beauty, utterly beguiling behind the curtained, plant-filled windows. The nice streets are a shimmer of light and power, taxis and doormen, smiles and golden belief—an obstacle in their foreignness, their dreamy protection and unassailability. Great sophistication, vigilance, imagination are needed to storm these heights, and the very young, poor criminals do not often possess that felonious knowledge and experience. The clever criminals of the old school are like figures in a film comedy. They drive up to expensive hotels in limousines, dressed in dinner jackets, in order to plunder the safes filled with diamonds, acting always swiftly and efficiently, and above all, mannerly, out of consideration for the quality of the loot.

Here in the city the worst thing that can happen to a nation has happened: we are a people afraid of its youth. One's own memory—the memory of a girl— was of turning about on a dark street at night, fearful of footsteps coming closer, turning and saying, Oh, it is only a boy. Relief. Now for a young man to be in his twenties or thirties, out of jail, is in some way a guarantee of accommodation to society—at least in the mass, if not of course in particular cases.

For the sick and dangerous young, the idea of "treatment" is a cliché, the joke of a psychiatry which does not know how to treat such devastating deviations, such appalling dislocations, such violence that baffles by its fecklessness. There is no will to undertake reconstruction of society. Not only is the imagination lacking just now, but the very terms of the reconstruction, the extent of it, freeze speculative thought and reasonable recommendation.

Revolutionary societies destroy or brutally "reeducate." Some countries like India have long ago learned to look upward and inward as they step around filth and hunger. The torpor of the Indian millions is a blessing for the prosperous. Here, among the poor, there is a political accommodation, or at least no symptom of organized revolt. Instead there is random crime. Random—a felicitous phrase that gives no substance to the devastation.

The wild growth of dangerous criminal insanity in the cities is a comment on the meek young with their ashrams in old brownstones, on Moonies in costly hotels and country estates, on clean-cut groups quietly meditating. Poverty and its abuses to children have their transforming power. Young persons stab and kill, throw each other off the roof, beat each other to death on the playing ground, rape, mutilate, set buildings on fire. To allow the facts to enter the mind is a guilty act, as if one were recording the scene of a porn film with a suspicious degree of imagination. And from the public pathetic screams for protection, when there is no protection. In the cities there has been a profound derangement of whole generations of the urban poor.

We cannot take it in. All we had planned on was Appalachia and the sweet, toothless smiles, the pale, white faces, ragged dresses, bare feet, hungry glances. No matter—a vibrant, ferocious, active, heart-breaking insanity is as much a part of the seventies as intimacy, retreat to the private.

It is always a relief to return to the middle classes, to ponder the way culture, economics, fashions work upon these citizens who are a mirror, returning what society puts before them.

To think of our domestic life is to ask what sort of person is actually needed by society. What parents, what children, young adults, workers? What makes sense—the tough and practical, the unsure and idealistic? The inner-directed and the outer-directed, to use David Riesman's terms, seem merely private, accidentally characterological, as one may be stingy or generous. The work ethic describes one who lives in a society that invests work with great spiritual and historical necessity, seeing in toil, advancement, tenacity, a virtue beyond material reward—the definition of self. All must work, but how hard and at what and with what motivation beyond dollars? In the late sixties many young people answered the question of dollars by casual work quite unrelated to advancement, to their preparation, their interests, and their future: driving cabs, working as waiters, making jewelry, teaching transcendental meditation, walking dogs, playing the guitar. Marginal occupations are suitable to prosperous times and have little reality in inflationary, unstable periods.

"I love long life better than figs," Charmian, Cleopatra's attendant, says in Shakespeare's play. If things go on as we reasonably expect, young people will experience long life as an unruly challenge to morals, possibilities, fantasies. They will, in huge numbers, live way up into their seventies and that means they will have three lives, with each one perhaps wiping out the one before as though it had never been. Who can easily imagine a young son or daughter marrying and living with the same person for close to fifty years? Or with two for twenty-five years each? This is not the way of hearts in love with the shifting demands of the ego, with painful pressures for new experience, second and third chances, lost hopes that are an accusation to self-esteem.

In a long life in which little can be taken for granted, it is not reasonable to project a fearful clinging to the known on the part of the contemporary sensibility—so far removed from the peasant-like stasis of times past. Instead, a nomadic search for the new waters and pastures of each period of life leads one on, running from the dryness of the past. Hell is no exit—and without sanctions few would wish to stay in the closed cell.

It is no wonder that with parents, authority seems to have become a burden. Part of it is the peculiar melding of parents and young adults in the way they look and dress, in their common reverence for sexual experience, which they have been told need never end for the good and the healthy. Custom is shattered by the parents' fear of age and the children's disaffection about age's wisdom, difference, and virtue; by the vacation spirit of a people who are not sure that society needs its work, by the blurred future of the species—on and on. Coolness rather than domination is the complaint of children against parents, neglectful confusion rather than insistent assertion. Those who imagine that this can be reversed by the will, by mere opinion, are not credible because the will to rule has itself collapsed along with the painful recognition of limits everywhere of every kind.

The women's movement has crystallized in domestic life changes that have been going on for decades. Historically, the political and social expression of the themes of women's liberation coincides with the needs of a world in which there are almost as many divorces as marriages, with smaller families, longer lives, the economic expansion desired by the average household for which two incomes are required, education of women, diminishment of the need for heavy muscular work, which means that the lives of men and women—talking on the phone, sitting at the desk, managing—became more and more alike.

The inner changes within women can scarcely be exaggerated. Ambition is natural to new groups freed, or demanding to be free and equal. No group demands equality for nothing, as a simple adornment of status. The arrival of women's ambition, transforming as it does private life, inner feeling, and public life is not at all simple but instead resembles the subtle shiftings of human thought and life brought about by enormously challenging ideas such as evolution and Freudianism. Many hang back; just as many would stand on the literal truth of Genesis; but no matter what the ideological reluctance may be, every life is an inchoate but genuine reflection of the change. We begin to act upon new assumptions without even being aware of the singular changes.

Society does not want women to lead a long life in the home. It is not prepared to support them and cannot give the old style true sanction. Children do not want their parents' lives to be given to them forever. Husbands cannot take the responsibilities for wives as an immutable duty, ordained by nature. Women's liberation suits society much more than society itself is prepared to admit. The wife economy is as obsolete as the slave economy.

But more than dollars are at stake. Power, the most insidious of the passions, is also the most cunning. The women's movement is in some respects a group like many others, organized against discrimination, economic and social inequities, legal impediments: against the structural defects of accumulated history. Perhaps it is that part of the movement the times will more or less accommodate in the interest of reality. The other challenges are more devastating to custom, uprooting as they do the large and the small, the evident and the hidden. The women's movement is above all a critique. And almost nothing, it turns out, will remain outside its relevance. It is the disorienting extension of the intrinsic meaning of women's liberation, much of it unexpected, that sets the movement apart. It is a psychic and social migration, leaving behind a violently altered landscape.

In the 1970s the insecurity of life, the rapid using up of resources, the alienating complexity of every problem from nuclear proliferation to falling reading scores, can scarcely fail to bewilder and lacerate relations between people in the family, in the streets, among the classes. When one tries to think of "domestic manners"—all of the rules and customs and habits which people have assumed as a group—one cannot imagine just who is sure enough of his ground to pass on the beliefs that grow out of reasonable certainty. And to whom are they offered, these beliefs and customs? The life of the young is far more complicated and murky than the life of those older. One thing looms out of the shadows: the reluctance of so many *promising* young people to have children. Where is the future?

REFERENCES
   [1]Richard Sennett, *The Fall of Public Man* (New York: Knopf, 1977).
   [2]"The Narcissist Society," by Christopher Lasch. *New York Review of Books* (September 30, 1976). Also "The Waning of Private Life," *Salmagundi* (Winter 1977).
   [3]Philip Rieff, *The Triumph of the Therapeutic: Uses of Faith after Freud* (New York: Harper and Row, 1966).
   [4]Morton Hunt, *Sexual Behavior in the 1970's* (New York: Dell Paperback, 1975).

SYDNEY E. AHLSTROM

National Trauma and Changing Religious Values

A new America? The question raises a host of imponderables. One remembers Ralph Waldo Emerson's misgivings in the early 1850s. "It chanced during one winter a few years ago, that our cities were bent on discussing the theory of the Age. By an odd coincidence four or five noted men were each reading a discourse to the citizens of Boston or New York, on the Spirit of the Times." Emerson, however, could not join the dialogue. "We are incompetent to solve the times. Our geometry cannot span the huge orbits of the prevailing ideas, behold their return and reconcile their opposition. We can only obey our own polarity." He spoke of the Turk's sense of preordained destiny and of the Hindu's patient resignation. "Our Calvinists in the last generation had something of the same dignity. They felt that the weight of the Universe held them down to their place." "Providence," he said, "has a wild, rough, incalculable road to its end, and it is of no use to try to whitewash its huge mixed instrument in the clean shirt and white neckcloth of a student of divinity."[1]

Despite such warnings, however, we again undertake to solve the times. If there be a current underrunning the course of events, we seek to discern its direction—and perhaps its significance. Yet in this enterprise we are sure to be baffled and balked, for unless we know the contexture of the whole, our interpretations are very incomplete. We draw our conclusions *in medias res* according to the explanatory principles of our own little spot of time. We know that the specious present in which we live is a product of the whole past; and as if that were not enough, we dimly recognize that without a view of the whole future, we have little grounds for ascertaining the significance of anything. Perry Miller showed an awareness of this predicament when he said that the one circumstance which might explain such advances as he had made in the study of Puritanism over those of the nineteenth century's scholarly giants was that he, unlike them, was fully capable of envisioning the entire American experience as of no greater material significance than the ephemeral empire of the ancient Parthians. In formulating his view in just that way, Miller must have been at least partially shaped by his life-long study of Johnathan Edwards, for whom the future was both ineluctable and unforeseeable. "Providence," Edwards had said, "is continually bringing forth things new in the state of the world, very different from what ever was before. . . . And the scheme will not be finished or the design fully accomplished, the great event fully brought to pass, till the end of the world and the last revolution is brought about."

Insofar as we have absorbed Robert Jay Lifton's conception of a new historical situation after Hiroshima, we too can now entertain the end of human history, which gives us at least something in common with Edwards which the
intervening generations lacked.[2] We can entertain human history as finite and
thus better understand Ernst Troeltsch's conviction that all things human are
historical—without remainder. The purpose of this essay, however, is not to
sound yet another apocalyptic warning but to delineate the religious situation of
the American people as they enter the third century of their national experience. Its subject matter will thus embrace (somewhat ridiculously) the beliefs,
aspirations, ethical views, and ecclesiastical commitments of over 215 million
people living in thousands of divergent contexts, many of which are profoundly
shaped by living traditions that reach back into the most remote antiquity.
They or their ancestors came to America from every part of the world. Contrary to the expectations of St. John de Crèvecoeur, moreover, no melting pot
has transformed them into a uniform race, nor have the passing centuries eliminated their religious diversity.

American civilization was founded in an epoch of divisive religious ferment.
During the nineteenth century, amid numerous denominational schisms, countless indigenous sects and cults arose. Even new religions were founded. The
later twentieth century has experienced yet another explosion of spiritual unrest, and now the newest immigration, from across the Pacific, is deepening the
nation's pluralism. It is hardly surprising that even the efforts of scholars to
describe an American character have foundered, one after the other, on the
rocks of ethnic, racial, cultural, and religious diversity. One really has no alternative, therefore, but to accept Emerson's insistence. I must follow my own
polarity.

The first necessity is to frame an inclusive religious category, for otherwise
one would be tempted either to lose oneself in a welter of details or to over-
emphasize that minority of Americans who are formally affiliated with the institutions of the Judaeo-Christian tradition. One must see religion as a virtually
universal aspect of being human. Integrated personhood intrinsically consists of
a felt relation to the environing world, a more or less ordered structure of values, some sense of the transcendent, and at least a rudimentary notion of personal or collective destiny or purpose. One can hardly imagine a person, either
now or in times past, whose religious commitments could not be described if
serious conversations could be arranged or personal records studied.

Hegel was one of the earliest to define religion in terms of ultimate concern,
but many have done so since, notably Paul Tillich and H. Richard Niebuhr,
each in his way. Indeed, Tillich's little book on *The Religious Situation*, published
in a translation by Niebuhr in 1932, to some degree suggested the approach in
the present essay: "Religion is the substance of culture, Culture is the form of
religion."[3] In this light it would seem that no one age is more religious than any
other, though some do experience far more excruciating demands for change
and adjustment than others even dream of. What changes are the modalities of
religious feeling and the forms of organization and expression.

In any case one must bear in mind the remarkable degree to which the values
and behavior of members of the larger denominations tend to parallel those of
the nonaffiliated, if due allowance be made for ethnicity, regional tendencies,

vocation, and class. Even on a central moral issue such as racial justice, for example, church members show only a slightly greater tendency to racism than nonmembers, though this is in part balanced by evidence that "dedicated" members show greater sensitivity on this issue than "nominal" members.[4] We thus do well to recognize that the culture of a nation, which is to say its collective behavior, reflects its dominant ethical and religious impulses. As it happens, one of the very best illustrations of this interrelationship is provided by those seventeenth-century developments in Britain and colonial America which engender and maintain the most decisive single characteristic of American civilization: its commitment to libertarian principles and its becoming thereby the world's great exemplar of what Marx would define as the bourgeois revolution. This first of the West's great social revolutions was animated, led, and morally justified by a determined Puritan constituency which under Oliver Cromwell's leadership overturned many of the chief institutions of the old order, from Roman Catholic holy days to sacral kingship.

In England, to be sure, the fabric of English life was considerably restored, but in America a truly glorious revolution was slowly carried out. Bernard Bailyn can justly claim that by the 1730s substantially all of the liberties to be demanded in 1776 were practical realities of American life, except that legal guarantees were lacking.[5] Intrinsic to this entire accomplishment, moreover, was the way in which Puritan piety and ethics undergirded and animated the new social order. As the nation grew prosperous, the larger Protestant churches brought strong and persistent theological support to this ideology. Gradually this blending of religion, social ethics, and politics became a unified gestalt or value configuration. Americans not only likened themselves to old Israel but insisted that their country was God's New Israel. Timothy Dwight in his anthem for the new nation in 1777 knew no restraint. He hailed Columbia as "queen of the world and child of the skies." Its reign was to be "the last and the noblest of time." The founding fathers themselves showed the same confidence. "Heaven smiles upon our undertakings," says the national seal: NOVUS ORDO SECLORUM. A generation later Lyman Beecher would declare that "the Mosaic institute more resembled our own than any government on earth ever did or does."[6] Gathering all of these ideas together in a way that brought peculiar satisfaction to the people was Francis Samuel Smith's hymn, "My Country 'Tis of Thee," written hurriedly in 1832. Through all vicissitudes this tradition maintained itself. Julia Ward Howe's "Mine eyes have seen the glory" survived the Civil War and became a national song. Fifty million immigrants aroused nativist responses, yet the newcomers in the long run strengthened the impulse, and Irving Berlin's "God Bless America" is appropriately the last (so far) to win wide popular acceptance.[7]

One thing, therefore, remains certain: that the essentially religious notion of this country as an Elect Nation with a Manifest Destiny is an overwhelmingly important factor that any study of recent decades must ponder. For the vast majority of Americans, the Union has always been an object of veneration with rites and symbols of its own. It has been apprehended as a source of moral norms, which, if not absolute, nevertheless transcend individual desires. Only very rarely, moreover, have even the strictest ecclesiastical authorities or other critics denounced these tendencies as idolatrous or illicit. It was amid the massive social, moral, and economic dislocations of the Gilded Age, however, that something like a continuous movement of dissent began to emerge. Not until the Great Crash of 1929 and the depression which followed did the magnitude of public policy changes become sufficiently great to effect changes in the public orthodoxy. By the end of World War II a moderate form of the "welfare state" had won widespread popular acceptance. With these developments in mind we proceed to a consideration of the last decade and a half of the republic's second century, remembering that it was while it was approaching the Bicentennial that the nation's sense of purpose fell to its lowest ebb.

That we may better understand the rude transitions that brought us to this condition it is useful to revisit a time when a quite different spirit pervaded the country, and for this purpose the Eisenhower years may serve very well. In the nostalgic memories of most it was a halcyon time. The decade's most sensational corruption scandal involved a Columbia professor and a popular television quiz show, unless it was the vicuña coat that led to the resignation of the president's chief adviser. College students of the sixties remembered those years as a time of bobbysoxers in pleated skirts; whereas those of the seventies who read Will Herberg's well-received study, *Protestant Catholic Jew* (1955) find that world so remote from their own experience that they confuse it with the world of Tolkien's *Lord of the Rings*. Some reflection on the fifties, therefore, may sharpen our perceptions of what the next fifteen years would do.

The Placid Decade

At the risk of oversimplification one may say that the Truman administration was primarily concerned with the gargantuan tasks of postwar reconstruction and that it was the good fortune of President Dwight David Eisenhower to ride the crest of a postwar boom. Fulfilling a campaign promise, the victorious General's first deed was to negotiate a treaty that ended the enormously divisive war in Korea. The gates of the temple of Janus were closed, and Americans, as the pundits so often said, had the father figure they wanted. In tune with the trend of the times, Eisenhower was also permissive—even to the length of giving the country's most unprincipled demagogue, Senator Joseph McCarthy, enough rope to hang himself in 1954, thus ending a rampage that had begun in 1950. His basic role was to be an indulgent guardian of a nation bent on getting and spending.

The vast unsatisfied needs and desires developed during the depression and war years could now be produced and sold with all the ingenuity that new technologies and new forms of corporate organization would make possible. Under the aegis of a friendly administration American industry experienced a decade of unprecedented economic growth. While bulldozers opened the way for equally unprecedented additions to America's urban sprawl, visions of affluence and expectations of upward social mobility made status-seeking a topic of journalistic and sociological investigation.

Against this roseate background the distinctive spiritual tone of the decade unfolded. Because "normalcy" was again in vogue much of the country's traditional religious life went on in its customary way, though television was now reaching new and receptive audiences. Yet gradually the "Eisenhower Revival" took on a character of its own. Most pronounced was a general heightening of religious interest in forms which were discontinuous with the more familiar types of American revivalism. To some degree this was even true of the Billy Graham Evangelistic Association, which was incorporated in 1950. Though harkening back in many respects to the techniques that Charles G. Finney had developed before the Civil War and which Dwight L. Moody and Billy Sunday had continued to use, Graham's crusades were different. Television seems to have reshaped the message. There was now a far larger use of public-relations techniques, a more studied avoidance of controversial topics, and an absence of doctrinal specificity which antagonized many of the more strict fundamentalist leaders.

More important than Graham's influence was a surprising and almost unsolicited increase in church membership that affected almost all denominations, whether liberal or conservative. At least in statistical terms this trend brought an end to the extended "religious depression" which had set in during the 1920s. This growth took place chiefly in the sprawling reaches of suburbia, where former denizens of American cities were now adjusting to new modes of living. So marked was the trend that Gibson Winter would speak of *The Suburban Captivity of the Churches* (1951).

For many people the resort to the churches may not have been profoundly motivated but it was, nevertheless, a very reasonable effort to break through the anonymity of suburban living and to search for friends, a phenomenon which contemporary critics often derided as a lust for togetherness. Marshall Sklare, in an important study, found these social conditions conducive to the rise of Judaic "Conservatism" as a middle tradition between Orthodoxy and Reform. Will Herberg, on the other hand, probably with primary concern for the Jewish experience, emphasized the degree to which church going provided a means for the "third-generation immigrant" to reclaim his religious heritage. He pointed to the Triple Melting Pot, where each of his three main groups established their identity as Americans by means of religious participation. He thus attributed the increased popularity of American religion chiefly to a desire to celebrate the American Way of Life. Like so many Americans of the period, he paid little attention to the momentous changes going on in the great migrations of black Americans which were then going on; but there is little doubt that he touched on a very prominent feature of the times. Even the American Legion sponsored a widely advertised Back-to-God hour. President Eisenhower himself was baptized in a private ceremony; and in a famous public statement he insisted that "our government makes no sense unless it is founded on a deeply felt religious faith—and I don't care what it is." In a like spirit prayer breakfasts and other religious meetings were often held in quasi-governmental contexts. More official were the acts of Congress which declared IN GOD WE TRUST to be the national motto and amended the Pledge of Allegiance to include the words "under God."

Behind all these developments was a growing recognition that the nation's new affluence entailed increasingly urban modes of living that had profound implications for the personal composure and social relations of very many Americans. Two works of social analysis found particular acceptance during these years. Perhaps most widely quoted was *The Lonely Crowd* (1953) by David Riesman, Nathan Glazer, and Reuel Denny, which described the "other-directed" conformists who predominated in the newly competitive American scene. William Whyte's *The Organization Man* (1956) dealt with rapidly growing numbers of middle-class Americans "who have left home spiritually as well as physically to take the vows of organization life." He was referring to those who work in and belong to "the great organized enterprises" that "will set the American temper." One of his more forcefully made points was that the trends being set were extinguishing the Protestant ethic. His final counsel was to "fight the Organization." Needless to say, the fight never got off the ground, nor did many seek to gain the "autonomy" that Riesman et al. had rather unrealistically prescribed for the Lonely Crowd. Instead one beheld an unexpected increase of new forms of middle-class alienation.

Nobody knows just what all of these people did for their uneasiness of spirit, but many of them, no doubt, helped swell the church rolls. More certain is it that millions of them turned to the consolatory literature that Americans had been producing in ever greater abundance since the Gilded Age, when many authors and movements responded to the public's growing need for harmonial inspiration. The first great postwar best-seller in this field was *Peace of Mind* (1946) by Rabbi Joshua Loth Liebman of Boston, whose thoughtful blending of religious counsel and Freudian insights made the book something of a landmark in the field. Enormously more popular, however, were the efforts of the Reverend Norman Vincent Peale, whose *Guide to Confident Living* (1948) and *The Power of Positive Thinking* (1952) broke all records for the genre and for many other genres as well. Peale in fact made himself into a multimedia institution with his endlessly repeated formulae designed to put people on the road to composure and success. To what extent he deepened the anxiety of a status-conscious people can only be guessed.

Fortunate both for millions of readers and for the reputation of the decade, however, was the appearance in 1955 of Anne Morrow Lindbergh's *Gift from the Sea*, a minor classic that addresses the problems of modern living. Lindbergh combines her own insights on the meaning and uses of solitude with the thought of both ancient and modern writers. Written primarily for women, it also anticipates many insights of the next decade. The *Zerissenheit* or "torn-to-piecehood" of American society which she addresses—and which Dr. Peale exacerbated— may be seen in retrospect to be a major revolutionary feature of a decade often depicted as halcyon. It is perhaps a disease of bourgeois society whose symptoms began to appear in the early Renaissance with the construction of town clocks, the precise measuring of time, and the rational synchronization of human activities. Henry Ford's assembly lines would be a later sign. During the fifties the age of the organization clearly arrived in America, with a suddenness that made it a landmark in human history and a warning to the whole world.

Marx, to be sure, had warned that "the constant revolutionizing of the instruments of production" would throw humanity into "the icy waters of egotistical calculation," and Christopher Caudwell had described the moral and artistic implications of the "constant revolution." Max Scheler had also diagnosed the *ressentiment* which this new industrialized and mechanized social order would arouse.[8] Now it became the American people before any others in the world who moved out onto this new frontier of technocratic values; and it is hardly surprising that they affirmed the very values that were passing away. In

1951 John W. Aldridge, who gained wide attention in his *After the Lost Genera-tion*, saw "an unstable and insecure relativism as threat to serious art: the frame-work essential to the writing of novels was disappearing." While the police were struggling with violent gangs in the rapidly growing urban slums, the college professors who dealt with an increasingly affluent middle class complained about a "listless generation" of students. Against this background neither the new interest in church membership nor the widespread search for spiritual com-posure need be interpreted as superficial unrest, but rather as a symptom of a creeping malaise of latter-day capitalist civilization.

In fact one sees in these attitudes and interests of the fifties a premonitory sign of the secularizing theologies of the sixties. And in President Eisenhower's expression of alarm over the growing power of "the military-industrial com-plex" one may see an intimation of the next decade's radical protest. Yet there can be no mistaking the prevailing complacency with which moral and religious trends were being viewed. Because a nation does not oblige historians by chang-ing sharply at ten-year intervals, the same judgment would have to be applied to the Camelot years, when John F. Kennedy sought to rejuvenate the nation's aspirations. In unexpected ways, however, his short term of office marked the onset of a new time of calamities that included his own assassination.

The Traumatic Era

The late Richard Hofstadter declared that if he ever undertook to write a history of the United States during the 1960s he would entitle it "The Age of Rubbish."[9] It is understandable why a professor who experienced the tumults at Columbia University would be led to that judgment, and he no doubt could have found many collaborators from other universities. But it might well have been a parochial book—and it is probably fortunate that he never wrote it. Every decade, to be sure, has its share of rubbish; but the dominant concerns of the sixties were of momentous import.

The turbulent period to be assayed is that which lies between the election of John F. Kennedy in 1960 to those days in April 1975 when an unelected Presi-dent inaugurated the Bicentennial Era at Lexington and Concord while news of the collapsing American regime in Vietnam poured in upon him. Nobody is likely to deny that these years were tumultuous, troubled, and traumatic, and that the fifties by comparison were serene. In the realm of religion and ethics one could justify the adjective "revolutionary." Never before in the country's history have so many Americans expressed revolutionary intentions and active-ly participated in efforts to alter the shape of American civilization in almost every imaginable aspect—from diet to diplomacy; from art to the economic order.

Richard Bushman in his excellent collection of documents on the Great Awakening of the eighteenth century stresses the importance of that colonial upheaval by likening it not to the Billy Graham "crusades" but to "the civil rights demonstrations, the campus disturbances, and the urban riots of the 1960s combined." In another of his works he referred to that Awakening as a "psychological earthquake that had reshaped the human landscape."[10] Now we may reverse the comparison, and see the sixties as another Great Awakening which also left the human landscape profoundly changed. In the realm where values, hopes, fears, and cosmological attitudes are shaped, the period was profoundly disturbing; its coincidental relation to the Bicentennial deepened its impact because of the unusual amount of thoughtful reflection which ensued. Contrary to the expectations of many, the great anniversary—like the national election which brought it to a close—was a relatively somber affair. Throughout the country, despite the BUYcentennial temptations and officially sponsored celebration, organizations and institutions of every sort (universities, churches, professional societies, and not least the American Academy of Arts and Sciences) sponsored serious programs of analysis and reappraisal.

Moral shock, the sudden discovery that dry rot has weakened the supporting members of a very comfortable structure of values, is a traumatic experience often followed by religious doubt which then yields, gradually or suddenly, to a new religious and ethical outlook. For a great many Americans the era was traumatic in just this sense. That is why it may be understood as a Great Awakening even though it was a time of fear and trembling for many Americans. The issues which occasioned all this private and collective consternation were very numerous, and each of them could be subdivided. There were at least five, however, that gained massive public attention, and it is hard to see one as more important than the others.

They can be briefly listed: (1) race and racism, (2) war and imperialism, (3) sex and sexism, (4) exploitation and environmentalism, and (5) government and the misuse of power. Underlying all of these was the fundamental question of Justice, which is the first virtue of any society. Because young people took such an unprecedented role among those who were active in these interconnected moral campaigns, the nature and function of educational institutions also became prime objects of concern—and sometimes of overt assault. Serious contention on some of these questions is as old as the Judaeo-Christian tradition, others (notably 3 and 4) had emerged much more recently. But all of them were revived with great urgency during the era under discussion. If these several protest and reform movements are seen as a whole they constitute a full-scale critique of the American way of life: both the social injustices of the system itself and the ideological, philosophical, and theological assumptions that have justified and legitimated the existing social order. In this "nation with the soul of a church" these injustices and assumptions are so deeply implicated in the nexus of religion and the moral life that they must be seen as essential to this essay. Most immediate and direct in their impact were those movements which brought the churches and their members—especially the clergy—into active participation, often at the price of alienating large portions of the constituency as a whole.

In this category the civil-rights movement is by all odds first and most important. It might even be said to have been initiated in the churches during the Great Awakening and the British evangelical revival; in America it was spurred by the Revolution, but it was not really effective until the great antislavery revivals of the 1830s. After the Civil War it was the Radical Republicans who led the struggle until the Grand Old Party's chieftains bade farewell to the Bloody Shirt in the 1890s. The Supreme Court decision of 1954 was the decisive twentieth-century event, but it was only with the Montgomery boycott of

1956 and the voice of Martin Luther King that a nationwide interracial movement became a sustained reality; and during the ensuing decade no one person contributed more than King to the nation's moral dignity.

The movement peaked at Selma in 1964. Then followed the time of burning cities and finally the emergence of Black Power in 1966 after the shooting of James Meredith turned his march from Memphis to Jackson into an ambulating conference of the movement's black leadership. By the time of King's assassination the old civil-rights movement had come to an end, but not without having precipitated a crisis of conscience in white America and an awakening of self-consciousness in black America. Nothing quite like it had happened anywhere else in the world.

The anti-Vietnam War movement began gathering strength as a direct response to President Johnson's drastic escalation of the war during the spring of 1965 with the sense of betrayed campaign promises adding to its bitterness. An outmoded and unfair conscription added further grounds for anger. Many others saw the war as a disastrous abandonment of the civil-rights movement. And gradually, among youth especially, there developed an intensity of feeling that is probably unique in the country's history; by 1968 it had so grown in volume and intensity as seriously to challenge the country's sense of public order. It was accompanied by a deep animosity for persons, agencies, and institutions that in any way supported the military effort. Finally in 1968, after Senator Eugene McCarthy had impressively challenged the war policy, a proud, ambitious, and stubborn President decided not to run for a second term. The agitations continued, however, for yet another half decade, with domestic atrocities such as those at Kent State University in the spring of 1970 increasing their tempo and intensity. The lack of a military or political settlement meanwhile continued to widen the dissenting constituency. Finally, after the traumas of Watergate and the resignation of President Nixon, the American regime in Vietnam simply collapsed. The objective of the long protest was finally gained, but in a context and for reasons that led to confusion rather than to hope.

Compared to the violence and divisiveness of the struggle for racial justice and antiwar agitation, the new feminist movement, often dated from Betty Friedan's *The Feminine Mystique* (1963), and the environmental awakening, similarly linked to Rachel Carson's *Silent Spring* (1962), were relatively peaceful in their outward aspect. Both of them, however, owed much to the provocations and questioning of American values that arose out of the civil-rights and antiwar movements. These two issues, on the other hand, raised questions that challenge the most fundamental assumptions and most basic institutions of Western (or for that matter world) civilization. They lead, moreover, to reorientations of attitude and behavior that make serious assessment of the entire biblical tradition almost inescapable. One might say, indeed, that the aims of neither could be attained without basic revisions, both personal and collective, of the most time-honored American attitudes toward religion and morality.

It was the wide range of questions dealing with sexual attitudes and practices that aroused the deepest consternation and the most controversy. Before long most of the state legislatures, all levels of the judicial system including the Supreme Court, and nearly all of the churches were in one way or another wrestling with questions of birth control, sterilization, abortion, divorce laws, homosexuality, pornography, and the immensely difficult and controversial problem of defining and then establishing the rights of women. Underlying and complicating these issues are four particular problems: the deep theological, psychological, and social roots of male chauvinism in Western culture; the effects of changing attitudes on the family, as well as the needs and rights of children; the adaptation or adjustment of men and women who are seriously threatened by this social revolution; and finally, the difficulty of accepting personal responsibility for choices caused by the precipitous loss of the churches' moral authority and the manifest incapacity of "experts" to agree in their counsel. It is this last consideration, incidentally, that reveals the difficulty if not the folly of making sharp distinctions between the "religious" and the "secular."

In the long run it is probably the ecological issue, including the problems of resource depletion and energy shortages, that will require the most excruciating policy decisions and personal adaptations in the world's most technologically advanced nations. When Robert L. Heilbroner describes *The Decline of Business Civilization* he is not writing a scenario of social revolution but of the stark necessity for modifying exploitative attitudes and practices; and the same contention is present in Michael Harrington's *The Twilight of Capitalism*, though Harrington places more emphasis on the incapacity of the present system to achieve social justice and a reasonable level of equality. Quite aside from these inescapable demands for reform, however, one can only marvel at the degree to which less immediate environmental concerns for water, air, noise, ugliness, and natural open spaces have entered the American consciousness, changed ways of living, and motivated the foundations of countless reform organizations—nearly all of this in a fifteen-year period.

As for the whole long crisis of confidence in American government that began with the infamous credibility gap of the Johnson administration and continued on down through the Pentagon Papers affair to the collapse of the Nixon administration and the final Vietnam debacle, it was somehow the ultimate trauma of the era under discussion. The era was marked throughout by a steady deterioration of national trust of a dozen different kinds depending on as many grounds of dissatisfaction. Inequities in the military conscription system, racial discrimination, the impersonality of big government, the venality of small government, corruption in high office, desolated cities, the harshness of the police, and official dishonesty about the war—all of these played their part. And everyone over the age of thirty years remembers the disenchantment they created. Because deep suspicions remain, reformist zeal and political concern is replaced by self-seeking and privatization, even though the need for reform and political activism is greater than ever. From the vantage point of the later seventies, however, the most important result is a profound alteration of the American "civil religion."[11] Ideological confusion and disbelief have taken its place. This circumstance in turn leads toward a consideration of traditional religious institutions whose situation reflects many of the same characteristics.

The obvious place to open our consideration of instituted religion in America is with the nearly simultaneous election of America's first Roman Catholic President and the election of Pope John XXIII. The impact of these two events was immense, and it would be intensified three years later when the young man who had so utterly belied the idea of a "Catholic peril" was assassinated. Almost at once the old Know-Nothing syndrome faded away, and in 1964 the Republican Party, despite its nativist heritage, nominated a Catholic for Vice President. By this time the effects of Pope John's revolution began to enter into the life of the world, partly because of his own charismatic qualities but also because he summoned an ecumenical council which even in its first session brought the Counterreformation to an end and set the church to the manifold intellectual and institutional tasks of aggiornamento. Protestants, Jews, and Communists alike were affected by the kinds of dialogue that ensued. Very soon there was hardly a city or village in America that had not experienced a drastic change in religious relationships.

For Roman Catholic Americans the combined effects of Vaticanum II and rapid changes in their social situation had created grounds for extreme forms of disorientation. The classic Catholic ethos forged after the Reformation at the Council of Trent evaporated. The old defensive stance of the "immigration era" was replaced by a new sense of responsibility for American policy. Catholic scholars, meanwhile, led an assault upon the "ghetto mentality" created by the church-controlled educational system. At the same time came sudden transformations of the Mass, the passing of many traditional forms of catechetics, devotion, and obedience—even fish on Friday. More troubling still were changes in theology and moral philosophy. At precisely the time when the country was being deeply agitated by a wide range of "sexual" questions, a new emphasis on the individual conscience gained importance. Long-suppressed dissatisfactions of the clergy and other religious also came into the open, and many reforms in seminaries and religious orders were instituted, though even these measures did not prevent innumerable demissions of priests, nuns, monks, and even bishops.

Accompanying these trends was a marked decline of interest in entering religious vocations, and hence the closing of seminaries and convents as well as the secularizing of schools and colleges. All of these changes, meanwhile, were made even more confusing by the reactionary pronouncements and encyclicals of Pope Paul VI, whose *Humanae Vitae* (1968) against birth control has been judged by some to be the most fateful encyclical since Pope Leo X's excommunication of Martin Luther. One need not agree with Malachi Martin's sensational prediction that "well before the year 2000 there will no longer be a religious institution recognizable as the Roman Catholic Church of today," but one can confidently say that no part of the American population has had to accommodate itself to more drastic changes in the realm of theology, morals, and customary practice than "the Catholic quarter."[12] And to make matters more difficult, the values of Protestantism, which so many Catholics were viewing with newly deepened respect, were themselves being drastically challenged.

In contrast to the ways in which the acts of popes and councils were fundamentally altering major features of Roman Catholicism, the parallel changes experienced by Protestants were ecological. They had been going on in all the realms of theology, behavior, and institutional life for centuries, and had been accelerating for decades. Then in the sixties amid many violent and radical challenges, but yet for reasons not easily fathomed, church people of very diverse types—clergy and laity, young and old, learned and unlearned—seemed to recognize a disjunction between received tradition and present belief. Questions were raised about central assumptions of theology, ethics, ecclesiastical polity, and the relation of all of these to the social order and personal comportment. Most alarming to conservatives were the criticisms leveled at the biblical tradition as a whole—its encouragement of exploitation, male chauvinism, racism, and intolerance. There were also pervasive doubts about America's alleged providential destiny and ability to mitigate racism, poverty, and hunger. Throughout the entire period there was also a marked estrangement between pastors and the national hierarchies on the one hand and the average church member on the other. As a result ministers and seminarians in large numbers either changed their vocation or sought out new forms of ministry which twenty years ago would not have been regarded as clerical.

Deserving more detailed comment are the widely publicized challenges to traditional theology and habitual forms of worship and the religious life. The "erosion of traditional faith" so often noticed during the 1950s continued to deepen in the years that followed, with Catholics being almost as much affected as Protestants. These changes in attitude and in denominational loyalty were, for understandable reasons, first reported by college and university chaplains, who during the 1960s found it increasingly difficult to rally their former constituencies. Among the scholars and theologians soon to follow was a radical criticism of both the churches and their traditional doctrines. H. Richard Niebuhr's *Radical Monotheism* (1960) was serving as an inaugural address to the decade. It was an austere statement that revealed a line of thought that owed much to Kant, Spinoza, Hegel, Edwards, and Josiah Royce. For Niebuhr the value center of human being was the principle of being itself; it referred not to one reality among the many but to the One beyond the many. Gabrial Vahanian's Nietzschean and existentialist *The Death of God in Our Contemporary Culture* (1961) also described how the acculturation of biblical religion posed the alternative of either an "almost inconceivable reconstruction of Christianity or the emancipation of Western culture from Christianity." The book that more than any other brought these concepts out of the academy and provided an agenda for further controversy was *Honest to God* (1963) by the English bishop J. A. T. Robinson, who took with full seriousness the call of Dietrich Bonhoeffer for a theology and an ethics that was suitable for "a world come of age." This meant the abandonment of incredible articles of faith and the questioning of traditional rules of middle-class morality. In both respects he called for respecting the maturity of the modern mind.

Even more widely read in America was Harvey Cox's *The Secular City*, which took seriously this same call for a secular understanding of biblical language while also upholding a "new morality" that reinforced a growing tendency in ethics to stress context rather than traditional rules. From a Judaic standpoint the most widely read work in this genre was Richard Rubenstein's *After Auschwitz* (1966), which saw the Holocaust as terminating the theological enterprise; and from the Catholic, Leslie Dewart's *The Future of Belief: Theism in a World Come of Age* (1966). The tendency which all of these, and many other, works represent was above all to defend modern thought and to insist that church members read and hear a theology that is not fenced off from their everyday modes of interpreting society and the environing world of nature. Theologians and biblical scholars alike lost confidence in the manner by which neo-orthodox theologians such as Karl Barth had met (or glossed over) the challenge of modern religious ideas. In this light we may more clearly see that the proposals of the so-called "Death of God theology" and Rudolf Bultmann's program for demythologizing biblical languages, were essentially continuous with a tendency that Max Weber had ascribed to Calvinistic theology in general and to Puritanism in particular: "the elimination of magic from the world" and the repudiation of "all magical means to salvation as superstition and sin."[13] These proposals, nevertheless, were disquieting to many—even to those whose commitments to traditional doctrine were very attenuated. These nominal or merely habitual members who see the churches as a vicarious guarantor of traditional beliefs and values may, indeed, be a very important conservative force in American life. A very considerable minority, on the other hand, was no doubt deeply relieved to find more meaningful ways to express their faith and order their lives. The larger effect of these challenges was an increased polarization of conservatives and liberals which considerably augmented the country's evangelical constituency.

Yet the concept of polarization by itself is too simple to explain the obvious enlivenment and increased militancy of evangelical religion. Highly significant as well was the sense of a world gone awry and the deep erosion of many time-honored modes of behavior. Those who upheld the old Puritan values came to apprehend themselves as an endangered species. Sensing the dissonance between their lives and the larger public orthodoxy they asserted themselves more forcefully than ever, and like the Catholicism of the Counterreformation sought to develop institutions of their own, including schools and colleges. Like all other Protestants, moreover, they were deeply affected by various trends that were undermining the status of the old Protestant establishment, notably the election of a Catholic president and those decisions of the Supreme Court which corrected the overrepresentation of rural Protestants in political elections (1962) and prohibited religious ceremonies in the public schools (1963). Having a reverse effect, no doubt, was the presidential campaign of 1976, in which both candidates testified to their evangelical convictions. Yet not even this assurance could hide the degree to which various kinds of pluralism—moral, religious, ethnic, and racial—were challenging the hegemony of the Judaeo-Christian tradition to an unprecedented degree.

American Protestantism, however, is anything but monolithic, and the impact of theological and ethical radicalism has varied accordingly. In churches that were never part of the nineteenth-century Protestant establishment, such as the Lutheran and the Christian Reformed, the effects have been far less noticeable; and this is even more true of the country's conservative or fundamentalist and Pentecostalist constituency, which is scattered in dozens of separate denominations and sects, often as dissident minorities, both black and white, within the mainstream churches. Countless theological and practical issues divide this vast body of believers, and it may be that in any given year as many are alienated by its narrowness of mind as are reanimated by revivalism and the charismatic movement; but the national election of 1976, if nothing else, serves as reminder of the great significance of their views. On most moral and social issues they are traditionalists. In their churches personal piety and evangelism outweigh the quest for social justice in importance. Since the later nineteenth century their millennial view has tended to be pessimistic. Among evangelical seminarians and college students, however, one may discern a very considerable social awakening, and a thoughtful evangelical President might well augment their numbers. Among black evangelicals the 1960s were a time of social awakening, in urban areas especially.

Jews are a small but extremely influential religioethnic component of the American nation which is never easily compared with the Christian components. Viewed as a whole Judaism is overwhelmingly humanistic though with powerful religious memories which were awakened to a kind of defiance by the Holocaust and constantly animated during the postwar years by the founding and ongoing problems of the state of Israel, and by the problems of survival in America under conditions of waning anti-Semitism and a rapidly growing incidence of interfaith marriages. In the campaigns of the sixties for racial justice and against the Vietnam War the Jewish contribution was disproportionately large, despite a certain amount of black anti-Semitism. Some Jewish radicals also had misgivings about Israel's becoming merely a middle-eastern satellite of capitalism. The Six-Day War of 1967, on the other hand, occasioned an enormous awakening of the reverse sort—as well as a certain estrangement from Christians. As for radical theology, it had for so long been so endemic in Jewish thought as to be an almost inconsequential aspect of the decade's turmoil.

An inflowing tide of new and nontraditional religion, along with a corresponding emergence of countercultural lifestyles, was another major expression of the disenchantment and disorientation which Americans experienced during the Traumatic Era. To some degree the new religions were also part of a radical critique of the moral and theological attitudes of the Judaeo-Christian tradition.

One might even say that the protest movement as a whole, including a vast peripheral group that was sympathetic but not actively engaged, was held together by a set of attitudes and enthusiasms that marked it off as a distinct religious phenomenon. It existed for a brief but memorable period between the early sixties and early seventies. At once joyous and angry, serious and critical, it was shaped by disaffection with conventional America and pervaded by a strong awareness of a generation gap. Most of its adherents were under the age of thirty years. Rage and disappointment led some to violence, but interpersonal warmth and affection and a desire for authentic personal relationships were everywhere apparent. Wide sympathy for the poor and the abused and hopes for a new America were widespread. It was the age of the guitar. This whole generation was animated by a new popular music that was in diverse ways deeply ideological. The incredible Beatles almost defined the movement's time-span, but Bob Dylan, Joan Baez, Peter, Paul & Mary, Simon and Garfunkel, and many, many others provided a meaningful hymnody. Woodstock was a mount of transfiguration for the fortunate thousands who could say that they were there. And the elegy for this "generation lost in space" was *American Pie*, released by Don McLean in 1971.

In the midst of this decade of turmoil, however, many particular religious commitments were formed and new religions adopted. Many of the religions to which people turned were in at least two respects not new. Some of them had maintained a lively existence since ancient times. Even in America the fascination with Eastern religions dates back to Emerson, Thoreau, and the Transcendentalists, who found it a welcome and rational alternative to both the "pale negations of Boston Unitarianism" and the doctrinaire theology of New England orthodoxy. Along with this turning to the religions of India and the East, and for similar reasons, came a more esoteric revival of gnosticism, kabalism, astrology, theosophy, and "heretical" forms of mysticism, some of which had been organized movements in America since the Gilded Age. Among black Americans an "Islamic" movement had been discernible since the 1920s, though it was only in the 1960s that the Black Muslims, chiefly because of Malcolm X, made their greatest impact on the social order.

It is an unquestionable fact that the country has in recent years experienced a veritable explosion of new forms of religious organization and expression. Furthermore, they continue to proliferate in all parts of the country, and by no means only among the young. A vast literature of explication has come into being; scholarly conferences are devoted to the subject.[14] The Graduate Theological Union in San Francisco is founding an institute to foster further study of the phenomenon. Lending even greater interest to such investigation is the corollary fact that all of the major "mainstream denominations"—Presbyterian, Methodist, United Church of Christ, and Episcopal—have during the same period experienced losses of membership in the magnitude of 10 to 20 percent, with the result that these churches too are studying the new religious situation.

In the midst of this fermenting situation the place of conservative evangelicalism is somewhat ambiguous in that large parts of its scattered constituency are themselves, and by overt profession, a religiously and socially deviant subculture, which in some of its manifestations takes on almost the character of a new and radically charismatic religion. Some evangelical youth movements, for example, share many organizational and ideological characteristics of Mr. Moon's much criticized Unification Church. When seen in a full perspective, therefore, the phenomenon of America's new religions becomes so valuable an index of the elements of change in the moral and religious realm that it is worthwhile to attempt a brief summary statement.

1. Extreme diversity of religious belief and of correspondingly distinctive ways of life have from the earliest times been a characteristic feature of the American experience. A growing commitment to libertarian individualism encouraged this tendency even in later centuries even after governmental intervention in the social order had become necessary. Denominational schisms, as well as the founding of sects, cults, and new religions, became prominent aspects of American life.

2. Immigration, migration across the continent, and very diverse forms of rapid social change led to the formation of innumerable large and small subcultures whose life situations and religious traditions varied accordingly. In these myriad contexts charismatic religious leaders could and did attract followings of extremely diverse types.

3. The new industrial revolution that followed World War II created still other grounds for religious discontent as older forms of *Gemeinschaft* yielded to more impersonal forms of living together, and these tendencies to alienation accelerated during the 1960s. In the antitechnocratic countercultural ethos that

then emerged, neither the moral attitudes nor the traditional theology of the major denominations had much appeal. The religious establishment was apprehended as both conventional and authoritarian.

4. The positive result of mounting dissatisfaction was a widespread and highly variegated turn toward other-minded religious movements according to principles of elective affinity, and usually in ways that if not formally communal were at least responsive to a pervasive desire to share and express a meaningful structure of moral and religious values.

5. Amid the shocks and disappointments of the 1970s the militancy of American dissent waned, but in almost no ways had it lead to a rebirth of confidence or hope. As a result new religions continue to multiply and flourish. American dissent has waned, but there is little or no evidence of a rebirth of confidence, and the future is more uncertain than ever. As a result the new religions continue to subdivide and flourish. As usual their diversity was extreme, ranging from Satanism to disciplined forms of Zen. Most nearly traditional is a noticeable attraction to evangelical groups, which have always encouraged meaningful small-group relationships, and which are themselves in a broad sense countercultural in outlook. By and large, therefore, the new religions tend to exhibit an untraditional tendency: opposition to dogmatism and code morality; a strong disapprobation of the exploitative mentality, pollution of the biosphere, and the wasting of natural resources whether by industry or through the country's endemic gluttony. They tend to feel and express a sense of oneness with the natural world which is conducive to a mystical approach to reality that may verge on pantheism or on the esoteric. A discountenancing of racist and sexist stereotypes and behavior is almost everywhere apparent, as is a strong emphasis on warm and authentic personal relationships. When seen as a whole, the new religions in many ways perpetuate the aims and ideals of the older counterculture. They do not, by and large, reinforce the social attitudes engendered by the Puritan ethic. They try to ameliorate the ways in which monolithic institutions and materialistic striving tend to dehumanize the social order. If this analysis is to any considerable degree accurate, therefore, one may say that the new religions in concrete and very intense ways instantiate, or at least suggest, the less intense but nevertheless pervasive and enduring impact of the Traumatic Era on American attitudes and behavior.[15]

If we take a broader view of the years since President John F. Kennedy issued his spirited summons to the nation, the overwhelming fact is that the entire religious realm—moral, spiritual, and attitudinal—has been so fundamentally altered that a negative response to the question with which this essay opened is unthinkable. A new and comprehensive agenda of expectations and reform has gradually taken shape. Yet the evaluations and priorities placed on these new goals for the republic are very diverse. For many people, especially those with long memories, John Donne's sense of "all coherence gone" is the dominant reaction. A well-behaved America has passed away, and with it the certitudes that had always shaped the nation's well-being and sense of destiny. For as many others, and especially those who in various ways had supported the movements of protest and reform which made the era memorable, the sense of disorientation is far less deeply felt. For most of them urban decay, high levels of crime, gross inequalities, and malfunctioning institutions are simply constitutive of the American way of life. Rapid social change and shifting mores are the normal conditions of existence. Even among the more thoughtful elements of this latter constituency, however, there is neither exultation nor a feeling of triumph, but rather widespread doubts as to the possibilities for significant institutional change or of any basic shifts of power in the economic order. Thus for this constituency as well as for the other, America has a clouded future. Because such a convergence of views is indeed new for America, the legacy of the Traumatic Years can be interpreted only as at once both momentous and unresolved.

REFERENCES

[1]*Fate*, an essay by Ralph Waldo Emerson (1852) that is included in many editions and anthologies. I quote from the first few pages.

[2]Perry Miller, "The Social Context of the Covenant," *Bulletin of the Congregational Library*, 6 (2) (January 1955): 17–19. Jonathan Edwards, *Miscellanies*, no. 547, quoted from Sydney E. Ahlstrom (ed.), *Theology in America* (Indianapolis: Bobbs-Merrill, 1967), pp. 188–189. See also Robert Jay Lifton, "Notes on a New History," *The New Journal*, 3 (1) (1977).

[3]Paul Tillich, *The Theology of Culture* (New York: Oxford University Press, 1964), p.42.

[4]See James E. Dittes, *Bias and the Pious* (Minneapolis: Augsburg Publishing House, 1973), Chap. 5 and the works he cites.

[5]"The Revolutionary ideology could be found intact—completely formed—as far back as the 1730's." Bernard Bailyn, *The Ideological Origins of the American Revolution* (Cambridge: Harvard University Press, 1967), p. xi.

[6]Lyman Beecher, *Works* (Boston, 1852), vol. 1, p. 176.

[7]Irving Berlin was born in Russia in 1888 and was brought to the United States in 1893.

[8]Max Scheler, *Resentment* (New York: Schocken Books, 1972). The final German edition was published in 1915.

[9]Quoted by Ronald Lora (ed.), *America in the 60's* (New York: Wiley, 1974), p. vii. This is a valuable collection of documents.

[10]Richard L. Bushman, *From Puritan to Yankee* (Cambridge, Mass.: Harvard University Press, 1970), p. 187; Richard L. Bushman (ed.), *The Great Awakening* (New York: Atheneum, 1970), p. xi.

[11]On the concept and history of American "civil religion" see two works of Robert N. Bellah: "Civil Religion in America," *Daedalus*, 96 (1) (Winter 1967): 1–21; and *The Broken Covenant: The American Civil Religion in Time of Trial* (New York: Seabury, 1975). See also Russell Richey and Donald G. Jones (eds.), *American Civil Religion* (New York: Harper & Row, 1974) and Conrad Cherry (ed.), *God's New Israel: Religious Interpretations of American Destiny* (Englewood Cliffs, N.J.: Prentice-Hall, 1971).

[12]Malachi Martin, *Three Popes and the Cardinal* (New York: Popular Library, 1972), p. 9.

[13]Max Weber, *The Protestant Ethic and the Spirit of Capitalism* (London: Allen & Unwin, 1930), pp. 105, 117.

[14]Among many others see Jacob Needleman, *The New Religions* (Garden City: Doubleday, 1970); Irving Zaretsky and Mark P. Leone (eds.), *Religious Movements in America* (Princeton: Princeton University Press, 1974); Robert S. Ellwood, *Religious and Spiritual Groups in America* (Englewood Cliffs, N.J.: Prentice-Hall, 1973); Edward A. Tiryakian (ed.), *On the Margin of the Visible: Sociology, the Esoteric, and the Occult* (New York: Wiley, 1974), and Theodore Roszak, *The Unfinished Animal: The Aquarian Frontier and the Evolution of Consciousness* (New York: Harper & Row, 1975). On aspects of Evangelicalism see Robert M. Enroth et al., *The Jesus People: Old-Time Religion in the Age of Aquarius* (Grand Rapids: Eerdmans, 1972); and David F. Wells and John D. Woodbridge (eds.), *The Evangelicals* (Grand Rapids: Eerdmans, 1977). For statistics and analysis of recent trends in church membership see Dean M. Kelley, *Why Conservative Churches Are Growing: A Study in the Sociology of Religion* (New York: Harper & Row, 1972). On the polarizing attitudes and strategies among extreme conservatives, see Elmer L. Towns, *America's Fastest Growing Churches: Why Ten Sunday Schools Are Growing Fast* (Nashville: Impact Books, 1972). Peter Berger links the new positive emphasis on "secularity" in religion to the dramatic economic recovery that followed World War II in both America and Germany. He also describes the process by which a "conservative cognitive minority" fortifies itself within its own institutions of nurture. See *The Sacred Canopy* (Garden City: Doubleday, 1969), pp. 164–165; 152–153, and passim.

STEVEN MULLER

A New American University?

WE ARE NOT where we were. That much is obvious on every campus. We are moving, but not as yet with clear purpose, direction, or confidence. Most palpably evident still is our sense of loss: the American research university yearns to return to the 1950s and early 1960s. After that period came the great upheaval. We survived. But even though we know ever more clearly that the crisis of the late 1960s marked the end of a time during which we flourished, we search still for a new beginning. Where we are is uncomfortable. Perhaps the most revealing fact about us is our acute resentment of our discomfort. We have yet to accept again the reality that discomfort is normal for universities. The fact is that we were spoiled. We took a great deal for granted—affluence, growth, the respect of society, a clear sense of purpose—all now diminished. We are not where we were, and there is no going back. A new American university is taking shape. Its features are still obscure. The traits that will define those features are becoming describable.

I

Already under way is a painful and wrenching change in the relationship between the American research university and the federal government. They need each other. The great postwar partnership between them turned sour after 1968. The relationship between them that has since emerged is in part almost adversary. The new American university cannot afford either the embrace with the federal government that characterized the decades of affluence, or open hostility between itself and government. Required are the terms of a new partnership, more distant than that of twenty years ago, less abrasive and potentially sterile than that of the present.

The yearning for the recent past by the American research university is still so great as to inhibit the needed evolution of a new partnership with the federal government. Therefore what must be understood is that the quarter century between 1941 and the mid-1960s was abnormal. In an overall sense the American university was mobilized for war by the federal government in 1941, and demobilization did not occur until twenty-five years later. When the United States went to war in 1941, so did the American research university. Some faculty and students served the war effort off-campus; others were involved with on-campus training, such as ASTP, V–5, and V–12; research was needed, and

31

new laboratories were founded for the purpose, with federal funds and under university auspices.

War's end brought not demobilization but the Cold War. National defense research continued, still under university auspices, as the era of nuclear weapons, unmanned missiles, and space flight unfolded. After Sputnik federal sponsorship of research in basic science became for a time a national security priority. For a few years Korea was the scene of a return to real war. The Cold War enveloped the Third World. Here also the universities were enlisted. Foreign-language and area studies under the National Defense Education Act; assistance to less developed nations by faculties under contracts and grants from the Agency for International Development; and even the training of Peace Corps volunteers by university staff, on and off the campus—all were evidence of the continued mobilization of the American university in the national security interest. So also was the continued involvement of the university community with the national intelligence establishment, which began but did not end with the Office of Strategic Services of World War II. In this very general sense the still-mobilized American university was drawn into Vietnam as the United States became more and more deeply committed there. The disaster of that commitment troubled the partnership between government and university; in large part produced the student revolt of the late 1960s; and ended in the partial demobilization of the 1970s, and with a distance between government and university that was not in fact new but that had not existed during the preceding twenty-five years.

To speak of the American research university as having remained in a large sense mobilized by the federal government for so long must in no way be taken to mean that the university was enslaved. Quite the contrary: mobilization for the most part reflected a partnership entered into with enthusiasm, first at the outbreak of a war that was nearly unanimously regarded as just, and later sustained by the prevailing preference of both parties. The cooperation of the university was consistently less demanded than volunteered. The idealism of the international assistance effort in general, and of the Peace Corps in particular, was sincere and honorable. Dissent on the campus was not stifled. If any proof were needed that the university remained mobilized by choice it can easily be found in the fact that when Vietnam changed the university's choice the partnership of mobilization came to an end.

No, a quarter century of mobilization did not enslave the university. It brought with it, from government and society, unprecedented and sustained support, prestige, encouragement of growth, and prevailing confidence. But for all that, a price was paid. The consequences of prolonged mobilization—largely voluntary—and of resulting splendor in the government's service were excessive university dependence on government; exaggeration within the university of the virtues of applied research; and a pervasive university expectation of affluence. The price of these consequences was paid—willingly or unwillingly—at the time. As is customary, the accounts were rendered only later. They became due in the 1970s. They are hell to pay.

II

By now, the American university knows the penalties of excessive dependence on the federal government. Ambitious programs of basic research, foreign-language and area studies, and graduate education are shrinking because support once lavishly given was abruptly withdrawn. At the same time, the federal government is using the power of its purse to regulate the conduct of universities, attaching ever new conditions and requirements to its programs of support. On the campus yesterday's partner now appears increasingly as today's oppressor, indispensable but stingy, and ever more intrusive. To date the university's reaction has been mostly a futile mixture of pleas for renewed or increased support, undercut by sharpening protest against the rising flood of regulation. There is the appearance of a confrontation—even talk of crisis. But there is also the prospect of a new relationship which may not be as difficult for the new American university to achieve as present pain might indicate.

The federal government and the American research university continue to need each other. Even though the government's mobilization of the university, and the university's readiness to remain mobilized, have ended, a high level of national interest in the university's services remains, and still includes a substantial national security component. As for the research university, its dependence on national government for support of much of its large-scale research is natural and unavoidable.[1] The issue for the university, therefore, is not dependence on government, but the degree and conditions of an inevitable dependence. A nonmobilized community of research universities can and should be more cautious and selective with respect to initiatives from government for new research activities, and more insistent that government support be granted on conditions that preserve the integrity of the university institution. With the clarity of hindsight, some principal flaws in the relationship between government and university during the long mobilization period can now be seen. They include the assumption by government that the research university was obliged to respond without reservation to every offered initiative deemed to be in the national interest; the overeagerness of the universities to respond that way, based in part on university assumptions that ever-increasing government support and unlimited growth had become the norm; and the error of both parties in agreeing to do so much in common on the basis of short-term, nonpermanent funding.

The new American university will seek to receive federal support for research on the basis of substantial long-term funding. An effort will be made to designate selected universities as major research centers and to obtain endowment for them as such. In order to include the largest possible number of research universities, this effort may take the form of suggesting that major research centers be designated by area of research rather than on a universal basis; so as to make it possible, for instance, for one institution to be endowed as a major research center in one area, such as cellular biology, whereas another university might be endowed for a quite different area, such as environmental engineering. The universities will answer the argument that such endowments are expensive and perhaps too permanent, pointing out that buildings have both of these characteristics but have already been funded by government to house major research activities. They will argue that the time has come to make as durable a commitment to the people needed for research and training as has already become customary for the facilities in which they work. As for research initiatives from government that involve entirely new activities and/or levels of commitments that preclude endowments, the new American university will attempt to bargain for a scale of effort and guaranteed term of funding that will not place the internal and fiscal stability of the university at risk, as a result either of sudden overgrowth or of sudden abandonment of support with inadequate lead time. The federal government is likely to respond positively at least in some measure to these university suggestions. They are practical and reasonable, and government remains dependent on the major research universities for research and training in the national interest. Therefore, government has its own unavoidable stake in the viability of the new American university, as well as in the continued desire of the university to engage in needed research and training.

III

The new American university will also resist the tendency of the federal government to attach a growing body of regulations and conditions to its measures of support for higher education. The need of the university to do so is more fundamental than either the substance or motivation involved in such conditions or regulations propounded by government, or the financial costs also imposed. At stake is the essential need of the university to maintain the unfettered freedom of the human mind to apply its powers and methods of reason. On the one hand it is precisely the unfettering of reason which occurred in the Enlightenment of the eighteenth century that permitted the development of modern science, and which allowed the university to become the mighty and productive engine of science represented by today's great academic research institutions. On the other hand, the free exercise of reason means not loose speculation, but disciplined, rigorous, relentlessly unprejudiced testing of ideas against observable reality and, therefore, is totally dependent on the existence of standards for the conduct of work and the selection of participants that promote rational competence and defy the inhibitions of prejudice (meaning prejudgment not founded in rational analysis) in every form. It is not accident but cause that the modern research university has flourished within societies whose governments are limited in their powers to impose the tyranny of orthodoxy on research and teaching. Nor is academic freedom in this sense self-serving in the sense of being self-indulgent. It spells self-preservation—preservation of the ability of the university to select and promote faculty and students, and to maintain standards of research, in accord with criteria insulated as much as possible from the pressures of public sentiment that otherwise would restrict the free and full exercise of reason.

Such brief and ineloquent words do inadequate justice to so vital a need. However, leaders of the university have dealt with the subject more effectively many times and should and will do so in future. What the new American university must realize is that, on the issue of freedom of reason, exposition and persuasion alone will not suffice. The tendency of representative government to impose in all respects the prevailing sentiments of the public majority is as natural and fundamental as the need of the scientific university to resist that tendency directed against itself. The key word is *resist*. Excessive dominion on the part of government seldom results from malevolent will that is ruthlessly enforced. It grows from the frailty of resistance on the part of the governed, who accept successive mixtures of benefits and burdens until it is too late and they have become subjects rather than remaining citizens. Fear of the tyranny of the majority evoked the concept of limited government. Obviously this occurred without thought being given to the university specifically. But the American university is uniquely blessed both by a constitutional framework and a political tradition and climate that can sustain its resistance to excessive impositions by the federal government—if the university itself has the need and the will to resist.

In this crucial context the conclusion that the American university is only just demobilized assumes special importance. Mobilization implies a relationship between government and university that transcends mutual benefit. The root of mobilization is the assumption that a higher public cause governs all, including the government-university partnership. Under that assumption, government—representing the national interest institutionalized—is an overpowering partner, in both practice and spirit. For the demobilized new American university, partnership with government should once more be based, not on the abnormal assumption of mobilization, but on the normal assumption of mutual need and self-interest. Such a partnership is less unequal but also less cohesive. Within its terms, the university can stake out its own inviolable conditions of participation. Only to speak to these, however, may not suffice. Therefore the university must have the will and determination to reject and do without selected aspects of partnership with government that invade essential university prerogatives. At the end of what is here characterized as an overlong period of mobilization this is doubly difficult for the university: first, because it means a relationship with government that is permanently full of tension, requires tenacious negotiations without end, thus denying even the prospect of ever reaching calm and safe waters; second, because it puts increasingly at risk the affluence to which the university had become accustomed.

Nowhere is it ordained that the university institution shall be richly well supported and untroubled—especially not the modern research university committed to free science and reason in the midst of human societies that at their best tolerate reason and freedom only within limits. The first reaction of the demobilized American university to the altered relationship with the federal government therefore still suffers from the shock of restored normalcy and its consequences. The new American university's emergence has to be based on full rerecognition that affluence too is a relative good. Self-preservation may depend more on freedom retained than on funding, no matter how desirable or urgent the need for such funding may appear. The integrity of free science is of greater fundamental importance than the resources at its disposal. The power of the purse may have to be opposed by the power of penury put at risk.

In the extreme these dichotomies, of course, would be suicidal for the university. But in present American society the extreme is unlikely. The federal government has a declared, profound, and irreplaceable interest in the universi-

ty and need for its research and training programs. When the federal government trespasses too far on the ability of the university to maintain standards
essential to itself, a few refusals of support will count for far more than arguments. The short-term risk involved in such refusals is great. They require
courage, especially because they imply acceptance of an enduringly uneasy
partnership. But the long-term risk is not great. Representative government
comprehends resistance, especially from an institution upon whose services
both government and the public are dependent. The new American university
must cultivate a new and lasting assertiveness, and abandon abnormal expectations not only of affluence but of harmony in its relations with government.

IV

Another consequence of prolonged mobilization, noted earlier, is an imbalance within the university caused by excessive emphasis on the application of
science and research. This presents a problem of vexing complexity which the
changing American university is only beginning to address. Again the issue
involves a question of degree. The generation of applicable knowledge—and
training—is a natural and desirable component of university work. Equally natural and also legitimate is the priority which government and society at large
attach to the usable fruit of research. All that is first suggested here is that
during the period of mobilization both government and university prized the
applicable results of rational inquiry so highly and for so long that the reward
system within the university became distorted. Support for research and salaries became most readily available for scholars whose work had the appearance
of social applicability. For a time government support of basic research and the
overall affluence of the university that derived from steadily rising enrollments
moderated the distortion. More recently, when federal support of basic research
dwindled and enrollments ceased rising, the university found itself with an internal reward system less oriented to pure merit of scholarship than to the social
utility of scholarship. Applied research, however, can in the long run maintain
high quality only when rooted in the rich soil of pure and basic research. This
alone demands a readjustment of the university's internal system of reward.

But other facets compound the problem. Emphasis on socially applicable
research within the university during the period of mobilization combined with
an unplanned and virtually unacknowledged deemphasis on values within the
university, as well as with a diminution of the university's most traditional role
in the transmission of fundamental values to successive generations of students.
The decline of emphasis on values was in so many ways related to the period of
mobilization that it must be regarded as a negative legacy of mobilization which
a changing American university must overcome.

Between 1945 and into the 1960s the American university was possessed by
an ideology in general best described as that of the New Deal. This ideology
rested around two basic concepts. First, society is best governed by a pragmatic
process of political compromise that allows popular majorities, on the one hand,
to insist on policies that favor the most urgent interests of the greatest number
and, on the other hand, to coalesce around such compromises as are necessary to

keep the social system working and to avoid outraging political minorities. Second, a society so governed has the capacity to solve not only all of its own problems over time but is also capable of solving the problems of other societies—at best by the imitation by others of the American way, at worst by benign intervention to encourage such imitation.

The accent in the first concept is on the word *pragmatic*, which elevates pragmatism into ideology, while denying the need for theory or philosophy. In the second concept the accent is on the capacity to solve social problems, denying the intractability of historic and human conditions, and perceiving all social phenomena as problems, subject by definition to solution. The real triumph of the New Deal came not in the 1930s but after the war, and its basic concepts constituted the orthodoxy of the university at that time. To the confidence of a university that had served society in war, knew itself to be needed in the Cold War, and was rejoicing in expansion, there was added the zest of an ideology that called for even greater recognition, because so much of the knowledge needed to solve the problems of America and the world emanated from the campus.

Protracted mobilization of the university would not have been possible without a prevailing rationale. This ideology provided the rationale, and so dominated the university as to constitute orthodoxy. Its dominance was partially obscured by an intriguing paradox. The university, suffused with pragmatism, luxuriated in more theory than ever before. "Luxuriated" is the right word: the university could afford theory because in the face of the dominating orthodoxy it did not matter; it was not even controversial. The sources of theory were unique. Before, during, and after the war, the American university absorbed an exceptional infusion of talent that had fled Hitler and his works.[2] That talent included some of the finest social philosophers of Europe, who were duly respected and installed on American campuses. Respected and installed, yes; listened to, scarcely. These men and women were truly refugees, not only physically but intellectually. The American university succored them, but precisely when the applause was loudest the indulgent audience was at its most deaf. No matter whether the alien thinker was a Marxist or a monarchist: he or she was alien, distinguished, admirable, and irrelevant. One may cherish the overwhelming confidence of American pragmatism that swept other philosophy aside or find cruel irony in the fact that the wisdom that understood Hitler was discredited, not only because of its perceived irrelevance but because it had been powerless to stop Hitler. The certainty remains that the greatest flowering of social philosophy in the history of the American university occurred when, and perhaps because, no one really gave a damn.

In the context of mobilization rationalized by ideology and adorned with the paradoxical richness of social theory, the American university appears to have suffered an inner erosion of values that went far beyond a simple, if protracted, overemphasis on the virtues of applied research. The chain of events began with the extraordinary success of physical science, in the early part of the century, most notably in physics and mathematics. Science produced new marvels of technology. To the extent that Russia and America won World War II as nations, so did technology as a phenomenon. Inevitably, science—a form of human creativity—became somewhat confused with technology, the application of science to human and material conditions. In the past there had been science without immediate technological consequences. In the twentieth century it was no longer commonly so. So much technology had resulted from science that technological consequences were expected from new science as a matter of course. It came to seem now that any science that produced no new technology might, solely for that reason, lack validity. '

Science itself is the fruit of brilliant human reason coupled with intuition. It deals with matter, and is therefore largely susceptible to rigorous testing and evaluation of the material results it predicts. Admirable as are its reasoning and intuition, even more admirable are its inflexible standard of proved authenticity and—in our time—its ultimate technological benefits. In this admiring spirit, it is merely logical to ask why the study of man and society should not also be science, subject also to the same measured proof and rewarded equally by resultant technology. The American university did more than ask the question. It answered, "Why not?" and gave a solid try.

In the years after 1945, a spectacular change took place on campus in the disciplines grouped together as social science. With the assistance of academic European refugees already versed in the work of Weber, Durkheim, Mannheim, and others, sociology developed a new theoretical framework and added the sophisticated new technologies of quantitative measurement. Economics exploded into new realms of mathematical abstraction, system modeling, and statistical evaluation. Political science turned from its classical tradition and adopted the theories and methods of sociology. Anthropology also adopted sociological theory and methodology and became an applied field in a wholly new sense, as American anthropologists studied less developed peoples in pursuit of patterns of social modernization as well as for the sake of research. Again with the help of academic European refugees, psychiatry emerged as a vigorous new field of its own; social psychology also turned wholly to quantitative techniques; behavioral psychology was already primarily a laboratory science. This transformation of the study of man in society into social science had a single guiding aim: scientific objectivity, or at least that degree of objectivity with which physical and biological scientists treated animate and inanimate matter. The banner that flew over the social sciences read "value-free." The leading social scientists were those best able to point with pride to the objective and carefully measured quality of their analysis.

One would have expected that this development in the social sciences would have caused at minimum extreme tension, and at maximum open conflict, between them and the disciplines grouped together as the humanities. But this did not happen. In fact the reverse happened, because the humanities attempted as best they could also to become sciences. Long before the designation of disciplines as arts and sciences became common, the old university had had only a faculty of philosophy, traditionally alongside a faculty of law and a faculty of medicine. In those days the precursors of today's arts and sciences disciplines were moral philosophy (humanities), social philosophy (social science), and natural philosophy (physical and life sciences). At least historically, the field of philosophy occupied a central place within the evolution of the university. After 1945, the discipline of philosophy in the American university was in a new and interesting condition. Even though ethics, the history of philosophy, logic, and other traditional aspects were still being taught, the discipline had become pre-occupied with the problems of linguistic philosophy that had just been imported from the British universities. Nearly all of the best young talents in philosophy took their stations along this new frontier. No criticism or disrespect is intended, but the effect was the conversion of philosophy into a discipline that at least for the moment had less to say to other fields than in the past. The philosophers did not speak of being value-free, but their newly identified problems of articulation severely reduced their discussion of values.

In the other fields of the humanities, particularly English and literature, the temptation to apply quantitative techniques to criticism was inevitably followed. History, astraddle the boundary between humanities and social science, found new rewards in the application of sociological methods to its material. Whereas a few disciplines, such as classics, and many older scholars failed to make the adjustment—and in some cases suffered perceptions of intellectual isolation to the point of paranoia—the bulk of the humanities followed the social sciences toward the adaptation of scientific method and quantitative techniques for testing hypotheses. They neither resisted the trend nor opposed it.

The American university that is newly emerging in the wake of demobilization is making a start toward the correction of the fundamental imbalance which has occurred. Viet Nam and Watergate put an end both to mobilization and to the prevailing ideology that lent it justification. It is also once again becoming clear that there can be no such thing as a value-free university. That this is so in practice became painfully evident during the crisis of American university of the late 1960s. During that crisis it became apparent that the common core of values, to which students and faculty might have rallied, had substantially disintegrated.[3] The university, therefore, has since been engaged in the difficult effort to rebuild consensus on the campus and has recognized the practical need for this purpose of a restored system of values. And of course, a value-free university is also not possible in principle.

There is no value-free science. The confusion that has arisen on this point is stupid and damaging. The scientific method is emotion-free. In its perfect application it proceeds rigorously regardless of values to which there may be deep emotional reactions pro or con. But that does not make it value-free. Science is nothing more than the application of human reason in the most logical manner possible. Therefore, reason is a value upon which it rests. And because it is human reason that is involved, science also is founded inextricably upon human life as a value, and upon the rational conduct of that life. The inner core of values of the modern university is therefore founded upon reason and its rigorous application.

The health of the new American university depends on its ability to strike a new and sound internal balance. Basic research and pure scholarship must once again be accorded their due. Fundamental values within the university must receive reemphasis. The traditional function of the university in the transmission of values must be restored. Even though it is necessary to perceive and comprehend those aspects of the recent past that have resulted in imbalance, it would be in vain to look to them also for future guidance. The trend that will most mark the emerging features of the new American university is found in its curriculum. Because self-renewal must be animated by innovation, needed curricular revisions are likely to compose the vehicle for a university reformation.

V

One of the imperatives that impels the American university toward curricular revision is correction of another imbalance: the present overemphasis on vocational and professional preparation in the training of students.[4] Recognition of the problem is already widely shared; corrective measures are already being attempted; little elaboration, therefore, is required on what is already obvious. Students in the university have been instructed in highly specialized knowledge to an ever more intensive degree. This has been the natural result of the rapid diversification and sophistication of the state of knowledge and the unavoidably allied tendency of faculty expertise also to become diversified and sophisticated, and in the process also fragmented. At least four adverse consequences for students have recently become apparent. They increasingly tend to lack command of a common core of basic knowledge; in part because they are encouraged to specialize too soon, in part also because faculty interest and competence in the teaching of basic knowledge has been diminishing. Students in the university are also being prepared up to the most advanced state of their specialized field of instruction; but although great effort is expended to acquaint them in detail with the ultra-latest state of their art, the further refinement of knowledge continues to develop so rapidly that what students learn so thoroughly in the final and most intensive phases of university preparation is superseded by new advances within a decade or less. At the same time, the number of openings for employment or further study for which intensely specialized preparation is required has been declining; and those students who as a result are not placed in such desired openings are then doubly frustrated, both because such an extensive and demanding investment of effort has been in vain, and because its very intensity defies its alternative applications. Finally, the joy of learning and the intellectual stimulus for students has been undercut by the growing tendency to regard university education purely as vocational or professional preparation; with the result that it has been described more and more exclusively as an economic investment, to be judged solely on the basis of ultimate economic return; and that in the process it has also attained increasingly the aspect of an economic competition among students.

These very same perceived negative consequences of the regular university curriculum have also already led to the rapid expansion of a new curriculum of the university that serves the purpose of continuing education.[5] Earlier part-time university curricula for working adults had been designed primarily for those who had missed the opportunity for full-time higher education before taking employment, or for those who wished to pursue their specialized studies further while at the same time retaining employment. Recently, however, university graduates in accelerating numbers have been returning for part-time study with additional and different motives. The most highly specialized graduates have begun to return to catch up once more with the advances in the state of their art that may have revolutionized their specialty during the relatively short interval since they took their degrees. Numbers of them have found their field superseded altogether by new knowledge and technology, so that they return to transmute their old specialty into a more applicable new discipline. Still others have discovered themselves to be too narrowly trained. They return for at least part of the general education that was earlier sacrificed to premature over-specialization.

In response, the American university is newly preoccupied with attempts to rebuild general liberal education within the regular curriculum on the one hand, and to realize on the other hand the full potential of changing and expanded demand for continuing education. But promising as these attempts may appear to be so far, they must be viewed as merely the stage of infancy of the new American university that is emerging. The first efforts to revive general liberal education are still encumbered by preliminary difficulties. General liberal education is so closely linked to a value system that its restoration must go hand in hand with the reemphasis on values within the university which, as noted earlier, is only just beginning. Effective reemphasis of basic knowledge is also indispensable to general liberal education and requires a changed commitment from the faculty. That may become easier to achieve in the new context of sharply restricted faculty mobility, which has resulted from economic scarcity and the arrest of growth within the university. There is, furthermore, legitimate argument as to the substance of general liberal education, particularly because a mere return to much of the curriculum as it existed years ago would appear to be essentially reactionary. The efforts on the other hand to develop new curricula for continuing education is making more rapid progress. It may be seen to suffer in part from being campus based, which puts it at times in awkward geographic relation to the places of employment and domicile of its clients.

The future is unpredictable. Nevertheless, the best assumption appears to be that the new American university is at the threshold of a curricular revolution whose consequences will define its novelty. The chief agent of this revolution—in two very different ways—will be technology. New educational technology is already becoming a vital force in the development of curricula for continuing education.[6] Film, radio, television, computers, and recordings are all already in use as educational tools. One tends to forget how relatively recent these technologies are; how natural it is that their applications should be manifest first in society at large rather than in the university; and how much the economies of miniaturization are in fact contemporary, not even recent. The pocket calculator is one example of how cheap and personally accessible the new technology can be. The television recording, the video-telephone and other refinements appear imminent. Computer-based instruction is less and less experimental and expensive. For years the fear among educators has been that technological devices might replace the human element in education and should be resisted. Now it is becoming more credible that these technological devices are no more than tools of the teacher, and in fact may free him or her to interact personally with numbers of students in a manner superior to their encounter without technological assistance. It is possible to envision the teacher or tutor with the burden of mass instruction not only shifted from the book to new technology, but once again individualized and personalized for each student even when large numbers of students are involved. One may even speculate that American society might solve the problem of democratic mass education without lowering standards, because the promise of the new educational technology is an achievable common standard at an extraordinarily high level.

The new American university may thus emerge as an institution liberated significantly from earlier constraints of space and of human age. The campus will continue to exist as a cluster of talent, of laboratories, of resources, as a community of some students in residence, and as a communication center. But the outreach of the university will become vast. Members of its faculty will be able to interact personally by means of new communications technology with colleagues and students across the world, ultimately without doubt across barriers of language as well as space. One implication is that the relationship between matriculant and university will become life-long, regardless of geography. Allied to that is the implication that what the youthful student first learns in residence can be truly basic, because he or she will remain literally a life-long student who can tap the resources of the university not only by returning there, but at home and on the job. Another implication is that the discipline of learning can once again be placed squarely on the student, where it must be, in that the student's progress can be tested and reinforced at every step by technology, relieving the teacher of some of the most time-consuming and least rewarding disciplinary obligations. The technological capacity to motivate, reinforce, and instruct is also potentially so varied and sophisticated as to call up a vision of high common standards of knowledge attained by almost every citizen.

On a far more profound level, technology may also become a major ingredient in the redefinition of general liberal education. It is an observable fact that university students may at their best be literate, numerate, and highly competent in their specialty; but also in large numbers they are profoundly ignorant of the technology already in daily use. The same assertion holds true for most faculty and, indeed, most citizens. Bygone is the era of the tinkerer. How many highly educated people today understand the inner workings of their televisions, their calculators, their microwave ovens, or even their automobiles and telephones? Behind such a question is an awareness of alienation from indispensable ingredients of everyday life that raises a host of other troubling questions. If we are daily so alienated from the fruits of science, will we long respect science? If this alienation means ignorant dependence, are we not subjects rather than masters of technology? Can one expect self-confident individualism from persons ever more dependent in their daily lives on tools which they comprehend only in their uses and can neither explain nor repair? Can human reason continue to flourish in a society whose most widely used artifacts, even though derived from applied reason in the form of science, seem to their users to be mysteries that to them—the users—defy analysis, understanding and, to a perceivable extent, control?

These are rhetorical questions. They point, however, to the apparent need for a new humanism. The essence would be to close a circle by refamiliarizing the individual once again with the familiar technology that is the fruit of science. Its goal would be to restore to the human person mastery of technology, to liberate the individual from ignorant dependence. If this suggestion is valid, it may have profound implications for a new university curriculum in general liberal education, and indeed for the American university institution. A new humanism of individual comprehension of technology might become the catalyst around which the value system of the university would revive in new form. It might also be the catalyst of a new liberal curriculum. In such a curriculum such essentials as literacy, numeracy, command of history, and other basic ingredients of education would have their necessary place, but the driving animus would be the effort to build individual mastery of the most essential components of everyday life. Just as the liberated mind must be free to use the tools of language and mathematics, so must it be free to use common technological tools with ready ease, and without the handicaps of mystery or alienation. The effort toward full confidence in the use of technology could and should begin in schools, but the high level of technological development implies that its full realization could occur only at the stage of higher education. The assumption of such a new humanism would be that it is as crucial today to learn to comprehend the mysteries of everyday technology as it was long ago in the university to study the Scriptures or the law.

If that is true, more should be added to a new liberal curriculum. For example, it is as alienating to live in an incomprehensible society as it is to live with incomprehensible technology. The fact that society is undergoing rapid, drastic change is well understood and closely studied within the American university. But the focus of such study is still essentially national rather than international, and that is becoming an indefensible anachronism. Global interdependence is easy to demonstrate: picture the not atypical American, with a German car, a Japanese camera, a shirt made in Hong Kong, Italian shoes, a television set assembled in Taiwan, drinking Colombian coffee, driving on Middle East oil—the inventory could go on and on. The company he works for is probably part of a multinational corporation, the bank he uses depends in part on foreign business, his investments and pension involve a stock market increasingly affected by overseas funds, what he produces probably is sold abroad as well as at home, and his security depends at least as much on international as on domestic tranquillity. But the American university remains heavily parochial in teaching the social sciences within a predominantly American context. For those Americans who do not travel abroad the real world is portrayed fitfully by the news media. They present instant news of foreign crises out of context. They do not prepare the traveler for the fact that the railroad station of Frankfurt looks and sounds more Turkish than German; for Teheran's traffic; for London's racial problems; for Brazilian industrialization; or for the countless other aspects of an international reality from which no person on the globe is insulated. This is no slap at the news media. They are not expected to substitute for higher education. The fact is that international studies remain too much a specialized field in the American university. Begun during the period of mobilization for the sake of training specialists, international studies should now at last take root in the curriculum of the newly emerging American university. Humanism never squared with nationalism; a new humanism should educate for familiarity with the reality of an international society as well as with technology. One world is neither vision nor ideal. Politicoeconomically, one world is hard, unsettling, radicalizing fact—already sensed by most, albeit understood by too few.

VI

We have ourselves now come a long way. Perhaps we have exceeded the real portents of the present. A conclusion must be attempted. It is that a new American university is indeed beginning to manifest itself, and that its prospects appear to be both brighter and very different from what is currently perceived. A major preoccupation of the university at the moment is its relationship to the federal government. We have suggested that this relationship was both abnormally close and imbalanced during the twenty-five years after 1941 that we have called the period of mobilization. Although these were years of growth and achievement, they were not necessarily golden years. A new partnership between government and university is in view—less close, more balanced—demanding of the university a ceaseless struggle to maintain support while retaining autonomy. In this respect the immediate challenge to the new American university is to shake off nostalgia for a recent past in which too much was wrongly taken for granted, and to regain self-confidence.

The great dread of the American research university in the wake of demobilization is stagnation. Fear abounds that lack of growth, declining enrollments and support, lack of faculty mobility, and the resulting aging of faculties almost entirely vested with the rigidity of tenure will in combination produce a university institution deprived of self-renewal. This fear is matched by concern that in a climate of dejection and reduction internal rivalries within the university will further traumatize a governance structure still shaken by the trauma of the late 1960s; especially because no internal consensus of values has yet been recreated in the university. Such fear and concern stem from real problems that we have not discussed.[7] Instead our conclusion is that the new American university is already beginning to be shaped according to a new agenda that will solve such problems over time. The visible opportunity to strive for a new curriculum, inspired by the values of a new humanism, realizing the potential for the university of the new technology of education is the opening door to the future. We are not where we were. We can see where we are going. It is worth getting there. We are already moving. It is time to pick up the pace.

REFERENCES

[1]See, for example, in Bruce L. R. Smith and Joseph J. Karlesky, *The State of Academic Science: The Universities in the Nation's Research Effort* (New York: Change Magazine Press, 1977). It is interesting to contrast the tone of this study, done in 1976, with the tone of one produced a decade earlier in Stephen Strickland (ed.), *Sponsored Research in American Universities and Colleges* (Washington, D.C.: American Council on Education, 1967).

[2]Even though this phenomenon is well known and virtually gave rise to a new institution in the form of the New School for Social Research in New York, it has never to my knowledge been fully documented. There is, however, an excellent background study done by Enid Bloch in an unpublished doctoral dissertation, *The Inverse Cultures: Politics Versus Philosophy in America and Germany* (Cornell University, 1973).

[3]This point is unfailingly made in studies of the crises that occurred at individual institutions. For example, *Crisis at Columbia: Report of the Fact-Finding Commission Appointed to Investigate the Disturbances at Columbia University in April and May 1968* (New York: Random House, 1968), and Cushing Strout and David I. Grossvogel (eds.), *Divided We Stand: Reflections on the Crisis at Cornell* (Garden City, N.Y.: Doubleday, 1970). In more general terms the point is made in Theodore Roszak, *The Making of a Counterculture: Reflections on the Technocratic Society and Its Youthful Opposition* (Garden City, N.Y.: Doubleday, 1969).

[4]This is, for example, a significant thesis in Joseph Ben-David, *Centers of Learning: Britain, France, Germany, United States*, an essay prepared for the Carnegie Commission on Higher Education (New York: McGraw-Hill, 1977).

[5]See, for example, the institutional study *The Lifelong University: A Report to the President* (Michigan State University, 1973), or the more general thesis in Theodore M. Hesburgh, Paul A. Miller, and Clifton R. Wharton, Jr., *Patterns for Lifelong Learning* (San Francisco: Jossey-Bass, 1973).

[6]See, for example, John Fralick Rockart and Michael S. Scott Morton, *Computers and the Learning Process in Higher Education*, a report prepared for the Carnegie Commission on Higher Education (New York: McGraw-Hill, 1975), and Judith Murphy and Ronald Gross, *Learning by Television* (New York: Georgian Press, 1966).

[7]I am conscious of having avoided almost the whole of the current agenda of problems confronting higher education, not because the problems are not of urgent importance but because I believe them to be—at least to a large extent—solvable only within the next context which I see in the emerging stage. These problems include equal opportunities for minorities, the handicapped, and women; faculty unionization and other aspects of change in university governance; uncertainties of federal funding under the higher education amendments of 1972 as further amended and amendable; the impact of federal regulation by any number of agencies such as the Veterans Administration or the Internal Revenue Service, or in pursuit of such new legislation as the Occupational Safety and Health Act and the Employment Retirement Income Security Act; the increasing tendency to resort to litigation in the resolution of campus-based problems; the new intervention at the level of the states which is represented by the efforts of state-wide coordinating agencies; the financial crisis produced by inflation; the tuition gap between the independent and the state-supported sectors; the potential adverse impact of tax reform proposals; the prospect of decreased full-time enrollments produced by declining birth rates; and a host of others.

ROSABETH MOSS KANTER

Work in a New America

TIMES OF AFFLUENCE carry with them emphasis on leisure and social reform. In the 1960s, despite the continual undercurrent of protest and youthful political energy unleashed, the cultural emphasis—in the media, in the Democratic administrations' social programs, in the expressed concerns of youth—was on personal and social improvement: the expansion of consciousness, the development of self, the discovery of vehicles for personal and spiritual fulfillment. Even the building of social movements (in the 1960s a complex of civil-rights activism, Vietnam War protests, student militancy, "flower children," and media interest in communes, cooperatives, and progressive schools) was in an important sense a leisure pursuit, to be followed by those for whom basic economic security was not in question. But times of recession change the cultural mood. In the 1970s high rates of unemployment, continuing inflation, and increasing competition for high-paying jobs have brought a very different and more sobering emphasis on material security, on jobs, on work. Work in America in 1977, then, has not only academic interest as one of a number of aspects of life in the society to be understood in its continuing and changing faces; it is a central public issue in its own right. Tackling unemployment has continued to be a major plank in the Carter administration's platform.

Neither interest in work nor the work ethic has disappeared in America. But, as I will present data to indicate, a concern for first, the meaning of work, including the compatibility of jobs with cherished life values, and second, individual rights in work (neither of them new ideas) have continued to grow stronger over the past twenty years, particularly as the composition of the work force and government policies have shifted. However, it is also clear that the issue of work and the conditions of work are perceived differently by different groups in the population, depending on sex, age, race, education, and occupation.[1]

The Basic Data

First it is important to look at the basic data about work in America over the last few decades: who works, at what kinds of jobs, under what kinds of laws, regulations, and policies, and how they feel about it. What has changed, and what has remained the same? Table 1, following the text of this article, presents those indicators of major work variables that show little change from the 1950s, that have remained constant, that have leveled off, or that have shown neither upward nor downward trends, instead fluctuating with economic conditions. As one would expect in a changing society, there are not many such important stable variables, although it is important to note that self-employment has stopped declining and that workers on the average have not become more likely to go on strike or to leave jobs but rather, on these matters, to respond to economic conditions. Table 2 presents those aspects of labor-force composition, job conditions, and employee attitudes that have been declining in the past decades; Table 3 shows indicators that have been increasing in magnitude and new policies or programs introduced.

It is not generally significant that Table 3 is longer than Table 2, for most indicators can be offered in either positive or negative terms; for example, a decreasing percentage of union membership among the work force is obviously also an increase in unorganized labor. But in the area of policy and work conditions, the additions do outweigh the declines; we can see that there have been many new developments added to a large number of existing rules and programs, without evidence of decline in previously won benefits or beneficial practices.

The Trends

What general trends can be identified in these data?

WOMEN AND WORK

The biggest change, both proportionally and in magnitude, involves the vast increase in women's labor-force participation over the past twenty-five years. The large increase in the number of women in the labor force offsets the slight decline in men's labor-force participation so that, overall, since 1950 the proportion of the population 16 years of age and over in the labor force has increased by a percentage point or two. Women also gained a bigger share of multiple-job holding during the recession period of the 1970s, indicating that women are working harder than ever before. The biggest increase is in white married women; the labor force participation rate of that group has nearly doubled since 1950. This also means an increase in the number of two-worker families, a phenomenon growing faster among whites than among blacks, who traditionally have had the larger proportion of two-worker families.

However, the larger numbers of women working and the passage of legislation outlawing sex discrimination have not necessarily resulted in great changes in the opportunity structure for women. Women have continued in the last twenty years to be clustered in the occupations in which they already dominated, such as clerical and other "female" occupations; clerical work is also among the fastest-growing occupations of the last decade, growth which is projected to continue into the future. There was a small increase in the proportion in women's share of professional jobs, up 4 percent in the period from 1962 to 1974, a change that is hardly significant given women's influx into the labor force. The proportion of female lawyers and judges and physicians and surgeons just about doubled, but the percentages are still small compared to men's share of such jobs. The largest increase was in women's share of college and university teaching jobs, which increased from 19 percent to 31 percent during this time. These represent primarily gains for white women, for the black women's proportion of total professional employment went down slightly. At the same time, there was an increase in the early 1970s in the percentage of women on sample surveys reporting sex discrimination in employment, a measure, of course, of a change in perception rather than a change in objective discrimination. There was also an increase in litigation as a result of enabling legislation and publicized settlements.[2]

A YOUNGER, MORE EDUCATED LABOR FORCE

The labor force has been getting younger, not only as a result of the youth bulge in the late 1960s and early 1970s, but also because of several other trends: the decline in labor force participation of older people, including older women, in part a function of retirement benefits and policies, and a large increase in teenage labor-force participation, growing two and a half times faster than the teenage population as a whole since 1964. This is also a more educated labor force. The median educational attainment over the last ten years has shown a small increase, to 12.6 years, but a bigger and more significant increase for blacks, from tenth grade to some college. Though professional, technical, and other white-collar jobs have been increasing during this period, increased educational attainment has also filtered into the blue-collar ranks, so that there is a more educated blue-collar labor force. The proportion of male crafts workers and other blue-collar workers with a year or more of college has doubled since 1966, so that nearly a fifth of all crafts workers and a tenth of other blue-collar workers have had at least four years of college.

These trends take on significance for worker attitudes and behavior, as well as for labor force composition, for this is much recent evidence that younger workers are the most restless and dissatisfied. On Institute for Social Research surveys, younger workers have the highest rates of expressed dissatisfaction with their jobs: 37 percent, as compared with about 20 percent for the overall sample of employed workers.[3] Younger workers also have the highest rates of job seeking and of unscheduled absence from work; they were the largest population group by age among the third of the labor force that changed occupational category between 1965 and 1970.[4] National surveys have also indicated a curvilinear relationship between education and job satisfaction, with dissatisfaction highest among those with some college, particularly in comparison with college graduates.[5] Although there has been little hard empirical evidence of rising worker discontent over the last twenty years, the shift toward a younger, more educated labor force of people who bring a different set of expectations into work, may have significance, a phenomenon we will explore later. Less educated teenagers are also the hardest hit by unemployment.

SOME SMALL GAINS FOR BLACK JOB HOLDERS

Even though more blacks than whites are unemployed, those blacks employed in the labor force have taken a slightly increased share of the good jobs.

The number of blacks in managerial jobs has more than doubled over the past fifteen years, but they still represent only 4 percent of the employees in such jobs; similarly the black men's proportion of total professional employment has also nearly doubled, but still represents a low figure. With the increased educational attainment and slightly better proportion of desirable jobs, it is not surprising that the expressed work satisfaction of black workers has shown a great increase since 1949, the same period during which the work satisfaction of the total labor force rose slightly and then leveled off and showed some declines in the late 1960s and early 1970s. It should be noted, however, that expressed job satisfaction of blacks is still lower than that of whites overall. Furthermore, the increase of black men in professional jobs has not been uniform; the biggest increase was in physicians, engineers, and accountants, whereas the smallest was in college and university teachers.[6] Black women, meanwhile, lost a small part of their share of total employed professional women, because of the vast movement of educated white women into the labor force.

INCREASED FRINGE BENEFITS AND GOVERNMENT ATTENTION TO WORK CONDITIONS

Since World War II, fringe benefits have gradually been extended, in kind, in quality, and in number of workers covered. Employee health benefits have increasingly included dental as well as medical benefits. Maternity leave options with pay and/or reemployment provisions have been developed; workmen's compensation insurance coverage has been extended; and work options such as job sharing, flexible work hours, or staggered hours have been highly publicized, though the growing numbers of employed persons enjoying such conditions is still a very small proportion of all workers. Legislative and government policy changes to enable alternative working hours and arrangements was the subject of Senate hearings in April 1976.[7]

A greater amount of federal and state activity in the past decade has concerned job safety since the development of the Occupational Safety and Health Administration in 1970. Some unions, such as the United Auto Workers and the Communications Workers of America, have also bargained for reduced work weeks or for flexible hours; successful attempts around flexible hours include the American Federation of Government Employees at the U.S. Social Security Administration and the Association of Engineers and Scientists at Pacific Gas and Electric.[8] But it should be noted that the impetus for such actions varies considerably: for employees, they may be seen as fringe benefits affecting the quality of out-of-work life; for employers, they may be seen as meeting needs for work arrangements that assure greater motivation and productivity; or, for the unions, they may be seen as making possible the avoidance of layoffs by spreading the available work.

At the same time that fringe benefits have been growing, so have expectations. The percentage of the labor force expressing a desire for more fringe benefits on national surveys has remained about the same despite an increase in benefits.

A SLIGHTLY SHIFTING POSITION OF ORGANIZED LABOR

Since 1960, union membership as a proportion of the nonagricultural labor force has declined, but, at the same time, collective bargaining has been extended into new sectors. In a number of states, collective bargaining was extended to health-service workers and public employees, and there has been an increase in public-employee unionism since World War II. There is evidence that such white-collar unions may emphasize work options and labor-management problem-solving committees more than have unions covering primarily blue-collar workers; the flexible hours bargaining reported above occurred in white-collar unions. Between 1970 and 1977 the number of collective-bargaining agreements with provisions for joint management-labor committees rose from 44 to 97; this change was particularly noteworthy in the federal sector, where 44 percent of negotiated agreements contained such provisions, in contrast to the private sector, where less than 5 percent of agreements covering a thousand or more workers stipulated joint problem-solving committees.[9] If the proportion of the population employed by federal, state, and local government and in white-collar occupations more generally continues to increase, the issues for organized labor could also begin to shift.

THE QUESTION OF WORK-FORCE DISCONTENT

One of the controversial topics of the 1970s has been the question of whether or not there is rising worker discontent requiring government action. The 1973 Task Force Report to the Secretary of Health, Education, and Welfare, *Work in America*, was severely criticized for exaggerating the extent of the "blue collar blues" and "white collar woes." Similarly, 1972 Senate Labor Committee Hearings were published under the title "Worker Alienation," but even the senators involved recognized the controversial nature of their position. Senator Edward Kennedy opened the hearings with the following statement:

> The Secretary of Labor, James Hodgson, was on the Today Show this morning. He said that the only two things that workers are interested in are their paychecks and their families. I think they are also interested in the content of their jobs and about what they do when they go through the plant doors. I think the Secretary has misread what has happened across this land, if he does not understand workers are increasingly dissatisfied by working conditions, even if they are satisfied by their paycheck.[10]

As Kennedy indicated, there were also politicians and union leaders just as vociferously expressing the opposite point of view. The General Vice President of the International Association of Machinists and Aerospace Workers said, for example, "To enrich the job, enrich the paycheck."[11] (But this could also express a cynicism about whether certain jobs could ever be improved.)

The trend data presented above are far from unequivocal on the issue of changes in work satisfaction. Over the last 20 years, a large number of surveys have indicated that the approximate percentage of the labor force reporting job satisfaction has remained steady at about 80 percent, although the Gallup Poll found the decline between 1964 and 1973 after an increase in job satisfaction from 1958 to 1964. It is only attitudinal measures that show slight evidence for small increases in job dissatisfaction; behavioral measures tend to show little change over the past twenty years—or, more accurately, fluctuations with the general economic situation. Quit rates have fluctuated inversely with unemployment. Strike activity showed a sharp increase in the late 1960s but peaked in the early 1970s and returned to earlier levels. Recession and inflation in the 1970s have been associated with an emphasis on job security and on material benefits in work, countering the tendency in the late 1960s and early 1970s for respondents on surveys to stress the content, interest, or importance of work.

On the other hand, national probability samples do indicate that job discontent, by some measures, reached a high from about 1970 to 1973. The proportion of employed men who said they would continue to work despite having enough money dropped between 1953 and 1971 from 80 percent to 74 percent.[12] Interesting work overtook steady work as the most important thing employed workers said they wanted from their jobs, between 1957 and 1969.[13] Yet, the 1972 Institute for Social Research survey of working conditions showed high overall levels of satisfaction with a large number of aspects of work conditions, except for an increasing proportion of workers between 1969 and 1973 reporting problems with inconvenient schedules, a larger proportion of women complaining about sex discrimination, and a larger proportion of union members complaining about democracy or management in their union. Reviewing the data they had collected, Robert Quinn and colleagues at ISR criticized the *Work in America* report for exaggerating the increase in dissatisfaction that did not exist. At the same time, they also commented: "It is comforting to think that at least matters are not getting any worse, but there remains the question of why they are not getting any better. The few bright spots that emerge in comparisons of the 1969 and 1973 data are mainly confined to financial matters."[14]

If the trend data are equivocal with respect to discontent, they at least point to the fact that the period from about 1967 to 1973 represented the height of concern. It is interesting to note, however, that even on the ISR surveys, although overall quality of working conditions did not decrease between 1969 and 1973, the quality for women increased, whereas the quality for men declined.[15] It may be, then, that whatever dissatisfaction existed was much more prevalent in the ranks of white men than of either black men or of women. Furthermore, most of the evidence for increasing discontent covered a rather short time period, and also a time that opened with relative affluence, showed a bulge in the youth population, and contained the protest over the Vietnam War and general youth movements known as the "counterculture." It was in 1972, for example, that college graduates from five Pennsylvania colleges saw themselves as placing a different emphasis on work from their parents; the students were interested in the nature and purpose of jobs, whereas they saw their parents as placing most emphasis on salary and job security.[16] But by 1976, after several years of high unemployment and inflation, 1976 Stanford Business School graduates were most interested in material factors in their work, rather than in intrinsic content or importance.[17]

Thus, 1977 is probably no worse in work conditions or worker attitudes than 1957; indeed, in objective conditions there is evidence for some improvement. But expectations also rise to keep pace with improvements, as we saw in the case of fringe benefits; and it is not, for example, workers with the lowest education and poorest objective job conditions that express a proportionate large amount of dissatisfaction. We must also, therefore, question the meaning of job satisfaction as expressed on public opinion surveys.

"Job satisfaction" is not usually a very good indicator of how people really think about their work or of what they would do if offered an alternative; I have criticized the concept and its measurement elsewhere.[18] As we have seen, expressed job satisfaction is rather high in the United States and has been for decades. In ten major population studies of job satisfaction, from 1935 to 1967, covering nearly 10,000 adults, not more than 23 percent expressed dissatisfaction, and that figure was reached only by including neutral and ambivalent responses; the average in these studies was under 15 percent.[19] Though very few workers express direct dissatisfaction in attitude surveys (less than 10 percent on a recent University of Michigan national survey), a much higher percentage tends to report that they would seek another occupation if they had a chance—up to 60 percent. And even though most people responding to a magazine questionnaire said that they liked their own job (84%), only half felt that most people liked their jobs.[20] There is also ample evidence that aspirations are a function of the opportunities for advancement people see at work, so that they might report immediate job satisfaction (making their peace with limited opportunity) while withdrawing their psychic investment from work.[21] People in low-opportunity situations, then, may become indifferent to the jobs, so they report no major dissatisfaction as long as the paycheck keeps coming. Thus, satisfaction is not a straightforward matter; responses are a function of expectations, opportunity, and the groups to whom people decide to compare themselves. We cannot, therefore, conclude from survey data about worker attitudes that there are no problems with work in America, or no new expectations.

Furthermore, some of the shifts in labor-force composition, in legislative actions, and in public discussions of work innovations may signal some changes in the general expectations people bring to the workplace, even if their level of discontent has not, objectively, increased. We are left with the question of whether the last few years represent a return to pre-1967 "normalcy" or a temporary dip in a long-term trend, in which more people who work also increasingly expect more from it.

THE NEW THEMES

With all the data put together, what general picture emerges? Two themes can be said to characterize the ambience of work in America in 1977—some parts of which represent continuous threads and ongoing trends since World War II, but others that are new developments or stronger tendencies. One theme can be called cultural or expressive: the concern for work as a source of self-respect and nonmaterial reward—challenge, growth, personal fulfillment, interesting and meaningful work, the opportunity to advance and to accumulate, and the chance to lead a safe, healthy life. The other can be called political: the concern for individual rights and power, for a further extension of principles of equity and justice into the workplace and into the industrial order, for equality and participation both in their general symbolic manifestations and in the form of concrete legal rights. Neither theme denies the extent to which concerns about income and basic material security still dominate the lives of many Americans and propel them into long hours and second jobs. But even in recent years, when unemployment and inflation increased many people's basic economic worries, and higher earnings was clearly the major reason job holders looked for another job (34% cited this), the themes were present as an undercurrent: 10.6 percent of job seekers wanted better working conditions, 9.8 percent wanted better advancement opportunities, and 9.3 percent wanted a job that would better utilize and develop their skills; no other reasons received as frequent mention.[22]

A more educated work force—as ours has become—is simultaneously a more critical, questioning, and demanding work force, and a potentially more frustrated one if expectations are not met.

The Concern for Work as a Source of Self-Respect and Nonmaterial Rewards

Post-World War II sociological and psychological evidence has continued to support the proposition that work is a basic source of meaning in life, and surveys of the American population indicate popular agreement with the professionals. On an often-quoted 1953 survey, most respondents (80%) reported that they would continue to work even if they had enough income to make it possible to stop; in 1971 the figure was still 74 percent among men, 60 percent overall.[23]

The hard-core unemployed have also responded positively to questions about working anyway, even if they could live comfortably without it (84% in one survey).[24] A Brookings Institution study in 1972 found that even long-term welfare mothers and their teenage sons continue to have a strong work ethic, associating their self-esteem with work just as strongly as the nonpoor and the working poor, and expressing as much willingness to work even if they had an adequate income. (But what does differ is their weaker belief in the effectiveness of their own efforts to achieve job success and their greater willingness to accept welfare if unable to earn enough money.)[25]

In the writings of professionals over the past decades, work has continued to be found central to health and psychic well-being, as a source of prized self-image and validating experiences.[26] Declaring after a study of 1,156 employed men that "employment remains a symbol of one's place among the living," Harold Wilensky wrote:

> In rich countries of the modern era, work, whether it is becoming more or less central as a source of personal identity and social solidarity, still remains a necessary condition for drawing the individual into the mainstream of social life; wherever work ties are severed, there is a decline in community participation and a related sense of isolation.[27]

The unemployed, and also those low in expressed job satisfaction, appear notably less satisfied with their lives in general and with their housing and community, less trusting, more concerned that they will have a nervous breakdown, and more out of control of their own lives, according to a 1971 national survey.[28]

Though to a somewhat lesser degree, these psychological relationships between paid work and well-being hold for women as well as men, despite a
traditional (but now questioned) nonlabor force option for women. Indeed, a
growing body of evidence suggests that unemployment (in the sense of non-
participation in the paid labor force) may be nearly as large a psychological
problem for women as for men. Working women, in comparison to non-
employed women, have been shown to exhibit more self-acceptance, and satisfaction with life, greater freedom from emotional disturbance, and fewer
physical symptoms.[29] A study of longevity, looking at who beat their life expec-
tancy as calculated by actuarial tables, and by how much, put housewives far
down on the list, well behind blue-collar workers.[30] Intensive studies of depressed women have shown that women who worked outside the home while
depressed were less impaired in their functioning than housewives, and that this
was not a function of differences in severity of the illness, leading the researchers to conclude that there was "something protective in the work situation."
(These relationships are modified, of course, by whether the woman feels that
she is working by choice or by necessity, and—even as for men—by how she
regards her job.)[31]

The trend data show, in fact, that paid employment may be becoming more
important to women as it very slightly declines in importance for men. The
increase in women's labor-force participation has been responsible for the increase in the employed proportion of the population; men's labor-force participation and expressed interest in continuing to work even if not economically
necessary has been dropping. Furthermore, it is no longer primarily poor or
single women who work. The labor-force participation gaps between black and
white women, between married and single women, and between wives of professionals and wives of laborers, have been steadily closing, as we saw in Tables
2 and 3.

And work remains an indicator of social importance, in specific as well as
general terms. Social-class position is still derived primarily from occupation
rather than income, and attitudes about occupational prestige have remained
rather constant over the past few decades, despite a closing of the income gap
between some professional jobs (such as college professor) and some unionized
blue-collar jobs (such as truck driver).[32] Those for whom occupational prestige
is higher are also more likely to report that work is a more central life interest;
out-of-work life takes precedence primarily for those with blocked mobility or
nonorderly, interrupted careers.[33] It can be argued that part of the social outcast
status of the elderly in America derives from their work deprivation; as we have
seen, in the twentieth century, and especially after the passage of the social
security legislation, the labor-force participation rate of older people has been
steadily declining.[34]

The objective sense in which work is associated with meaning in life is more
than matched by an expressed expectation, on the part of workers and potential
workers, rising since the mid-1960s, that jobs ought in fact to be a source of
meaning. Daniel Yankelovich has pointed to a growing tendency to expect to
find self-fulfillment through meaningful work, a trend carried by younger
people and women. His surveys of college students in 1973 provide dramatic
demonstration of the desire to find meaning in work. Respondents identified

major influences on their choice of a job or career: "challenge of the job" was endorsed by 77 percent; "able to make meaningful contribution" by 72 percent; "ability to express yourself" by 68 percent. Money, job security, and the chance to get ahead were still chosen by over half of the respondents, but only 28 percent were interested in the prestige or status of the job, and only 22 percent that it lacked pressure and was not too demanding.[35] For the rest of the youth population (the 70% of those between 18 and 25 who do not finish college), Yankelovich argued that the idea of meaningful work produced ambivalence and confusion. The notion that work should have meaning has diffused to them at the same time that they lack the opportunity to do meaningful work. This split within the youth generation is far more significant than any split between the generations, because the tendencies of younger workers to be less satisfied with their jobs, and for those with some college education to be more discontented than college graduates, are added to the growing number of more educated blue-collar workers, all increasing the expectations for jobs—but also the frustration potential.

There is similar evidence from studies of adults. Detroit Area Surveys in 1958 and 1971, which asked respondents what they would most prefer in a job, found the following rank order both years: (1) "The work is important and gives a feeling of accomplishment"; (2) "Chances for advancement"; (3) "High income"; (4) "No danger of being fired"; and (5) "Working hours are short, lots of free time." Although there was some shift in relative popularity from 1958 to 1971, with short hours and high income gaining, the overall ordering remained.[36]

Thus, the self-respect theme—the idea that self-esteem comes through the act of working—seems alive if not well in contemporary America. Whatever turning away from jobs as the source of esteem exists may reflect disillusionment with the potential of these jobs for individual interest or achievement. The supposed erosion of this portion of the "work ethic" might be more apparent than real among production workers, too. The highly publicized Lordstown strike has been reinterpreted as a response to speed-ups on the line that interfered with the capacity to carry out the work.[37] Indeed, it seems to be a piece of recurring managerial ideology to complain of the lack of interest in and devotion to work shown by workers. At least since Frederick Winslow Taylor and his "scientific management" movement at the turn of the century built into management thinking a view of workers as hedonistic, materialistic, unstable, childlike, and requiring direction, similar concerns have been expressed by the captains of industry.

Labor leaders, understandably, take a different position. In a recent survey of 563 members of the American Management Association and 69 union leaders, the contrasting views were predictable. Among managers, 79 percent agreed that "the nation's productivity is suffering because the traditional American work ethic has eroded," a statement endorsed by only 35 percent of the union spokespeople. Similarly, about one-fourth of the managers agreed that "workers don't care what they produce or how they produce it—as long as they are well paid" and "the average unskilled worker is interested in doing as little as possible," in comparison to only about one-tenth of the labor leaders. In general, union leaders, much more often than managers, were inclined to see many more ways of improving worker attitudes and motivation—that is, they were likely to believe it was there in the first place to be improved.[38] So one's view of the state of the work ethic is a function of which side of the fence one is sitting. It might also have something to do with the degree of nostalgia indulged in, even though what we romanticize as a "work ethic" may have instead been a "mobility ethic" for earlier generations. Yankelovich also argued that there is a trend away from postponing self-gratification in order to ensure the upward mobility of one's children.[39]

Further support for the willingness of people to continue to work hard— regardless of how they feel about it—comes from the fact that high proportions of the labor force continue to prefer work (or the income associated with it) over leisure. Even if this is explained by economic necessity, it at least undercuts the notion that distaste for hard work is at an all-time low. As Stanley Lebergott pointed out, "The tendency to exchange more income for more leisure was apparently checked by the end of the mid-1930's. Workers thenceforth took productivity gains almost wholly in money rather than partly in leisure."[40] A number of reports, including Lebergott's, make clear that even though hours of work scheduled by work establishments have been declining through the century, and part-time opportunities have increased, such reductions in official work times may not be matched by a decline in the overall hours worked by individuals. The decline in the work week for the United States economy as a whole over the past hundred years may be offset somewhat by dual-job holding, which increased, for example, from 3 percent in 1950 to 5.3 percent in 1957, remaining steady at about that rate (fluctuating between 4.5 and 5.7%).[41] The reasons for multiple-job holding are also revealing. In 1974, 38 percent of the men and 18 percent of the women were self-employed on their second jobs. Although 32.1 percent said they had more than one job in order to meet regular expenses, the second largest group (17.9%) said they did it because they enjoyed the work.[42]

Hours for individuals have also not necessarily declined. According to 1965 Bureau of Labor Statistics reports, 40.1 percent of employed men between the ages of 25 and 44 years worked overtime on a given job, and another 8.2 percent had two or more jobs, averaging 39 hours in their primary jobs and 13 in their secondary ones.[43] Of full-time employees in May 1974, 16 percent worked 5½ to 7 days a week.[44] Although long hours declined in the recessionary period of 1973 to 1976, still one-fourth of all full-time employees worked more than 40 hours a week in May 1975.[45] The long hours put in by executives and some professionals are notorious; in 1975, nearly half of the managers and administrators had extended workweeks. It may be true that the only occupational segment for which working hours have actually decreased are white-collar jobs, such as clerical and low-level administrative positions.[46] Although goods-producing industries have reduced hours more than service industries, blue-collar workers are also more likely to moonlight.[47] In addition to hours spent at paid work, volunteer work also indicates the extent to which people are willing to work hard. Informal surveys in several cities indicate that volunteering still remains an important avocation, and many agencies have no trouble finding volunteers, although volunteers do seem to be themselves asking for more meaningful and less routinized work.[48]

Given these trends toward long hours of work, where was the impetus for the concern exhibited with work dissatisfaction by the HEW task force and the Senate Labor Committee in 1972? During the late 1960s, partly as a result of youth movements, the "work ethic" did appear to be losing ground to the desire for personal fulfillment and social activism among young people. This was also the time of the Lordstown strike, called by some a sign of increasing revolt by younger workers. Yankelovich polls found disillusionment with the "success" theme, especially among college students, in the early 1970s. What declined during that time was the belief that work pays off and produces such rewards as home ownership, a high standard of living, and position in the community.[49] It was also at this time that "corporate dropouts" received public attention, and interest peaked in exploring self-sufficient, perhaps land-based, communes and other forms of self-employment as an alternative to more conventional jobs. But cynicism, on the Yankelovich surveys, reached its height around 1971, and career orientation among college youth grew from 1967 to 1973. Whereas for a time physicians, lawyers, business executives, and politicians fell in public esteem as stories of corruption—Watergate, Lockheed, and Medicare payment scandals—there is no evidence that such high-prestige occupations became less attractive. If anything, increasing job competition and student populations have raised enrollments in professional and business schools.

But the late 1960s did bring attention on a variety of levels to some human costs of work. Public interest focused on the quality of work conditions and their effect on psychological as well as physical health. Popular media themes, as well as governmental attention, are illustrative. Some of these involve costs of success. If once people were considered virtuous by working hard, they now may be considered "sick" if they work too hard; "workaholic" has entered the vocabulary. If providing material benefits for one's family was once the raison d'être of breadwinners, now material goods may be considered hollow, and families seen to suffer if work absorption removes the breadwinner as emotional participant in the family. The ailments associated with high-stress occupations have also been increasingly in the public eye: from heart disease through alcoholism. The Occupational Safety and Health Administration began in 1970 to monitor job safety, and state legislation for safety and health soon followed. Recent court decisions have extended workman's compensation to executives, managers, and other white-collar workers, as well as to widows whose husbands had fatal heart attacks while under executive pressures.[50]

Work, then, may still be important to Americans for self-respect and meaning in life—but not just any work, and not under just any conditions. For a sizable segment of the population, work is expected to provide more than merely material rewards, and the cost of material rewards themselves should not be too high. At the very least, work should be a source of pride, and it should contribute to the realization of cherished personal values.

There is one final aspect to the concern for meaning in work also connected to the changing view of success: a concern for work as part of the total life situation, and thus, an interest in how work relates to life as a whole. Both the social critics of the 1960s and the more recent women's movement encouraged awareness to the context in which work occurs. The increase of women in the paid labor force, especially married women with children, focused attention for policy-makers on how work connects with family life and the extent to which work systems make it possible to maintain effective participation in both worlds.[51] A rise in the number of single-parent families has similarly directed attention to the question of how the organization of work might change to permit a bridging of the work world and the rest of life, particularly for those people who must both work to financially support a family and take responsibility for that family's personal care and feeding. Many people, on surveys, desire an organization of work which acknowledges and facilitates what they must do (and want to do) in the rest of their life. Work is no longer to be the inflexible core around which the other parts of life must bend.

One indicator of this developing expectation that work accommodate to the rest of life comes from the 1969 and 1973 ISR Surveys of Working Conditions. The greatest increase in problems of 19 labor standards areas was reported around inconvenient hours. Excessive hours almost disappeared as a complaint; scheduling was the issue. One-fourth of the reported problems in 1973 concerned the interference of work schedules with home life; in 1969 this was mentioned so infrequently that it did not constitute a coding category. Furthermore, the big increase in reported problems came from men, not women. Though complaints were associated with children in the home, the association was not limited to women.[52]

The organized women's movement began to formulate concrete requests in these areas in 1972 and 1973. Some are still a part of the platform of the National Women's Agenda (which reflected the consensus of 100 women's organizations in 1977) and such continuing groups as NOW, Women's Equity Action League, and the National Women's Political Caucus: child care services at work; maternity and paternity leaves without loss of seniority or benefits; part-time work (with benefits) and flexible work hours; and an end to nepotism rules when they discriminate against women.[53] Some of these are already being established, although very slowly. Maternity leave benefits grew in the 1970s, but a recent Supreme Court decision in *Gilbert v. General Electric* excluded pregnancy from disability benefits. Innovative arrangements have been developed which permit couples to work together, or two people to share a job—although such arrangements are probably available to only a minute fraction of the work force at this time.[54] There has been only a slight but still a steady increase in voluntary part-time employment: from 9.3 percent in 1957 to 13.5 percent in 1972, with women comprising 67.5 percent of the part-time workers in 1972,[55] although Massachusetts is one state to have passed legislation requiring a proportion of state jobs to be part-time by 1978.

Flexible work hours are gradually being extended in the United States after a slow start. In 1976 the U.S. Comptroller General's office estimated that 4-day, 40-hour weeks were in use in 3,000 firms employing more than one million people.[56] Ironically, protective labor legislation, as well as employer reluctance, has been one of the barriers to flexible hours in America. Flexible hours permit some workers choice of when to put in their hours, except for a fixed "core time."[57] They thus allow a greater chance for participation in valued parts of life outside of work, from family to recreation to politics, as well as for accomplishing tasks that need to be performed during conventional working hours.

The contemporary cultural challenge to economic organization, then, can be summarized as follows: a concern that work have meaning, provide self-fulfillment, express cherished values, and permit a healthy, balanced life.

The Concern for Individual Rights

The past decades have witnessed an increase in public policy pronouncements directed toward rights at work, as well as in job holder expectations in this area. On both fronts the issue is the extension of basic civil rights assumed to be guaranteed by a democratic society into organizations which have operated without making all of them explicit—the creation of more "organizational civil rights." The concerns involve equity, on the one hand—fairness, justice, an even chance to obtain the position for which an individual worker is qualified; and discretion, on the other—greater employee control, a larger say in decisions, more power over work conditions.

Equal-employment opportunity and affirmative-action programs are only one instance of a tendency, throughout the twentieth century, for more and more governmental and judicial intervention in the internal practices and policies of employing organizations, on behalf of unorganized as well as unionized employees; and collective-bargaining rights have been extended to important groups of white-collar workers, such as public employees. Since the Civil Rights Act of 1964, and despite the failure of the Equal Rights Amendment to pass in the requisite number of states by the time of this writing, there have been a growing number of state antidiscriminatory statutes and agencies.[58] In 1976, Congress passed a bill dealing with federally funded public works programs that imposed the first criminal penalties for failure to comply with anti-job bias provisions.[59] Other individual employee rights, such as jury service without employer retaliation, were also guaranteed by new statutes.[60]

Thus, from the perspective of policy makers, the public interest is seen to require a scrutiny of employment practices and an extension of individual rights, because of the centrality of organizations as producers of jobs as well as of products—jobs that have important individual and social consequences. Philip Selznick phrased the legal rationale this way:

> In recent years we have seen a transition from preoccupation with freedom *of* association to a concern for freedom *in* associations. This renewed awareness stems from a realization that the private organization can be more oppressive than the state. The loss of a job, or the right to pursue a profession, or the opportunity to continue one's education, may be far more hurtful than a term in jail. When these deprivations are inflicted arbitrarily, and there is no recourse, a gap in the legal order exists. We become more sensitive to that gap when the decisions are made by organizations that seem large, powerful, and impersonal, and by men who have the look of officialdom.[61]

In this perspective, then, the women's issue is one example of the pressure for development of appropriate concepts of individual rights inside workplaces as well as structures that maximize the exercise of these rights.

Yankelovich labeled the worker demands that parallel such governmental attention a "psychology of entitlement," which leads to the creation of new social rights as the boundary between the public and private sectors becomes increasingly fuzzy. For example, the college students he studied in 1973 believed, in these proportions, that they were entitled to as a social right: "participation in decisions that affect one's own work" (56%); "a secure retirement" (37%); "the right to work" (27%); "a minimum income" (26%); and "an interesting job" (17%).[62] Certainly militant women's-rights organizations, such as the coalition of over twenty of them led by The National Women's Political Caucus that lobbied President Carter to offer more jobs for women, are not content with the mere appearance of greater opportunity for women; they expect concrete results—so many people in so many jobs. And, the argument runs, if organizations do not provide both positions and access to opportunity, they should be forced to do so.

Union leaders are also more likely than management to favor an increase in rights—in worker power and control—as a method for improving employee attitudes, although unions have not tended to make these part of their platforms (despite such well-publicized experiments as the job-enrichment innovation at Harman Industries conducted by management and the UAW). However, when asked, some union leaders do support the issues. In much higher proportions than managers, union officials in one recent survey stressed such issues as greater job security, improving working conditions, protecting workers from arbitrary and unfair treatment, better treatment by supervisors, providing greater opportunities for advancement, and giving workers more autonomy on the job.[63] From the other side, some union members would like more of some of these things from the union itself; between 1969 and 1973 complaints about union democracy and leadership on the ISR survey doubled.[64]

Among social scientists concerned with work, there is a great deal of interest in the extension of worker rights and justice in the workplace in the form of participation. A rather old idea, that began with "human relations in industry" studies in the late 1920s, is beginning to take new form: the idea that workers are more satisfied (and perhaps, though not necessarily, more productive) if they have a chance to participate in the decisions affecting them. Until recently, unlike the European experience, "participatory democracy" in American organizations tended to be confined both in scope and in the people it affected. It often meant a human-relations emphasis on more communication from management and more chance for employees to discuss impending changes or tinker with their details; even then, it was often restricted to upper white-collar ranks. But "participation" today, as expressed by the National Quality of Work Center in Washington or the Work in America Institute, increasingly means structural support for a larger degree of worker control. And the request implies such major organizational change as flattening the hierarchy, generating self-directed work teams, and providing employees with more job-related information necessary to make decisions.

In short, such proposals (few are as yet implemented in many organizations) encompass a variety of basic "organizational civil rights"—the extension of such legal safeguards as due process, free speech, and open access to information into the workplace. Making such proposals particularly significant is the fact that only about one in five workers in the labor force is a union member, and only about one in nine is covered by a major collective bargaining agreement (those covering 1,000 or more workers.)[65] Whether collective bargaining will extend further as the major vehicles for power, or whether organizations will ensure more rights on an individual basis (or both), remains to be seen. Access to information is particularly interesting as a right, for a higher managerial or professional monopoly on information is one of the ways workers and even middle managers or paraprofessionals are disenfranchised and disempowered. Thus, the push for equal-employment opportunity on the part of minorities and women may work not only to ensure equity but also to make work systems more transparent. As employment records are subpoenaed and data are collected for court cases, as employment practices are scrutinized for fairness by outside agencies in compliance reviews, then the stage is set for people inside the organization also legitimately to demand and receive more information.

The expectation of more rights in the workplace is given fuel by those social science studies which find the degree of power and control over one's work a major predictor of a range of personal outcomes. These studies are significant for several reasons. First, the evidence has been accumulating with only rare contradictions. But more importantly, sociologists and psychologists are employed as management consultants and as witnesses in legislative hearings; the 1972 and 1976 Senate Labor Committee hearings called on a large number of social scientists. Third, the control theme is not only a leftist issue; it shows up in studies of job satisfaction, alienation, mental health, political attitudes, and family relations. For example, men low in job autonomy were found to be more severe and hostile toward their sons, confirming a "displacement of frustration" hypothesis.[66] Blue-collar workers in low control jobs (with limited participation and self-direction) were less democratic in their politics and less creative in their leisure compared with those in similar jobs at the same pay levels but with more control at work.[67] Two of the best predictors of work alienation, in another series of studies, were an organizational setting which provided little discretion in pace and scheduling, and a blocked and chaotic (i.e., out-of-control) career.[68] In still another survey of over 3,000 male workers in all occupations, alienation was more directly affected by the degree of occupational self-direction than by ownership or hierarchical position.[69] My own investigations of work behavior in a large industrial firm lend confirmation to the notion that powerlessness among administrative and managerial personnel (accountability without discretion and with little capacity to independently mobilize resources) was associated with rigid, controlling, rules-minded, and coercive behavior.[70] Indeed, Melvin Seeman pointed out, in a major review of research on alienation, that most reports of increasing self-estrangement at work and desire for meaningful work fail to distinguish between discontent stemming from the absence of intrinsic fulfillment in work, and that derived from lack of control at work. He argued that control aspirations seem to be involved in most major outbursts, such as the strikes at Lordstown and Luton in France.[71]

All such studies provide back-up, then, for rights-enhancing policy scrutiny such as the Senate hearings. What they do not do, however, is document the extent of the problem.

Even though it is possible to identify an overarching sense of entitlement and a rights-extension theme, these issues also have complications and problems that are not expressed in the same way, or with equal force, by all segments of the population. First, and most importantly, what happens when rights conflict, or when one group feels its job rights are being violated by another's? The interpretation of antidiscrimination statutes and decisions to involve compensation for past discrimination has come into conflict, in recent years, with other hard-won rights, such as seniority; but a 1977 Supreme Court decision struck a blow against retroactive seniority, perhaps beginning the reversal of a trend toward attempting to remedy the effects of past as well as present sex or race discrimination.[72] Conflict can also center around such special privileges as preference for war veterans in hiring, struck down in Massachusetts in 1976.[73] So even though the rights of some groups have been advancing, other groups have been complaining.

Second, power and participation themes have been expressed most vociferously by college students, by people in high-prestige occupations, and by educated young workers. But even here, it is not clear how to interpret the data: as indicating a concern for greater job security by increased "entitlement" in the jobs? for less rules-bound, more flexible work conditions? for more voice in management and organizational decisions? or for more autonomy and self-direction? The available evidence points to the first two, at least for the bulk of the working population, rather than the latter two. In this sense, "rights" might mean to most people (other than the educated elite) the traditional bread-and-butter issues of protection from arbitrary job or income loss for which unions have been fighting since their beginnings.

Autonomy and self-direction, though stressed by many social-science professionals, have not yet emerged as high on average workers' preference orderings. Studies of occupational prestige, for example, have found relatively low-autonomy jobs inside organizations accorded more prestige than jobs with comparable pay that are self-directed but may also involve risk—for example, office-machine operations and bookkeepers ranking higher than small independent farmers, and assembly-line workers higher than taxi drivers.[74] This is compatible with the 1969 ISR Survey of Working Conditions, in which advancement opportunity and loose rather than tightly controlled supervision correlated most strongly with job satisfaction, whereas autonomy and "enriching" demands ranked seventh and eighth in terms of ability to predict job satisfaction.[75] Anecdotal, but well-publicized, evidence also comes from the month-long visit of six American auto workers to the innovative Saab-Scania plant in Sweden; these workers were indifferent or negative to the worker participation plan and the self-directed assembly-team arrangements.[76] Of course, as commentators have pointed out ever since "participatory democracy" was first suggested as a work option, participation is very time consuming and unlikely to be appealing to people who do not see the direct benefits to them or who are not very committed to their jobs in the first place.

Finally, certain organizational innovations with employee rights and power implications may be opposed by unions if introduced by management, particularly if there is the suspicion that the move is antiunion or another way to increase productivity without increasing pay.[77] There is also no clear-cut agreement, even among social scientists promoting participation or autonomy-enhancing schemes about the best ways to do this. As for affirmative-action and equal-employment opportunity programs, there is little consensus about specific steps to take or changes to make in work conditions other than hiring and promoting more members of any discriminated-against groups. Thus, the rights and power issue remains fuzzier and more controversial than matters such as pay, fringe benefits, or flexible work hours.

However, one conclusion that can be drawn is that the political issues of rights and power continue to be involved in American jobs in the 1970s. As rights are extended, contention (such as grievance filing or litigation) also increases. But we are witnessing a predominantly individual phenomenon: a change in job holders' views of what they are entitled to, rather than an increase in strident demands or organized activism.

Workplace Realities

How do the concerns with meaning and with rights stack up against the realities of the distribution and content of jobs?

In some basic sense, it is true that American society, having moved a century or so ago from agriculture to industry, is now moving from the production of goods to the production of services as the major component of the economy. A large proportion of the labor force can now be called "white collar," like the professional, technical, and kindred workers, salaried administrators and managers, sales workers, and clerical workers that together made up 45 percent of the employed persons in 1974.[78] In the period from 1972 to 1985, professional and technical workers will be the fastest-growing occupations, according to the Labor Department's *Occupational Outlook Handbook*.[79] But at the same time that more service jobs exist, the supply of college graduates is already beginning to outstrip the demand, a gap that labor forecasts see as widening in the future. Two consequences are not difficult to imagine: increasing competition for preferred jobs, and increasing numbers of overqualified workers with poor work morale. Manpower agencies could find themselves with incompatible clientele: (1) well-educated workers seeking high-status jobs; and (2) employers seeking workers for low-level jobs.[80] Thus, despite a shift toward white-collar, service jobs with more comfortable working conditions, labor supply and demand incongruities can lead to pressure for even more job up-grading.

Furthermore, a close look at the jobs considered to be part of the service sector changes the picture about an overall shift to desirable jobs. There are at least three sources of confusion. First, the census occupational category bearing the label "service workers" includes such jobs as janitors, waiters and waitresses, police, and beauty parlor workers. Very few of these have the pay, the status, or the humanistic tinge usually associated with the myth of the service society. In many cases, these jobs are already heavily mechanized and involve a closer relationship to machines than they do to people; an AFL-CIO spokesperson called the service economy a "nation of hamburger stands and soda jerks."[81] Only factory and construction workers such as craftsmen and foremen, operatives, and nonfarm laborers fall within the formal "blue-collar" category; yet, many of the "service" occupations are blue collar in all but name.

Also contributing to the misleading picture is the labeling of service industries. Service-producing organizations cover, of course, a much wider range than hospitals, schools, law firms, welfare departments, and research organizations. Transportation and communication make up a large portion—and, in some instances, the most rapidly expanding portion—of the service sector; here is where we find truck drivers and turnpike toll-takers and machine operators for the media. Again, "services" hide a large number of blue-collar or working-class jobs.

Even within the white-collar and professional ranks, in those areas and those jobs we could all agree represent the essence of human services, routinization and mechanization have moved factory disciplines from the manufacturing to the service sector. White-collar employees have become the production workers of service industries—the "army of paper handlers" noted by C. Wright Mills in the 1950s, as a major post-World War II phenomenon.[82] More recently, Harry Braverman argued that the logic of the labor process under monopoly capitalism required a gradual extension upward in the occupational hierarchy of the minute and mechanized division of labor which de-skills workers and puts them under the control of externally imposed work rhythms.[83] In hospitals, for example, there seems to be a trend toward breaking down and standardizing work as hospital administrators attempt to rationalize the system to make more "efficient" use of labor power. Time-and-motion studies, the legacy of turn-of-the-century scientific management which created the modern factory, have entered the hospital; the Phlebotomist Manual of Boston University Hospital gives phlebotomists, who take blood samples, six minutes to approach a patient, stick in the needle, and get the blood before going on to the next patient.[84]

At the same time, it can be shown that a large part of the growth in jobs in human service i ıdustries and the "professional, technical, and kindred occupations" which staff them can be attributed to the invention of lower-level technical support functions rather than to a growth in the elite jobs at the top. Most dramatic has been the increase in salaried health workers who are production-line workers for hospitals: technicians, technologists, and a variety of paraprofessionals. Such allied health workers have tripled in number since 1950, but the proportion of health jobs in hospitals with high skill and income content declined from 34 percent in 1950 to 25 percent in 1960.[85] Similarly, the development of paralegals has increased the number of law-related jobs without necessarily broadening access to the most desirable statuses. The positive side of the development of these fields is that they do help meet the growing demand for services at the same time that they reduce the monopoly of the elite professions over every aspect of service delivery. But the negative side is that these groups tend to take over the most routine—and thus the most boring, repetitive, and factory-like—aspects of the elite professional's work.

Finally, within the blue-collar ranks themselves, the monotonous jobs seem to be increasing faster than the desirable ones. In the coming decade, the need for semiskilled workers will increase faster than that for craftsmen. In absolute terms there will continue to be many more operative jobs, because this category is much the larger of the two.[86]

Such phenomena have led many writers on the left to challenge the myth of the service society and to insist, instead, that what is growing in the United States is a "working-class majority." One young scholar, using Census statistics, estimates the size of the "proletariat" in America—those nonsupervisory employees and others in noncomplex jobs who lack control over their own labor power, the resources of production, or the accumulation process—at 41 to 54 percent of the working population. This group does not include the 13 to 23 percent who are lower managers and foremen or the 5 to 11 percent of "semi-autonomous employees" (such as college professors) who may also work in highly disciplined, routinized settings where they have limited discretion.[87] One does not have to share the political critique from the left in order to see that the behavioral gap between traditional production workers and many white-collar employees has been closing in recent years. Unionism has spread to health and government workers. Strike activity has spread to college faculties.[88] And the rate of unscheduled absenteeism in services, public administration, and education rose to match that in manufacturing from 1967 to 1972.[89]

Some economists have pointed out that work can be truly reformed only by a shift in aggregate demand for labor; otherwise, no amount of shuffling of assignments or restructuring of organizations can fully change the basic nature of the work involved. And none of the seven largest expanding occupational groups in 1973 (that therefore supplied a large proportion of today's jobs) were undergoing rapid technological change which would provide upgrading[90]:

Secretaries	3.8 million
Retail sales clerks	3.1 million
Precollege teachers	2.7 million
Restaurant workers	2.5 million
Drivers, delivery personnel	2.4 million
Bookkeepers, cashiers	2.4 million
Cleaning workers	2.2 million

At the same time, most people continue to work in very large organizations. Not only has self-employment continued to represent a very small proportion of the labor force, but the numbers employed in relatively small-scale organizations has continued to decline. Nearly 20 percent of the total nonagriculture-employed labor force works for local, state, or federal government. Another 30 percent are employed by business enterprises with more than 500 people on the payroll.[91] And this half of the labor force in government and big business does not include a variety of other large organizations that cannot be called "businesses" but are often increasingly run like them: private universities, private hospitals. Over 12 million Americans work in firms which employ over 10,000 people. In manufacturing, the dominance of large organizations in providing jobs is even more striking. Recently, 60 percent of all persons employed in manufacturing were in firms with at least 1,000 people, 42 percent in companies with over 10,000 employees. Over 3 million people work in firms employing over 100,000 people.[92]

Despite the growing interest on the part of some policy makers and employees, discussed earlier, in increasing work flexibility, meaningfulness, and individual rights, there is little to suggest that large employing organizations have become less routinized, bureaucratized, and hierarchical or that very many organizations have been affected by schemes for employee participation, "job enrichment," or other proposals, such as self-managed work teams, rotation of repetitive tasks, responsibility for larger portions of the job, or removal of supervisory levels.[93]

Aside from questions about the efficacy of such proposals in raising work satisfaction or productivity in the absence of real power and opportunity given to employees,[94] such innovations are much more prominent in professional conferences than they are visible in practice. Hard data on the frequency of work innovations are difficult to find. But a recent *New York Times* estimate was that only 3,000 workers were under job-enrichment schemes in the United States.[95] Descriptions of organizations with innovative rights and meaning-oriented personnel practices use non-American examples or talk about the same two or three famous experiments: the Gaines (General Foods) pet food plant in Kansas, Harman Industries in Tennessee. And, in large organizations, these innovations run up against organizational politics, regardless of their contribution to productivity. The Gaines experiment in autonomous work teams with minimal outside management, begun in 1971, showed bottom-line benefits to the company (unit costs down by 5%, turnover less than 8%, three and one-half years without an accident). But it was steadily eroded by management indifference and hostility, as well as by worker complaints that they were not sharing sufficiently in the financial gains of increased productivity. By 1977 many jobs at Gaines had returned to their "pre-enrichment" form.[96]

In short, job market and organizational realities do not fully match the growing concerns with quality of work conditions and desires for high-status, non-routinized jobs for women as well as for men.

Work in America, 1977: A Summary

Six major labor trends have been identified: (1) a large increase in women's labor-force participation; (2) a shift toward a younger, more educated labor force; (3) some small gains for black job holders; (4) increased fringe benefits and government attention to work conditions, especially health implications and schedules; (5) a slightly shifting position of organized labor, especially in the growth of white-collar unions; and (6) equivocal and controversial data on job satisfaction and whether work-force discontent has increased or remained a steady, small proportion. In a time of inflation and high unemployment, the overwhelming need for jobs can overshadow all other considerations. But a growing undercurrent of changing cultural expectations about work can be identified: a concern with meaning and quality of life by means of work, and a concern with individual rights and power.

I am arguing, in short, that part of the cultural and political legacy of the post-World War II period, and especially of the 1960s, has reached the workplace, not in the form of overt protest or militancy but in actions of government, the writings of professionals, and the psychology of some segments of the labor force. What seems to me to define the issues around work in America today more than anything else is the fact that people continue to want more even as they get more: a lag between the realities of work possibilities and expressed or latent job holder concerns. A strain toward congruency in society as well as in the lives of individuals could lead to a lowering of expectations—though once hopes are raised, it seems difficult to turn back—or to a gradual bending of the organization of work to accommodate the concern for meaning and the concern for rights. My own view is that it is work—not workers—that will have to change.

TABLE 1

WORK-FORCE COMPOSITION AND WORK CONDITIONS SHOWING NO CHANGE OR
FLUCTUATIONS

Period	Phenomenon	References
ca. 1945–1973	Self-employment other than ownership (e.g., professionals, craftsmen, real estate brokers)—leveled off since World War II	97
1960–1970	Proportion of nonfarm laborers and farm workers in the labor force	98
1962–1974	Clustering of women in clerical work and other "female" occupations, and continuing low proportion in management	6, 99
1958–1972	Quit rates (fluctuates inversely with unemployment)	37
1962–1975	Multiple-job holding (after increasing 1950–1957)	41; 45 pp. 7–12
ca. 1960–1973	Strike activity (sharp increase late 1960s, peaking early 1970s)	37
1945–1975	Amount of leisure time for overall work force	100
ca. 1955–1973	Approximate percentage of labor force reporting satisfaction with jobs in response to a general question on a sample survey	37
1958–1971	Rank order of factors preferred in a job, with "work is important" first, and "lots of free time" last, by respondents in sample surveys in Detroit	36
1969–1973	Percentage of labor force in a national probability sample wanting more fringe benefits (despite an increase in benefits during this period)	2, Quinn, Mangione, and de Mandilovito

Source: Periods are those for which data were available; data other than sample survey statistics were from Bureau of Labor Statistics reports.

TABLE 2

WORK-FORCE COMPOSITION AND WORK CONDITIONS SHOWING DECLINE OR DECREASE

Period	Phenomenon	Magnitude of Shift	Reference
1950–1970	Labor-force participation rate of men 16 and over	86.8–80.6%	101
1940–1975	Labor-force participation rate of older people		34, Lebergott, pp. 97–144
1970–1975	Proportion of women 55 and over in the labor force	25–23%	101
1962–1974	Black women as proportion of total employed professional women	12.6–12.4%	6
1965–1975	Gap between proportion of black and white families with two or more workers (number of white families increased faster than number of black families)		102
1927–1977	Self-employment, after reaching peak in 1926–1927		34, Lebergott, pp. 97–144
1870–1977	Proportion of population running own business, farm		97
1960–1976	Union membership as a proportion of the nonagricultural labor force		103
1948–1975	Average number of hours worked per week by nonagricultural labor force (but may reflect changes in labor force composition, increasing numbers of women and students)	40.9–38.1 hours	100
1948–1975	Average number of workweeks per year		100
1948–1975	Average number of work years for men		104
1973–1975	Long hours and extended work weeks (short-term trend, perhaps reflecting effects of recession)		45
1965–1977	Antinepotism rules prohibiting employment of relatives		105
1953–1971	Proportion of national probability sample of employed men who say they would continue to work despite having enough money	80–74%	12

TABLE 2

WORK-FORCE COMPOSITION AND WORK CONDITIONS SHOWING
DECLINE OR DECREASE *(continued)*

Period	Phenomenon	Magnitude of Shift	Reference
1964–1973	Expressed work satisfaction, in response to general question, on Gallup poll, after increasing from 1958–1964 (though other polls show little change)		2, Quinn, Mangione, and de Mandilovito; 3, Yankelovich
ca. 1965–1975	Interest in money and security as prime aspects of jobs for college students, on sample surveys		16

Source: Periods are those for which data were available; data other than sample survey statistics are from Bureau of Labor Statistics reports.

TABLE 3

WORK-FORCE COMPOSITION AND WORK CONDITIONS SHOWING INCREASE, DEVELOPMENT,
OR INTRODUCTION

Period	Phenomenon	Magnitude of Shift	Reference
1950–1970	Proportion of overall population, 16 and over, in the labor force	59.9–61.3%	34, Lebergott, pp. 97–104
1964–1974	Teenage labor-force participation	2 ½ times faster than population	106
1950–1974	Labor-force participation rate of women, 25–54, working or seeking work	37–54%	99
1950–1975	Labor-force participation rate of married women	24–44%	102
1970–1975	Proportion of multiple-job holders who are women	16–24%	41, Michelotti
1950–1975	Families with two or more workers (increasing faster among whites than blacks)	36–49%	102
1950–1975	Two-worker married couples in which husband is a professional rather than a factory worker		102
1965–1973	Number of children with working mothers, though the number of children in the population declined		107
1962–1974	Female employment in clerical jobs (where women are already clustered)	Up 4.8 million	6
1962–1974	Women's proportion of total employed in the professions (small increase, after declining since 1930)	36–40%	6
	Lawyers, judges	3–7%	
	Physicians, surgeons	6–10%	
	College, university teachers	19–31%	
	Women entering professional training		
1966–1976	Median educational attainment of labor force	12.2–12.6 years of schooling	108
1966–1976	Median educational attainment of blacks in labor force	10.5–12.3 years of schooling	108

TABLE 3

WORK-FORCE COMPOSITION AND WORK CONDITIONS SHOWING INCREASE, DEVELOPMENT
OR INTRODUCTION *(continued)*

Period	Phenomenon	Magnitude of Shift	Reference
1962–1974	Number of blacks in managerial jobs (more than doubled, but at highest held only 4% of such jobs)	184,000–380,000	6
1962–1974	Black men as a proportion of total professional workers	3.6–6.6%	6
1966–1976	Proportion of male craftsworkers and other blue-collar workers with a year or more of college (doubled)		108
	Craftsworkers	9–18%	
	Other blue-collar	5–10%	
1960–1970	Rise of clerical workers as largest single census occupational category, replacing operatives		98
1960–1977	Professional, technical, and kindred jobs		98
1960–1970	Clerical and service jobs for women (women's growth greatest in those jobs already dominated by women)		98
1950–1968	Average percentage of life spent in retirement	11.9–15.6%	100
1967–1972	Unscheduled absence and scheduled vacation absence from work		4, Hedges
1900–1970	Average number of job changes over the work lifetime	6–12	34, Lebergott, pp. 97–144
1966–1975	College and university faculty strikes (not necessarily related to faculty unions)		87
1970–1977	Extension of collective bargaining to health-service workers, public employees, by state action		58
1970–1976	Union bargaining for reduced work week (e.g., United Auto Workers, Communication Workers of America)		8, 109
1970–1977	Number of employees on flexible work hours or staggered hours		56

TABLE 3

WORK-FORCE COMPOSITION AND WORK CONDITIONS SHOWING INCREASE, DEVELOPMENT, OR INTRODUCTION *(continued)*

Period	Phenomenon	Magnitude of Shift	Reference
1965–1977	Publicity for work options such as job sharing (and, perhaps, the frequency of such arrangements—a provision of union contracts since the 1930s, to avoid layoffs, but seldom used)		7, 110
ca. 1950–1977	Employee health benefits, both level and kind (from cash alone to services, from medical only to dental, greater employer contribution)		111
1969–1973	Maternity leave options, with pay and/or reemployment provisions		2, Quinn, Mangione, and de Mandilovito
1970–1977	Extended workmen's compensation coverage, to more occupational categories, including private household workers, to dependents, by state actions		112
1970–1977	Number of collective bargaining agreements with provisions for joint management-labor committees for special production problems, particularly in the federal sector (44% of negotiated agreements) but not in the private sector (less than 5% of agreements covering 1,000 or more workers)	44–97	9
1970–1977	Monitoring of job safety through OSHA, increase of protective action by states, concern with prevention and not compensation only		113
1964–1977	Federal and state legislation barring employment discrimination by race, sex, age, or physical handicap		58
ca. 1950–1977	State legislation on employee rights, such as jury service without employer retaliation		58

TABLE 3

WORK-FORCE COMPOSITION AND WORK CONDITIONS SHOWING INCREASE, DEVELOPMENT
OR INTRODUCTION (continued)

Period	Phenomenon	Magnitude of Shift	Reference
1957–1969	Ratings given to interesting work, in contrast to steady work, as the most important thing employed workers want from their jobs, on a national sample survey		75, 114
1969–1973	Proportion of workers on a national probability sample survey reporting problems with inconvenient schedules	+ 9%	2, Quinn, Mangione, and de Mandilovito
1969–1973	Proportion of women on a national probability sample survey reporting experienced sex discrimination in their jobs	+ 5%	2, Quinn, Mangione, and de Mandilovito
1969–1973	Proportion of union members on a national sample survey reporting complaints about union democracy or management	26–35%	2, Quinn, Mangione, and de Mandilovito
1949–1969	Expressed work satisfaction of black workers on Gallup polls	55–76%	13

Source: Periods are those for which data were available; data other than sample survey statistics are from Bureau of Labor Statistics reports.

REFERENCES

The author wishes to thank Lynn Joy for research assistance.

[1]Work also does not necessarily mean paid work, though here I am confining my discussion to employment for money. Also for convenience I use the term "worker" for people in the labor force, so that it includes managers, professionals, and the self-employed as well as nonmanagerial employees on wages.

[2]Robert P. Quinn, Thomas W. Mangione, and Martha S. Baldi de Mandilovito, "Evaluating Working Conditions in America," *Monthly Labor Review*, 96 (November 1973): 32–41. Kristine A. Rosenthal, "Women Focused Events, 1970–1976," *Review of Grant-Making for Women's Issues: Report to the Coordinating Committee on Women's Programs* (New York: Ford Foundation, 1977).

[3]Quinn, Mangione, and de Mandilovito, "Evaluating Working Conditions in America"; Daniel Yankelovich, "The Meaning of Work," in Jerome M. Rosow (ed.), *The Worker and the Job: Coping with Change* (Englewood Cliffs, N.J.: Prentice-Hall, 1974), pp. 19–48.

[4]Carl Rosenfeld, "The Extent of Job Search by Employed Workers," *Monthly Labor Review*, 100 (March 1977): 58–62; Janice Neipert Hedges, "Absence from Work: A Look at Some National Data," *Monthly Labor Review*, 96 (July 1973): 24–30; Dixie Sommers and Alan Eck, "Occupational Mobility in the American Labor Force," *Monthly Labor Review*, 100 (January 1977): 3–19.

[5]Quinn, Mangione, and de Mandilovito, "Evaluating Working Conditions in America."

[6]Stuart Garfinkle, "Occupations of Women and Black Workers, 1962–1974," *Monthly Labor Review*, 98 (November 1975): 25–35.

[7]*Changing Patterns of Work in America, 1976*, Hearings before the Subcommittee on Employment, Poverty, and Migratory Labor of the Committee on Labor and Public Welfare, U.S. Senate (Washington, D.C.: U.S. Government Printing Office, 1976).

[8]Herman A. Gadon, Fellow of the National Academy of Labor Arbitrators, personal communication, 1977.

[9]James E. Martin, "Union-Management Committees in the Federal Sector," *Monthly Labor Review*, 99 (October 1976): 30–32; Edgar Weinberg, "Labor-Management Cooperation: A Report on Recent Initiatives," *Monthly Labor Review*, 99 (April 1976): 13–22.

[10]*Worker Alienation, 1972*, Hearings before the Subcommittee on Employment, Manpower, and Poverty of the Committee on Labor and Public Welfare, United States Senate (Washington: U.S. Government Printing Office, 1972), p. 8.

[11]William W. Winspinger, "Job Enrichment: A Union View," *Monthly Labor Review*, 96 (April 1973): 54–56.

[12]Angus Campbell, Philip E. Converse, and Willard L. Rodgers, *The Quality of American Life: Perceptions, Evaluations, and Satisfactions* (New York: Russell Sage Foundation, 1976), pp. 287–318.

[13]H. Roy Kaplan, "How Do Workers View Their Work on America?" *Monthly Labor Review*, 96 (June 1973): 46–48.

[14]Quinn, Mangione, and de Mandilovito, "Evaluating Working Conditions in America," p. 38.

[15]Quinn, Mangione, and de Mandilovito, "Evaluating Working Conditions in America."

[16]"College Students and the Meaning of Work," *Monthly Labor Review*, 96 (November 1973): 42.

[17]Report of Graduate School of Business, Stanford University, 1976.

[18]Rosabeth Moss Kanter, *Men and Women of the Corporation* (New York: Basic Books, 1977), esp. pp. 161–162.

[19]Executive Office of the President: Office of Management and Budget, *Social Indicators, 1973* (Washington, D.C.: U.S. Government Printing Office, 1973), p. 145; Campbell, Converse, and Rodgers, *Quality of American Life*, p. 299.

[20]Ben J. Wattenberg, *The Real America: A Surprising Examination of the State of the Union* (Garden City, New York: Doubleday, 1974), p. 128.

[21]Robert S. Blauner, *Alienation and Freedom* (Chicago: University of Chicago Press, 1964); Kanter, *Men and Women of the Corporation*.

[22]Rosenfeld, "Extent of Job Search."

[23]Nancy C. Morse and Robert S. Weiss, "The Function and Meaning of Work and the Job," *American Sociological Review*, 20 (March 1955): 191–198; Campbell, Converse, and Rodgers, *Quality of American Life*, pp. 291–292.

[24]H. Roy Kaplan and Curt Tausky, "Work and the Welfare Cadillac: The Function of and Commitment to Work among the Hard-Core Unemployed," *Social Problems*, 19 (Spring 1972): 475.

[25]Leonard Goodwin, "Welfare Mothers and the Work Ethic," *Monthly Labor Review*, 95 (August 1972): 35–37. See also Leonard Goodwin, *Do the Poor Want to Work? A Social-Psychological Study of Work Orientation* (Washington, D.C.: Brookings Institution, 1972).

[26]Harold L. Wilensky, "Work, Careers, and Social Integration," *International Social Science Journal*, 12 (1960): 543–560. Lee Rainwater, "Work, Well-Being, and Family Life," in James O'Toole (ed.), *Work and the Quality of Life* (Cambridge, Mass: M.I.T. Press, 1974).

[27]Harold L. Wilensky, "Varieties of Work Experience," in Harry Borow (ed.), *Man in a World at Work* (Boston: Houghton Mifflin, 1964), p. 148.

[28]Campbell, Converse, and Rodgers, *Quality of American Life*, p. 313.

[29]Sheila Feld, "Feelings of Adjustment," in F. I. Nye and L. W. Hoffman (eds.), *The Employed Mother in America* (Chicago: Rand McNally, 1963).

[30]Erdman B. Palmore and Virginia Stone, "Predictors of Longevity: A Follow-up of the Aged in Chapel Hill," *Gerontologist*, 13 (Spring 1973): 88–90.

[31]Myrna M. Weissman and Eugene S. Paykel, *The Depressed Woman: A Study of Social Relationships* (Chicago: University of Chicago Press, 1974).

[32]Peter M. Blau and Otis Dudley Duncan, *The American Occupational Structure* (New York: Wiley, 1967).

[33]Wilensky, "Work, Careers, and Social Integration"; Kanter, *Men and Women of the Corporation*, pp. 140–147. Richard Sennett and Jonathon Cobb's finding of a deprivation of dignity of some members of the working class because their work was not accorded social prestige is suggestive; see their *The Hidden Injuries of Class* (New York: Knopf, 1972).

[34]Stanley Lebergott, "Labor Force and Employment Trends," in Eleanor Bernert Sheldon and Wilbert E. Moore (eds.), *Indicators of Social Change: Concepts and Measurement* (New York: Russell Sage Foundation, 1968), pp. 102–103.

[35]Yankelovich, "Meaning of Work."

[36]Otis Dudley Duncan, Howard Schuman, and Beverly Duncan, *Social Change in a Metropolitan Community* (New York: Russell Sage Foundation, 1973), pp. 73–74.

[37]Harold Wool, "What's Wrong with Work in America? A Review Essay," *Monthly Labor Review*, 96 (March 1973): 38–44.

[38]Raymond A. Katzell and Daniel Yankelovich, *Work, Productivity and Job Satisfaction* (New York: Psychological Corporation, 1975), pp. 98–101.

[39]Yankelovich, "The Meaning of Work," p. 25.

[40]Lebergott, "Labor Force and Employment Trends," pp. 101–102.

[41]Joseph S. Zeisel, "The Workweek in American Industry, 1850–1956," *Monthly Labor Review*, 81 (January 1958): 23–29; Allyson Grossman, "Multiple Job Holding in May 1974," *Monthly Labor Review*, 98 (February 1975): 60–64; Kopp Michelotti, "Multiple Job Holders in May 1975," *Monthly Labor Review*, 98 (November 1975): 56–61.

[42]Grossman, "Multiple Job Holdings in May 1974"; Michelotti, "Multiple Job Holders in May 1975."

[43]Lebergott, "Labor Force and Employment Trends," p. 105.

[44]Janice Neipert Hedges, "How Many Days Make a Workweek?" *Monthly Labor Review*, 98 (April 1975): 29–36.

[45]Janice Neipert Hedges, "Long Workweeks and Premium Pay," *Monthly Labor Review*, 99 (April 1976): 3–8.

[46]See Rosabeth Moss Kanter, *Work and Family in the United States* (New York: Russell Sage Foundation, 1977), pp. 31–32.

[47]Hedges, "Long Workweeks and Premium Pay."

[48]Virginia Lee Warren, "Plenty of Takers for Jobs without Pay," *New York Times* (January 29, 1977): 24.

[49]Eric Morgenthaler, "Dropouts Revisited," *Wall Street Journal* (December 27, 1976): 1–7.

[50]Lawrence Stessin, "Fixing the Liability for Work Pressures," *New York Times* (April 25, 1976): III–3.

[51]Kanter, *Work and Family in the United States*.

[52]Quinn, Mangione, and de Mandilovito, "Evaluating Working Conditions in America."

[53]Rosenthal, "Woman-Focused Events, 1970–1976."

[54]*Changing Patterns of Work in America, 1976* (Senate hearings).

[55]Executive Office of the President, *Social Indicators, 1973*.

[56]Comptroller General of the United States, "Legal Limitations on Flexible and Compressed Work Schedules for Federal Employees," *Report to the Congress*, in *Changing Patterns of Work in America, 1976* (Senate hearings).

[57]Barry A. Stein, Allan Cohen, and Herman Gadon, "Flextime: Work When You Want To," *Psychology Today*, 10 (June 1976): 40–43, 80.

[58]Deborah T. Bond, "State Labor Legislation Enacted in 1976," *Monthly Labor Review*, 100 (February 1977): 25–38; Bond, "State Labor Legislation Enacted in 1975," *Monthly Labor Review*, 99 (January 1976): 17–29.

[59]Rosenthal, "Woman-Focused Events, 1970–1976."

[60]Bond, "State Labor Legislation Enacted in 1976," and "State Labor Legislation Enacted in 1975."

[61]Philip Selznick, *Law, Society, and Industrial Justice* (New York: Russell Sage Foundation, 1969), p. 38.

[62]Yankelovich, "The Meaning of Work."

[63]Katzell and Yankelovich, *Work, Productivity, and Job Satisfaction*, p. 98.

[64]Quinn, Mangione, and de Mandilovito, "Evaluating Working Conditions in America."

[65]U.S. Department of Labor, *Employment and Training Report of the President, 1976* (Washington, D.C.: U.S. Government Printing Office, 1976), p. 19.

[66]Donald Gilbert McKinley, *Social Class and Family Life* (New York: Free Press, 1964).

[67]William R. Torbert, with Malcolm P. Rogers, *Being for the Most Part Puppets: The Interaction of Men's Labor, Leisure, and Politics* (Cambridge, Mass: Schenkman, 1973).

[68]Wilensky, "Varieties of Work Experience," p. 143.

[69]Melvin L. Kohn, "Occupational Structure and Alienation," *American Journal of Sociology*, 82 (July 1976): 111–130.

[70]Kanter, *Men and Women of the Corporation*, pp. 189–197.

[71]Melvin Seeman, "Alienation Studies," *Annual Review of Sociology*, 1 (1975): 105–106.

[72]James E. Jones, Jr., "Cost-Sharing in Gaining Equal Employment Opportunity," *Monthly Labor Review*, 99 (May 1976): 39–40.

[73]Rosenthal, "Woman-Focused Events, 1970–1976."

[74]Paul M. Siegel, *Prestige in the American Occupational Structure*, unpublished doctoral dissertation, Department of Sociology, University of Chicago, 1971, Table 5.

[75]George Strauss, "Workers: Attitudes and Adjustments," in Jerome M. Rosow (ed.), *The Worker and the Job: Coping with Change* (Englewood Cliffs, N.J.: Prentice-Hall, 1974), pp. 73–98.

[76]Arthur S. Weinberg, "Six American Workers Assess Job Redesign at Saab-Scania," *Monthly Labor Review*, 98 (September 1975): 52–53.

[77]Winspinger, "Job Enrichment: A Union View." He also expressed the Union suspicion that "job enrichment" might be another name for time and motion studies, substituting the sociologist's questionnaire for the stopwatch.

[78]U.S. Bureau of Labor Statistics, *Handbook of Labor Statistics, 1975* (Washington, D.C.: Department of Labor, 1976).

[79]U.S. Department of Labor, *Occupational Outlook Handbook, 1974–1975 Edition* (Washington, D.C.: U.S. Government Printing Office, 1974); Max L. Carey, "Revised Occupational Projections to 1985," *Monthly Labor Review*, 99 (November 1976): 10–22.

[80]Harold Wool, "Future Labor Supply for Lower Level Occupations," *Monthly Labor Review*, 99 (March 1976): 22–31.

[81]Andrew Levison, *The Working-Class Majority* (New York: Coward, McCann and Geoghegan, 1974), p. 263, quoted from *The Federationist*.

[82]C. Wright Mills, *White Collar: The American Middle Classes* (New York: Oxford University Press, 1951); see also Norman Birnbaum, *The Crisis of Industrial Society* (New York: Oxford University Press, 1969).

[83]Harry Braverman, *Labor and Monopoly Capital* (New York: Monthly Review Press, 1974).

[84]Harold M. Goldstein and Morris A. Horowitz, *Restructuring Paramedical Occupations*, Report to the Manpower Administration, U.S. Department of Labor (Boston: Northeastern University Department of Economics, 1971).

[85]"Allied Medical Education," *Journal of the American Medical Association*, 234 (December 29, 1975): 1379; Jeffrey Weiss, *The Changing Job Structure of Health, Manpower*, unpublished Ph.D. dissertation, Harvard University, 1966.

[86]U.S. Department of Labor, *Occupational Outlook Handbook, 1974–1975*.

[87]Levison, *Working-Class Majority*; Erik Olin Wright, *Class Structure and Income Inequality*, unpublished Ph.D. dissertation, Department of Sociology, University of California, Berkeley, 1976; Erik Olin Wright, "Class Boundaries in Advanced Capitalist Societies," *New Left Review*, 93 (1976): 3–41; Erik Olin Wright and Luca Perrone, "Marxist Class Categories and Income Inequality," *American Sociological Review*, 42 (February 1977): 32–55; Reeve Vanneman, "The Occupational Composition of American Classes: Results from Cluster Analysis," *American Journal of Sociology*, 82 (January 1977): 783–807.

[88]Bill Aussieker, "Faculty Union Strike Activity: Reasons and Measures, 1966–1975," *Monthly Labor Review*, 99 (October 1976): 32–33.

[89]Hedges, "Absence from Work: A Look at Some National Data."

[90]S. A. Levitan and W. B. Johnson, "Job Redesign, Reform, Enrichment Exploring the Limitations," *Monthly Labor Review*, 96 (July 1973): 35–42.

[91]Bureau of Labor Statistics, *Handbook of Labor Statistics, 1975*; U.S. Bureau of the Census, *1967 Enterprise Statistics, Part I, General Report on Industrial Organization, January 1972* (Washington: U.S. Government Printing Office, 1972) pp. 164–165, 124.

[92]U.S. Bureau of the Census, *1967 Enterprise Statistics*.

[93]Richard Walton, "Innovative Restructuring of Work," in Jerome M. Rosow (ed.), *The Worker and the Job: Coping with Change* (Englewood Cliffs, N.J.: Prentice-Hall, 1974), pp. 145–176.

[94]Kanter, *Men and Women of the Corporation*, pp. 265–287.

[95]Levison, *Working-Class Majority*, p. 307.

[96]"Stonewalling Plant Democracy," *Business Week*, no. 2476 (March 28, 1977): 78–82. For background and early reports of the Gaines program, see Walton, "Innovative Restructuring of Work."

[97]Robert N. Ray, "A Report on Self-Employed Americans in 1973," *Monthly Labor Review*, 98 (January 1975): 49–54.

[98]Constance Bogh Dicesare, "Changes in the Occupational Structure of U.S. Jobs," *Monthly Labor Review*, 98 (March 1975): 24–34.

[99]Doris Pisetzner Klein, "Women in the Labor Force: The Middle Years," *Monthly Labor Review*, 98 (November 1975): 10–16.

[100]John D. Owen, "Workweeks and Leisure: An Analysis of Trends, 1948–1975," *Monthly Labor Review*, 99 (August 1976): 3–8.

[101]Beverly Johnson McEaddy, "Women in the Labor Force: The Later Years,"*Monthly Labor Force*, 98 (November 1975): 17–24.

[102]Howard Hayghe, "Families and the Rise of Working Wives—an Overview," *Monthly Labor Review*, 99 (May 1976): 12–19.

[103]Jack Barbash, "The Labor Movement after World War II," *Monthly Labor Review*, 99 (November 1976): 33–37.

[104]R. Fullerton, Jr., and J. J. Byrne, "Length of Working Life for Men and Women, 1970," *Monthly Labor Review*, 99 (February 1976): pp. 31–35.

[105]"Company Couples Flourish," *Business Week* (August 2, 1976): 54–55.

[106]Allyson Sherman Grossman, "Women in the Labor Force: The Early Years," *Monthly Labor Review*, 98 (December 1975): 3–9.

[107]M. Waldman and R. Whitmore, "Children of Working Mothers, March 1973," *Monthly Labor Review*, 97 (May 1974): 50–58.

[108]Kopp Michelotti, "Educational Attainment of Workers, March 1976," *Monthly Labor Review*, 100 (March 1977): 62–65.

[109]Joann S. Lublin, "The Four-Day Week," *Wall Street Journal*, 189 (February 16, 1977): 1, 27.

[110]"Job Sharing Catches On," *Business Week* (October 25, 1976): 112E; Liz Roman Gallese, "Two for the Price of One," *Wall Street Journal* 186 (April 19, 1974): 3.

[111]Kevin G. Wetmore, "Improvements in Employee Health Care Benefits," *Monthly Labor Review*, 95 (August 1972): 31–34.

[112]H. S. Hribal and G. M. Minor, "Workers' Compensation—1975 Enactments," *Monthly Labor Review*, 99 (January 1976): 30–36.

[113]Alexander J. Reis, "Three Years of OSHA: The View from Within," *Monthly Labor Review*, 98 (March 1975): pp. 35–36; see also Joe Collier, "Inspection and Enforcement at the Workplace," *Monthly Labor Review*, 96 (August 1973): 35–42; Nicholas Ashford, "Worker Health and Safety: An Area of Conflicts," *Monthly Labor Review*, 98 (September 1975): 3–11; Sylvia Weissbrodt, "Changes in State Labor Laws in 1972," *Monthly Labor Review*, 96 (January 1973): 27–36.

[114]George Strauss, "Worker Dissatisfaction: A Look at the Causes," *Monthly Labor Review*, 97 (February 1974): 57–58.

JOHN T. DUNLOP

Past and Future Tendencies in American Labor Organizations

AMERICAN LABOR ORGANIZATIONS today reflect primarily the influence of long-term continuities with gradual changes and adaptations to evolving problems and opportunities. They are shaped much more basically by events of the past century than by the forces of the last fifteen years. Their dominant method is collective bargaining, which has grown substantially in scope and complexity in new sectors and circumstances. Legal enactment, including administrative proceedings, and participation in political elections are supportive and collaborative secondary methods which have also expanded to meet new contingencies and opportunities. The American labor movement and our industrial relations system are distinctively American, quite different from those of Europe, and even though our arrangements would not work elsewhere, they have served this society and economy well.[1]

The central directions of the past are likely to continue into the future because labor organizations and collective bargaining reflect well the character of American workers, managements, economy, and larger society. This view rejects the aspirations of those who would like to see the AFL-CIO become what is called a "genuine social movement," modeled after European labor movements, rather than the "political arm for market-unionism."[2]

It is conceivable that fundamental changes in the traditional methods of collective bargaining and legal enactment and in the directions of labor organizations could arise, however, should certain unlikely developments occur, in particular, should top labor leaders lose touch with local union officials and the rank and file of active members; should major employers operating under collective agreements launch a concerted attack on the legitimacy of unions; should the political leaders of both parties refuse to make accommodations to the aspirations of the labor organizations; or should a period of prolonged economic stagnation and inflation preclude advances in wages, benefits, and other rules of the workplace. Such drastic changes in the American environment appear remote, but should they occur they could well produce a marked shift to the ideological left and to a social movement closer to those constituting the labor movements of Western Europe.

The first three sections to follow consider Structural Features of American Labor Organizations, The Method of Collective Bargaining, and The Method of Legal Enactment and Political Action. In each instance the discussion is to portray the fundamental course of American labor organizations and to ascertain the extent of new tendencies and directions, if substantial, in the past decade or two. A fourth section, Issues for the Future, considers the extent that new elements, or new magnitudes, are likely to change the course of American labor organizations and their methods. Four substantive areas are explored: Workers' Attitudes, Participation in Management, Economic Policies and Consequences, and International Interactions.

Structural Features of American Labor Organizations

American labor unions, together with employee associations such as those among police, professional athletes, nurses, and teachers that behave like unions, probably aggregate 24 or 25 million members, approximately 30 percent of nonagricultural employment; almost 3 million are in the employee associations. Although American labor organizations approach double the absolute size of their counterparts in Great Britain and Japan, the percentage of nonagricultural employees in unions is over 50 percent in Great Britain, and 35 percent in Japan and in Germany. In Scandinavian countries the percentage probably ranges from 60 to 80 percent.[3] The percentage in labor organizations in the United States has remained relatively stable over the past decade but has slipped about five points below the level of the first decade after World War II. Absolute membership continues to grow slowly save in periods of significant breakthroughs in particular sectors or regions. Union membership alone approximated 3.4 million in 1930, 8 million in 1940, 16.6 million in 1960, and between 21 and 22 million in 1976.

The American labor movement is very decentralized. There are more than 175 national unions with 71,000 affiliated local unions, and 35 national employee associations with almost 14,000 local chapters. More than 60 percent of the national unions are affiliated with AFL-CIO; and 85 percent of the local unions are in these national unions. The 12 largest national unions, with a half-million members or more, encompass approximately half the union members of the country[4]; the other half are distributed among more than 160 national unions.

Labor-organization membership is very unequally distributed among sectors and regions. Transportation, communications, public utilities, parts of construction, and such manufacturing industries as basic steel and automobiles are highly organized. On the other hand, finance, real estate, most retail trade, and services are very lightly organized. Government employees, who were relatively poorly organized with some notable exceptions prior to 1960, have had a significant surge to union membership since then. Approximately one-half of state and local government employees and two-thirds of civilian federal government employees now are estimated to be members of unions or similar associations. The five most highly organized states in the country are New York (45.4 percent of nonagricultural employees are members of unions or similar associations), Michigan, West Virginia, Pennsylvania, and Washington. The five least organized states are Florida, Texas, Mississippi, South Carolina, and North Carolina with the lowest figure (9.8 percent).

White-collar membership of unions has grown from 13.6 percent to almost 18 percent of all members over the past 20 years; the level is 24.3 percent if association members are included. Women similarly have grown as a percent of union membership from 16.6 percent to almost 22 percent in the past 20 years; the level is 25.0 percent if association members are included.

American labor organizations assess their members relatively high dues compared to those applied in other countries. Membership payments are about 1 percent of the annual earnings of unionized workers,[5] who support a much larger paid staff and organization than unions do abroad; one study suggests that American unions have one paid officer to 300 members compared to one to 3,000 members in Great Britain.[6] The decentralized collective bargaining arrangements in the United States, with private grievance handling and private arbitration rather than with labor courts or government inspectors, increase the need for union staff familiar with the workplace.

It is estimated that in 1969 American unions at all levels had income of $3.2 billion and assets of $2.6 billion compared to an estimated $300 million of assets for British unions. (These are, of course, small sums compared to those common in the corporate world.) In keeping with our decentralized industrial-relations arrangements, it is significant that the income and wealth of unions are almost equally divided between national unions and local organizations. The AFL-CIO raises by per capita payments less than 1 percent of all the union dues income of its affiliates.

Each local or intermediate labor organization conducts its internal affairs and makes its decisions under its constitution and procedures, subject to applicable law, the Labor-Management Reporting and Disclosure Act of 1959. It holds elections, arranges for appointed representatives and staff, negotiates and ratifies agreements, collects or receives dues, processes grievances, engages in job training and administers medical care plans alone or with employers under agreements, publishes papers or journals, engages in organizing activities, affiliates with other labor bodies, participates in community, educational, and social affairs, and engages in various political activities under the general guidance of the national labor organization from which it holds a charter. The autonomous national unions may in turn be affiliated with the federation, AFL-CIO. There is wide variation in the governance of local and national unions depending on industry, collective bargaining patterns of centralization and decentralization, leadership, and internal traditions.[7]

The American Federation of Labor (AFL) was founded in the 1880s on two fundamental constitutional principles relating to its constituent unions: the autonomy of each affiliated national union and the exclusive jurisdiction of each national union specified in its charter from the federation. The principle of autonomy means that the federation is not to interfere in the internal political life, operations, or collective bargaining of its affiliates. Although the federation may render assistance when requested, it is not staffed for a major role in collective bargaining. The AFL-CIO (Congress of Industrial Organizations, founded in 1938) is not authorized to negotiate collective agreements with management groups (except for directly affiliated local branches) or incomes policies with government. Nor does it seek such authority. In the merged federation constitution of 1955 the original principle of autonomy was qualified to permit suspension of an affiliate by the Executive Council, upon a two-thirds vote, on a showing of corruption or domination by the purposes of the Communist Party or by any fascist organization or other totalitarian movement.[8] The corruption procedures have been largely preempted by the law since 1959, and there has been no occasion to use the Communist or other totalitarian proviso.

The constitutional principle of exclusive jurisdiction has been transmuted, under the necessities of government policies in the Wagner Act (1935) and the Taft-Hartley Act (1947), into the principle of constitutional respect for an "established collective bargaining relationship" and a prohibition of raiding any affiliate. This principle is enforced by an internal arbitration procedure, and appeal to the Executive Council, with the threat of all affiliates to be authorized to raid a violator guilty of noncompliance.[9] Prior to merger, the AFL held that a worker should join only the union specified by the AFL jurisdiction. Since then the internal rules of the federation comport in the main with public laws, and workers are to join only the union with an established collective-bargaining relationship with the worker's employer. "Exclusive jurisdiction" has lost its constitutional application, replaced by "an established bargaining relationship."

The locus of collective bargaining, organizing, and community activities in American labor organizations is lodged in national unions and their constituent local unions, with distributions of responsibility that vary widely among national unions. The federation may play a coordinating role in a few negotiations or organizing campaigns. In legislative and political questions, and in international labor and public affairs, its role is greater although not preemptive.

Although the basic characteristics of U.S. labor organizations have been largely unchanged in the past several decades, a few developments are significant. The AFL-CIO merger in 1955 has continued and the internal disputes plan replacing "exclusive jurisdiction" has worked reasonably well—surprisingly well in view of the history of jurisdictional problems in the federation. Both developments are tributes to George Meany. Walter Reuther withdrew from the merger after helping to put it together, but Leonard Woodcock and Douglas Frazier, the new president, have expressed a desire to see the United Auto Workers (UAW) reaffiliate in the interest of a stronger national labor center. The aspirations for merger of constituent unions have not been fully realized, although more than 50 mergers of national unions or associations have taken place since 1955, most often as a consequence of financial problems. Labor organizations continued to grow slowly in absolute numbers in these two decades, with relatively more women and minorities as these two groups have entered more industries and occupations. The period saw a dramatic expansion of membership in the public sector, with an orderly means of recognition in many states and localities still unspecified, the role of collective bargaining in public employment largely still fluid, and management capacity grossly undeveloped.

The Method of Collective Bargaining

The American labor movement regards collective bargaining as its major business. George Meany has defined collective bargaining in the following perceptive way: "On its philosophical side, collective bargaining is a means of assuring justice and fair treatment. In the economic realm it is a means of prodding management to increase efficiency and output, and of placing upon trade unions great responsibilities to limit their demands to practical realities. A failure to recognize the unique role of collective bargaining is a failure to understand the distinctive new nature of American private enterprise as it has evolved over the past seventy-five years."[10]

Collective bargaining, in common parlance, is used in this country to refer to at least three separate forms of labor-management activity: (a) periodic negotiations for a new collective agreement that may take place yearly or every two or three years depending on the duration of the agreement setting compensation and other terms and conditions of employment; (b) the day-to-day administration of the provisions of an existing agreement, including the vital steps in the grievance procedure and arbitration provisions; and (c) in some relationships, informal joint consultations and conferences that may take place outside agreement negotiations to explore common problems, to improve productivity, and to review broad questions of common interest in the industry or locality.

In the industrial-relations system of the United States the no-strike, no-lockout clause in an agreement developed concomitantly with the provision for binding arbitration over disputes arising during the term of the agreement, or more narrowly, over disputes as to the meaning and application of the agreement. The British, in contrast, generally have not made the distinction between periodic negotiations and administration, between issues of interests and rights; and accordingly almost any issue may be raised at any time on the shop floor and pressed to a work stoppage.

The collective-bargaining arrangements in this country are peculiarly the product of American unions, workers, and managers in the setting of our institutions; more recently and to a small degree, they have been constricted by legislation. The U.S. labor movement did not arise with the Wagner Act, nor were the fundamental features of collective bargaining created by government. Collective bargaining is a highly decentralized and diversified accommodation to union structure, managerial independence, market and locality forces, and the size of our country. Moreover, collective-bargaining institutions have changed gradually with developments in these features. There are probably more than 200,000 separate collective agreements, and negotiations are designed to address the problems of each pair of parties, including their employees (members). As Thomas R. Donohue has said, "Each of these agreements is of paramount importance to the workers involved—no matter whether it is Firestone Rubber or a small electrical shop, whether it's New York City or Kalispell, Montana."[11] The individual parties are not entirely free, of course, to consider alone their preferences. The collective bargaining processes compel them to pay attention sooner or later to the practical realities of market competition, to industrial relations developments in closely related negotiations, and to legal constraints.

For an appreciation of the decentralized quality of American collective bargaining it would be well to compare the texts of agreements in a variety of sectors—airplane pilots, seamen, railroad engineers, basic steel workers, construction pipefitters, insurance agents, TVA employees. The methods of wage payment; fringe benefits; rules on hiring, transfers, promotions, and layoffs; grievance procedures; and arbitration—each one reflects the problems of technology and markets posed to workers and managements and their organizational histories. No government agency could ever promulgate rules of the workplace with such diversity or adjust them so well to changing conditions. Within some sectors collective bargaining is relatively centralized on a national basis, at least on key questions such as compensation, as is the case in the basic steel industry, railroads, and motor freight trucking. In other industries, negotiations may be conducted on a regional or locality basis as in maritime occupations, construction, and paper, whereas in still others agreement making is decentralized to the establishment level.

American collective bargaining is distinguished from European and Japanese industrial relations systems in that there is generally a single line of responsibility on the union side from the national level to the immediate workplace, local unions, and workers. In this country one agreement between management and the local or international union, or both, sets the full terms and conditions of employment. Elsewhere the works council, enterprise organization, or shop steward constitutes a more or less independent authority. Negotiations take place in several tiers at varying levels with wage drift and separate provisions as each level negotiates additional items.

Each agreement in the United States typically specifies a grievance procedure, or steps in which representatives of the two sides seek to resolve disputes or differences over the meaning or the application of the agreement that arise during its term. Agreements also tend to specify an arbitration process, including the selection of arbitrators or umpires; they may also provide that certain issues may be resolved by the controlled resort to strike or lockout, as in the case of production standards in the automobile industry. In this way the grievance procedure provides a way for responsible officers to review the operation of the agreement, to clarify the application of new provisions, and to consider questions of interpretation that had not been anticipated. The industrial jurisprudence that develops is shaped by the particular parties rather than by government agents; management supervision and workers and stewards participate in resolving most issues at the work level. In this process our industrial relations system has developed a large cadre of private arbitrators with wide understanding of plant-level issues.

One of the most significant—and often overlooked—effects of collective bargaining in the United States has been its influence on management generally as well as on unorganized or nonunion establishments, particularly of large size. Fifty years ago there were much sharper differences in wages, benefits, and conditions of work than now prevail in American industry between workplaces that are under collective bargaining and those that are not. In part to keep unions out and in part because multiplant companies may have to deal with employees in both unionized and unorganized plants, these differences have been narrowed, even with regard to procedures for discharge, discipline, or layoff. "The challenge that unions presented to management has, if viewed broadly, created superior and better-balanced management, even though some exceptions must be recognized. . . . If one single statement were sought to describe the effect of unions on policy making, it would be: they have encouraged investigation and reflection."[12]

The American collective bargaining arrangements purport to perform a wide range of vital functions in the society—it is a decentralized means of setting compensation and benefits; it sets the vital rules of the workplace relating to hiring, discharge, transfer, layoff, retirement, and promotion; it establishes procedures to review these decisions under collective agreements with resort to third-party neutrals; it provides means for plant-level employees and supervisors to participate in many decisions; it provides means of communications by means of the enterprise hierarchy; it constitutes a means to resolve many industrial conflicts; and it permits periodic review of rules and bargaining arrangements in the light of new technological or market conditions. These are primarily activities of local and national unions.

Although the basic features of collective bargaining have continued through the past several decades, several new features are to be noted. The scope of bargaining, in the sense of the subjects bargained about and incorporated into agreements, has grown. Health and welfare plans and pension arrangements have expanded to cover both more people and more situations. Some negotiations improve the retirement benefits of those already retired. Supplemental unemployment benefits and enhanced job security in numerous ways have been specified. Special training provisions and some modifications of the units in which seniority and rights are exercised have been developed to agree with the requirements of law respecting equal employment opportunities. The steelworkers and the basic steel industry imaginatively created an experimental agreement to avoid the costs of instability for both sides that grow out of a normal expiration date. A legal services benefit has been negotiated in a few situations. Collective agreements have grown more detailed and much longer. The greater complexity and technical nature of issues has introduced more experts and specialists on each side in some phases of the bargaining process. The negotiations process is continuing to concern itself with the greater intrusion of government into the employment relationship by means of statutes and regulations concerned with health and safety, pensions, affirmative-action programs, and the like.

But collective bargaining is not a cure-all of social and economic problems. It does not apply to a majority of workplaces, although its influence is widespread. It is not a principal means to eliminate poverty, to change the distribution of income, to reform the production process, to eliminate discrimination, or to reform the health-care delivery system, although it may make major contributions to all these purposes. Collective bargaining should not be demeaned because it is not an all-purpose social tool, but no one should prescribe for works or the workplaces of America without knowledge and experience with collective bargaining and consultation with the parties.

The Method of Legal Enactment and Political Action

The method of legal enactment, to use the phrase of Sidney and Beatrice Webb,[13] has been used extensively by American unions from their earliest days. The principal committee of the federation at its outset in the 1880s was the Legislative Committee, later the Executive Council. A bill of grievances, formulated by a conference of national unions in 1906 and presented to President Theodore Roosevelt and leaders of Congress, called for legislation to curb immigration, to restrict the sale of products made by convict labor, to ensure maritime safety, to provide relief from injunctions in labor disputes and the antitrust laws as applied to labor, to establish a House Committee on Labor, and to enact child labor laws and suffrage for women. The pursuit of legislative objectives for union members and trade-union institutional purposes, for all workers and for broader social objectives has been a major preoccupation from the outset for both state federations and local central bodies.[14]

From their outset labor organizations in this country have debated the issue of formal political organization and mobilization of the electorate. The question arose in the early days of the federation as to whether the socialists or the Socialist Labor Party should have a special relationship to the AFL, similar to the relations in Great Britain and Germany between the unions and the socialist parties. In the 1890 convention it was argued that "there is this fundamental difference between the old plutocratic [Republican and Democratic] parties and the S.L.P., that the former are notoriously the machines of the employing class, and as essential a part of the whole machinery through which they control, rob and oppress their wage-workers as is their industrial and commercial machinery; whereas the Socialist Labor Party is owned and controlled by wage-workers like yourselves. . . ."[15] But Gompers and the convention by a 3-to-1 vote would have none of it: "We hold that the trade unions of America, comprising the AFL are committed against the introduction of matters pertaining to partisan politics, to the religion of men or to their birthplace. We cannot logically admit the S.L.P. to representation, and shut the door in the face of other political organizations formed to achieve social progress." As Gompers said almost twenty-five years later: "The AFL has an independent political policy—a policy so politically independent that it is independent of the Socialist Party, too."[16] Reward your friends and punish your enemies was its formulation.

The constitution of the merged federation adopted the principle: "While preserving the independence of the labor movement from political control, to encourage workers to register and vote, to exercise their full rights and responsibilities of citizenship, and to perform their rightful part in the political life of the local, state and national communities."[17] The Committee on Political Education (COPE) is the coordinating mechanism for these activities in the federation.

The Federal Election Campaign Act has left intact the capacity of labor organizations and COPE to play a significant role in political campaigns. Although money derived from dues may not be used for contributions or expenditures for a candidate for public office, such funds may be used to communicate with union members and their families, to encourage and organize registration, and to get out the vote. In a polity in which machine organization has declined and voters appear more independent, these activities can have a significant impact. Voluntarily contributed funds can, of course, be used for direct support of a candidate.

The 1976 COPE activities surpassed earlier efforts in registration, voter participation, funds raised, and extent of activity with minorities (COPE Minorities Department and A. Philip Randolph operations) and with women's groups. COPE mobilized 120,000 volunteers in programs of registration and getting out the vote; 80 million pieces of literature were distributed to union members; 700 films were in the field by mid-September. A large number of full-time union representatives and officers were released from their regular work and were mobilized in critical states and districts in the weeks before the election. A number of national unions developed their own programs. About 80 percent of union members registered compared to about 70 percent of the voting-age population; also a higher percentage of union members voted compared to the electorate generally. In the Senate, 19 of 28 COPE-endorsed candidates were elected, and in the House of Representatives 259 of 365 COPE-endorsed candidates won. Although it is difficult to appraise precisely the independent effect of these activities, the effort is substantial and increasing over the years, and its leaders believe that it is becoming more effective.

Since the 1952 election, unlike its prior practice, the federation has generally endorsed the presidential candidate of the Democratic party; however, in 1972 the federation refrained from endorsing McGovern, and the endorsement of a number of national unions was split between the two major candidates.

Despite the considerable efforts of the federation and COPE to encourage political participation and involvement in federal elections, there remains marked diversity in the activities of the thousands of local unions in local and state politics. As Edward C. Banfield and James Q. Wilson remark: "Some unions want nothing more from city government than assurance that the police will not interfere with pickets during strikes. Others aspire to take possession of the city government and to run it as an adjunct of the union. Between these extreme positions there are many intermediate ones."[18] The rapid growth of organization among state and local government employees with their special interests in elected officials has further compounded this diversity.

Activities to influence the electorate have had their counterpart in lobbying legislative bodies and concentrated efforts to secure desired decisions from administrative agencies. From their earliest beginnings unions have advocated measures ranging from institutional concerns such as rights to join unions and limitations on suits against union funds, to issues of broad concern to all employees such as worker compensation for accidents, public works jobs, and social security, to matters of general social and national interest such as the elimination of discrimination, educational opportunities, consumer protection, and national defense. One historic illustration of these wider involvements is provided by Title VII of the Civil Rights Act of 1964. When the legislation was introduced, the Kennedy administration had not included a title on discrimination in employment, fearing defeat of the legislation as a whole. George Meany promptly urged the inclusion of equal-employment-opportunity provisions, and the federation carried on a vigorous campaign for legislation. This vital role of the federation was fully recognized by the National Association for the Advancement of Colored People.[19]

The AFL-CIO is a federation of autonomous national unions, each of which not only conducts its own collective bargaining but takes its own public position on issues of major concern. The federation is at times engaged in developing a consensus, or permitting diversity, on conflicting questions such as the dispute over pipelines or railroads as a means to carry coal, or competing routes for gas lines involving sea or land. Individual unions may seek public policies for their industries, as compulsory arbitration in local and state government, only to find that the federation is unwilling to endorse such proposals on grounds of possible adverse effects on the right to strike more generally. There are likewise competing priorities for legislative programs and efforts. The federation is comprised of small unions, such as the Horseshoers with 390 members, to ones as large as the Steelworkers approaching 1.5 million; 30 unions with members in public employment and 80 with only private-sector interests; industrial unions and craft unions; unions in export industries and those adversely affected by imports; the regional concentration of members varies a great deal as does their distribution among sectors. A federation requires consensus building and accommodation.

The federation takes positions by resolutions on major issues of domestic and foreign policies, just as state organizations do on many state and local issues. With the assistance of particularly concerned affiliates it seeks alliances in the legislative and electoral processes that may be more or less stable. Civil rights groups have often been aligned with it on questions of minimum wage, welfare, and legislation on discrimination despite tensions on some other questions. On the issue of strip mining of coal and much of the clean air issues, the federation has sided with environmentalists, whereas on nuclear power and related questions it has often taken positions close to that of industry. On many international issues it has been strong on defense and suspicious of detente. The federation has developed particularly over the past two decades a very considerable familiarity with the operations of the federal bureaucracy and the legislative process.

However one appraises the effectiveness or the consequences of the method of legislative enactment and participation in political elections at national, state, and local levels, there can be no doubt that these activities are a major feature of American labor organizations. The representation of workers in their dealings with employers is the prime concern, but "social unionism, the effort to improve the general condition of their members by improving the general condition of everyone in the community,"[20] is a vital secondary function.

Issues for the Future

Sumner Slichter's judgment as to our past is correct: ". . . I think the United States should consider itself lucky. It possesses a system of industrial relations that, in its basic characteristics, fits conditions here reasonably well. The system has been developed without being planned. Perhaps that is why it represents a pretty good adaptation to conditions. . . . We seem justified in being grateful that we have been favored by fortune and perhaps also in taking modest pride that we have pursued opportunistic policies with considerable flexibility and good sense."[21]

But what about the future?

WORKERS' ATTITUDES

Widespread attention is attracted from time to time to the view that the American work ethic has eroded, that dissatisfaction is increasing rapidly at the workplace, and that union rebels are "mining a deep vein of worker discontent." After a long strike the phrasing is likely to continue, "relations between management and labor have degenerated into bitter parochial conflicts incapable of resolving the mutual discontents."[22] But the evidence is clearly that these conclusions are in the eye of the beholder and in phrase-makers of "blue-collar blues" and "lunch-pail lassitude" rather than in the workplace or work force. It would seem that if any events call for explanation in our times it is not so much the occasional wildcat strike at Lordstown, Ohio as the fact that the great inflation of 1973–1974, with declines in real income, and the large-scale unemployment of 1975–1977 have produced so little industrial unrest or protest.

Periodic polls have asked employees, "On the whole, would you say you are satisfied or dissatisfied with the work you do?" An overall response for 1973— 77 percent satisfied, 11 percent dissatisfied, and 13 percent no opinion—is rather characteristic of responses from those with paid employment over the past quarter century.[23] The study of more substantial behavioral measures such as productivity, quit rates, absenteeism, accidents, and strikes reflects that their changes over time are explained by conventional economic determinants, and there is no basis to ascribe any role to changes in worker attitudes and motivation.[24] The Survey Research Center at the University of Michigan made careful surveys for 1969 and 1973 that conclude that there were no major changes in overall job satisfaction for the labor force as a whole or for any major demographic subcategories between 1969 and 1973.[25]

There are, of course, differences among employees in different types of jobs as to their job satisfaction, whatever the term "satisfaction" may mean. Younger workers appear to reflect more dissatisfaction than older workers, but the jobs they hold as newcomers pay less well and are probably less challenging than jobs they subsequently achieve. Moreover, the proportion of the labor force below the age of 25 years has begun to decline, and absolute numbers in this age group may well decline in a few years. The evidence indicates that women are less satisfied than men with the financial rewards and challenges of their jobs, but their overall satisfaction scores do not differ significantly from those of men. Racial differences in job satisfaction appear pronounced, although differences within occupational and age groups are much less. Job dissatisfaction among racial groups and among women in part reflects resentment at discrimination.

Changes in the workplace over time seem, if anything, gradually to have been favorable. Unskilled work has declined relatively, and professional, technical, and clerical positions have increased substantially.[26] Higher wages, fringe benefits, and legislation provide increased protection against risks not only of the workplace but of modern life in general. An emphasis on education and retirement and changes in the schedules for working hours and increased opportunity for part-time work have tended to mitigate job dissatisfaction. Company policies in large enterprises in general have become concerned with people at the workplace, reflecting in part the consequences of professional personnel functions and in part the effects of labor organizations on management. These changes are not frozen; they continue to be made in response to aspirations, pressures, and the opportunities of economic growth. Indeed, it is likely that as wages, leisure time, and educational attainment rise along with progressive income taxes, employees in the future may well seek to take a higher fraction of their rewards in improved conditions of work. These are opportunities for collective bargaining and some legislation, not the seedbed of worker rebellion or a revival of the class struggle.

PARTICIPATION IN MANAGEMENT

Worker participation in industry has received widespread public attention in recent years, and European developments appear to be extending significantly worker participation in management. Participation is urged as a solution to such widespread problems of industrial society as worker alienation, low productivity, industrial conflict, and political unrest. It is also said to contribute to effective management and productive efficiency.[27]

German codetermination was adapted in 1976 from the iron and steel industry to provide nominally equal worker and management representation on the supervisory boards of companies employing more than 2,000 people. At least one of the worker members is to represent plant-level supervision; in the event of a stalemate in the board, the management chairman is to cast the deciding vote. German law also provides, as does that of many other European countries, for an elected worker council for plants, and for company-wide councils comprised of all segments of the work force to meet with management and supervision over plant-level issues. German authorities are keen on the results of codetermination and hold that it has contributed significantly to German labor peace, stability, and productivity.

The Bullock Report in Great Britain, presented to Parliament in January 1977, proposed to place worker directors in the boardrooms of enterprises with 2,000 or more people, estimated to comprise the 738 largest firms, when unions demand it and when endorsed by a vote of all the work force.[28] It is argued that this form of union participation is essential to improve the deep-seated industrial-relations malaise of Great Britain. "It is our belief that the way to release those energies, to provide greater satisfaction in the workplace and to assist in raising the level of productivity and efficiency in British industry—and with it the living standards of the nation—is not by recrimination or exhortation but by putting the relationship between capital and labor on a new basis which will involve not just management but the whole workforce in sharing responsibility for the success and profitability of the enterprise."[29]

The Sudreau Report of February 7, 1975 represents President Giscard's concern with *reform de l'enterprise*. The commission rejected German codetermination on the grounds that it is not suited to present-day France, where it is essential to preserve management's responsibility to direct the daily affairs of the enterprise. But there exists a need for conscious participation by all in the organization of the work. A radically different approach to participation by employees in the boards of companies is held to be necessary. It proposes that consideration be given to a one-third worker participation in supervisory boards or boards of directors with supervisory functions, a new form of participation designated cosupervision. In view of general misgivings, cosupervision should be introduced gradually. The report contains a number of other areas of company reform, including means of strengthening work councils.

In the United States, labor organizations have not only failed to show interest in codetermination, but they are hostile to such ideas. They also look unkindly toward stock ownership as a means to interest workers in management. Our unions regard collective bargaining as an adequate means of influencing management. The words that follow are those of Thomas R. Donahue, George

Meany's Executive Assistant, but the views are widespread: "We do not seek to be a partner in management—to be, most likely, the junior partner in success and the senior partner in failure. We do not want to blur in any way the distinctions between the respective roles of management and labor in the plant. . . . And we probably bargain on as many, if not more, issues than the number we might have any impact on as members of a Board of Directors."[30]

ECONOMIC POLICIES AND CONSEQUENCES

The economic consequences of labor organizations can be briefly considered under three headings: conflict, productivity, and inflation. In the period immediately after World War II, as after World War I, the concern over disruptive economic strikes reached a peak. The national emergency provisions of the Taft-Hartley Act (Title II) were enacted in 1947. The statute was seriously defective from the perspective of labor-management relations (e.g., the role of the board of inquiry and the last-offer vote). Emergency disputes have ceased to be perceived as a significant problem, if they ever were one.[31] On rare occasions, however, one may continue to expect a sticky situation as in a chaotic coal organization or in public employment. Protection of the public interest in private employment is likely to be better served by bargaining of the parties, informal influence of senior labor and management leaders, imaginative mediation, and the forbearance of Congress with ad hoc legislation designed for the particular dispute as a final resort, than by the patent solutions of compulsory arbitration or the application of antitrust laws. In local and state government employment, state legislatures and courts are in the process of experimenting with a variety of procedures, and in due course the complex issues of the competing interests of taxpayers and public employees will be brought under more clearly delineated procedures.

Alfred Marshall[32] well understood, as few contemporary economists do, that labor organizations have materially increased productivity by their effect on training, morale, methods and forms of compensation, safety, support of orderly procedures, and discipline at the workplace and in the work community. The favorable influence by the "prodding of management" (Meany's phrase) or "the making of exacting demands on management" (Slichter's phrase) is recognized to be very considerable by those familiar with the processes of management organizations. These influences are a continuous process and may be expected in general to continue. Moreover, in a growing number of enterprises formal labor-management production committees outside the bargaining mechanism are operating to reduce waste, to improve quality and performance, and to tap the ideas of workers regarding the production process.[33] These joint efforts are likely to be significant in only a minority of situations with special problems, opportunities, or leadership.

The net impact of labor organizations and collective bargaining on productivity is obscured in public discussion by a few outdated work rules such as that requiring a fireman on a diesel locomotive. The elimination of obsolete practices is a continuing function of periodic bargaining, and the view has been widely accepted in American collective bargaining that such practices are a form of property-right of workers to be purchased or traded in negotiations if they are realistically to be eliminated. In the interests of efficiency, American managers with some exceptions have done well in this process.

The inflationary potentials of collective bargaining have been obscured in recent years by the worldwide inflation in 1973–1974 derived from food and energy. But with the leading collective bargaining settlements in recently negotiated agreements averaging 9 to 10 percent (at 6 percent increase in the cost of living) out to 1979 and 1980, the persistent concern with wage-cost inflation has already revived. As Arthur Okun of the Brookings Institution sees it, "a happy ending to the stagflation story *must* involve some incomes-policy or social-compact arrangement."[34] It is well that economists of both political party-persuasions now recognize that wage and price guideposts cannot be effective without full consultation with labor and management, but they have little experience, and one might add capacity, in the art of consensus building in this area.

In the United States an incomes policy or a social contract, as those terms are understood in Europe, are not a viable policy save in a dire national emergency. The decentralized federation has no capacity to commit its constituents, and they in turn have little authority or disposition to control their members on vital collective-bargaining matters. The ultimate test of any wage-restraint policy is what happens when a union strikes against the policy, as the Heath government discovered in the coal industry in England. Moreover, the use of a single yardstick (be it 3.2 percent of the Kennedy-Johnson guideposts or 5.5 percent of the Pay Board) is a crude and inappropriate measure to distinguish inflationary from noninflationary settlements. Noncompliance with these so-called voluntary standards creates strong pressures for controls. Inflationary periods distort the wage structure, and the primary task of effective stabilization as wage agreements come open is to achieve a result in which different amounts are negotiated for variously situated parties in order to restore the wage relationship and to eliminate continuing efforts to catch up or to move ahead of closely related groups. A single guidepost number is incapable of producing wage stability.[35]

The alternative policy for the United States is the identification of sectors with severe wage and price problems, to diagnose the underlying difficulties, and to work with the labor organizations, managements, and government agencies involved to moderate the structural inflationary pressures, be they labor supply and training, plant capacity, collective bargaining structure, or productivity.

INTERNATIONAL INTERACTIONS

American labor unions have a long tradition of interest and involvement in international labor affairs. Gompers was a leading figure in the founding of the International Labour Office. American unions continue to participate actively in the various international trade secretariats which deal with international standards in various industries such as the transport and metal trades. The federation vigorously opposed the spread of Communist influence in the labor organizations of Western Europe after World War II; it has sought to encourage and support the growth of democratic trade unions in the developing countries. Although the federation has withdrawn from the International Confederation of Free Trade Unions in a dispute over policies, it has expanded its activities to assist leadership development, education, technical assistance, housing, and medical and other social programs in developing countries through the American Institute for Free Labor Development (Latin America and Caribbean), the African-American Labor Center, and the Asian-American Free Labor Institute.

The labor unions of the United States could be an extremely important resource in the policy aims of the country in international relations. In Western European and some other countries many government officials are former labor union leaders, and the complex interactions of labor unions, labor, and allied democratic parties and their governments are intertwined in ways more readily understood by those sensitive to the labor scene. Personal relations in labor forums often go back many years. Among a number of developing countries, the influence of our labor organizations, both direct and by associates in third countries, can make a contribution to the emergence of institutions more compatible with our long-term interests and values. It may not be remiss to note that among Western countries, there is none that enjoys more loyalty and security from its labor movement.

There is no more contentious issue for the future in this field than trade policy and taxes on corporate earnings abroad. The severe unemployment has exacerbated the concern in labor groups over imports and created in many communities deep hostility to the trade negotiations envisaged by the 1974 act. These developments have occurred despite the fact that the devaluation of the dollar against the currencies of trading partners and greater inflation abroad have increased the relative competitiveness of American enterprise. The magnitude and spread of adjustments required by expanded imports in the projected economic climate in such industries as clothing, shoes, electronics, and speciality steel are certain to create strong economic and political reactions favoring bilateral restraints on imports.

It is naive to assume that workers are fungible and that one can simply add up the employment gains and losses or the gross national product effects from trade and be persuasive in a trade policy. Trade adjustment assistance in the 1974 act in the form of a measure of higher unemployment compensation, retraining grants, and moving allowances is an improvement over earlier policies. Workers affected, however, do not see why they should bear the material and psychic costs and risks of adjustment. Their labor and community leaders, particularly in the present and projected economic climate, are persuaded that the United States is simply accommodating to subtle forms of autarky abroad which encourage American firms to locate abroad and to keep out American exports, with resulting damage to American employment, while at the same time the foreign autarky subsidizes in various ways the costs and exports of its own enterprises. The state trading companies of Communist countries and government-operated enterprises elsewhere have compounded the problem. Until labor leaders are much more deeply involved in the formulation and execution of policy in this area, beyond the formalism of advisory committees, and until responsible officials are prepared to carry on a much more vigorous campaign against autarkical forms abroad, there will be little change in the present hostile policies and attitudes among labor leaders. These developments will require a long time and much new and detailed data.

A concomitant major issue concerns the growth in this country of people without documents, to use the language of diplomacy, or simply illegal aliens. Various informed estimates now place the figure in the 8 to 10 million range with significant effects on competition for jobs, wages, and benefits, and welfare among the least skilled. A country of immigrants and relatives has difficulty facing the issues. Police action is ineffectual. The economic interests of some employers combine with civil rights interests against identification cards that may be used in a discriminatory manner to preclude strong legislation. Population pressures in other countries combined with large wage differentials is an invitation to movement across borders, temporarily or more permanently. It has been suggested that citizens may not be willing to perform menial jobs and illegal aliens are essential for many activities.[36] Serious attention to this area, including further negotiations with our neighbors, is a major item on the agenda for the future likely to affect as well labor attitudes toward trade.

The American labor movement and collective bargaining are well-established institutions, deeply rooted in the character of the American worker, the economy and its structure of markets, and our political system. They have the virtue of pragmatism rather than ideology, and they respond gradually to new challenges and opportunities at the workplace and in the polity.[37]

Any appraisal of the past performance or future prospects of labor organizations in this country decisively depends on the expectations that are applied. Some have expected labor unions to perform activity for which they were ill designed and never intended to accomplish, and which they abjured. Some have looked to unions for the working-class revolution; often labor organizations have been urged to adopt the mutually inconsistent objectives of radical reform and economic responsibility; others have hoped for a new political party. Consider the following aspirations: "Labor had no more urgent job in the '60's than the focusing of its political energies on the conquest of want, illiteracy, intolerance; the building up of both health and decent housing; the realization of limitless promise of the scientific golden age. And apart from their general social necessity, these undertakings would be vastly more inspiriting, to union membership and leadership alike, than the present ever more routine function of the policing of day-to-day plant grievances and the writing of mechanized contracts.[38] Labor unions will undoubtedly gradually continue to make some contributions toward some of these objectives primarily at the workplace and secondarily by social and legislative activities. But in the depreciation of collective bargaining and grievance handling, and the enhancement of political methods, there is a serious misreading of the nature of American workers, their organizations, and the practicalities of the American economy and society.

As memories of the Viet Nam and the 1968 and 1972 election conflicts recede, a window of opportunity emerges for a more civil and possibly productive direct dialogue between labor representatives and intellectual groups. In the university world, now almost devoid of contacts with established labor leaders, there are again students and younger faculty interested in labor union institutions and how they actually work. There is a long agenda of potential common interests—union growth in new areas, the effect of government regulation, foreign labor issues in Western countries and in developing nations. Despite the deep-seated tensions, there are some opportunities for a degree of accommodation.

REFERENCES

[1] Sumner H. Slichter, "The American System of Industrial Relations: Contrasts with Foreign Systems," January 1955, reprinted in John T. Dunlop (ed.), *Potentials of the American Economy, Selected Essays of Sumner H. Slichter* (Cambridge, Mass.: Harvard University Press, 1961), pp. 285–286.

[2] Daniel Bell, *The End of Ideology* (Glencoe, Ill.: The Free Press of Glencoe, 1960), p. 213.

[3] U.S. Department of Labor, Bureau of Labor Statistics, *Directory of National Unions and Employee Associations*, 1975. Also see Everett M. Kassalow, "International Labor Standards—Their Comparison and Implementation," unpublished paper (December 14–16, 1976): Table 1. There are numerous problems involved in such comparisons, including the handling of migratory workers and the meaning of membership. Attachment to labor organizations might be tested by voting in representation elections, regular payment of periodic dues, willingness occasionally to demonstrate, support of a long strike, or voting a labor ticket in public elections. The number of persons governed by collective agreements is still another concept which encompasses more employees than union membership. The significance of such indicia varies among countries. The figures cited in the text for the U.S. exclude Canadian membership. They also exclude a growing number of retired union members with whom many unions keep in touch by pension arrangements and political education committees.

[4] In order of size in 1974 these unions were the Teamsters, Autoworkers, Steelworkers, Electricians (I.B.E.W.), Machinists, Carpenters, Retail Clerks, Laborers, State, County and Municipal Workers, Service Employees, Meat Cutters, and Communication Workers. Among associations, the largest, the National Education Association, would rank third if rated on the list of unions.

[5] Leo Troy, "The Finances of American Unions, 1962–1969," in *Explorations in Economic Research* (2) (Spring 1975): 223. The income of the federation has been about $17 or $18 million a year recently. See also Charles W. Hickman, "Labor Organizations' Fees and Dues," *Monthly Labor Review* (May 1977): 19–24.

[6] Seymour M. Lipset, "Trade Unions and Social Structure: II," *Industrial Relations* (February 1962): 93.

[7] See Lloyd Ulman, *The Rise of the National Trade Union* (Cambridge, Mass.: Harvard University Press, 1955). Also review the history of various national unions, for instance, Mark Perlman, *The Machinist* (Cambridge, Mass.: Harvard University Press, 1961), or Martin Segal, *The Rise of the United Association, National Unionism in the Pipe Trades, 1884–1924* (Wertheim Committee, Harvard University, 1970).

[8] Constitution of the AFL and CIO, 1975, Article VIII, Section 7. *Proceedings and Executive Council Reports of the AFL-CIO*, San Francisco, October 2–7, 1975 (Washington, D.C.: AFL-CIO), p. 451.

[9] Article XX, Constitution of the AFL and CIO, pp. 462–466. Also see Arthur J. Goldberg, *AFL-CIO Labor United* (New York: McGraw-Hill, 1956), pp. 103–154.

[10] George Meany, "What Labor Means by 'More,' " *Fortune Magazine* (March 1955): 92, 93, 172, 174, 177.

[11] Thomas R. Donohue, "The Future of Collective Bargaining," International Conference on Trends in Industrial and Labour Relations, Montreal, Canada, May 26, 1976, *AFL-CIO Free Trade Union News* (September 1976): 6.

[12] Sumner H. Slichter, James J. Healy, and E. Robert Livernash, *The Impact of Collective Bargaining on Management* (Washington, D.C.: The Brookings Institution, 1960), pp. 951, 952.

[13] Sidney and Beatrice Webb, *Industrial Democracy* (London: Longmans, Green, 1914). The Webbs regarded the Trade Unionists as achieving their objectives by three main instruments or levers: Collective Bargaining, Legal Enactment, and Mutual Insurance (p. 150; see also pp. 247–278).

[14] For the activities of the California federation, see Philip Taft, *Labor Politics American Style: The California State Federation of Labor* (Cambridge, Mass.: Harvard University Press, 1968).

[15] *Proceedings of the Tenth Annual Convention of the American Federation of Labor*, held at Detroit, Michigan, December 8–13, 1890. The issue in the convention was the issuance of a charter to the Central Labor Federation of New York, which included as one constituent member the Socialist Labor Party. There was an extended and formal debate. Gompers opposed the charter.

[16]Morris Hillquit, Samuel Gompers, and Max J. Hayes, *The Double Edge of Labor's Sword, Discussion and Testimony on Socialism and Trade-Unionism Before the Commission on Industrial Relations* (New York: Socialist Literature Company, 1914), pp. 134, 152.

[17]Constitution of the AFL and CIO, Article II, 12.

[18]Quoted in Charles M. Rehmus and Doris B. McLaughlin, *Labor and American Politics* (Ann Arbor: The University of Michigan Press, 1967, reprinted), p. 267.

[19]See Derek C. Bok and John T. Dunlop, *Labor and the American Community* (New York: Simon and Schuster, 1970), p. 124; Ray Marshall, *The Negro Worker* (New York: Random House, 1967), pp. 40–41; and J. David Greenstone, *Labor in American Politics* (New York: Knopf, 1969), pp. 342–343.

[20]Donohue, "The Future of Collective Bargaining," p. 5.

[21]Slichter, "The American System of Industrial Relations: Contrasts with Foreign Systems," pp. 285–286.

[22]Solomon Barkin, "A New Agenda for Labor," *Fortune* (November 1960).

[23]George Strauss, "Workers: Attitudes and Adjustments," in Jerome M. Rosow (ed.), *The Worker and The Job, Coping With Change*, The American Assembly (Englewood Cliffs, N.J.: Prentice-Hall, 1974), pp. 74–75. There are technical difficulties with the Gallup Poll. See Robert Quinn, Thomas Mangione, and Martha Madilovitch, "Evaluating Working Conditions in America," *Monthly Labor Review* (November 1973): 39. Also see in the same American Assembly volume, Peter Henle, "Economic Effects: Reviewing the Evidence," pp. 119–144.

[24]Robert J. Flanagan, George Strauss, and Lloyd Ulman, "Worker Discontent and Work Place Behavior," *Industrial Relations* (May 1974): 101–123.

[25]See Quinn, Mangione, and Mandilovitch, "Evaluating Working Conditions in America."

[26]See *Employment and Training Report of the President* (Washington, D.C.: U.S. Department of Labor, 1976, pp. 147–157 ("The Changing Nature of Work").

[27]Arnold S. Tannenbaum, "Systems of Formal Participation," in George Strauss, et al. (eds.), *Organizational Behavior, Research, and Issues* (Madison, Wisc.: Industrial Relations Research Association, 1974), p. 78.

[28]*Report of the Committee of Inquiry on Industrial Democracy*, Cmnd. 6706 (London: Her Majesty's Stationery Office, 1977); *TUC Guide to the Bullock Report on Industrial Democracy* (London: The Trade Unions Congress, February 1977); B. C. Roberts, "Participation by Agreement," *Lloyds Bank Review*, no. 125 (July 1977): 12–23; *The Economist* (November 13–19, 1976): p. 105.

[29]*Report of the Committee of Inquiry on Industrial Democracy*, p. 160.

[30]Donohue, "The Future of Collective Bargaining," p. 6.

[31]John T. Dunlop, "The Settlement of Emergency Disputes," *Proceedings of the Fifth Annual Meeting, Industrial Relations Research Association* (December 28–29, 1952): "I believe that in twenty-five years the emergency dispute will have ceased to be a serious question."

[32]Alfred Marshall, *Elements of Economics of Industry* (London: Macmillan, 1893), Chapter 13, "Trade Unions," pp. 374–411.

[33]National Center for Productivity and Quality of Working Life, *Directory of Labor-Management Committees* (Washington, D.C., October 1976). For a discussion of Scanlon plans and other systems of encouraging productivity, see Paul Pigors and Charles A. Myers, *Personnel Administration* 8th ed. (New York: McGraw-Hill, 1977), pp. 356–377.

[34]Arthur Okun, "Conflicting National Goals," in Eli Ginzberg (ed.), *Jobs for Americans*, The American Assembly (Englewood Cliffs, N.J.: Prentice-Hall, 1976), p. 81.

[35]John T. Dunlop, "Wage and Price Controls as Seen by a Controller," Industrial Relations Research Association, *Proceedings of the 1975 Annual Spring Meeting* (May 8–10, 1975): 457–463. See also Committee for Economic Development, *Fighting Inflation and Promoting Growth* (August 1976): 62–77.

[36]Michael J. Piore, "The 'New Immigration' and the Presumptions of Social Policy," *Industrial Relations Research Association, Proceedings of the Twenty-Seventh Annual Winter Meeting* (December 28–29, 1974): 350–358.

[37]On several occasions I have sought to outline the future course of development of American unions and collective bargaining. See John T. Dunlop, "The American Industrial Relations System in 1975," in Jack Steiber (ed.), *U.S. Industrial Relations: The Next Twenty Years* (East Lansing, Mich., 1958), pp. 1–24; "Future Trends in Industrial Relations in the United States," a paper presented to the Third World Congress, International Industrial Relations Association, London, September, 1973 (unpublished).

[38]A. H. Raskin, "The Obsolescent Unions," *Commentary* (July 1963): 18.

NANCY NEEDHAM WARDELL

The Corporation

THE CORPORATION—an association of individual people created by law having an existence independent of the existence of its members, and powers and liabilities distinct from those of its members—is a major institutional form in America and the primary means for the production of goods and services and the distribution of wealth. Despite the fact that business firms so organized are clearly essential to the functioning of the economy and the well-being of the public, they often are perceived as inimical to the public interest. They do not enjoy a position of high repute, and corporate managers are not held in esteem.[1] Why is this so? Do our negative perceptions reflect accurately what corporations are and what they do, or do we suffer from a lack of understanding?

The Corporate Population

The American corporate population is vast; by 1970 there were nearly two million corporations. If such a number is to be understood, some method of categorization is essential.

First, firms can be sorted into big versus small and then according to their product strategy—to whether they manufacture one product (single-product firms), one major product or vertically integrated chain of products (dominant-product firms), or many different products (diversified firms). Compared to the past, some differences become immediately obvious. In sheer size, the American firm is considerably larger than it was forty years ago. Testimony given in the late 1930s at the Temporary National Economic Hearings in Washington showed that only 0.2 percent of the American corporations had assets in excess of $50 million.[2] Today there are hundreds of firms whose assets are worth hundreds of millions of dollars. AT&T has $86 billion and the "smallest" (e.g., number 500) firm on the *Forbes* magazine list of the 500 largest corporations has $993 million in assets. The foundations of our antitrust laws were established in the late nineteenth and early twentieth centuries, and many of our regulatory agencies were founded in the 1930s. These laws and government institutions were directed at firms which were big in one era but which would be considered small today. Do the present increases in scale imply the need to reexamine the regulations? Or, alternatively, do we need to question the urge to attempt to return today's large firms to sizes of our yesteryears?

The *Fortune* list of the 500 largest industrial corporations together with the product strategy method of classification reveal a shifting population since World War II, from a preponderance of single-product firms to a preponderance of diversified firms. Studies on the organization and performance of these firms by students and faculty at the Harvard Business School concluded that the single-product firms have declined from about 30 percent of the total *Fortune* 500 in 1949 to under 10 percent by 1969; that the dominant-product firms have continued to comprise about 40 percent of the *Fortune* 500 firms; and that the growing form has been the diversified firm.[3]

The trend toward diversified companies was accelerated by the merger movement, which flourished in the 1960s and which is still continuing. Leaving aside the question, for a moment, of why the trend in corporate development has been toward diversification, it is possible to speculate on the implications of these corporate strategies for the internal organization of the firms.

Most single-product and many dominant-product firms are organized on a functional basis. For example, there are managers who focus on control and finance, managers in charge of marketing, managers in charge of manufacturing. The president or chief executive officer of such a corporation is usually astute in the operational aspects of the business and often concerns himself with marketing to a very great extent. Numerous oil-company and steel-company presidents are shirtsleeves men who worked their way up the ranks and who are considered to be top "oil men" or "steel men." Not surprisingly, these men who have worked their way up often think alike about their industry; after all, there are only so many ways to make steel, produce paper, or market oil. Sharing a common "industry viewpoint," however, does not mean that personnel move back and forth among companies; on the contrary, longevity with one company is both a fact and a requisite virtue.

In a well-developed economy such as that of the United States, the market for basic materials, particularly those like steel, is often limited in growth potential. And a prime preoccupation of firms in such markets is, not surprisingly, the maintenance of market share. "Old" industries may decline, relatively and even absolutely. If increased sales are not found abroad, a company such as a steel company may find itself tied to a growth rate in sales that roughly parallels (slightly above or below) the growth rate in GNP. Spectacular increases are rare. So these firms lumber onward. When investments are made, they are often investments in incremental capacity or new technology so that the firm can keep up with its competitors domestically and worldwide. Such investments usually are made to reduce costs and often show a more attractive return on investment than alternative investment opportunities requiring, for example, longer start-up times or the acquisition of new management skills.

Unlike dominant-product firms, diversified firms are usually organized not by function but by division. The divisional organization makes sense given that this type of company has different types of products operating in distinct product "markets," each of which might require varying marketing, manufacturing, or financing techniques. The division form, furthermore, permits the company president to see which division, or products, are profitable and which are not. The president's role becomes one where he allocates funds to the winners, eliminates the losers, and pulls cash from the old reliables that may chug along providing little glamor but a steady income stream. What may be chiefly a "political process" in the dominant-product firm can be chiefly an economic one in the diversified one—which is not to say that politics is absent. As might be expected, the president of such a company does not have to be a production or marketing expert for a particular product, but he does have to be a good financial strategist, and a marketing generalist. He does not have to come up from within the company; he does not think of himself as a man wedded to any particular product.

In diversified firms, managers competing for promotion do not compete on the basis of market share, for how can one compare the market share of a paint division with the market share of a rental-car division or the international division? For one market, a tiny increase in market share may have taken superhuman skill; for another, growth may occur because the market itself is expanding and the share of market could remain fixed. But managers do compete on the basis of earnings, the one measure that can be used as a yardstick across divisions related or unrelated and which brings with it great stress for managers precisely because it ignores extenuating circumstances.

The major firms are not only significantly larger in size; they have developed new strategies and enjoyed better earnings in comparison to the older style firms.[4] If single-product and dominant-product firms are significantly different from diversified firms, decisions about how to modify their behavior might well vary despite the fact that both types may be "big." Such government regulators as the Federal Trade Commission or the Department of Justice, Antitrust Division, however, are geared philosophically to thinking about firms in the big-small and industry categories; and the diversified firms remain a challenge that is not well understood. When firms in a particular industry (and it is often difficult to determine industry boundaries) are perceived as having become "too big," and by inference or observation "powerful," then the battle is on. Trotting out the traditional antitrust measure—structural disemboweling of one version or another—is still standard practice. Its utility is questionable.

Take, for example, the case of Procter and Gamble and its purchase of the Clorox company, which the owners wanted to sell to an established company. After a lengthy court battle which stretched over much of the 1960s, the Supreme Court upheld the government's position and Procter and Gamble was ordered to divest itself of Clorox. The government's case was in part based on the argument that the public interest would have been better served had Procter and Gamble not purchased Clorox but had waited in the wings as a potential competitor (thus, presumably, putting fear and loathing into the hearts of existent bleach makers and spurring them to greater heights). In the end, when Clorox was indeed divested, it was quite clearly a small clone of Procter and Gamble, which made a substantial profit on the bleach sales while it owned Clorox and an even greater profit on the divestiture. In the end, no other diversified firm was much better able to deduce what the government believed was right or wrong with mergers, except to have some cautious idea that buying the leader in the field (which Clorox had been in the bleach business) was not a good idea. From the public interest point of view, what was apparently wrong with this merger (and mergers in general by large firms) was that it made one firm "too big" and "too powerful" in the bleach industry.

A current antitrust case of interest to most businesses is that being waged against the cereal companies. The government has cast the issue of the public interest with respect to cereals into a structural argument based on there being too few cereal companies and too many brands. To get at the issue of brand proliferation (and by inference, quality and nutrition) by means of structural arguments, the government has put forward the as yet unvalidated notion of a "shared monopoly" (which must share the honors for internal inconsistency with "half-truths" and "partial virgins"). But the point here is that the government's view of corporations depends on a limited classification scheme—big-small—the government's remedies are too often structural; and the government does not recognize or understand what a diversified firm is or how to prod or encourage it to behave in ways consistent with whatever has been determined to be in the public interest.

The pressure to chop up the oil companies into small pieces (assumed thereafter to be more honest, more economical, less "bad") reflects both our national antitrust reflex whenever we feel that corporations are out of control, and our mythic belief that small is good. But splitting up oil companies, which now with respect to foreign oil have been relegated to middlemen between the American public and the oil-producing nations, is a little like punching the ticket seller when the play is bad. Neither action affects the supply. The oil companies are now conduits for Middle East prices and the time for antitrust action was, if at all, in 1952 when the Justice Department first documented the seven multinational oil companies' practice of dividing up the oil production and thereby allocating market shares among themselves. Today OPEC does the production dividing, and the target of our foreign oil supply policies ought to be the producing countries rather than the companies. The companies require transformation, not amputation.

Professor Bruce R. Scott, of the Harvard Business School, has conducted research on corporate structure and strategy which has led him to conclude that the public interest would be better served if even more firms were diversified, if government regulators encouraged dominant firms to merge with other firms and to acquire new product lines.[5] His rationale is that it is in the public interest to have firms capable of generating high earnings. His views are diametrically opposed to those of many influential legislators. For example, one of the major pieces of legislation suggested in the past few years has been the so-called Hart Reorganization Bill; after hearings that covered many of the nation's industries, Senator Philip A. Hart sponsored a bill, again premised on the big-small method of categorization, that would have had the effect of restructuring firms in eight major industries. His proposals are basically a variant of the antitrust approach. It is a testament to the profound lack of communication and agreement among groups in our society with respect to the appropriate government influences on business that the proposal offered by one business educator and one legislator are so antithetical. The divergence in their proposed solutions relates not only to their different preferences but to their different methods of categorization. Hart used the big-small industry approach and Scott the product strategy approach and their solutions were cast in terms of their categories.

Categorizing firms reveals commonalities and differences among various corporate groups and is an exercise which leads one to ask what can be done to make one group be more like some other, more appealing group. Scott, as noted, finds the high-performing, diversified firms more attractive. Others might prefer high-technology firms; still others might want to make a distinction between high-technology firms such as IBM, which have predominantly nondefense customers, and firms that depend on government defense contracts for their survival. It could be argued that as our State Department pushes for more interdependence among nations (implying, among other things, the removal of tariff barriers), the high-technology firms whose growth, survival, and competitive strength rest on a combination of research and development and marketing acumen, are attractive candidates for competition in a global context and should be encouraged. Regardless of method, it is important that those persons capable of inducing or requiring change in the composition of the corporate population be aware of their categorization schemes and recognize those solutions to which a specific scheme is most amenable and those which it precludes.

Implicit in the idea of regulating business is the notion that once the public interest has been defined, there must be rules with which a firm can align itself in order to have its behavior congruent with the public interest as defined. The public interest, however, or at least definitions of it, changes over time. Thus, a firm's behavior must change. A firm's behavior changes in response to managers' perceptions of external pressures and their determination of which pressures are significant and which insignificant. Thus, how firms change and what they will look like in the future is a combination of the real pressures in the external environment and the nature of the managers themselves and their behavior within particular types of corporate environments.

The Corporate Managers

Who are the corporate managers and what do they think?

From the viewpoint of the public, they are unloved and not particularly respected. Not since the Depression has there been such public distaste for business. Consider some recent survey results.[6] Over a ten-year period, the Harris organization asked people whether or not they had a great deal of confidence in the heads of large corporations. In nine years the number of persons having a great deal of confidence dropped from 55 percent to 15 percent—a drop of 40 percent! A Yankelovitch survey which asked whether business strikes a fair balance between profits and the public interest showed a similarly large decline—from 70 percent in 1968 to 20 percent in 1974. Business executives, when compared with "small business" on "honesty, dependability, and integrity," received a high ranking from only 11 percent of the respondents, compared to the 28 percent rating for small business. A Gallup poll which asked people to describe their level of confidence in those institutions which comprise the United States power structure ranked educational institutions and organized religion first, then the military, Congress, the Supreme Court, and organized labor, and last of all, business.

To understand why there are such negative views of business, it is important to recall the high expectations for business in the 1960s. If business did not live up to these expectations, it may not have been that business was per se inadequate, but that some of those expectations were inappropriate in the first place. Implicit in the expectation that business would solve social problems while also producing products that were well made and low priced was an assumption that managers were the appropriate people to determine social needs and to set up nongovernmental policies to satisfy those needs. Further, a distinction must be made between being a "professional manager" with the responsibilities that that term entails and being a public policy maker or quasi-government; that distinction was not made. Most managers are, in fact, uncomfortable with the expansion of their role which is implied by such terms as "corporate social responsibility."

Over a period of years beginning in the 1970s, Professor George Lodge of the Harvard Business School has surveyed the men, and the very few women, who have attended the Advanced Management Program at the Harvard Business School. Lodge described the traditional American ideology as atomistic, individualistic, least government is best, Darwinian survival of the fittest, sanctity of private property, specialization.[7] According to his surveys, most of these managers (80 percent) feel comfortable with this description of the traditional ideology and would find it very close to their own personal ideologies. There have, however, been changes in society, and Lodge has described what he sees as the emerging new American ideology as organic, people as part of a social process, community rights, state (government) as planner, groups.[8] Interestingly enough, these same managers thought that this second ideology would be more effective in solving future problems and would be in force in 1985—not too far away. But they themselves still prefer the old ideology.

I have given this same survey to students in my MBA classes and their responses paralleled those of the older group, though with a smaller majority preferring the old ideology. Equally interesting to me is the fact that when I asked my MBA students some of the same questions about the reliability, integrity, and respectability of business, the students were just as cynical and disgusted as the national survey samples. Yet they are training to be managers! This ambivalence is bound to set up tensions for them. There will be no tension, of course, if there is no conflict between the manager's value system or ideology and that of his corporation. But often there are conflicts, and I suspect that there will definitely be conflicts between the old guard and at least some of the new.

Ironically enough, the debates over business school curricula are not with respect to the best ways to train managers for the year 2000, much less the year 1985, but whether teaching by the case method is superior to teaching a more theoretical, investment portfolio-management approach. In both instances, the education is perfectly suited to the 1950s. Neither the business schools nor the firms are particularly adept at long-range strategic thinking. Very few firms have strategic planning groups that address a time period longer than five years into the future. Even fewer firms have strategic planning groups that encompass political or social factors; many have mastered economic planning or can subscribe to one of the firms that peddle such forecasts. But strategic planning, in companies or in business school curricula, that encompasses political and social trends and translates them into meaningful "so what's" for corporations is in its infancy.

Business school education focuses primarily on how to manage such functional aspects of the business as marketing, production, finance, and control. The leading schools are beginning to develop courses that train managers to think about business-government relations and public policy, but often such courses are optional rather than part of the required curriculum. At present, the consideration of ethics, an area of great public concern with respect to business, is grafted onto business schools' curricula in the form of optional (and therefore irrelevant to most students) seminars. To be effective, it must be infused into the courses on control and finance (for much ethical abuse takes the form of financial machinations) as well as the other parts of the curriculum.

This same managerial education, which ignores for the most part business-government relations, also still treats international business as an optional field of study rather than as an integral part of the curriculum. But managers must be cognizant of others in the world and able to deal with our own and other governments over a host of issues. For example, whether or not a small glass manufacturer in Connecticut obtains the natural gas he needs for his product will be a function of the government's decisions with respect to importing liquified natural gas from Algeria, the resolution of the questions surrounding deregulation of domestic gas, and the availability of substitute energy. A decade ago, the same glass manufacturer would not have had to be troubled by Algeria, regulation issues, or the energy supply, with its obvious international links.

Whether the content of the manager's education is cause for concern depends, of course, on whether or not one feels that the pressures facing corporations are going to be different from the pressures of the past. The rise of diversified firms has provided ample evidence that the corporate population can and does change in response to pressures. The nonchanging firms may be constitutionally unable to evolve given the type of managers that inhabit them, or they may be constrained by such factors as the fear or actuality of government antitrust intervention. But why the diversified firms, for example, appear as they do reflects the process by which corporations change over time.

The Nature of Change

The pressures on American firms can be considered under such broad headings as technology, resources (human, material, and financial), and infrastructure. Populations were a significant factor in the development of business; waves of immigration from Europe to the United States provided both a labor force and a huge domestic market for manufactured goods, which would be readily made from available supplies of domestic raw materials. The push westward of this population was abetted by such technological breakthroughs as the steam engine, which, by providing a new energy source, freed factories from locations on the banks of rivers with their water power, to locations near population centers. The technology of the internal combustion engine again freed people locationally. With the development of the refrigerated railroad car, for example, Swift was able to build a far-flung meat-processing empire—an example of strategy in response to technology and preceding organizational restructuring that Alfred D. Chandler has documented in detail in his pioneering work on the strategy and structure of American firms.[9]

In terms of infrastructure, it was the development of the railroads that spurred the rise of professional managers, men who could coordinate the complicated business of shipping a variety of goods to a variety of places at a variety of prices. The pressure was there for some way of organizing, and the response was to set up cost-accounting systems and to begin to divide up the managerial tasks. The Depression was another large-scale pressure; from it there resulted among other things business practices designed to avoid in the future those tremendous inventory backlogs, to master the production activity so it could be accelerated and slowed at the manager's behest. Inventory control practices, the desire to even out business cycles (which had just been identified as such by economists like Joseph Schumpeter and W. C. Mitchell) led to an interest in an expanded product line, the fine tuning of the mass production factory during World War II—all of these being large-scale responses to large-scale external pressure.

Obviously there were many factors affecting the development of diversified firms, but it can be argued that financial pressures were paramount. In order to be self-sustaining, to regenerate when necessary and finally to grow, firms have to have financial resources—internal (earnings) or external (equity or debt). Most firms cannot be completely self-financing, but our capital markets, the source of external financing, appear to place high value on firms that show growth in earnings. One way to show such growth is to diversify into more promising markets domestically or abroad. Diversification can be through internal research and development or through acquisition; either way, the purpose is to increase earnings. As a society we have not fully addressed the question of how we will relate to those firms whose ability to grow is limited and which, therefore, may consistently face difficulties when trying to raise funds. Some we may prefer to see fail. Others we may, for reasons of national security, pride, or employment, prefer to see succeed. We do have electric and gas utilities and the telephone company, and we have made them regulated corporations. We have not decided whether steel, textiles, or mass transportation, to name a few with low earnings potential but high cash needs, constitute equally essential domestic industries that we will try to cram into the regulated-monopolies category, attempt to publicly finance or subsidize, or leave to survive in the arena with firms which by definition are going to have more appeal to investors.

Seen in this perspective, the pressure for funds since World War II has been monumental. It has stimulated changes in the basic structure of the corporate population and influenced firms' strategies. Against this background, the questions of corporate involvement in the cities, of the support of minority enterprises, of the promotion of women—the topics of great debate and interest in the late 1960s and into the early 1970s—shrink in significance as prods to action. These issues were indeed stimuli, but they were not sufficiently strong or central to the running of firms to induce major strategic changes and subsequent structural changes. Once such firms stopped worrying about being burned down or having their windows stoned by angry radicals, the pressure for action was off.[14]

Second, the drive to reform often was not followed by changes within the operations of the company. For example, one major aerospace and defense firm (with other nondefense divisions as well) hired a man to promote opportunities for minorities and women within the corporation but gave him no line authority and made no change in the reward and compensation systems in the firm. Shop foremen were still rewarded on the basis of how well they kept down costs, while at the same time they were being asked—but not tangibly rewarded for so doing—to bring the salaries of females on the production line into parity with those of the male workers. The foremen resisted these changes because, to them, they meant only increased costs, no corresponding rewards, and the potential for a lesser bonus (the latter were calculated on profits, which are a function in part of costs).

Although the issue of blacks has largely been superseded by the issue of women and both are at the forefront of personnel policy and practice, neither sexual nor racial discrimination receives much attention in business school curricula. In the corporations themselves, decisions on shaping and implementing affirmative-action plans are funneled into personnel departments and are no longer considered matters for continued top corporate involvement. This may represent the institutionalization of the issues surrounding minorities; a few firms are indeed now trying to tie compensation to the successful attainment of affirmative-action goals, but the latter are not among the most important features of corporate strategic thinking.

In fact, there are so few firms which are regarded as "forward looking," particularly with respect to social or public-policy concerns, that they are usually cited with almost monotonous regularity whenever the subject arises: Polaroid, Xerox, Cummins, Eastern Gas and Fuel to name several of the most prominent. Recalling that there are well over two million corporations, and that there is a readily identifiable group of the largest 500, the group of "anticipators" is small indeed. One feature common to these firms, however, is that they are leaders in their respective fields; their sales are sufficiently adequate to provide funds for such "social responsibilities" as corporate giving. Additionally, I suspect that the presence of dynamic chief executives who are personally committed to social roles for their corporations has been a critical factor.

In sum, firms respond to external pressure. One of the strongest and most sustained pressures for the last few decades has been the need for financial resources, and one response has been to diversify through a variety of means. The pressures of the 1960s with respect to what could be termed "social" concerns were not of sufficient intensity and duration to bring forth a corporate response of much magnitude or, in some instances, longevity.

The New External Pressures on the Corporation

What are the significant pressures that will face managers in the next decade? From the multitude which can readily be identified, three stand out: the questions of the boundary of American business, the issue of supply, and the issue of division of power between business and government.

The ideas of boundary and supply are intertwined. Since World War II we Americans have become more conscious of our loss of self-sufficiency and of our dependency on others for many raw materials. This awareness has been slow to come. Although the first national Commission on Materials (the Paley Commis-

sion) in the late 1940s pointed to our use of imports and tried to interest the
country in planning, it was to little avail. Subsequent government commissions
have noted our dependency on a wide variety of imported raw materials; public
awareness, however, did not surface until the Arabs embargoed oil in 1973.
There are over forty minerals designated as "critical imported materials" by the
federal government. During the postwar period another phenomenon was occurring, that of rising nationalism and a determination by producing countries
to alter the terms of trade.

Again, the example of oil is known to all. Other examples are less known.
From being a country that once exported steel and iron ore, we are now a net
importer. Over a third of our iron ore is imported; on average about 15 percent
of our steel is imported (not counting indirect imports of steel in the form of
manufactured goods, such as cars). The import figures are much higher (40
percent) for certain types of steel.[10] Without addressing the issue of the abundance or scarcity of these and other supplies, the fact remains that in our dealings with other nations in order to get supplies, we must contend with
heightened nationalism and our own slow-dawning awareness that our economy
is tied to the decisions of others.

Nationalism has been expressed in nationalization of assets and in increased
militancy on the part of governments with respect to raw material prices and
taxes. American businessmen did not, en masse, expect this phenomenon. European managers have decades of experience, as do the Japanese, with dealing
with foreign raw-materials suppliers from the perspective of a customer. The
initial expectation of most American businessmen dealing with foreign raw-
materials suppliers was that they could dictate the prices and, moreover, that
there would be American ownership of such supplies, rather than straight purchase from some other owner.

This mind-set toward equity ownership is changing only slowly. Executives
with whom I have talked about foreign raw materials have tended to express a
preference for equity ownership rather than purchase; accounting systems in
some industries (for example, the oil industry) and our own tax laws favored
equity ownership by permitting the companies to allocate costs, and therefore
profits, at particular points in the process (the crude production end rather than
the marketing end, for example).

Resource experts tend to speak of geologic availability (what material is in
place), and economic availability (the materials that will be available to the market at a given price under a given technology). To this I would add the term
"political availability," that is, the resources that the owners will permit to be
used and the terms attendant upon such use. For example, Australia has rich
deposits of uranium that could be economically produced given current prices
and technology. The government, however, made them unavailable for political
reasons.

The focus of most managerial education was and still is on the management
and manipulation of demand. Yet "supply management," with its implications
for political and social sensitivity, is being forced upon managers. The process
of obtaining supplies is now more political than it used to be; it is a process in
which governments of producing countries are more aware than previously and
less compliant; it is a process which will involve or at the least interest our own

government. What had been considered in many companies to be the province of the purchasing department will have to become a concern of top management.

The questions of boundary and supply relate to United States policy with respect to trade. The trend for the last decade has been to open up international trade, to remove trade barriers. Thus American firms will have to contend with increasing numbers of foreign competitors on our own shores. But when corporations—and it is interesting to note that it is often dominant-product firms which do so—call for import protection, public reaction is often that they are whining unduly. Many in government see such cries as unjustified complaints by technologically outdated firms which need the foreign competitors to keep them in line; such firms, in fact, may be technologically in the forefront but have to compete with foreign firms enjoying different cost structures because of their governments' tax or employment policies. Whether the cries are justified or unjustified depends on the particular industry or firm, but those bodies of the government that are charged with analyzing the American corporations—chiefly the Federal Trade Commission and the Justice Department—have an undeniably domestic focus. Thus we have the anomaly of the State Department pushing for internationalism and interdependence on the one hand (as opposed to isolationism) and on the other hand the Justice Department bringing antitrust suits against such vigorous and successful international competitors as IBM and basing the suit strictly on domestic data. Since Secretary of Commerce Peter Peterson left the Commerce Department, there has been no subsequent analysis of United States industry in an international context; and there was not much before him.

Finally, there is the issue of power, the question of who will control the corporations—the managers or the government. Historically business has had great freedom of action, a freedom that depended more on the ample supply of domestic resources and the vast domestic market for goods than on any agreement hammered out between business and government, although the business-government relationship, in fact, has been a continuous one over time. And government regulation of business has been part of the American way of life.

One prominent feature of the history of regulation of business is that much regulation by government has occurred in response to some public perception of corporate misbehavior. For example, the Securities and Exchange Commission and the Federal Power Commission (the 1930s version) came about in response to the excesses of the utility holding companies of the 1920s. The current Securities and Exchange Commission interest in forcing corporations to ever more disclosure of operating practices is both a response to the perception that some companies have been cheating, and part of a long-term trend toward expanding the concept of "material information." Likewise, regulation of environmental pollution activities indicates that pollution is becoming regarded as another example of corporate misbehavior.

The lesson here for corporations is that public dissatisfaction (which derives from the feeling that expectations raised are now being denied) becomes translated into calls for increased government intervention into management's territory. If such intervention is unwelcome—and to most managers it is because managers want to *manage*—then the message is clear that responsible behavior, ethical behavior, behavior that anticipates changing social pressures will be requisite for managers.

The question of supply will intensify the power struggle. As noted above, corporations used to making their own arrangements with foreign governments must now deal more cautiously. When the Canadian government decided to increase the export tax on its western oil going to the United States, the increased taxation was a matter of public interest, not just of American oil company interest. The increased prices that can be anticipated for many commodities coupled with the government's concern over inflation virtually guarantee that companies' decisions with respect to procurement of raw materials abroad and prices set for finished goods here will get increased scrutiny.

The power question will also arise with respect to social issues such as equal employment opportunity. Although the government has established regulations with respect to affirmative-action hiring, companies have been able to set their own goals. Thus some managers have been able simply to set low targets. The disparity in employment income between men and women[11] and between minorities and whites cannot continue forever. Yet, if corporations are expected to assist in the process of ethnic parity through personnel policies (some would argue that this expectation is inappropriate, but it is the law) there are bound to be differences of opinion on how best to do this. Current guidelines with respect to hiring the handicapped, which have not been enforced with any particular vigor to date, indicate that companies must recruit at schools for the blind and retarded, among many other requirements. Spokesmen for the Department of Health, Education, and Welfare announced that alcoholics and drug addicts could not be discriminated against if they were "qualified for the job."[12] Age discrimination is also being tackled by the government. The lack of vigorous enforcement of such regulations is a commentary on the government agency responsible. But because the regulations are extant and the public expectation has been raised, and because private enforcement by class-action suits is increasingly a substitute for ineffectual or nonexistent government enforcement of its own regulations, companies can expect that these issues will not evaporate.

The major pressures facing corporations in the future are of a nature different from that of the past. In addition to being economic, they are now more intensely sociopolitical in nature. The question of power and who will make the final decision in a business-government dialogue is one which is tied to the more philosophic question of the legitimacy and purpose of corporations as we know them. As more critics question the role of corporations, their taken-for-granted legitimacy will become less secure.

Whether corporations can respond adequately to these pressures is a function of the nature of the managers, the people who make the decisions about what the corporations will or will not do and a function of the way the corporations are perceived by those people who make policies affecting them.

Conclusions

Milton Friedman once wrote that "the business of business is business," an assertion which generated intense debate in the late 1960s and which, to its critics, was a call for callousness; his basic argument, however, was that the only "social responsibility" of business was to use its resources to compete fairly (e.g., to use no fraud or deception) and to increase its profits for its stockholders.[13] Such failures of business involvement in the cities as alluded to by Henry M. Morgan attest to the fallacy of business trying to do good apart from the basic purpose of making money for stockholders by the production of goods and services.[14] This is not to argue that business should be callous but that the more we confuse the roles of business manager with the roles of other professionals in society and thereby require managers to spend time doing things which they are not trained to do, the more failures we can expect. As a society we can ask whether or not it is realistic to think of training all-purpose professionals. Friedman's line of thought would suggest that it is not.

Further, the more we require managers to expend their efforts in nonproductive areas, the more we diminish the effectiveness of the firms. One major company, for example, calculated that it took 80 man-years per year and cost $5 million (its net earnings were $95 million after taxes) to fill in all the forms required by government regulations.[15] The more such nonbusiness activities we force upon business people, the more we will divert their energies from the production of goods and services, and the more will corporations come to resemble quasi-government bureaus.

The pressures facing corporations today are tied to internal organization, to foreign policy, to business-government relations in the United States, and to rising and continuing social demands; often they are beyond the ken of many managers given their ideologies and training. We do not train managers to be public policy makers, not do we vote them into office; we do not train them to be sociologists or psychologists; we do not train them to be sensitive to issues of boundary, supply, and power as these terms have been defined earlier. Business responds to pressures, but we cannot reasonably expect people to behave in ways which are foreign to them.

As business school education is presently constituted, there is very little said with respect to the responsibilities of a manager in a capitalist system. As a group, managers do not have a Hippocratic oath. Much is said about managerial rights, not enough about managerial responsibilities, and almost nothing about the overall relationship between managed organizations and the society which creates them and endorses the corporate existence. And finally, there is a certain ambivalence in managers, young and old, as they are pulled between their own beliefs and inclinations based on the practices of the past, and what they themselves consider to be the ideologies of the future.

There will be increasing conflict and confrontation because corporations are the economy. There is a limit to how far the government can control corporations before it destroys what it set out to save; but it is not clear that government regulators as a group understand what they are each doing individually.

There is a certain American tendency always to assume the best: to decide that business schools will amend their curricula; that government officials will modify their approach; that managers will realize the folly of clinging to an outdated ideology and replace it with a vigorous relevant new one. But where is the evidence to suggest that these good things will happen? There is far more evidence to suggest that we will muddle along, missing the broad trends and issues, constraining our corporations at ever more junctures, and ensuring that our corporations will be increasingly ill at ease in our society.

REFERENCES

[1]Leonard Silk and D. Vogel, *Ethics and Profits* (New York: Simon and Schuster, 1976); Marketing Department, *U.S. News and World Report, Summary Report 1976, A Study of American Opinion.*

[2]Investigations of Concentration of Economic Power, Hearings before the Temporary National Economic Committee, Part I, *Economic Prologue, December 1, 2 and 3, 1938* (Washington, D.C.: Government Printing Office, 1940), p. 229. Data based on a sample of 415,000 firms account for 85% of all corporations, but 98% of tax revenues.

[3]A summary of the research project is provided in Bruce R. Scott, "The Industrial State: Old Myths and New Realities," *Harvard Business Review* (March–April 1973).

[4]For details, including a discussion of the subcategories of diversified firms and the relative profitability of the various types, see Richard P. Rumelt, *Strategy, Structure and Economic Performance* (Boston: Division of Research, Harvard Business School, 1974).

[5]Scott, "The Industrial State: Old Myths and New Realities."

[6]Silk and Vogel, *Ethics and Profits.*

[7]Lodge's questionnaire is as follows:

CASE I. Society is atomistic. The community is no more than the sum of the individuals in it. Self-respect and fulfillment result from an essentially lonely struggle in which initiative and hard work pay off. The fit survive and if you don't survive, you are somehow unfit. Property rights is a sacred guarantor of individual rights and the uses of property are best controlled by competition to satisfy consumer desires in an open market place. The least government the best. Reality is perceived best through the specialized activities of experts striving for objectivity.

CASE II. Individual fulfillment and self-respect are the result of one's place in an organic social process—we get our kicks by being part of a group. If the group is well designed, it makes full use of our individual capacities. Property rights are less important than the rights which derive from membership in the community or a group, i.e. rights to income, health and education, for example. The uses of property are best regulated by community need which is often different from individual consumer desires. The state must plan, coordinate and set visions in order to define community need efficiently and effectively. Reality can only be perceived through an understanding of wholes and systems of wholes.

1. Although you may not agree fully with either statement, which Case more adequately describes your own feelings?
2. Which Case do you think is more dominant in America today?
3. Which Case do you expect will be more dominant in 1985?
4. Which Case do you think would be more effective in solving the problems of the future?

[8]Ibid.

[9]Alfred D. Chandler, *Strategy and Structure: Chapters in the History of Industrial Enterprise* (Cambridge, Mass.: M.I.T. Press, 1962).

[10]Nancy N. Wardell, *United States Iron Ore Imports and Sourcing Strategies for Steel Companies.* Harvard University, Graduate School of Business, unpublished doctoral thesis, 1977.

[11]Bureau of the Census, Current Population Reports, p. 60, no. 101 (Washington, D.C.: GPO, 1976).

[12]*New York Times* (July 6, 1977): A 14.

[13]Milton Friedman, "Monopoly and the Social Responsibility of Business and Labor," in Edwin Mansfield (ed.), *Monopoly Power and Economic Performance* (New York: Norton, 1968), pp. 105–116.

[14]Writing in the Spring 1974 issue of the *Journal of Contemporary Business* on the subject of corporate responsibility and the problems of the city, Henry Morgan described the involvement of three major American corporations in the inner city. The corporate efforts were initiated by the civil unrest of the 1960s, but after the initial fanfare and strong start, most petered out. Why? Morgan concludes: ". . . the vast majority of companies has not been willing or able to make large adaptive changes without outside stimuli. They respond strongly to strong stimuli . . . but they also promptly return to prior behavior when no longer prodded." Black issues are virtual nonissues today; the reason may lie in the fact that firms are no longer prodded; as Morgan noted, the nation is "temporarily free of riots." Henry M. Morgan, "A Look Back," *Journal of Contemporary Business* (Spring 1974): 72, 73.

[15]*Fortune* (November 1976): 118.

EDWARD K. HAMILTON

On Nonconstitutional Management of a Constitutional Problem

I

THE PAST FORTY YEARS of evolution in American governance are an impressive testament to the influence of pragmatism upon our social and political philosophy. Without any fundamental amendment of the Constitution, and with only two genuinely sweeping redirections of judicial interpretation, we have totally transformed the scope of purpose, the scale, and the order of complexity of the public sector, as well as the difficulty in holding government accountable. This masterwork of incrementalism confirms our post-Civil War talent for effecting major adaptation without doctrinal confrontations serious enough to threaten the fabric of the republic. It also owes much to the capacity of the Framers to sense how much they could not foresee, and their consequent care that all except the few most sacred propositions and structures could be changed without altering organic law.

However, the more durable part of the deep malaise now evident in popular attitudes toward government probably represents the price of sustained incrementalism. Such change depends upon a delicate balance between fact and myth. The greater the innovation, the more necessary that it be linked to a reaffirmation of traditional principles. The three great watersheds of change in this period have been crises of strikingly different kinds: the Great Depression, World War II, and the mid-1960s crisis of economic morality when we discovered that years of unprecedented general prosperity did not eliminate poverty or guarantee a decent level of public services. Each crisis produced a massive expansion in the role of government generally acknowledged to be legitimate. Each produced a corresponding enlargement in government operations and costs. But none resulted in major challenge to the average citizen's conception of the nature of the federal system and the relation of the multiplying numbers of governmental units within it.

Evidence now abounds that (1) the facts of federalism have diverged so far from the classic myth that the rhetoric of political persuasion is largely irrelevant to the real world; (2) unless ways are found to achieve consensus on revisions in the myth—without necessarily revising the Constitution—attempts to deal with our deepest social pathologies are likely to be ineffective and brutally expensive; and (3) even if this revision is achieved, there is substantial basis for doubt that the political and economic incentives created by the current division of labor and authority among jurisdictions can be blended into a satisfactory set of instruments for supplying the protections and services now generally demanded from government.

If this case can be made, a student of the Constitution might remind us, the straightforward remedy would seem obvious. The document contains an orderly procedure for amendment, or even for total revision. But few would maintain that the present strength of the American political consensus is sufficiently impressive to warrant confidence that a wholesale revision would yield more improvements than new defects. The problem is more subtle. It is to formulate, explain, debate, and solidify a new set of federalist principles to underlie a nonconstitutional revision of the nature of our union that has already partially occurred. Out of the ruins of the classical theory of separate levels of government, separately financed, the nation needs to develop either a broadly based rationale for the current jungle of inextricably intertwined units, or an effective constituency for reform. In this area as in many others, our national response to the question "A New America?" is subject to conscious influence only if we are better able to come to terms with the current state of the nation.

This essay attempts a modest exploration of the main directions of past change in the federal system, the critical characteristics of the current situation, the reasons that pressures on the federation may be somewhat different in the future than in the past, and the indicators which may most reliably suggest which direction we are taking. It closes with a brief discussion of major problems and options that seem likely to present themselves in the years immediately ahead.

II

The vast literature of judicial speculation on the intent of the Framers probably says nothing more accurate than that these people would be uniformly aghast at the living patterns which characterize twentieth-century America. The Framers did not construct a governmental framework for a predominantly urban nation. Quite the contrary, their writings suggest consensus on the distaste for urban civilization expressed some decades later by Tocqueville:

> In towns it is impossible to prevent men assembling, getting excited together, and forming sudden passionate resolves. Towns are like great meeting houses with all the inhabitants as members. In them the people wield immense influence over their magistrates and often carry their desires into execution without intermediaries. . . . I regard the size of some American cities and especially the nature of their inhabitants as a real danger threatening the future of democratic republics of the New World, and I should not hesitate to predict that it is through them that they will perish, unless their government succeeds in creating an armed force which, while remaining subject to the wishes of the national majority, is independent of the peoples of the towns and capable of supressing their excesses.

The Framers, an extraordinarily gifted assembly, did not indulge their antiurban sympathies to the extent of the national police force implied by Tocqueville's position. But they did take pains to vest all subfederal sovereignty in units of sufficient size and diversity to assure that the passions and other evil humors that they perceived as inevitable products of city life would be filtered through the more measured and balanced judgmental processes that they associated with rural culture before any governmental decision could be taken. Thus, they gave no constitutional stature to even the largest local governments; they prescribed no procedures for state cooperation in governance of contiguous urban settlements that crossed state boundaries; nor did they place any limits on the discretion of states in making their internal allocations of governmental labor and authority. Because the states were much more substantial entities than the union at the time, it is not surprising as a matter of practical politics that a Constitution achieved through their consent contains very few checks on their internal affairs. Still, it is important to understand that the leaders of the day viewed it as undesirable that urban concentrations develop which either would dominate state governments by the sheer size of their populations, or which would evolve a sense of local political identity separate from that of the state that might be translated into purely urban decisional mechanisms for governance of more than the most localized of public functions.

The structural expression of this point of view was, in the image developed by Morton Grodzins, "layer cake Federalism." The Constitution contemplated clear separation between state and federal governments, with each provided with the sources of public revenue necessary for support of the functions assigned to it. This emphasis upon separate powers over separate purses was elegantly phrased by Alexander Hamilton in his discussion of the division of taxing authorities in the *Federalist* (no. 31): "A government ought to contain in itself every power requisite to the full accomplishment of the objects committed to its care, and to the complete execution of the trusts for which it is responsible, free from every other control but a regard to the public good and to the sense of the people." Thus, the notion of major transfers of resources between the federal government and the states does not arise in the Constitution.

For the first 140 years of our history, a few important exceptions such as the land grants for state colleges to the contrary notwithstanding, the prevailing attitude was that expressed by President Franklin Pierce in 1854 when he vetoed a bill that would have provided federal land grants to the states to support facilities for the insane: "[Should Congress] make provision for such objects, the fountain of charity will be dried up at home, and the several states, instead of bestowing their own means on the social wants of their people, may themselves, through the strong temptation, which appeals to states as to individuals, become humble supplicants for the bounty of the Federal Government, reversing their true relation to this Union." One would hardly need to change a word to render this pronouncement suitable to express the first reaction of President Ford and a majority of the Congress to the New York City fiscal crisis of 1975. Yet the subsequent reversal of Ford's position and provision of direct federal aid to New York City signaled the very advanced state achieved by the transition, continuing in Grodzins' imagery, from "layer cake Federalism" to "marble cake Federalism."

This transition had begun to take shape in the late nineteenth century at the base of the "cake" in the relation between state and local governments. By and large state constitutions had placed more restrictive controls on executive authority than the national Constitution had placed upon the President. And, although state legislatures were clearly sovereign, local police powers, responsibility for minimal aid to the poor, and regulation of land use within incorporated areas (if any) were generally in the hands of local government, following the British tradition. State governments primarily concerned themselves with facilitating and regulating commerce, supervising the development of new land and the incorporation of new localities, administering justice, governing unincorporated areas, and providing for some public institutions (e.g., universities and mental hospitals) that clearly would not be provided by the ordinary workings of the market, by private industry, or by local governments. But the urbanizing effects of the industrial revolution and the surge of poor immigrants from Europe made this simple division of labor unworkable in the fastest growing states. From the political standpoint, the center of attention and relevance for most state politicians moved with the voters—into the cities. The shift of focus had major effects on all practitioners, from the governor in need of urban votes to the rural member of an unreapportioned (and therefore rural-dominated) state legislature striving to keep the cities in their place. From an economic perspective, the costs of providing even the most minimal care to the urban poor were more and more obviously beyond the revenues produced by the taxes that the states had authorized cities to levy, as the philosophical proposition that minimal care should in fact be provided was growing in strength, albeit over strong resistance. Meanwhile, the great scandals of the big-city corruption had severely undermined public confidence in the municipality as an efficient administrator.

Thus, both political and economic logic in the centers of subfederal sovereignty argued for a sharp increase in the state role in local affairs. The great weight of the traditional concept of federalism showed clearly in the effort to achieve this concept without obscuring the basically separate nature of state and local governments. Thus, as the welfare function became a state concern, its administration and financing were often shifted from cities to countries, the latter being designed, after the British shire, to serve as administrative outposts of the states. The local revenue base to meet the enlarged costs of traditional local services (police, fire, etc.) in the swelling cities was generally provided through grudging transfer of most property-tax authority from the states to localities, to be replaced in the state exchequers by sales and eventually by income taxes. Cities, for their part, launched major programs of annexation, and in a few cases of merger with surrounding counties, in an attempt to assure that the rapid increases in revenue-generating capacity created by the settlement of their outskirts would be available to support growing public-service costs in the urban cores. By 1934, therefore, 24 states had designated their counties as primary units for welfare administration, and 11 of the 20 counties of more than 500,000 population (including New York, Philadelphia, Baltimore, San Francisco, and Denver, among others) had completed some form of consolidation of city and county governments. In general, it could still be persuasively argued at that time that the functions of the three levels of government were distinguishable, that their revenue sources were largely independent, and that there was reasonable identity between the point of decision on spending and the point of publicly visible responsibility for persuading the people to support the revenue measures required to support that spending.

However, the Depression placed what eventually proved to be intolerable stress on the "layer cake" concept. The crash caught the nation in the early stages of transition from laissez-faire national economic governance to a somewhat more activist philosophy. The response was correspondingly ambiguous. On the one hand, it was evident that decisive action could not come from the states unless they were vested with very substantial new financial authorities, including the power to run a large cumulative deficit. (Because state finances are regulated by state constitutions, formal action to force this would probably have required an overriding amendment of the national Constitution.) In any event there was little patience for the delays, complexities, and presumed inefficiencies involved in attempting to address so pressing a national problem while maintaining strict financial separation among governments. On the other hand, the suddenness and depth of the collapse seemed to underscore the temporariness of the situation. It was tempting, both as an intellectual matter and as a matter of political salesmanship, to view the Depression as a short-term aberration that could and should be dealt with by brief suspensions of traditional federalist rules that could be lifted when normalcy had been restored. This perception made it possible to avoid the substantial problems evident in the two straightforward approaches suggested by adherence to the "layer cake" theorem: that the federal government turn over to the states the revenue-generating capacity necessary for them to support massive new income subsidies and pump-priming efforts, or that the national regime—the states and the Supreme Court willing—mount these operations as directly administered functions.

To be sure, the federal government did in fact administer some aspects of the recovery program. But the largest and most fateful share was provided through a hybrid, and avowedly temporary, approach to federal organization that could be justified both as a reaffirmation of state sovereignty and as a legitimate use of the constitutional power of the Congress to raise federal revenues and to supervise their use. The essence of the new arrangement was to abandon Alexander Hamilton's dictum and turn a growing portion of the federal government into what might be termed a bank for the states, granting and (later) lending matching money as the clients generated their contributions and proved their qualifications to receive federal subsidies according to federally set criteria which permitted very wide variations in policy and practice among the states. Overriding the objections of groups that urged a uniform national income maintenance policy, such as the 1935 President's Commission on Income Security, this banking concept was locked formally into place in the landmark Social Security Act passed in that year. By the end of the decade, the banker relation was the channel for more federal funds than had been contained in the entire federal budget only a few years before.

The parallel history within states was much more diversified, with the populous and industrialized states behaving more nearly according to the federal model. The development of state subsidies for local operations had begun some time before. However, in the decade beginning in 1932, the states doubled the share of local spending that they subsidized for education and highway purposes, and they multiplied their share of local welfare financing sixfold. The interpenetration of state and local budgets became pronounced in many of the larger states, but on the whole state resources were still carefully restricted to "areas of state interest," which did not include the traditional municipal service staples. There were several dozen municipal bankruptcies, and a number of very near misses—notably in New York City—which were largely dealt with through state and private measures advertised as temporary emergency steps.

The aftermath of World War II demonstrated that even though the national economy had mushroomed during the hostilities, the end of the Depression did not bring the end of the social problems to which the banking-type federal functions were addressed. Indeed, as the pace of urbanization quickened, the suburbs burgeoned, and the postwar readjustment effects—including the baby boom—emerged, the political pressure to extend federal-state matching, particularly in transportation and housing, became irresistible. It also became evident that the intervening decade of decentralized policy making had resulted in so diverse a collection of state social-welfare policies and benefits, most of which were federally subsidized, that uniform national standards would be extremely difficult and expensive to impose.

More important, however, there was little sense of need for such standardization. Diversity was widely perceived as an asset, representing the capacity of the American system to permit subnational communities to apply their own values and reach presumably more sensitive judgments about local standards of decency than could be dictated from Washington. This view also helped to explain the relative equanimity with which the country watched the major metropolitan areas splintered into a myriad of overlapping jurisdictions (e.g., nearly 1,200 in the Chicago area, more than 1,100 in and around New York) too complex for even the most determined citizen to hold in his mind the division of responsibility among them. But the politics of local administration were also influential. The psychology of flight from inner-city problems was the very heart of the suburban mentality. It dovetailed neatly with the perception of professional politicians that sole and visible responsibility for local administration promised no benefits to a budding career, but could easily destroy one if some snafu demonstrated that the officeholder could not "even" pick up the garbage or deploy policemen. This perception had long fostered the growth of the city manager system, which ironically had been initiated in part by the strong mayors. Now this consensus on the negative value of visible local administrative authority provided solid support not only for the proliferation of jurisdictions, but also for the plethora of plural decisional bodies—boards, committees, commissions, and the like—which provided a certain protection in the anonymity of individual members when trouble developed.

Some of the same factors underlay the simultaneous acceleration in the trend toward "privatization" of public-sector functions, which added another dimension of complexity to the organizational scene. With the exception of the Department of Defense, the federal agencies formed after the war were designed less as direct operators than as contract supervisors, overseeing huge collections of private enterprises engaged to perform stated tasks. The preference for corporate-style organization also included new and expanded public benefit corporations and free-standing public authorities at all three levels of government, along with a flood of special districts at the regional and local levels. In most cases, these districts overlapped preexisting local jurisdictions, and were governed by complicated mixtures of state-, local-, and district-selected officials.

Within the states, the great engine of state absorption of previously local financial burdens was the growth of elementary and secondary education, which produced unworkable public-school economics for many localities. In most areas, however, this did not in itself breach the state-local separation because school districts and local governments were separate jurisdictions. Expansions of state support in such areas as highway programs and public health efforts, however, did begin to signal a basic change in the nature of state support. Meanwhile, the capacity of states to raise revenue became more and more superior to localities as state after state enacted an income tax. The absence of any metropolitan level of revenue raising made the state the residual financier as the stresses of urbanization and intrametropolitan migration made the local tax base in older core cities unequal to the costs of maintaining services.

By the mid-1950s the syndrome of inner-city shrinkage and decay had begun to take clear shape, irreversibly tangling the aging urban cores with their respective states in a financial embrace as indispensable as it was unpleasant. Although metropolitan areas continued to expand rapidly, most of the core cities began a steady shrinking process that masked very brisk two-way traffic in which most of the leavers did not depart the area, but simply took their higher incomes to the suburbs. The combination of shrinking numbers, shrinking average incomes, and growing average per capita demand for public services added up to an impossible mismatch between revenue-generating capacity and the costs of vital services. Slowly at first, and then with growing momentum, the larger states expanded their banker roles toward localities. In the period 1954–1974 they expanded their share of financial support for local budgets by more than half; by the end of the period such states as New York were allocating more than 80 percent of state revenues to aid to localities. The banking function had become much the most financially significant state activity in most of the states which contained large cities, while in such states as South Dakota it remained relatively minor.

However, at no point in any state did this evolution proceed according to any long-term plan. States typically did not admit of the possibility of any increase in local subsidies in advance of a point of absolute and generally acknowledged desperation. This was as true before the Supreme Court forced reapportionment of state legislatures, beginning in 1962, as it was afterward, for the Court's decision moved the balance of power within most state bodies from rural areas to the suburbs, which were not noticeably more inclined to recognize state responsibility for city finances. As Gelfand has demonstrated, the ruling event in all principal state movements was perceived emergency and the correlative perception that no alternative existed. Rarely was the theory of state interest precisely enough defined so that a clear rationale for growth in the state share of local financial burdens could be discussed. Never was it widely admitted that the fiscal mismatch of the core cities was an inevitable consequence of the combination of poverty concentration and jurisdictional separation from access to the affluent sections of the metropolis.

Despite repeated experience to the contrary, state budgets continued to be planned and projected on the basis of current state-local burden-sharing arrangements, and city charters continued to contemplate that pressures for local expenditure increases could be met by local actions, without regular recourse to the state. When both premises proved faulty year after year, the event was typically treated as an unexpected and irregular happenstance which qualified for attention only if dire and immediate consequences would flow from inaction. When addressed, it was dealt with in a subsidy pattern which strove mightily to preserve the principle that the state had only limited and specialized interests in a few local service areas. The separation was also carefully maintained with respect to borrowing authorities, to the extent that states and their client localities often had quite different ratings applied to their bonds regardless of the degree to which their respective financial viabilities were linked.

But the resulting flow of services was far from adequate in the eyes of many. The superlative behavior of the macroeconomic indices in the period 1962–1966 served only to accentuate the plight of the poor, particularly those in the inner cities. It was clear that neither the traditional state and local resource base nor the crisis ad-hocery of emergency adjustment would make a dramatic improvement in their fortunes without imposing a tax burden upon both industrialized states and core cities which would drive out the revenue base that remained to them. This realization combined with the unique political circumstances of 1963–1964 to generate enactment of more than two hundred new domestic federal programs—many of them very sweeping—within the years 1965–1968. The same opinion trends contributed to a major change in public attitudes that had the result of drastically reducing the number of people who, although qualified for benefits and services, had previously chosen not to apply for them. Direct federal payments to states and localities rose from less than $3 billion in 1954 to about $60 billion in 1976, or from just over 11 percent of state and local revenues to nearly 30 percent. Moreover, the nature of federally subsidized programs became substantially more open-ended and even less connected to direct federal administration. Reacting in part to the administrative complexity inherent in the traditional categorical grant-in-aid form of federal-state banking relations (which Douglas Yates has fetchingly dubbed "ordeal by paper"), such newer benefits as Medicare, Medicaid, and food stamps were given the character of economic rights attached to individuals, theoretically to be provided without budgeted limit upon demonstration that the individual met the qualifications established for the grant.

As these new federal commitments unfolded, all levels of government were adjusting to a surge in labor costs, the dominant component in all of their budgets. The upward revaluation of public goods and services represented by the Great Society contained an element of recognition that public instrumentalities could not be expected to compete with the private sector for first-class talent when government salaries, particularly for middle- and upper-level managers, were not remotely comparable. In the federal case, this realization led to enactment of the Federal Pay Reform Act of 1963, which established the principle that the salaries of federal workers should be adjusted annually to maintain "comparability" with private-sector workers carrying similar responsibilities. In states and localities—whose employees averaged about 30 percent lower annual earnings than federal employees—upward movement was much more uneven and closely tied to other factors, notably the growth of collective bargaining; but the direction was the same, particularly in large states and urban governments. Brookings research has documented the fact that, as state and local employment tripled between 1955 and 1973 (rising from about 7½% to 12% of the national work force), average earnings progressed from about 92 percent of the average for all private industries to about 104 percent of that average. This still compared unfavorably with the 143 percent average achieved by federal workers, but it represented substantial change from the 88 percent recorded for subfederal workers in 1945. In historical terms, the adjustment largely restored the relative earning position that state and local employees had occupied in 1929 (when they were at 107% of the industrial average), but did not yet approach their position in 1939, when they received more than 116 percent of the industrial average.

Overall, the effect was an upward ratcheting of government salaries (along with those paid in universities, foundations, and most other elements of the nonprofit industry) at a rate about 20 percent higher than the growth in private-sector earnings. Thus, urban areas, especially core cities, were faced with the triple pressure of rising (and largely nonignorable) per-capita demand for traditional services, an explosion in mandatory and optional nontraditional services partially financed from other tax bases, and a powerful upward surge in the unit cost of the labor necessary to perform both varieties of service. If there had remained any question about the infeasibility of return to arm's-length relations between banker governments and their clients, the grotesque contrast between these pressures and the condition and prospects for the inner-city tax base should have removed all doubt.

The final abandonment of Alexander Hamilton's principle was signaled by the enactment of General Revenue Sharing in 1972, but the event seems not to have really registered upon the consciousness of most citizens until the New York City crisis of 1975. The enactment of Revenue Sharing was a historic but relatively untraumatic occurrence (at least as compared with the surmounting of previous major philosophical barriers to federal subsidy) that essentially reflected the plight of the states in the wake of the first recession since the budgets of many of them had become heavily dependent upon a revenue source—the income tax—that was susceptible to a very severe damage from sudden stagnation in the general economy. Unaccustomed to predicting or dealing with volatile revenue behavior, unequipped with reserves or other techniques for absorbing the shock of revenue shortfalls, without controllable, non-labor-related expenditures (other than aid to localities) that could be reduced easily and quickly, and deprived of the capacity to finance deficits in any way other than by cutting expenditures or raising taxes, the states almost uniformly found themselves in greater financial embarrassment at a time when political wisdom argued against imposing further taxes upon a frightened electorate in the grip of the first economic downturn in almost a decade. In most states and cities taxes did in fact get raised, but the associated clamor for national action was sufficiently loud to persuade a Republican President, and later a quite conservative Chairman of the House Ways and Means Committee, to sponsor legislation granting all states and cities an unappropriated lien on a portion of federal income tax proceeds.

This action should have thrown into sharp relief the scissors-like effect upon the federal structure of the 1960s commitment to governmental activism. Pressure on first city and then state tax bases in densely populated areas had steadily expanded the geographic breadth of revenue sources, while growing interest in more and more tailored public services had striven to bring the point of expenditure decision down closer to the local and even sublocal bodies that individual citizens might reasonably aspire to influence. The theoretical contribution of Nixon's "New Federalism," albeit modest, was largely to bless this divorce of revenue and expenditure decision bases as a natural and even traditional construction of the Constitution. The same concept had earlier been embodied in state relations with localities, as evidenced by the rise in general state support to local budgets from $600 million in 1954 to nearly $5 billion twenty years later. Again, however, the increase was concentrated in a few of the populous states and was apparently arrested during the sweeping retrenchment in state spending (from 4.6% annual increase to 0.6%) which occurred after the tax-raising shock of 1971.

However, two other elements were necessary to provide sufficient drama to intrude the breakdown of traditional federalism onto the crowded agendas of opinion makers. First, it was necessary that an important and identifiable jurisdiction be poised on the brink of a financial collapse that would severely damage its parent state and perhaps the financial integrity of the nation at large. Second, the nature of the peril had to be defined in terms of a manageable number of actors within a finite time frame, rather than the Tolstoyan exercise in historical process that had characterized management of annual fiscal emergencies during the previous fifteen years. The New York City crisis provided these elements in ample measure, and thereby awakened many opinion leaders to the reality of "marble cake" federalism. The sheer scale of New York City and its singular dependence upon short-term borrowing (a practice which had originally developed to compensate for late arrival of federal and state subsidies) crystallized in the minds of reluctant and unbelieving officials and citizens alike the financial stakes at risk for the entire structure of public and private finance. In time, it also demonstrated that the risk of total abandonment of troubled urban cores was no more tolerable than had been the threatened failure of one of the nation's largest industrial employers a few years before. Yet, once again, the response stopped short of formal recognition that the problem was based on long-term structural difficulties which were likely to generate many variations on the same theme in the years ahead. Clearly terrified by their brush with the maelstrom of inner-city finance, President and Congress—in the face of unanimous contrary urgings by all manner of local officials—declared the New York City crisis a regrettable but temporary condition resulting from the failure of a single city to "live within its means." The fact that no older inner city had met this standard for about three decades (if the standard implies providing local services only to the degree that they can be supported from the local tax base), was conveniently ignored. Subsequent events in Detroit, Cincinnati, and other cities suggested that this attitude simply pushed forward the day of reckoning and increased the probability that it would be dealt with in the traditional crisis atmosphere rather than on the basis of any concerted federal or state planning.

The New York City scenario also represented a continuation of unwillingness at the federal level to address the question of the net impact of federal policy upon jurisdictional form at the state and local levels. The "layer cake" view had exerted a strong disincentive against direct or overt approaches to this problem. In theory, it was simply none of Washington's business how states and localities arrayed themselves. This principle still carried substantial political power. However, it had been at least obliquely attacked in the Economic Opportunity Act of 1965, when the concept of community-wide action (usually meaning a base of action larger or smaller than the central city) had been put forward in a modest way, much to the distaste of most city officials. The rapid demise of this effort had been followed by a series of partially conflicting incentives and disincentives to metropolitanization that were independently administered by a variety of federal agencies, usually without the consent or cooperation of the affected states. These efforts also seemed to have little effect, with a few possible exceptions in such areas as health-facility planning and environmental pollution control. Following a mildly successful attempt to get the federal government's own house in order by systematizing the geographic regions used to administer its major agencies, another attempt was made to incorporate all relevant jurisdictions into the decision process (including, particularly, the state governors) through a review process (the so-called A-95 sequence) that was said to be a required component of many federal decision procedures.

Meanwhile, states and cities had moved in a modest way to create loose collectivities of governments in some regional and metropolitan areas. In general, these took the form of Councils of Governments (COG) that were typically without substantial decision authority, but that contained some minimal capacity to provide common staffing and a regional discussion forum for governments that wanted to make use of such facilities. Largely independent of the process of COG formation, a brisk traffic developed in the transfer of functions from local jurisdictions with narrower tax bases to ones (e.g., counties) of broader or more specialized revenue-generating power; a 1976 survey showed that about one-third of approximately 3,300 responding municipalities reported the transfer of one or more functions or components of functions during the previous ten years. The potential of the federal government to induce state and jurisdictional change was amply demonstrated by the rush to create and partially finance metropolitan transit organizations when Washington finally capitulated and began appropriating tiny sums for subsidization of first capital and then operating expenses of such enterprises. Nevertheless, in 1977 it is still fair to say that the basic right of federal authorities to engage in state and local jurisdictional architecture is by no means established, the jurisdiction-influencing policies followed by different federal agencies are very different, and no durable tendency toward metropolitanization of major functions, or of the generation of revenues to support these functions, has yet appeared in most states.

As reasonably solid data on demographic and income trends for the period after 1970 have begun to be available, it appears that major changes in the 1955–1970 pattern have taken place and may suggest a future quite different from the past. These trends and their implications will be discussed in Section IV.

III

The net legacy of these fits and starts is a federal "system" that bears little relation to the pre-1935 model or, more importantly, to the model that most Americans carry around in their heads. For purposes of domestic governance it is the most gigantic mechanism ever devised to transfer resources from the point of generation of income to thousands of categories of individuals and institutions eligible for public subsidy. The minority of this flow that is focused upon the poor has principally involved transfer from the outer rings of our metropolitan complexes to the inner cores, a feat of extraordinary difficulty where the supra-municipal jurisdiction is controlled by residents of the outer rings, and where those rings may not even be contained within the same state. Paradoxically, the very bulk of these huge transfer mechanisms obscures their visibility to most citizens. So many are the linkages, so fragmented the financing and authority, and so byzantine the decision channels that many citizens seem to be driven back to the "layer cake" perception in simple defense of sanity. The more thoughtful have long since abandoned hope for simplicity, an inevitable casualty of industrialization. There is, however, a yearning, as yet unfulfilled, for some set of consistent principles that can at the same time order the meshing of governmental fiefs and provide a rationale for their future evolution that promises to bear some reasonable relation to real prospects rather than to empty exercises in nostalgia.

As will be discussed in the next section, there is reason to believe that factors emerging during the most recent years make these future prospects quite different from past experience, and that these developments will make rationalization of the "system" even more difficult. Before proceeding, however, the analysis already presented supports the following heretical truths about the present federal framework.

1. The dominant domestic functions now performed by the "banker governments" (the federal and state levels), other than making formula payments to individuals, are to generate revenue and transfer it to narrower jurisdictions which either cannot or will not be self-sufficient.

2. This role is not temporary; neither does it show any signs of declining in significance. Federal aid now accounts for about 30 percent of state spending, and federal and state aid to localities supports more than 40 percent of big-city spending, including education. With the enactment and renewal of Revenue Sharing, this involvement extends to every aspect of subfederal governance. Allocative principles based upon restricted areas of federal or state interest are at least sick unto dying.

3. In the older and most populous states and cities, no policy change which involves any substantial increase in state or local spending can in practice be effected without intergovernmental consultation and financial cooperation. Once commenced, this cooperation becomes a very hardy feature of the budgetary landscapes of all parties concerned. This rule of involvement increasingly applies to such delicate matters as collective bargaining policies, state and local burden sharing, and the setting of state and local tax rates.

4. The rapidly expanding states (Texas, Arizona, Florida) and cities (Houston, San Diego, Phoenix) have more policy flexibility but thus far less politicocultural inclination to use it.

5. The extended initiation and control linkages in so large and diverse a "system," together with the long lead times implied by the necessity to coordinate so many unsynchronized units, has greatly reduced the influence of elected

officials upon real-world outcomes, and severely diluted the capacity for deliberate and predictable influence by any individual or faction. This problem has been compounded in recent years by a marked tendency toward shorter average tenure in elective and appointive office at all levels.

6. Many of the largest states and cities are so interdependent financially that questions of major default will expose them as a single financial entity in which one component's credit worthiness stands or falls with the other's. There are also strong links between all public jurisdictions in terms of the marketability of their securities, as was demonstrated when municipal interest costs rose across the nation by an estimated $3 billion (or half the annual yield of Revenue Sharing) in the wake of the 1975 New York City crisis.

7. The diversity of state policies and attitudes is profound, and, in practice, susceptible to change only by positive (that is, financial) incentives applied from the federal level. Sanctions on the states for noncompliance have been largely ineffectual. And even full federalization of functions has not necessarily been effective in reducing state spending, standardizing benefit levels, or eliminating administrative complexity, as was demonstrated by the 1974 federalization of programs to aid the aged, disabled, and blind.

8. Whatever discipline has been alleged to flow from the perceived lack of financial recourse by urban governments to umbrella jurisdictions in the event of fiscal distress has been severely diluted everywhere and may have largely disappeared in the poorest cities. Conversely, there appears to be a fairly strong disciplinary potential in the attitude of the private money market, although ways have not yet been found to standardize risk assessment for most types of public entities.

9. The commingling of governmental levels seems to have severely attenuated the link between the intent of voters and the postelection sequence of events, particularly at the local level. The "ambassadorial" function of local elected and appointed executives (to the state and the national capitals) is often as invisible to the electorate as it is critical to meaningful action. In general, candidates' programmatic platforms continue to ignore the necessity of intergovernmental cooperation to effect any major change, so that voters have little sense of how many cooks are required to produce edible broth.

Put in simplest terms, having been unwilling to recognize the existence, legitimacy, and permanence of bank-type relations among governments, we have been unable to learn how to control them or to manage them efficiently. We do not know how the banker governments should go about deriving program criteria and performance measures for local authorities that tread the thin line between helpful direction and inefficient meddling. We do not know how best to maximize the quantity and quality of governmental product when the point of finance is split and often two or even three levels removed from the point of final output. We do not know what disciplinary forces can resist impulses to excessive spending when the spender bears no responsibility for raising the revenue being allocated. And we do not know an effective means for providing policy-making and administrative traction to short-lived, politically chosen officials, and thereby to the voters who selected them. This is not to say that there is no useful research or experience on each of these questions. But the body of knowledge and hypothesis is pathetically small in comparison to the importance of the problem, and its utility is further limited by our basic unwillingness to accept the fact that the classical concept has been abandoned.

IV

The post-1970 statistics tracking national demographic trends point up some important differences in many of the factors which shaped developments during the previous fifteen years. Most critical, of course, is the dramatic reduction in the birthrate, which reduction shows some signs of durability. If so, prospects are that the age profile of the country will shift markedly upward, increasing the category of citizens who are most generously provided with public subsidies. The shift in concentration of population is also important; the 1970 census was the first in which more than 50 percent of the population was located within fifty miles of the East and West coasts, and the remarkable acceleration in the growth of the "sun belt" metropoles in the first five years of this decade indicates that entirely new migratory patterns are well under way.

As a result, as George Peterson has shown, not only do the inner cities of the Northeast and Midwest continue to shrink in population and, even more important, in employment opportunities, but some of their surrounding metropolitan areas (as of 1976, those around Cincinnati, Cleveland, Detroit, New York, and Pittsburgh) are shrinking as well. Similar but less pronounced phenomena seem to be occurring in a number of older Western urban complexes, notably San Francisco, Oakland, Los Angeles, and Denver. These developments include some complete turnabouts, such as the net out-migration of blacks from central cities that occurred during 1970–1974. But the figures also contain many reaffirmations of earlier trends, such as the fact that the average family moving into inner cities during this period had an annual income of about $1,200 lower than that of the average family moving out.

Demographic movements are complemented by changes in fiscal policies in the populous states, and by growing tension with and political estrangement from their needier client cities. It seems clear that 1972 was a watershed year for spending patterns at both subfederal levels, as the average annual spending increase of the previous decade was slashed by nearly 90 percent. Ironically, this occurred at the same time as the collection of revenue generated by the painful tax increases of the preceding year. This revenue, expanded by inflation and by the recession tendency to underestimate the tax yield that will be realized from a given rate applied during a recovery phase, was swelling their coffers to the extent of a $10-billion overall surplus in the state and local sectors. More significant, however, was the general signal from state capitols that the window dispensing subsidy increases to localities was shut and was unlikely to be opened to the late-1960s level for some time, if ever. The steady increases in state-aid formulas that had been a major escape valve for urban fiscal pressures during the 1960s became increasingly rare in the more industrialized states. Shaken by the realization that a recession, over which they could exercise no substantial control, could create volatile revenue behavior in the face of inflexible expenditure commitments, states took a number of other steps to shore up their fiscal shock absorbers, including more conservative projection of revenues and the regular budgeting of surpluses and reserve funds. These actions, together with the effect of Federal Revenue Sharing, were evident in the much lower order of distress that the states suffered during the subsequent recession of 1974–1975.

One particularly general device employed by states in their efforts to lessen fiscal risk was more aggressive use of the "transformers" by which they convert open-ended, entitlement-type federal subsidization of individuals into finite commitments which can be budgeted by subfederal governments that must provide substantial matching funds but have no means of financing major deficits if claims exceed resources. The usual technique was a flat ceiling on the portion of the statutory standard of need (e.g., for Aid to Families with Dependent Children) that would actually be paid to eligible recipients during a given year. In extremis, this could be converted into an immediate "ratable reduction" in the course of the current year. Rarely if ever was the need standard itself reduced, a difficult political task in the context of stagflation that was inflicting greatest hardship on the poor. But the level of actual payment fell below 60 percent of the standard in some states, and in only 20 states was the need standard fully met throughout the period. This practice was critical to the success of the states in holding the largest and yeastiest elements in their budgets (other than education) in check.

On the other hand, inner cities, plagued by the mismatch between tax base and service demand, were rather more ravaged by the second recession of the decade. Although they too benefited from Revenue Sharing, this source represented less than 2 percent of big-city budgets and was not sufficient to avoid major damage. Despite partially successful efforts to halt the growth in employee salaries and benefits, the disappearance of the option of increased state aid forced most of the declining urban cores to impose substantial degradations in services. Some were dramatic, as in the case of New York's dismissal of more than 40,000 employees, or Detroit's short-lived suspension of 20 percent of its police force. Most were less eye-catching, such as the major northeastern city that suspended all street maintenance for at least three years. Taken as a whole, however, the core city picture was one of steady, sometimes largely invisible disinvestment that raised the spectre of decline into what I have elsewhere termed general service default—the inability to provide a level of service consistent with the minimal requirements of prevailing community standards of decency. It was becoming evident that this form of decay could be at least as effective in discouraging job creation and maintenance as would be the higher tax rates necessary to allay it.

But both states and cities were reeling in the face of taxpayer reaction to fifteen years of state and local tax increases which had doubled the share of the national income devoted to these governments. Property owners were in particularly general revolt, and relief of their burdens was complicated by decisions in some major states (notably California and New Jersey) that basing the quality of education upon the differential capacities of school districts to generate property-tax revenues violated the equal protection clauses of state constitutions. Barring enactment of one of the as yet unaccepted equalization schemes that take into account the unusual service demand placed upon core cities, the prospect was that their relative paucity of schoolchildren would react in state aid formulas with their wealth of high-priced buildings to produce a greater local financial burden simply to maintain the same level of educational quality. There were also some signs of efforts to extend the "Serrano principle" (named for the plaintiff in the California school case) to other urban services, an extension well within the bounds of rational extrapolation if the basic principle were accepted. If such a movement were to develop, it would require the discard and replacement of the allocative principle now most widely in use for supporting and distributing local services.

The property-tax struggle was one component of a general trend toward divergence of the circumstances of older, declining core cities from those of most states and less afflicted municipalities. Indeed analysis of upward pressures on overall state and local spending in the 1960s led some scholars to pronounce them largely transitory and unlikely to recur, so that the aggregate state and local sector could look forward to taking in about 1 percent more revenue than needed to finance services of present scope and quality each year through 1986. The basis of this optimism lay in four key assumptions: (1) upward pressure on state and local expenditures will ease considerably because of the halt in growth of demand for services (particularly education) as population growth slows; (2) state and local capital needs will either be much more heavily subsidized by federal grants, or will simply be ignored; (3) no new problems will be addressed or services developed unless their costs can be entirely met by reductions in existing services; and (4) public-sector salaries will move back from the accelerated growth rate they have exhibited during the past fifteen years to a rate which is the same as the average in the private sector.

The controversiality of these assumptions is obvious, but it seems clear that they are most dubious when applied to the distressed inner cities. Thus emerges the prospect of an inverse relation between the degree of urban distress and the probability that the shrinking inner cities will be able to mobilize political support from sister jurisdictions on the basis of shared experience and interests. The bleak financial prospects of the distressed states and cities imply that others will be enjoying relative affluence and cannot be expected to be pleased to join in what will necessarily be ever more visible transfers (viz. the present New York City loan program) to less fortunate places. If it is deemed important that minimal living and service standards in core cities be maintained, the dangers are two: that the necessary resource transfers will not occur because of the absence of political support, or that the condition of any transfer to the needy will be nearly equivalent transfer to the nonneedy.

Thus, recent experience suggests that both the political and the economic strains on the federal structure will be more pronounced in years ahead than they have been in years past. Our past muddling-through has been heavily dependent upon rapid average rates of economic growth, relatively cheap energy, ample capacity for capital formation, and the capacity of the states to offset, however disparately and inadequately, the chronic fiscal mismatch in the core cities. None of these factors appears as favorable now as in earlier years. Differences among states are likely to increase, in terms of both attractiveness as places of investment and living quality acceptable to the middle class. The result could be a reverse of the past pattern in which the federal government has been willing to "carry" a high percentage of the costs of southern state governments as the price of much larger dollar (but smaller percentage) contributions to much more elaborate governments in the North. But it is not clear that the politics will work in reverse, particularly if the "sun belt" cities and states use their remaining advantages (e.g., transfer of functions to large counties, easy processes for municipal annexation) to avoid the worst of the aging problems that characterize cities in the Northeast quadrant. At the very least, such changes would exert stronger and more divisive pressures upon our jury-rigged federal linkages. The question posed is whether a federation formed to protect diversity among states can deal with increasing concentration of its have-nots in a small minority of state and local jurisdictions of steadily weakening political influence.

V

The key exogenous influence upon the evolution of federalism will clearly be the perceived economic and cultural utility of geographic proximity. So far, despite extravagant expectations of change from such technological innovations as cable television, this utility seems at a high and stable level—the level that has concentrated 75 percent of the population in 2 percent of the land area. As long as more than 80 percent of bank accounts, 75 percent of federal income tax collections, and 80 percent of the value added to manufactured goods are located in urban areas, the present stresses, or worse ones, will endure. Rapid urbanization has clearly mellowed into a fairly constant aggregate balance between urban and rural populations, but there is no current suggestion of a massive movement away from preference for densely settled areas.

Given continued stability in this balance, the most revealing benchmark is likely to be the relation between the point of financial responsibility and the point of control. Revenue Sharing, as we have seen, represents an almost complete separation of the two. About 25 percent of all other federal payments to states and localities are now provided in the form of "block grants" which at least theoretically allow more local discretion in their use, although sometimes on the condition of providing information (e.g., inventories of existing city housing stocks) that requires establishment of wholly new facilities and practices in state and local jurisdictions. Should this separation continue to gain momentum, the principal effect is likely to be steady enhancement of the role of the states, which can largely regulate effects upon cities irrespective of direct federal aid to them or of mandatory "passthroughs" of federal funds initially granted to the states. This control can be exerted through manipulation of state subsidies. If such measures become a serious problem, counteracting them may eventually require a difficult choice between what amounts to federal controls on state allocations of state resources, and the designation of the most distressed cities (or of core areas within them) as direct federal wards by some agreement with the relevant states.

In the near term, however, the main determinants of trends are likely to be (1) whether federalization of welfare finance is determined to entail federal administration and solely federal determination of benefit levels and eligibility standards; (2) how any program of national health insurance that may be enacted is financed and administered; (3) whether a general program of federal aid to inner cities (and/or guarantees for their securities) is developed, and what role is given to the states in its administration; (4) whether collective-bargaining rules governing state and local employees are established at the federal level as well as at the state level; and (5) whether the federal government develops a coherent policy with respect to its influence upon local jurisdictional forms.

Within the states, the critical question is whether—and for how long—state governments can increase subsidies to inner cities without (1) paying the price of equivalent subsidies to localities that do not need them, and (2) eschewing direct control of client government administration. The divorce between financial responsibility and control grows easier in direct proportion to the remoteness of the financier. Modern state governments still enjoy some degree of detachment from city administration, but this distance is clearly decreasing. As in the aftermath of the New York City crisis, it seems probable that it will be the inclination of the state, and of any private investors involved, to establish a semipermanent institutional bridge to major cities so as to maintain direct supervision of their most expensive clients. Over time this could produce a quite serious negative reaction from an inner-city population of steadily decreasing influence in the decision councils of the state. At some point this friction, in the absence of such preemptive federal action as that mentioned above, could lead some states to consider massive shifts of local power to larger jurisdictions, perhaps to counties. Ironically, this may be the only practical route to metropolitanization.

These indicators etch the outline of the options likely to be placed before us as the overburdened structures of traditional federalism groan under the strain of dealing with a population that refuses to deploy itself tidily within the governmental vessels provided for it. History suggests that the least promising option is also the most probable. Our instinct in such matters has been to treat the strain as a temporary imbalance, and our instinct is likely to be to go on doing so. But the weaknesses that seem to be developing in the adjustment mechanisms which have made that policy marginally viable suggest that the price of ignoring the gap between constitutional theory and operating practice is rising and will rise faster in future. Rightly reluctant to risk wholesale amendment of the Constitution to close the gap, our challenge is to effect a new consensus and appropriate modus operandi within the permissive framework afforded by the current form. This will require leadership and foresight of the same order as that exhibited by the Framers in setting forth the original structure, and possibly a higher tolerance for frustration, in that the results are unlikely to have the decisive and tangible characteristics of a single document. Whether these qualities of leadership are forthcoming will bear heavily on the nature of any "New America."

LOUISE WEINBERG

A New Judicial Federalism?

FOR A TIME it seemed that federal court orders governing our state agencies had become a curious characteristic of our country, our federalism, our time. To some no doubt it still seems so. Federal trial judges continue to order our sovereign states to reapportion their legislatures; under federal court orders state prisons are abandoned and hospitals rebuilt; whole populations of school children are shifted daily as under federal court orders the school buses roll.

And this unprecedented regime is only a point of high relief in the larger picture, a picture of proliferating litigation in the federal trial courts, extraordinary sorts of cases raising broad issues of public concern on behalf of huge classes of consumers or environmentalists or minorities.

But this massive federal judicial power, in its acute phase, may have informed only a brief chapter in the history of our federalism, a period coinciding roughly with the last years of the Warren Court. Today's heroic exercises of that power may with hindsight come to seem a phasing out and winding down. How did federal trial judges come to wield such powers? Is the Burger Court dismantling the engine? Are we to return to the status quo ante?

These inquiries will be advanced only in part by comparing the constitutional interpretations of the Warren and Burger Courts. Although it is a truism that an expansive view of rights will generate increased litigation, and that a restrictive view of rights will chill litigation, a more complete understanding can be had only by examining what the Supreme Court has done about federal trial-court power itself. By treating court powers as crudely distinct from legal rights, we can reach the sources of today's federal "judicial activism," trace the broader outlines of contemporary judicial federalism, and gain insights into the changes now occurring.

But there is an additional reason why the subject of judicial power, once more or less abandoned to the specialist, has become rather more interesting to others. A Supreme Court bent on retrenchment can accomplish only so much through head-on confrontation with Warren Court constitutional interpretations. The Court is not about to overrule *Brown* v. *Board of Education*. If retrenchment is to come then, it will tend to come not through rulings restrictive of rights, but more subtly, through rulings restrictive only of the powers of federal courts to enforce those rights. And in fact that has been the preferred method of the present Court.

In this essay I have singled out two cases in the Burger Court which limit federal judicial power. I have done this not so much to comment on the cases themselves as to illumine in a very brief space the origins, significance, and late decline of federal public interest litigation, and of the power of federal trial judges to govern the states by decree.

The latter power raises grave issues of federalism, and I have focused on those when dealing with the second case. But on a deeper level both cases, in restricting power, raise another issue of federalism, and a central question to be put to the present Court. Because the underlying premise, and, as one suspects, the raison d'être, of the current assault on federal judicial power is that substantive rights are to be left overtly undisturbed, the necessary implication of a contraction in federal jurisdiction is that the state courts are intended to effectuate the rights in question. Yet if this expectation proves too optimistic, limits on federal judicial power become the functional equivalent of denials of individual rights. From this perspective I have contrasted the approaches of the Warren and Burger Courts, and at the close offered a few personal observations about the Court's current course.

1. The Public Action, the Private Attorney General, and the Frozen Tundra of the North

The building of the Alaska pipeline has been one of those romantic enterprises one tends to associate with the nineteenth century rather than with ours. As a giant consortium of oil companies pushed the work across the tundra, job-seekers poured across the continent into oddly luxurious camps for six-week stints, eating steaks ad libidum and struggling to forge a chain between remote supply and insatiable demand at temperatures of 60 below. But the world is full of cynics (or idealists) who lack the spirit of romance. An organization of environmentalists, concerned about wildlife cycles, discovered that the consortium had not complied with federal environmental regulations, and that federal authorities had winked their eyes at the omission. The environmentalists sued the federal agency and the consortium, seeking an injunction against construction of the pipeline until compliance was obtained. As was perhaps to be expected, particularly in view of the Arab oil embargo, Congress bailed out the consortium with special enabling legislation. The litigation was mooted. Everybody had to go home.

But one issue remained, and the lawyers persisted with the case. That issue, as it finally reached the Supreme Court,[1] was the unglamorous question whether the federal trial judge had the power to order the defendant consortium to pay the environmentalists' lawyers' fee. The answer would profoundly affect a phenomenon we have set ourselves to explore here: the explosion of federal public interest litigation in our time.

Why should a party to a lawsuit ever be ordered to pay another party's legal fees? In the United States the practice has always been that each party pays its own lawyer. The fee shifting proposed in the pipeline case would make sense only where it was thought desirable as a matter of public policy to encourage litigation. Yet here again, in the United States it has been the general policy to

discourage litigation. And if the purpose of fee shifting was to encourage litigation, the practice could never be administered in an even-handed way. (Nothing
will so efficiently discourage lawsuits as the traditional English practice of making losing plaintiffs pay winning defendants' legal fees.) Yet one-way fee shifting had become commonplace in federal litigation by the close of the 1960s.
Three discrete events in the judicial history of the sixties are important to an
understanding of this pattern.

The first of these was the 1961 decision in *NAACP* v. *Button*. That case and
its progeny seemed to say that lawyers had rights under the First Amendment
to create litigation: to identify potential plaintiffs; to advise them of their rights;
to institute litigation on their behalf and on behalf of an organization or union of
which they might be members, or whose members were similarly situated. As
long as this litigation was group litigation in the public interest, the states apparently could neither prosecute nor disbar lawyers for conduct previously thought
unethical: "ambulance-chasing," "capping," "running," stirring up litigation
for private gain, buying up cases, paying the client's expenses; in short, lawyers
seemed to have a new constitutional right to commit the ancient professional
sins of champerty, maintenance, and barratry.[2]

The second event occurred in 1966 with the promulgation of new, revised,
updated rules of court to govern federal class actions. The event was not calculated to imprint itself upon the public consciousness. But two of these rules
made possible altogether new kinds of lawsuits.

Suppose that a giant corporation has bilked the public of millions in overcharges. In the conventional private litigation model, a consumer litigious
enough to sue for the small individual overcharge could do so only in small
claims court. No lawyer would take the case; one-third of an overcharge even as
large as $75 still amounts to $25, or about ten minutes of a trial lawyer's time.
Meanwhile, the $75 damages awarded to the plaintiff will fail to deter the corpo-
ration from further wrongful conduct, or to vindicate the public interest in fair
dealing in the national marketplace.

But after the 1966 class action for damages became available, and given the
1961 *Button* case, there was an alternative. In the new litigation model, counsel
would search public records and conduct investigations. Learning that illegal
overcharges had been made, counsel could search out a consumer, somehow
persuade that consumer to lend its name to a lawsuit in which it could have only
the most minimal interest,[3] and file on its behalf and on behalf of all those
similarly situated a modern federal class action for damages. One-third of three
million is, after all, a million. The corporation would be deterred, the public
interest vindicated, and counsel made rich. The modern consumer class action
was born.

These giant litigations, "Frankenstein monsters parading as class actions,"[4]
lumbered almost unmanageably through the federal courts, and a vigorous
"class action" or "public interest" bar sprang up to realize the profits. Federal
trial judges scrutinized and often themselves set the percentages of the damages
funds which were skimmed off the top for counsel. It was also necessary—and
was required under the new class action rules—to monitor settlements for
abuse. The defendant companies were not overly concerned about the size of
plaintiffs' attorneys' fees. But the class suit could leverage exposures to the point

where damages would exceed company assets. That was especially so whenever the allegedly violated statute authorized treble damages, as in the Clayton Act, or some fixed sum as minimum damages per violation, as in the Truth in Lending Act. Under such pressure, quick settlement would often seem to defendants their best strategy. Entrepreneur lawyers, having jockeyed the defendants into this position, could then sell out the interests of the class, together with the public interest in full deterrence, for a quick maximization of profits on investment. But the federal class action for damages had a number of conspicuous successes, and even a few of the state courts began to catch this fever.

The other new federal class action rule authorized suits for injunctions against continuing harms to a class. (The pipeline case fell into this category, and in the next section we will have a look at another example, a civil rights case, when we take up the question of federal court orders against a state agency.)

Now an injunction suit is in one crucial way very like a small consumer claim: it is not very appealing to a trial lawyer, who like everyone else must make a living. By scooping the consumer claim out of small claims court and "making a federal case out of it," the new class action for monetary relief had made the case worth a lawyer's time. But in creating a forum for suits seeking injunctions against group harms, the new rules had done nothing to make such litigation more feasible from a lawyer's point of view; the result of a successful suit could be only a court order, and that buys no shoes. Unless such a litigation were funded by an organization like the NAACP Legal Defense Fund or the ACLU it was unlikely to materialize.

That brings us to the third event. In 1968 the Supreme Court voiced approval[5] of the practice of ordering losing defendants to pay winning plaintiffs' lawyers in injunction suits. The Court pointed out that in such cases fee shifting might well serve the public interest. Agencies created by Congress to enforce federal rights could not always find time or resources for full enforcement. But given appropriate incentives, private lawyers could be created watchdogs of the public interest: "private attorneys-general."[6] And under the *Button* case, lawyers were more or less free to ambulance-chase this sort of litigation into existence; by hypothesis, it was group litigation in the public interest.

These separate strands conjoined were the genesis of the explosion of public interest litigation at the close of the sixties. Whether counsel in the role of knights on white horses jousted for first cuts from damages funds, or for fee awards to be paid by losing defendants, federal judges for the most part recognized that public interest lawyers were private attorneys-general, and rewarded them generously in the public interest.[7]

The federal class action for damages was done to death by the Burger Court in 1974, in *Eisen* v. *Carlisle & Jacquelin*. A lawyer's investment in class action litigation is always considerable; it is counsel, not the nominal client, that risks the expense of pretrial maneuvers; and making the litigation costly is a corporate defendant's usual strategy. Yet the nature of these suits is such that expensive investigation in the corporate files must be undertaken. Nevertheless the game remained worth the candle until in *Eisen* the Supreme Court upped the ante for entrepreneur counsel to the point of rendering prohibitive an investment in class litigation. The Court held that in a class action for damages each and every ascertainable member of the class must be notified of the pendency of the action, and that the named plaintiff must bear the expense of notice.[8] In *Eisen*, the named plaintiff had $70 at stake, and the estimated cost of notice was in six figures.[9]

Similarly, the Alaska pipeline case was the intended coup de grâce for the federal injunction suit. For there the Court held federal courts powerless to shift fees in injunction suits—powerless, that is, unless Congress authorized the practice, as it has for example in certain antitrust cases. It will be noted that the pipeline ruling was not about the *rights* of defendants, but only about the *powers* of federal courts. Thus, of course, both Congress and the state courts remain free under the pipeline case to provide for fee shifting.

I doubt that the Court was motivated by a perceived need for fairness to defendants. The defendants protected by the ruling ex hypothesi will have been found in violation of national law. Then, too, their conduct is likely to have injured not only the named plaintiff, but a broad segment of the public. These defendants in the nature of things will tend to be large corporations or governmental agencies, able to spread these costs to the public. In the ordinary injunction case, moreover, these defendants will have no damages to pay; their duty will be to obey a court order.

I also doubt that the Court was motivated by special antipathy to the sort of plaintiffs upon whom the case has had the heaviest impact: those individual litigants with a grievance great enough to impel them to seek out counsel, on the old litigation model. The least justifiable such impact was on the individual civil rights complainant unable to afford the costs of litigation and without access to group funds. Congress had already authorized fee shifting in school desegregation and job and housing discrimination cases, and in 1976 Congress legislatively repealed the pipeline case in a spectrum of other civil rights cases.[10] The largest class of civil rights injunction suits was not omitted from the legislation, suits (like that discussed in the following section) challenging the actions of state officials under the old Civil Rights Act.

The shock waves generated by Alyeska were also felt, of course, in the treasuries of public interest groups, from the NAACP through the firms providing legal services on grant money to the community organizations using the pro bono services of lawyer members. All have felt the loss of the potential source of help.

But hardest struck has been our friend, the entrepreneur, the private attorney general. Here appears to have been the Court's real target, in both *Eisen* and the pipeline case. These shots have found their mark, and the golden age of federal public interest litigation is over. The public interest in wider enforcement of national policy has been the unfortunate additional casualty.

I would not too quickly attribute such rulings to the evolving political outlook of the justices. An equally likely explanation for the pipeline case, and for the case following, lies in the justices' concern about crowded federal dockets. Chief Justice Burger is foremost among the distinguished authorities warning that the federal judicial system is approaching collapse, and that the explosion of litigation cannot be managed.[11] If Congress will not provide more federal courts and judges, the unspoken conclusion is that the Court will have to cut down on access to federal justice.[12] The pipeline case shows on just how broad a front the Burger Court's assault on federal trial court jurisdiction is being waged.

2. *"Principles of Federalism" and the Unwinning of the Civil War*

The 1976 case of *Rizzo* v. *Goode* is remarkable chiefly for a pronouncement by the Burger Court which undoubtedly represents the most extreme position it has yet taken on federal judicial impotence.

The grant of certiorari surprised observers. A federal trial judge in Philadelphia had ordered high officials of that city, including the mayor and police commissioner, to establish citizen complaint procedures in the police department. The order was based on proof at two long trials showing recurrent incidents in which the police had abused the rights of citizens, particularly of minority citizens; of failure on the part of the defendant officials to supervise police misconduct; and of official unresponsiveness to repeated citizen complaints. But the trial judge had rejected those of the plaintiffs' requests which demanded that he appoint a receiver to run the Philadelphia police department, and that he regulate by decree the way in which the police did their jobs. He had granted the order for complaint procedures in the hope that with time improved complaint procedures would ameliorate police conduct. A unanimous Court of Appeals had affirmed. But the Supreme Court capped its unexpected grant of certiorari by reversing. Among other things, the Court held that the trial judge's decree had offended "principles of federalism."

Viewed narrowly, as a curb on the flights of judicial remedial imagination, *Rizzo* simply will not square with what we know federal trial judges can do. If in a proper case they could order the police to institute procedures for hiring and firing personnel, why should they lack power in this case to order the police to institute complaint and disciplinary procedures for the same personnel? Of course the greater power might be held not to include the lesser in a particular case; but although *Rizzo* bristles with opportunities for justifying such a ruling,[13] Mr. Justice Rehnquist, writing for the five-man majority, seems to go out of his way to isolate the federalism issue and make it stand alone in striking down the decree.

My difficulty with "principles of federalism" as a rationale for the result is that such a rationale could do the same job in every case; that it would justify overruling that central but little-read decision in which the Warren Court created the modern federal injunction against a state, the second opinion in *Brown* v. *Board of Education*.

It will be remembered that in the first *Brown* decision in 1954, the Court at last struck down the states' power to segregate schoolchildren by race. But the rights thus generated were without precedent, and the Court ordered further briefs and argument on the way in which those rights could be enforced if need be. The following year it handed down *Brown II*.

Reading *Brown II* at a remove of a generation, one is struck by the Court's quiet accuracy and prescriptive power in outlining the permanent pattern of federal civil rights litigation. Failing voluntary compliance, desegregation of the public schools in our country was to be enforced through the filing of lawsuits against school boards in the federal trial courts. The trial judges would retain jurisdiction of these suits and continue to supervise the local desegregation process for its duration. They were to consider all the attendant difficulties, and then to fashion their decrees sensitively but imaginatively, if possible using plans negotiated between the parties. They were authorized to draw upon the affirmative injunctive powers they had exercised until then only in the framing of antitrust decrees; powers to restructure and then regulate whole industries would now be used to restructure and then regulate whole school systems and their populations.

So *Brown II* is in a strict sense the immediate source of that affirmative remedial power, not only in school desegregation cases, but in all civil rights cases, which continues to astonish the country. It seems to stand on the landscape of our current jurisprudence at the polar extreme from the position occupied there by "principles of federalism." It is surprising, then, that although the Burger Court has launched a powerful attack on *Brown II*, significantly limiting its force, until *Rizzo* federalism has not been the weapon. Rather, the Court has insisted on a punishment-to-fit-the-crime approach, limiting a federal injunction to the violation proved. And in cases after *Rizzo*, the Court has finessed opportunities to turn "principles of federalism" into a doctrinal limit on the scope of federal injunctions. At the close of this past Term, the Court approved a federal court order in the Detroit desegregation case which by mandating expensive remedial programs had created local fiscal exigencies. Yet, over the "principles of federalism" argument, the Court unanimously approved the Detroit decree.

It may be appropriate, then, to view *Rizzo* more broadly, as an attempt to confine not simply the *scope* of federal injunctions, but their *availability*. In this view, "principles of federalism" would be intended to establish a doctrinal limit on access to federal courts. Yet here, too, there is the same difficulty. "Principles of federalism" could do the same job in every case. It could shut down federal civil rights jurisdiction whenever what is sought is a court order against a state official. It would justify overruling the panoply of Warren Court decisions which opened federal courthouse doors to such cases.

It is no exaggeration of the achievements of the Warren Court to say that in civil rights cases against state officials the Warren Court did open the door to federal justice. It is not generally emphasized that much of the significant work of the Warren Court in fact took the form of simple door-opening rulings. From a civil rights lawyer's point of view the really great cases of the recent past may well have been these sorts of cases. *Baker* v. *Carr* (1962), of course, in striking down the malapportionment of a state legislature, was preeminently a colossus of constitutional interpretation; but that case also took a great issue of the day and authorized its adjudication in federal courts, despite the ancient barrier which had prevented federal litigation of such "political questions." Virtually all our state legislatures were malapportioned at the time, and federal court-ordered reapportionment, under *Brown II*, was the contemplated remedy. *Fay* v. *Noia* (1963) hacked away an underbrush of barriers, partly rooted in the concerns of federalism, which had stood between state prisoners and federal judicial scrutiny of the legality of their detentions. *Monroe* v. *Pape* (1961) cut a swathe through a similar thicket that had blocked civil rights challenges to state officials. These watershed events, with *Brown II*, are the link between Warren Court activism and the activism of ordinary federal trial judges in our own time.

The Burger Court has striven in direct and indirect ways to attack those cases. The pipeline case, of course, was a prodigious assault, its impact on civil rights injunction suits cushioned only up to a point by Congress. A heavy new burden of proof of discriminatory intent has seriously impaired the usefulness of *Brown, Baker*, and indeed most civil rights injunction suits in federal courts. *Fay* v. *Noia* has met with particularly rough treatment, the Court ruling last year that Fourth Amendment claims of state prisoners could not be heard in federal habeas corpus, and that in any event some of the old barriers to state prisoners' claims must be reinstalled. New immunities defenses have crippled the *Monroe* v. *Pape* civil rights action for damages. Older devices, like the formerly strict requirement of "standing to sue" in federal courts, have been dusted off for new service. And, as I mentioned, the Court has limited the injunctive power staked out in *Brown II* to the violation proved, in turn a function of the new "intent" requirement.[14]

Much of the Burger Court's door-closing has been in the avowed service of our federalism; *Rizzo* is one instance. But the Court has never set down standards by which we can try to determine in a given case whether the concerns of federalism outweigh the concerns underlying the Warren Court legacy. What is the test? Where does federalism end and federal enforcement begin? In *Rizzo* we need very much to know what the Court means by "principles of federalism," so that we can determine which civil rights injunction suits remain permissible and which do not. But the opinion, although emphatic, in the end suggests only a vague concern for the dignity and autonomy of the state—something of a feat, considering that Pennsylvania itself as amicus curiae had supported the trial judge's decree. So *Rizzo* rests mysteriously in the reports, at once a sign and a danger, like a loaded revolver tucked carefully away in a bureau drawer.

Whatever limitations and qualifications the facts of *Rizzo* suggest, it is now widely believed that under *Rizzo* police misconduct cases are "out." School desegregation cases—after a long period of breath-holding—are now seen despite *Rizzo* to be "in." Such results seem simply ad hoc.

Yet our federalism is important to us. A little reflection may enable us usefully to put into words some of its more powerful appeals. It will remain then only to ask whether any of these concerns seem compromised a priori by federal injunctive power against state officials.

Why should the work of the highest state officials and judges be reviewed, undone, prohibited, regulated, not by the state courts, not by the great national tribunal, but in the most undignified way, by ordinary federal trial judges? Why should the delegation of essentially local governmental tasks to local agencies—a virtue of our federalism—be frustrated, and the discretion of local authorities impeded as they work to deliver vital governmental services? Why should unelected federal judges with life tenure, answerable to no one, be able to govern the states, displacing duly elected state officials? Why allow a federal judge, representative of no electoral constituency, virtually to levy and appropriate taxes? A refusal to permit these inroads on federalism would mean the relinquishment only of a forum for certain lawsuits, not of underlying legal and constitutional rights. Since the state courts can enforce the Constitution, and under the Supremacy Clause are bound to do so, why should not the states be permitted to correct their own wrongdoing, always under the supervision of the Supreme Court? Certainly such arrangements would accord with the original understandings. We feel that the states would never have ratified the original compact had they believed that they could be governed by decrees of federal judges. The Eleventh Amendment, giving the states sovereign immunity from suit in federal courts, seems to embody this early understanding.

In bringing renewed prominence to these concerns of federalism, the Burger Court may seem to many to be returning to a judicial federalism more in keeping with our institutions and our history than the judicial federalism ushered in by the Warren Court. In this view the Warren Court's door-opening has been, on the whole, a mistake.

But such views somewhat overstate the present Court's aims and the previous Court's role, failing to take into account, as the Court must, great events in the history of our institutions. The Warren Court, of course, did not confer civil rights jurisdiction on federal courts. Only Congress could do that, and it had already done so, in the Civil Rights Act. After the Civil War was fought and won, Congress perceived the ante bellum institutions of judicial federalism to be utterly inappropriate to the tasks that confronted the country. The great problem for the radical Reconstruction Congresses was to impose national standards upon the states, to establish the rule of national law in this union. The Ku Klux Klan rode "unwhipped of justice" while freedmen and carpetbaggers looked to local authorities for protection and found none; looked to local courts for vindication and had none. Federal civil rights jurisdiction was created then.[15]

It is difficult to say that there remains today no further need for that jurisdiction. On the contrary, today there is broad consensus[16] among scholars, judges, and lawyers that the stand taken by Congress after the Civil War was in fact essential to our federalism. It is now widely understood that there must be power in federal courts to hear civil rights lawsuits against the states. The fundamental rights which that greatest of Reconstruction achievements, the Fourteenth Amendment, guaranteed to individuals *as against the states* for the first time, will never seem secure in the absence of a neutral forum for their adjudication. Thus, even the Eleventh Amendment, giving sovereign immunity to the states in federal courts, had to be subordinated to the goals of the Fourteenth Amendment. And this was done by the Supreme Court, not in the Warren Court era, but in 1908.[17]

In reflecting on the part played by the Warren Court, there is a sense in which its role, though decisive, was not at all on a heroic scale. In giving broad access to federal civil rights jurisdiction, the Warren Court was simply thrusting aside obstacles to federal justice erected by the Supreme Court in other days. But those obstacles accounted for the tragic ineffectiveness of the Fourteenth Amendment and the Civil Rights Act until our own time. What gave these technical moves their grandeur was that they helped make possible the Court's visible struggle in our lifetime to fulfill the promise of the Fourteenth Amendment and to give us back our national ideals.

That the Burger Court in fact has not returned us to the status quo ante is a measure of the consensus the Warren Court legacy still commands. The Court will not return us to a judicial federalism the Civil War was fought in part to restructure, and which time has taught us is inconsistent with the preservation of national standards in a federal union.

Of course there are principles of federalism which must temper the exercise of federal injunctive power. For this purpose federal judges have broad powers to invite the participation of affected parties, and to shape their decrees to accommodate such concerns. But little in our federalism should require deference to the freedom of state officials to violate or refuse to enforce national law without federal interference.

Rizzo, then, is not only a shot in the dark, but a misfire. However the case ought to have been decided, the "federalism" rationale, unique in that context and a sport in our law, ought never to have been advanced.

As I write this the controversy between the Philadelphia police and minority groups has flared up once more. At the time they filed the federal cases, the plaintiffs had correctly perceived that a class action for an injunction would not have worked in Pennsylvania state courts. But Goode brought an individual action for damages there, and this was ultimately settled for a modest sum. As for the federal injunction suit, the police never did institute grievance procedures along the lines mapped out by the trial judge. The minority plaintiffs moved to obtain their attorneys' fees, but that effort collapsed under the double barrage of the pipeline case and their own defeat in the Supreme Court. The litigation goes on: the city is now seeking to recover from the plaintiffs its costs in defending the suit. Meanwhile, a series of articles in the *Inquirer* appears to have sparked fresh concern, and a federal grand jury is now sitting in Philadelphia to investigate continuing charges of police brutality. Two hundred members of the Philadelphia police force have paraded to demonstrate their opposition to these charges. Although it is most unlikely that the remedy granted by the federal trial judge would have produced any dramatic result, it seems as unclear now as it did when the Supreme Court handed down the *Rizzo* opinion how federalism was served by aborting his attempt to adjust this controversy.

In this pair of brief studies of Supreme Court cases, both prosaically dealing with remedial power rather than legal rights, we have traced to the Warren Court some of the sources of contemporary federal judicial power, and have seen some of the ways in which the present Court is limiting access to that power.

The emerging pattern of judicial federalism will be one of decreasing access to the federal trial courts for the enforcement of federal rights, and increasing pressure on the state courts. For a number of reasons that pressure may well fail to reallocate the jurisdiction of public interest litigation and civil rights cases to our state courts in anything like the degree which the current Court seems to anticipate.

What the Court may have to face up to here is a crisis of confidence, not in the Supreme Court, but in the county courts of our states.

The underpinning of the argument that jurisdiction of federal claims ought increasingly to be confided to the state courts is the ultimate benign stewardship of the Supreme Court. But the Supreme Court today cannot possibly protect all federal claims dealt with adversely in the state courts. These days the Court takes jurisdiction in less than 15 percent of all cases petitioning for review. Yet even if the state courts without such supervision would zealously effectuate federal claims asserted there, they can no longer as a practical matter do so. Today federal courts have moved far ahead of state courts in development of remedial power. Federal courts have broad, massive, affirmative injunctive powers which many of our state courts have long held themselves incapable of exercising; can consolidate multistate litigation; can hear suits on behalf of nationwide classes, and can decree nationwide relief. Thus, to deny access to federal courts today may be to deny, over a broad range of claims, any effective remedy to those aggrieved. The suitors denied federal injunctive relief because of "principles of federalism," or debarred from federal adjudication by the indirect expedient found in the pipeline case, will have been denied any day in court—unless they can bring their cases in one of those few state courts that today are ready and able to manage what may well be essentially federal litigation.

The argument is being made that the states can, and should, ready themselves to take up these important tasks.[18] The improbability of securing Supreme Court review is seen to be an advantage by advocates of the rights of minorities and consumers today; it is even suggested that the states can triumphantly avoid review in a conservative Supreme Court by grounding their decisions on state law. But the long road the states would have to travel to do the whole job is not generally perceived. Ideally, their courts will have to begin to allow fee shifting; to hear modern class actions embracing nonresident members of the class; and to exercise not only the affirmative injunctive power but in addition the unitary administration[19] these cases require. The states need to draft, promote, and adopt uniform legislation enabling their courts to consolidate duplicative litigation and to require and simplify enforcement of each others' decrees.

But even if the states could meet these challenges, equipping themselves superbly and adjudicating civil rights and other public interest cases with uniform and sympathetic concern for the national interest, it is hard to see what we gain by denials of access to the optional federal forum provided by Congress.

We lose a great deal. At a minimum we lose the appearance of fairness. Principles of federalism cannot really require that the minority citizens in cases like *Rizzo* be forced to sue the mayor and police commissioner in the local county courts. And it is too late in our history to indulge the presumption that those courts will always be vigorous in guarding the interests of such plaintiffs as the environmentalists in the pipeline case in the teeth of extremely powerful local opposition. Certainly in a case raising racial issues, or even one in which one of the parties may be a member of a minority race, the records of the state courts in our very recent past make it inappropriate to deny to these parties access to an alternative federal forum when Congress has provided one. And whatever value one may place upon the Supreme Court's new "principles of federalism," in civil rights cases surely Congress has weighed those principles, struck the balance, and found a concurrent jurisdiction needful. Federal courts have no basis for abdicating this jurisdictional responsibility.

If we face up to these realities, we perceive that cases like *Rizzo* and the pipeline case will not so much shift litigation from the federal to the state courts as discourage it altogether. Then we lose not only remedies, of course, but rights. And thus the supreme national tribunal cannot continue actively to discourage civil rights and other federal public interest litigation without taking real toll of our national ideals.

That being so, the judicial federalism emerging from the Court's current course rests on assumptions that are—regrettably—much too brave, and places at risk stakes that are much too high.

REFERENCES

[1] *Alyeska Pipeline Service Co.* v. *The Wilderness Society* (1975).

[2] Very briefly, champerty is a lawyer's buying up an interest in the outcome of a lawsuit. Maintenance is a lawyer's investing in the outcome of a suit by payments to a client; however, such payments are unavoidable in some personal injury litigation where a contingency fee is all the client can afford, and there are medical or other expenses to be covered in the interim. Barratry is a lawyer's solicitation of cases.

[3] Perhaps for this reason named representatives in large consumer class actions frequently seem to be relatives or associates of counsel.

[4] I paraphrase Judge Lumbard's *cri de coeur* in the second Court of Appeals opinion in the *Eisen* litigation, discussed in the text shortly.

[5] *Newman* v. *Piggie Park Enterprises, Inc.* The scope of *Piggie Park* remained unclear, however, because an act of Congress there conferred discretion on the trial judge to make the fee award. What was useful about *Piggie Park* in other cases was its language and rationale.

[6] The phrase seems to appear for the first time in a 1943 federal appeals court opinion by Judge Frank.

[7] These days, in the wake of an influential Court of Appeals decision, lower federal courts and state courts active in such litigation compute fees on the basis of time, skill, and risk. The large percentage fees of the past are infrequent. Unfortunately, the result makes less sense in this context than might appear. These suits would not have been brought but for counsel. The absentees have too little at stake to have filed suit, and do not care whether or not they recover. The purpose of the suit is deterrent, not compensatory; and the purpose of the large percentage fee is to place a real premium on such litigation.

[8] I overstate this somewhat. Consumer class actions in which the absentees are unascertainable would be available after *Eisen*, because notice to these absentees could be provided relatively cheaply by publication. However, the Court all but eliminated such class actions in the spring of 1977, holding that retail consumers could not sue manufacturers under the antitrust laws, until then the chief vehicle for federal consumer class actions.

[9] Here, too, the result is untenable. No consideration of fairness requires notice to absentees who by hypothesis have so little at stake that individual suits would not have been brought. They simply have nothing to lose. Absentees with extraordinary interest in the subject of the litigation under these circumstances would not be bound anyway by an adverse ruling. The federal court rule's mandatory notice requirement should have been judicially modified, especially in view of the fact that the Supreme Court itself had ruled thirty years before that in a class action adequacy of representation was sufficient to bind the absentees to a judgment.

[10] Clumsily, Congress chronically authorizes fees to prevailing parties rather than plaintiffs. The Supreme Court has recently agreed to decide in an employment discrimination case whether a federal trial judge under such a provision can actually order losing plaintiffs to pay winning defendants' fees. Because such a practice would undercut the legislative intent to encourage private enforcement in such cases, the lower courts have usually treated such provisions as providing fees for winning plaintiffs only.

[11] This is the recurrent theme of the Chief Justice's annual State of the Juduciary Addresses. See H. Friendly, *Federal Jurisdiction: A General View* (New York and London: Columbia University Press, 1973), Part II. Civil filings in the federal trial courts have doubled since 1969.

[12] See, e.g., 123 Cong. Rec. S95, 201-205 (daily ed., Jan. 10, 1977) (remarks of Sen Mathias); Statement, Board of Governors, Society of American Law Teachers (Oct. 9, 1976); see also Lewis, "The Doors of Justice," *New York Times* (Mar. 29, 1977), p. 29.

[13] The plaintiffs failed to show that the named defendants intended to violate their constitutional rights, and the patrolling officers actually responsible for trespassory invasions of their rights were not joined as defendants. In any event, *Rizzo* concerned police misconduct, which the Chief Justice had recently described as virtually unadjudicable in a federal injunction suit; and the decree set up a quasi-judicial remedy; the Court has ruled that federal courts may not regulate the general conduct of state tribunals. See *O'Shea* v. *Littleton* (1974).

[14] For example, if intentional discrimination has been proved in one school district only, a federal court now lacks power to order busing of school children between that district and a second one not shown to lie within the scope of the intentional violation.

[15] (1871). Federal jurisdiction to grant habeas corpus to state prisoners was conferred in 1867; and, in a parting shot, general jurisdiction over all cases arising under federal law was conferred in

1875. With the Fourteenth Amendment (1868), these achievements of Reconstruction were intended to shift judicial power over cases arising under federal law from the state courts to the federal, and in particular, to authorize federal lawsuits against state officials.

[16]Judge Friendly, in his book cited at note 11, seems to recognize this; see p. 75. See also C. Wright, *Law of Federal Courts* (3rd ed., St. Paul, Minn.: West, 1976), pp. 208–211.

[17]In the great case of *Ex parte Young. Young*, however, accomplished this result at the behest of railroad interests seeking relief from allegedly confiscatory rates. The case was brought in the general jurisdiction over federal questions, not, of course, in the civil rights jurisdiction.

[18]Brennan, "State Constitutions and the Protection of Individual Rights," 90 *Harv. L. Rev.* 489 (1977).

[19]In many states trial judges are assigned not to cases, but to sessions, and frequently ride circuit among the various counties.

MARVIN E. WOLFGANG

Real and Perceived Changes of Crime and Punishment

Deviance and Crime

THE DEFINITION OF crime is culturally subjective. So is society's response to persons who commit crimes.[1] Crime is an act that is believed to be socially harmful by a group that has power to enforce its beliefs and that provides negative sanctions to be applied to persons who commit these acts.[2] Although crime, like pornography, may be in the eye of the beholder, subjective perceptions about crime are closer to universality and retain a more temporal stability than do definitions of obscenity and pornography.

At least this generalization applies to serious crime and the meaning of seriousness. Acts that are defined in American culture as crimes which contain no personal victims and which do not involve physical injury, theft, or damage to property have a wider range of perceived seriousness; acts that involve injury, theft, or damage have a narrow range of seriousness and considerable stability over time in their rank order of gravity.[3]

It is commonplace to refer to the cultural relativity of crime and to mention that the crime of yesteryear is noncriminal today. What is less trite and certainly not trivial is Emile Durkheim's notion that crime is normal, not pathological.[4] Durkheim said that even in a society of saints there would still be crime, by which he meant that if all acts we know as crime were eliminated, small differences in behavior that now appear to have no moral significance would take on a new and important meaning. Slight breaches of manners and good taste could become serious crimes. In his terms, crime involves acts that offend strong collective moral sentiments. If these sentiments weaken, then what were formerly considered to be serious offenses would be considered less serious; when the sentiments grow stronger, less serious offenses are promoted to a more serious category. The degrees of enforcement and severity of sanctions are correlated with the intensity and degree of commitment to the collective moral sentiments.

Even though deviance may have both inevitability and elasticity, we are currently experiencing in America, perhaps in Western society, an expansion of acceptability of deviance and a corresponding contraction of what we define as crime. The total quantity of criminal and noncriminal deviance may be constant, both in value definitions and in statistical frequency; but the line of demarcation between criminal and noncriminal deviance is being positioned at a different point in the total line segment we call deviance.

By a contraction of what is deemed delinquent, the criminal law will be made more enforceable. The more narrow range of behavior considered criminal will mean a stronger link of consistency with history, for the persistently serious offenses like homicide, rape, and thefts, which have almost everywhere and always been viewed as criminal, will constitute the hard core of criminality, and the actors will continue to be viewed as criminals.

The Increase and Decrease of Crimes of Violence

Since 1930, the major method for determining the amount of crime in the United States has been the Uniform Crime Reports (UCR) of the Federal Bureau of Investigation. These annual reports are produced from the collection of police reports in departments of cities and county jurisdictions across the country. There are twenty-nine categories of offenses, but only the first seven are used for what is known as a crime index, a classification analogous to the consumer price index, the cost of living index, and the index of economic productivity. These seven include criminal homicide, forcible rape, robbery, aggravated assault, burglary, larceny of $50 and over, and automobile theft, and are referred to as "offenses known to the police." All the remaining twenty-two offense categories are reported only in terms of the number of persons arrested.

There has been much critical commentary over the past forty-five years about the validity of the crime index, both from traditional scholars who use the crime index reports and from Marxists who deride the data and deny the validity of a capitalist system that fails to take into account the criminogenic forces of the economic and political power of the state. Putting aside those issues and admitting that except for the new series of data known as "victimization rates," collected by the Bureau of the Census in cooperation with the Law Enforcement Assistance Administration, there is little other basis upon which scholars or public officials have for determining whether crime rates are increasing, decreasing, or remaining stable.

Using the UCR data,[5] it can be said that since 1960 crimes of violence have increased 180 percent. The fear of crime, as indicated in a variety of localized studies, has probably increased in even greater proportions than the recorded reality of crime. That many crimes are unrecorded, that reporting procedures have varied over this time, and that more crimes may be reported now—particularly rape—than in earlier days are issues that are difficult to test empirically.

Nonetheless, there appears to be some consensus among the community of criminologists who examine criminal statistics that the amount of real criminality has considerably and significantly increased during the past fifteen years. That there have been equally high rates of crime and crimes of violence recorded in earlier eras of the history of the United States has been asserted by using such long-time series data as Buffalo and Boston provide and as are recorded in the Task Force Reports of the National Commission on the Causes and Prevention of Violence.[6] Crimes of violence in the latter part of the nineteenth century were as high or higher than even the currently reported rates of crimes of violence.

The issue, however, is that within the memories of the current living population of the United States, since the early 1960s, there has been such an upsurge in crimes of violence, or street crimes, that social concern, governmental budgets, and public policy are increasingly affected.

Explanations for the assumed increase are varied but usually embrace such issues as unemployment, broken homes, inadequate education, housing, racial injustice, relative deprivation, lack of law enforcement, and leniency in the courts. Our purpose here is not to be explicative, but descriptively analytical.

We do know that there have been significant demographic changes directly related to the changing crime rates. High fertility rates immediately after World War II, known as the "baby boom," produced a significant alteration in the age composition of the United States population, such that a swelling of the age group between 15 and 24 years occurred in the early 1960s.

For example, in 1940 and 1950, 15–24-year-olds constituted 14.7 percent of the total population. By 1960, 1965, and 1970, the proportions of the same age group were respectively 13.6, 15.7, and 17.8 percent.[7] Because this age group is the most "criminogenic," meaning that this age-specific group contributes more than any other to the rates of crimes of violence for the total population, it has been asserted that the sheer increase in this age group has been the major contributor to the increase in crimes of violence. Studies designed to factor out statistically the contribution of this demographic change have generally supported the assertion that no matter what social interventions may have been made to control, prevent, or deter crime, the changing age composition of the population has been importantly responsible for the increase in crimes of violence.

In an econometric-type model of crime rates over time in the United States, James Fox has shown how the 14–21-year age group has significantly contributed to the rising rates of crimes of violence in the United States.[8] But he has also shown with carefully controlled demographic projections to the year 2000 what changes are most likely to occur (Figure 1). In the United States we are now at our lowest rates of fertility, and the reduction of fertility has already begun to be reflected in the reduced increase in crimes of violence. In 1976 we began to notice both relative and absolute decreases in crimes of violence. The rate of increase dropped, and in many major cities across the country there was an absolute decrease in crimes of violence. The proportion of the youthful group in the total population has decreased and the earlier "baby boom" generation is in the late twenties and early thirties, ages at which the commission of violent crime normally decreases. We should be witnessing from now through the mid-1980s a decline or stability in the amount of crimes of violence.

However, the postwar "baby boom" children, now grown, are getting married and will produce high fertility rates again despite the relative decline in the number of children per couple. Consequently, the 15–24-year age group will rise again in the 1990s, producing once more a rise in the amounts of violence. These claims are made without reference to any effect which greater amounts of law enforcement activity or changes in the criminal justice system may have on the reduction of crime. As a matter of fact, the weight of empirical evidence indicates that no current preventative, deterrent, or rehabilitative intervention scheme has the desired effect of reducing crime.

Two other points need to be made about the changing rates of crimes of violence. One is related to the increase in violent crimes since the early 1960s,

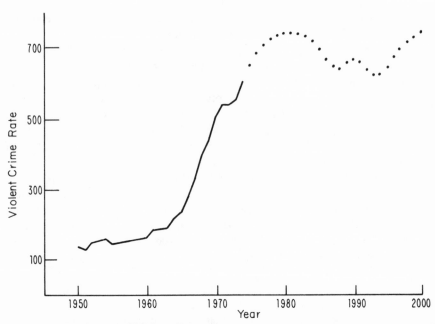

Figure 1. Prediction of Violent Crime Rate

Source: James Alan Fox, *An Econometric Analysis of Crime Data* (unpublished Ph.D. dissertation, University of Pennsylvania, 1976), Figure 8.1, p. 80. Reprinted with permission.

and the other is related to the expected decrease in crimes of violence from the late 1970s to the 1990s. First, it is not simply the increase in crimes of violence that has promoted public fear and increased expenditure of public funds to combat crime; it is the expansion of crimes of violence to groups that have "the power to enforce their beliefs," namely, the large middle class and the upper class in American society who have increasingly become victims of crimes of violence.

The major crime control system in Western civilization has traditionally been that of residential segregation. From the time of the ancient Greeks in Athens through classical Rome, the Middle Ages on the continent of Europe, and in the United States, the slaves, the "criminal classes," the beggars of society, and the lower socioeconomic classes—to use the more current traditional phrasing of social scientists—are the groups attributed with being the major crime committers of theft and physical injury; they have always been residentially kept within their own densely populated, propinquitous areas. Kept on the other side of the river, the canal, or the railroad tracks, the "criminal classes" have been segregated, and crime committed among these groups has either not been well recorded or reported, or it has been considered to be of relative inconsequence to the social structure that has been politically and economically powered by the aristocrats, nobility, or bourgeoisie.

In the United States, the under class, which has always included a high proportion of blacks since the days of slavery, has conveniently been residentially segregated from the middle class. Rapes, robberies, and homicides commited intragroup among the lower classes have been relatively unimportant to those groups in legislative, executive, and judicial power. With the increasing importance attributed to equality of opportunity, the breakdown of racially restrictive covenants in 1949 by a Supreme Court decision and the value placed upon political equality, the traditional residential segregation crime control system has been altered. Moreover, technological changes affording greater opportunities for physical as well as social mobility and interaction among groups have contributed to the breakdown of barriers that formerly existed. Consequently, even as there has been an increase in the amount of social interaction among social and ethnic classes and groups, there has been an increase in the amount of intergroup and interclass crime which has contributed to the greater victimization of middle and upper classes. Burglaries, muggings, rapes, and killings among the groups that define and rate the seriousness of crime and that have the power to enforce sanctions have increased their concern with crimes of violence.

So long as the poor and the blacks were raping, robbing, and killing one another, the general majority public concern with crimes of violence was minimal. Public visibility of concern with such crimes has been related to the more generalized victimization as well as to the rise in the rates of such crimes.

The second point dealing with the expected stability or decrease in crimes of violence concerns the change in public perspectives about seriousness of other kinds of crimes. For example, crimes of violence caused by what some of us call a "subculture of violence"[9] may be replaced by cunning and corruption. Lombroso foresaw some of this condition as he compared societies in the nineteenth century: "Civilization introduces every day new crimes, less atrocious perhaps than the old ones but nonetheless injurious. Thus in London the thief substitutes cunning for violence."[10] Georges Sorel's *Réflexions sur la Violence*, which first appeared in 1906, was in a similar vein.[11] Speaking for the revolutionary syndicalist wing of the labor movement, Sorel focused on the struggle for social power and suggested that reduction of overt acts of violence in social relations is correlated with an increase in fraud and corruption; fraud comes to replace violence as the means to success and privilege. Manipulation of persons and things, especially through economic institutions and the impersonalized relationships represented by money, increasingly is substituted for force. Men become interchangeable, alienation accumulates, minds are raped in subtle ways.[12]

With reduction in crimes of violence, major public concern about crime will probably shift to organized and white-collar varieties. In this transitional stage we will make the trade-off of violence with fraud. In the 1970s organized crime uses less violence than thirty or forty years ago. Monopolies of power in service industries are gained by legal purchase or fraudulent conversion. Accounting practices and legal services constitute the backbone of organized criminal business. Loopholes in regulatory law, purposefully retained, are exploited by legitimate and illegitimate business. Violent liquidation of competitive persons in organized crime gives way to incorporation of the adversary by buying him out or burying him in bankruptcy.

When professional and business crime is finally viewed as corporate dysfunctionality, as an attack on the body politic, such crime will then be more carefully scrutinized and placed under the focus of stringent governmental control and public appeal for action. The change is already occurring and will continue. The rise in the number and political and economic power of consumer interest groups, the increased perceived seriousness of political corruption, corporate criminality, and multinational bribery are already reflections of the changing emphasis in our society from crimes of violence to fraud and corruption. Pollution, bribery of public officials, and Medicaid and Medicare fraud may yet be viewed as being as serious as burglary or sexual assault.

NAM ET IPSA SCIENTIA POTESTAS EST

Part of this change is already being reflected in a new form of information or knowledge theft that is becoming a major type of criminality. Computer tape theft, computer program theft, and corporate information burglary are styles of crime that are already prominent. The theft of information in order to obtain positions of power will increase. The Pentagon Papers, the attempt to steal information from Daniel Ellsberg's psychiatrist, the entire Watergate scandal are among the more dramatic illustrations of this kind of theft.

But there are many others. Recently six persons were arrested in California in what is described as a "multimillion-dollar industrial espionage case" perpetrated against the International Business Machines Corporation.[13] An IBM engineer was arrested and charged with ten felony counts: four of conspiracy, three of theft of trade secrets, two of offering or accepting inducements to steal trade secrets, and one of receiving stolen property. The principal subject of the theft was an IBM-developed direct-access-storage device known as the Merlin, which comprises the data-storage portion of many computer systems.

This is not an isolated case, for many similar ones are coming to light. These, combined with consumer fraud, securities thefts, and political corruption constitute a growing form of major crime in our postindustrial era.[14]

The penal codes of socialist countries may more nearly represent this future condition in the United States. No inference is made that the socialist countries represent a further step in social evolution; whether the change suggested is upward, downward, or horizontal is irrelevant. The point is that economic crime—embezzlement, theft of corporate money and property—is considered in socialist countries as more serious than many, or most, crimes against personalized victims. The sanctions for the former are more severe; the frequency of committing either is apparently lower than in capitalist countries.

Explaining Crime

SYSTEM SHIFTS

Talcott Parsons[15] has provided a useful analytic model of three major systems: culture, society, personality. The culture system refers to values and norms, the social system to the structure or group and individual interaction, and the personality system to the biopsychological and psychiatric forces within the individual. These are interesting systems, idealized and isolated for analytic purposes. Each individual is a biological organism, a vessel of culturally transmitted values, a member of some social groups who thereby interacts with others. The three systems are, in reality, meshed and merged, but disciplines of knowledge and of science focus on different aspects of each system.

Both in academic criminology and in the public mind, shifting system emphases can be noted. If the modern scientific analysis of crime and the criminal can be said to be dated from the writings of Cesare Lombroso in the last quarter of the nineteenth century, then the emphasis in the early stage may surely be said to have been on the personality system. He wrote, for example, about the atavistic, or born, criminal, who was a biological throwback to an earlier stage of evolution, a genetic anomaly characterized by marked physical traits like the prognathous jaw, long arms, and sloping forehead.[16]

Psychological studies, such as those from William Healy[17] in 1915 to contemporary ones, have emphasized the mental condition of the *individual*. The main task of such studies was to devise a typology of personalities, with one or more types susceptible to deviance in general, or to some specific type of deviance. Mental aberration was a central point in Healy's eclecticism.

A move toward the *social system* emerged in the writings of W. I. Thomas in the 1920s: " 'Environment' is no longer regarded as a scene of action for the person, but as material out of which the personality itself is built."[18] Thomas's emphasis on social psychology as the "subjective side of social culture" places him in the interactionist approach to personality and culture. People have attitudes, or propensities to act; values are external to the individual and the objects toward which people have attitudes. Certain social drives, such as the desire for security, response, recognition, and new experience are universal, but in varying strengths and weaknesses in different personalities. Thomas's explanation of prostitution took this social-psychological form which required use of the learning process to explain behavior.[19]

With the notion that learning is part of a response pattern leading to deviance, Edwin Sutherland's differential association,[20] which further emphasized the social system and interaction between the individual and his group, found fertile intellectual soil for growth in 1924. One now became criminal because of frequent, long, intense, or early associations with others who were criminal, compared to those who were not criminal. Differential association indeed shifted American criminology from a focus on the personality system to the social system. There developed a variety of psychodynamic theories of criminality, of deviance in general, that brought to the fore such concepts as sex-role identifications, ego strength, dependency needs, defense mechanisms, and other psychoanalytic notions of individual response to social interaction. The learning process emphasized the way that external values were differentially ingested into the personality by means of the social system.

But there was yet a further shift to come, one that firmly placed the burden of explanation on the larger ambience, that drew upon macroforces and made the individual offender more a captive of historical, political, and economic determinism than of his biology or personal interaction with others.

Clifford Shaw and Henry McKay, in the early 1930s,[21] exemplify the "cultural transmission" approach and the changing focus from how criminogenic forces get inside individuals to what those forces are and the gradient degree of their appearance in the environment outside the individual. We are told, for example, that "delinquent behavior is related dynamically to the community" and that "all community characteristics, including delinquency, are products of the operation of general processes. . . ." Delinquent conduct of children in a city is surely due not to a personality maladjustment but to a much larger social disorganization. The "differential rates of delinquents," Shaw and McKay asserted, "reflect the differences in social values, norms, and attitudes to which the children are exposed." And, "from the point of view of the delinquent's immediate social world, he is not necessarily disorganized, maladjusted, or antisocial. Within the limits of his social world and in terms of its norms and expectations, he may be a highly organized and well-adjusted person."[22]

Emile Durkheim[23] had much earlier (1895) provided a *culture system* emphasis. His social "facts" possessed an exteriority to the personality and social systems that influenced generations of scholars. Sociological inquiry, suicide, and other phenomena were to be explained in a style reminiscent of the earlier work in social physics. Anomie was borrowed from medical literature to describe norm conflict, normlessness, and general social states of anxiety. Robert Merton[24] expanded the notion of anomie in the 1950s and introduced a means-end schema that emphasized structured social strain and stress, the disparities between what was wanted and how it could be achieved. Aspirations and achievement gaps and variations were viewed not from the point of individual frustration but from a higher level that saw cultural systems with conflicts.

Thorsten Sellin[25] drew attention to this emphasis when he spoke of "conflicts between the norms of *cultural systems* or areas," and in this phrasing itself helped to transform research interests to the current focus.

The link to contemporary sociological thoughts about crime and delinquency that push the culture system approach further is fairly obvious. Albert Cohen introduced a kind of Hegelian antithesis with his description of the delinquent subculture: "The delinquent subculture is not only a set of rules, a design for living which is different from or indifferent to or even in conflict with the norms of the 'respectable' adult society. It would appear at least plausible that it is defined by its 'negative polarity' to these norms."[26] With this note on a delinquent subculture, Cohen took us beyond the point of raising questions about an emphasis on personality or on a social or cultural system. The culture system was assumed from the outset as the generation of forces producing delinquency, or at least the predominant mode of delinquency.

Cohen argued that a delinquent subculture arose because of conflict with middle class culture and was oriented to deliberate violation of middle class norms. Walter Miller took the position that gang delinquency emerged directly from, and in response to, a set of norms in the lower social-economic class, which constituted a culture system of its own, an idea similar to that of Oscar Lewis. Delinquency was not a directed negativistic and malicious attack on the middle class. "In the case of 'gang' delinquency," Miller said, "the *cultural system* which exerts the most direct influence on behavior is that of the lower class community itself. . . ."[27]

Richard Cloward and Lloyd Ohlin[28] differentiated three subcultures—criminal, conflict, and retreatist—with the vector of illegitimate opportunities. Combining anomie, role theory, and cultural transmission traditions, they asserted that not only are legitimate opportunities (access to normatively acceptable means) differentially distributed in the social structure, but so are opportunities to achieve cultural goals by illegitimate means. Deviant responses were in subcultural forms depending on the types of opportunities available in various communities.

Wolfgang and Ferracuti[29] emphasized the culture system approach with their contention that a clustering of individuals who have allegiance to and share in the resort to violence in many situations of interaction constitute a subculture of violence. The major thrust of their position is that a subcultural system tolerates, encourages, and even requires the use of violence under prescribed circumstances, and that high rates of aggressive offensivity are due to the value system, not to instinctual aggressive drives or to idiosyncratic motivation or drives.

The recent basic assumptions of the "labeling school," or the symbolic interactionists, take the culture system approach even further. At the same time, emphasis is placed on the dynamics of social psychology by the claim that the definers implant a conception of the self in the self. Criminal deviance occurs, says Kai Erikson, by reason of the assignment of labels by the "social audience." As he claims: ". . . deviance is not a property *inherent* in certain forms of behavior; it is a property conferred upon these forms by the audiences which directly or indirectly witness them. The critical variable in the study of deviance, then, is the social audience rather than the individual actor, since it is the audience which eventually determines whether or not any episode of behavior or any class of episodes is labeled deviant."[30]

One of the chief elements in the manufacturing of criminal deviance is the official labeling by the public response agents—police, court agents, correctional personnel, the guild of therapists. The social organization of the criminal justice system also imposes behavioral restraints that support and confirm the conferred label of deviance. There are many more important features of labeling, but each reaffirms the passivity of the deviant who is defined and processed, who is stamped with social stigma. The act or actor is dethroned from importance and a position of initiation; the reactors and the reaction process are paramount.

The major thrust of social thought has thus been from the personality to the social to the cultural system in an effort to explain. No set of explanations of social phenomena moves in phalanx style; there is usually some overlapping. The claim here is only that these have been the dominant modes of explanation represented in the sequence described.

Neoclassic Revival

NEW WINE IN AN OLD BOTTLE

The major purposes of punishment historically have been retribution, expiation, deterrence, reformation, and social defense. Throughout history, an eye for an eye, the payment of one's debt to society by expiation, general deterrence of crime by exemplary punishment and specific or special deterrence of an individual offender, reformation of the individual so that he will not commit further crime, and protection of society against criminality by detaining or imprisoning offenders have been the principal rationales for disposition of criminal offenders.

In 1764 Cesare Beccaria, in his classic book *Dei delitti e della pena* (*On Crime and Punishment*), wrote that there should be a scale of the seriousness of crime with a corresponding scale of the severity of sanctions. In the Age of Reason in the eighteenth century, with an emphasis upon the rationality of man, deterrence was the principal purpose of punishment. And Beccaria wrote poignantly about this rationale. One of his major statements—which surely has contemporary value—was that it is not the severity but the certainty of punishment that deters.

Since that time and through the nineteenth century, Western civilization encountered a different and new rationale for disposing of criminal offenders: rehabilitation. In the nineteenth century there was an increase in psychiatric concern with criminality. Isaac Ray[31] (1838) wrote in his famous treatise on medical jurisprudence about insanity and criminal responsibility. Following him were the writings of Sigmund Freud and others that increased the psychiatrization of the criminal law. The medical guild linked with the legal guild in criminal justice and convinced the administrators of criminal law that offenders could be reformed, rehabilitated, remolded, resocialized, and thereby produce a decrease in criminality. In 1870, the American Prison Association met in Cincinnati, Ohio, and declared that the principal purpose of punishment was reformation. From that time on, through six decades of the twentieth century, criminal justice was primarily oriented toward this rationale.

Around 1960, careful studies began to evaluate the efficacy of the rehabilitation model. As these studies increased in statistical sophistication, they increasingly reported negative conclusions, namely, that intervention techniques from individual to group therapy, reduced case loads for probation and parole officers, and other intervention models had no significant effect in reducing recidivism.[32] In 1975, a major report of 289 studies of rehabilitation and intervention was made showing that no therapy significantly contributed to the reduction of recidivism.[33] Since that report and Robert Martinson's article in the *Journal of Public Interest* entitled "What Works?" there has been an increasing disillusion with the rehabilitation model.[34]

The Struggle for Justice[35] was a major report by the American Friends Service Committee that had earlier questioned the rehabilitation model and was primarily concerned with the enormous disparities in criminal sentencing and suggested greater uniformity. Since that time, and with the impact of articles by distinguished authors like Francis Allen[36] and Herbert Packer,[37] there has grown a social policy assertion that the uniformity of sentencing and a decrease in judicial discretion are necessary attributes for promoting greater justice in our criminal policy. The Goodell Committee for the Study of Incarceration, whose report was recently published by Andrew von Hirsch[38] under the title *Doing Justice*, has expressed explicitly the growing public concern and disillusion with rehabilitation and a desire to produce a criminal justice system based upon the "just deserts" model, which means that criminals should be punished not for what they might do in the future but for what they have done in the past. This "just deserts" model is in much conformity with the eighteenth-century writings of Cesare Beccaria and the later works of Jeremy Bentham and his felicific calculus regarding risks, rewards, and punishments.

Current thinking among many jurists, police, and legislators, well articulated by James Q. Wilson,[39] is that we cannot do much about the "root causes" of crime, nor that government at any level can legislate love or affect the rate of broken homes. Unemployment, low levels of education, poor housing, and similar social problems among the working classes are issues that the government can and should try to change sui generis with only secondary reference to crime and only because they are major issues concerned with social welfare.

On another level, the criminal justice system is capable of direct manipulation, and federal and state governments should make efforts to effect change. These changes involve the following: increase in the probability of arrest and conviction and a positive sanction of incarceration for offenders who have committed offenses of injury, theft, or damage; elimination of the indeterminate or indefinite sentence by judges and reduction of judicial discretion at the point of sentencing; inclusion of the juvenile record for adults who are convicted and about to be sentenced so that the seriousness of crimes committed as juveniles will be considered in the sentencing discretion; decrease of judicial discretion, which should be substituted by a uniform sentencing process based upon the seriousness of the crime committed rather than on characteristics of the offender.

A new bill submitted to the Congress by Senators Gary Hart and Jacob Javits is in agreement with many of these suggestions. The bill recommends the establishment of a Federal Sentencing Commission which would base its guidelines for sentencing on the seriousness of the crime alone.

A relatively small cadre of persons is responsible for most of the crimes of violence in America. In one study[40] it was noted that only about 6 percent of an entire birth cohort of 10,000 boys born in 1945 and followed through their years from 10 to 18 were responsible for the many street crimes about which the public is so fearful. It follows that a social criminal policy designed to incapacitate for three to five years persons upon conviction of their second or third violent assaultive offense could have a significant effect upon the total rate of crimes of violence.

Under the "just deserts" conceptualization there is no expectation of rehabilitation. In fact, David Rothman,[41] who gave us one of our best histories of asylums, refers to the concept of a failure rather than a success model as being more appropriate to punishment. However, under the current mode of thinking, therapy and service programs should continue to be available but on an optional basis, and participation in those programs should have no effect on the time of release for any convicted offender. Because of the excessive and intolerable number of false positives, the prediction of dangerousness would remain as an academic exercise only and should not be included in a criminal justice system. Even if we were able to predict future violent behavior, it would be inappropriate for us to determine the length of a sentence or the degree of restraint based upon future expectations. Offenders should be punished for what they have done, not what they might do.

Punishment, even retribution, now becomes acceptable as a basis for justice. The Durkheimian conceptualization is reintroduced as a reinforcement of the community moral sentiments and not necessarily as a vengeful reaction by the madding crowd. Humane treatment in and out of prison is highly emphasized, as is the likelihood of fewer prison sentences, and then only or mainly for violent, assaultive offenders. The use of fines such as "income days," restitution to victims, and the right to be treated as well as the right not to be treated would be fundamental principles of the system. Definite sentences rather than indefinite or indeterminate sentences constitute a core item in the agenda, whereas parole or aftercare from an institution would be eliminated as an institutional procedure and a part of the criminal justice bureaucracy. Helping agencies that currently exist could be augmented for assistance to persons released from prison, but not under coercion.

The deprivation of liberty is a punishment sufficient unto itself in a democratic society that places high value on liberty and freedom of movement. Such a proposition implies that capital punishment is an unnecessary and unjust sanction. Retribution does not require it; neither proportional sentencing nor just deserts suggests the death penalty.

We should recall that throughout most of the history of Western civilization, jails, prisons, and detention quarters were used for purposes of detaining suspects awaiting trial or convicted offenders awaiting some form of corporal punishment, exile, or banishment. The use of prisons as penitentiaries, as loci of restraint, as a punishment per se, is a relatively new invention. The Eastern State Penitentiary in Philadelphia (1829) was not the first prison to be used as punishment, but it had few antecedents and few that resulted in the cultural diffusion of the idea of imprisonment as a form of punishment.

TRIUMPH OF THE PUBLIC MIND

Vilfredo Pareto,[42] the Italian sociologist, spoke about culture imitation and the diffusion of folkways, mores, and social inventions from the leaders of society downward through social classes to the masses. Ideas generated by the nobility, intellectuals, and the powerful migrate downward and broaden their base until they strike the lower classes. Pareto's sociological theorizing may have been more appropriate in earlier periods of history, for we have witnessed, particularly in America with the technology of mass media, many examples of reverse diffusion. What has happened is that concepts of crime, criminality, and justice that have existed in the general public mind have had stability over the centuries and are now merging with the current thinking of the social scientific community, criminal justice analyzers, and administrators.

When Beccaria wrote his famous essay 200 years ago, he exemplified an elite rationalism that quickly spread among the leaders of Western society, including Benjamin Franklin and Thomas Jefferson, who were well aware of his writing when they were working on their own independence and creation of a new government.[43] This classical school of criminology and criminal justice took hold among the less learned primarily because the ideas were expressions of the grievances of most people. Whimsical, arbitrary, capricious administration of criminal law benefited the wealthy and the nobility; the poor were punished and tortured severely.

But early in the nineteenth century the Philadelphia Quakers, the elite leaders, introduced at the old prison in Cherry Hill what came to be known as the Pennsylvania, or separate, system. In that prison all inmates, all convicts were kept in solitary confinement from the moment they arrived until the moment they left the institution. With humanitarian intentions to promote self-reformation and to eliminate the effects of social contamination from other convicts, this philosophy and correctional movement were imposed on the criminal justice system and enforced, as Rousseau would force men to be free, on the unfortunates caught in a network of the administration of criminal law.

Charles Dickens visited the famous Philadelphia prison in 1842. At first he was complimentary, but when he put his impressions into writing he was very critical, and his perspective is as current as the critics of today who are opposed to coercive therapy: "In its intention I am well convinced that it is kind, humane and meant for reformation; but I am persuaded that those who devised the system and those benevolent gentlemen who carry it into execution, do not know what it is they are doing. . . . I hold this slow and daily tampering with the mysteries of the brain to be immeasurably worse than any torture of the body; and because its ghastly signs and tokens are not so palpable to the eye and sense of touch as scars upon the flesh, because its wounds are not on the surface, and it extorts few cries that human ears can hear; therefore I denounce it as a secret punishment which slumbering humanity is not roused to stay."[44]

Coercive reformation thus began and later changed its language but not its style. The invasion by medicine, especially psychiatry, of the philosophy of responsibility and of the "reasonable man" changed sin and evil to sickness and disease. The subconscious and unconscious came to dominate cognitive reasoning, and offenders were to be treated rather than punished. It was not the sin in the soul but the disease in the mind that needed to be changed, and mind-altering mechanisms were invented to remold, refashion, and reform the offender for his own good as well as for the protection of society.

It is doubtful that this model and these messages of reform were ever fully accepted in the popular culture. But when the heavy weight of authority from the well-respected academies of medicine and law joined to promote policies of criminal justice, the voices of punishment and retribution from the folk culture remained hushed for over a century.

Only now, with the revival of the eighteenth-century classical position, are these muted tones being heard and articulated by leaders in social science, criminal law, and public policy. Neoclassicism was born from the popular culture and is now nourished by sophisticated research. Deterrence, retribution, and punishment, never abandoned by the populace, have once again become acceptable to those "with power to enforce their beliefs." Reformation, although still accepted as desirable, is dethroned from its position of dominance and is subordinated within a more retributive penology.

Rehabilitation will surely continue and will be researched but in a non-coercive style. Imprisonment should be used as infrequently as justice can design, and humane concern for involuntary victims, by means of such programs as victim compensation and counseling, as well as concern for captured criminals, should govern our democratic justice system. The public, the police, the judiciary, and legislators are now joined by many social scientists in an ethical stance that requests retribution, not revenge, as the definition of justice; that requires an emphasis on stability rather than law and order; that looks to certainty rather than severity of punishment. California, Indiana, and Maine have already passed legislation reflecting these views, and many more states and the federal government can be expected to follow these changes in the perceptions of crime control and the meaning of justice.

REFERENCES

[1]This section includes some remarks presented at the Fifth National Conference at the Institute of Criminology, University of Cambridge, England, on July 5, 1973.

[2]This is essentially John Louis Gillin's definition of crime in his *Criminology and Penology* (New York: Appleton-Century, 1945).

[3]Thorsten Sellin and Marvin E. Wolfgang, *Delinquency: Selected Studies* (New York: Wiley, 1969).

[4]Emile Durkheim, *The Rules of Sociological Method* (Chicago: University of Chicago Press, 1938), pp. 67–71.

[5]*Uniform Crime Reports* (Washington, D.C.: Federal Bureau of Investigation, 1975).

[6]Donald J. Mulvihill, Melvin M. Tumin, and Lynn A. Curtis, *Crimes of Violence*, vol. 11 of the staff report submitted to the National Commission on the Causes and Prevention of Violence (Washington, D.C.: U.S. Government Printing Office, 1969).

[7]*Census of Population: 1970*, "General Population Characteristics," Final Report PC(1)–B1, U.S. Summary (Washington, D.C.: Bureau of the Census, 1972).

[8]James Alan Fox, "An Econometric Analysis of Crime Data," Ph.D. dissertation, University of Pennsylvania, 1976.

[9]Marvin E. Wolfgang and Franco Ferracuti, *The Subculture of Violence: Towards an Integrated Theory in Criminology* (London: Tavistock, 1967).

[10]Cesare Lombroso, *Crime: Its Causes and Remedies* (Boston: Little, Brown, 1912), pp. 34–35.

[11]Georges Sorel, *Réflexions sur la Violence* (Paris, 1936).

[12]See my earlier comments on this topic in "A Preface to Violence," *The Annals of the American Academy of Political and Social Science* 364 (1966):1–3.

[13]*The New York Times* (June 30, 1973).

[14]Thomas Whiteside, "Annals of Crime: Dead Souls in the Computer," *The New Yorker* I (August 22, 1977):35–65; II (August 29, 1977):34–64.

[15]Talcott Parsons, *The Structure of Social Action* (Glencoe, Ill.: Free Press, 1949); *The Social System* (Glencoe, Ill.: Free Press, 1951). Portions of this section are drawn from an earlier paper entitled "The Viable Future of Criminology," *Criminology in Action* (Montreal: University of Montreal, 1968), pp. 109–134.

[16]Lombroso, *Crime: Its Causes and Remedies*, pp. 34–35.

[17]William Healey, *The Individual Delinquent* (Boston: Little, Brown, 1915).

[18]W. I. Thomas, "The Relation of the Individual to the Group," *American Journal of Sociology* 33 (1927):814. The statement quoted is embodied in a notice to the American Sociological Society, of which he was then president. The notice was designed to justify his selection of the general topic to be discussed at the next meeting of the Society.

[19]W. I. Thomas, *The Unadjusted Girl* (Boston: Little, Brown, 1923).

[20]Edwin H. Sutherland, *Principles of Criminology* (Philadelphia: Lippincott, 1934). The first edition of Sutherland's textbook appeared under the simple title *Criminology* in 1924.

[21]Clifford R. Shaw and Henry B. McKay, *Social Factors in Juvenile Delinquency*, vol. 11 of the National Committee on Law Observance and Law Enforcement, Report on the Causes of Crime (Washington, D.C.: U.S. Government Printing Office, 1931); and *Juvenile Delinquency and Urban Areas* (Chicago: University of Chicago Press, 1942).

[22]Shaw and McKay, *Juvenile Delinquency and Urban Areas* (rev. ed., 1969), pp. 315–316.

[23]See especially Emile Durkheim, *Suicide* (translated by J. A. Spaulding and G. Simpson, Glencoe, Ill.: Free Press, 1951); and *The Rules of Sociological Method* (translated by Sara A. Solovay and John H. Mueller, Glencoe, Ill.: Free Press, 1950), 65–73.

[24]Robert Merton, *Social Theory and Social Structure* (Glencoe, Ill.: Free Press, 1957).

[25]Thorsten Sellin, *Culture, Conflict and Crime* (New York: Social Science Research Council, 1938).

[26]Albert Cohen, *Delinquent Boys* (Glencoe, Ill.: Free Press, 1955), p. 28.

[27]Walter B. Miller, "Lower Class Culture as a Generating Milieu of Gang Delinquency," *Journal of Social Issues* 14 (1958):5–19, at p. 5, emphasis added.

[28]Richard A. Cloward and Lloyd B. Ohlin, *Delinquency and Opportunity: a Theory of Delinquent Gangs* (Glencoe, Ill.: Free Press, 1960).

[29]Wolfgang and Ferracuti, *The Subculture of Violence*.

[30]Kai T. Erikson, "Notes on the Sociology of Deviance," *Social Problems* 9 (1962):308.

[31]Isaac Ray, *A Treatise on the Medical Jurisprudence of Insanity* (Boston: Little, Brown, 1838).

[32]Walter C. Bailey, "Correctional Outcome: An Evaluation of 100 Reports," *Journal of Criminal Law, Criminology and Police Science* 57 (1966):153–160; R. G. Hood, "Research on the Effectiveness of Punishments and Treatments," in *Collected Studies in Criminological Research*, vol. 1 (Strasbourg: Council of Europe, 1967), pp. 74–102; David A. Ward, "Evaluations of Correctional Treatment: Some Implications of Negative Findings," in S. A. Yefsky (ed.), *Law Enforcement, Science and Technology* (Washington, D.C.: Thompson, 1967), pp. 201–108.

[33]Douglas Lipton, Robert Martinson, and Judith Wilks, *The Effectiveness of Correctional Treatment: A Survey of Treatment Evaluation Studies* (New York: Praeger, 1975).

[34]Robert Martinson, "What Works?—Questions and Answers about Prison Reform," *Journal of Public Interest* 6 (June 1974):22–54.

[35]*Struggle for Justice*, A Report on Crime and Punishment in American, prepared for the American Friends Service Committee (New York: Hill and Wang, 1971).

[36]Francis A. Allen, "Criminal Justice, Legal Values, and the Rehabilitative Ideal," *Journal of Criminal Law, Criminology and Police Science* 50 (1959):226–230.

[32]Herbert L. Packer, *The Limits of Criminal Sanction* (Stanford: Stanford University Press, 1968).

[38]Andrew von Hirsch, *Doing Justice: The Choice of Punishments* (New York: Hill and Wang, 1976).

[39]James Q. Wilson, *Thinking about Crime* (New York: Basic Books, 1975).

[40]Marvin E. Wolfgang, Robert M. Figlio, and Thorsten Sellin, *Delinquency in a Birth Cohort* (Chicago: University of Chicago Press, 1972).

[41]David Rothman, *The Discovery of the Asylum: Social Order and Disorder in the New Republic* (Boston: Little, Brown, 1971).

[42]Vilfredo Pareto, *Mind and Society* (translated and edited by Arthur Livingston, New York, 1935), 4 vols.

[43]Marcello Maestro, "Benjamin Franklin and the Penal Law," *A Journal of Ideas* 36 (1975):551–562.

[44]Charles Dickens, *American Notes for General Circulation* (London: Chapman and Hall, 1842), pp. 119–120, cited by Torsten Eriksson, *The Reformers: An Historical Survey of Pioneer Experiments in the Treatment of Criminals* (New York: Elsevier, 1976), p. 70.

ADAM YARMOLINSKY

What Future for the Professional in American Society?

To be a professional in American society is somehow to be special. A professional is thought to have special knowledge, special skills, special resources, and special responsibilities. A professional is the object of special respect, special envy, and special demands. Individuals, and more recently organized groups, aspire to professional status—while that status is thought to be uniquely in the power of professionals to bind or to loose.

Yet there are reasons to believe that the status of the professional in America has begun to decline in recent years, and that current trends in American society will continue and even accelerate that decline, unless professionals modify their practices and their attitudes in response to these trends while maintaining a fundamental commitment to the intellectual core of the professional functions.

I

In a sense, professional status is self-defining. As a lady has been described as a person whom other people are willing to treat as a lady, so a professional is a person whom other people, inside and outside the professions, are willing to treat as a professional. But if we can identify the principal characteristics that tend to set professionals apart from the rest of humanity—other than historical accidents or hangovers—we can then speculate about the likely futures for the persons we now identify as professionals in America, and for their successors in interest.

The principal asset of the professional is specialized knowledge, and the professional's principal function is to use that knowledge for the benefit of individuals or groups with whom he or she establishes a relationship of trust and confidence. The professional may market his services directly to the user, or indirectly through a private or quasi-private employer, or through the state. In the United States, doctors, lawyers, and architects tend to fall into the first category; teachers, preachers, engineers, economists, and actors into the second category; and sanitarians, forest rangers, and county agricultural agents into the third category. Traditionally, self-employed professionals have tended to look down on colleagues who are mere employees—"in-house lawyers" has been a slightly derogatory term—but that distinction is eroding with the increasing bureaucratization of society. The limiting case is that of the military, who serve the nation-state through their own hierarchical organization, but who still manage to maintain a professional status that is not always accorded to their civilian opposite numbers.

In any event, the market for those services is peculiarly an imperfect one, because of the relative ignorance of the ultimate beneficiary. Characteristically, that beneficiary is not described as a customer, even where he purchases the services directly, but rather by a series of words like client, patient, parishioner, and even audience. All these words emphasize the benefits conferred, rather than the quid pro quo to the provider. And they all imply a kind of assumption of responsibility, on the part of the professional, as a provider of services; that responsibility, at least to some extent, makes up for the absence of a bargain among equals.

Professionals tend to establish their own systems of reward and punishment, internal to the profession itself. Although professionals in the United States lack their British colleagues' advantage of rendering their bills in guineas instead of plebeian pounds, the material rewards that American society provides for the professional have ranged from above average to extremely high. These rewards are supplemented by systems of honorific distinction, often highly organized, and controlled by members of the profession or of a group of professions. Typically, these honors are conferred not by decision of the profession as a whole but by those who have already been honored, thus leaving the definition of professional excellence in the hands of a small self-selected minority. It may be significant that when other groups, not ordinarily thought of as professions per se, such as businessmen or public officials, organize internal awards for excellence, they tend to insert the adjective "professional" in their description of the award.

Most professionals no longer wear distinctive uniforms, although medical residents can still be identified by the stethoscope bulge, and government counsel in the U.S. Supreme Court by their frock coats. The story is not apocryphal that a non-M.D. faculty member at a distinguished medical school on the U.S. East Coast gave up his appointment because his M.D. colleagues would not allow him to wear the traditional white coat around the school.

Professionals also exercise disciplinary control over their professional colleagues. Their specialized knowledge is thought to extend to judgments about standards for ethical behavior, and to appropriate relations between individual professionals and the outside world. The sanctions available to disciplinary bodies within a profession are generally limited to suspension or exclusion from professional practice; but this is a powerful sanction indeed. It is, to be sure, subject to varying degrees of judicial review, but the initiative for imposing the sanction lies within the profession itself—or within a governing body usually composed exclusively of professionals. The issue of Richard Nixon's disbarment, after his resignation, waited on the action of the governing bodies of the New York and California bars.

The disciplinary powers of the profession are closely related to the control over admission to the profession itself, which is also in the hands of a professional body. This control amounts to an extraordinary delegation to a private body of the determination not only that a person cannot hold himself or herself out as possessing a particular set of skills, but that that person is forbidden to practice those skills, at least in relation to the general public. Courts have intervened to insist on standards of fairness in the admissions process, but they have not intervened in the determination of substantive standards. And where questions have arisen as to the boundaries of professional authority, courts and legislatures have generally reflected the views of the professions themselves—or the balance of power among competing professions, as between doctors and nurses, or between lawyers and accountants.

The role of the professional in American society is in many ways an enviable one—respected, rewarded, independent, yet essential to the functioning of society. Yet it is a role that the professional has only recently assumed, at least on the basis of his contribution to society. Lawyers were so unpopular in nineteenth-century America that some state constitutions expressly authorized any citizen to practice law, or forbade any person to accept a fee for a court appearance. The idea of professional management in business or government did not really come into its own until the second half of this century. And serious writing about the professions did not begin to appear until the late twenties.

It was only with the phenomenon of Sputnik in 1957 that Americans embraced the ideas that knowledge is power, and that science, broadly construed to include social science and even language and area studies, would protect us from orbiting dangers. At about the same time the teaching profession was expanding in scope and importance as the tidal wave of post-World War II babies advanced through high school and on to college, the legal profession was riding the ascending curve of business expansion, and the medical profession was proliferating new facilities and new technologies. And within the military establishment, new professional skills in weapons development and systems engineering were so much in demand that professional services formerly performed within the military were contracted out to private civilian organizations, which then began to apply their new kinds of engineering skills to other social problems.

But the rising curve of professional ascendancy may be about to turn downward. Not that American society is any less in need of knowledge-based skills. Yet three kinds of challenge increasingly threaten the status and privileges of the professional. The first challenge arises out of the proliferation of knowledge. The second challenge arises out of the growth of bureaucratic institutions. And the third challenge arises out of the spread of democratic ideas and ideals. Together these three challenges will require some fairly fundamental restructuring of relationships between the professional and the society that he or she serves.

II

So long as the demand for professional skills is relatively limited, the professional class can remain a relatively small and privileged minority. But as the demand for these skills increases, in an increasingly knowledge-based, service-oriented society, the professional role is no longer so distinctive. Privileges must be shared, and pro tanto, diminished. At the simplest level, in a society where literacy is almost universal, there is no need for professional letter-writers. A generation or so ago, patients thought of health professionals as doctors, dentists, and nurses. There are now about 200 recognized Allied Health Professions with more than 1.5 million members according to the National Health Council (the term "paraprofessional" has been rejected by the practitioners of these skills) from hospital administrators to X-ray technicians and technologists. The physician may acquire some added prestige within the health-care community as the captain of an expanding team, but his relations with patients are bound to be more distant and less significant, and he himself seems less concerned with the patient's welfare.

Social work has only recently claimed the status of a profession, but its professionals are not only multiplying (from less than 40,000 in the thirties to over a quarter of a million today) but also dividing into subprofessions, like psychiatric social work and medical social work. A major addition has been the professional manager, who has succeeded (or supplemented) the owner-manager in all but the smallest businesses. As the professional class has grown, the numbers of quasi-professionals and would-be professionals has increased as well. A plumber is still a plumber (although he may earn more than most professionals), but airline pilots, accountants, real-estate brokers, travel agents, and insurance agents make up part of an increasing number of people who all perceive themselves, and are increasingly perceived by the public, as members of this professional group.

The dividing line between professionals and others is further blurred by the proliferation of proprietary schools offering career preparation in everything from computer programming to paralegal practice (the paralegals are one stage behind their health-care colleagues, still accepting the invidious prefix). At the same time, the numbers of applicants for professional training have multiplied, from just over 52,000 for medical and law schools in 1967 to almost 125,000 in 1974. How much the increase in applications is a function of overestimation of the prospects for professional careers—or simply of career fads—and how much it results from a generally rising level of career expectations, as more young people can take advantage of higher education, is hard to estimate. But whatever the mix, one consequence has been increased frustration among disappointed entrants into the professions, whether because they are denied admission into professional training, as in medicine, or because they cannot find professional employment after their training, as in law and in teaching. Either way they are likely to feel some resentment toward those who actually made it in their own chosen fields.

If the broadening of the knowledge base is increasing the numbers of professionals, it is also decreasing the scope of activity of the individual professional. Knowledge in depth takes the place of knowledge in breadth, so that the area of the professional's competence is less and less likely to be congruent with the area of the client's problem. A patient no longer has a single physician, but shuttles back and forth among the internist, the surgeon, and the psychiatrist, with occasional stops to visit a variety of subspecialists. An individual client no longer has a single lawyer, but consults an estate planner, a litigator, and a corporations expert. An architect, designing a structure of almost any size, must bring in a heating engineer, an electrical systems designer, and a landscape architect, to name only a few of the special skills required.

One consequence of this specialization is that the client does not see the professional as helping him directly with his problem, and the professional may be more interested in the problem as an intellectual exercise, rather than as a real-life concern of a particular individual. The orthopedist who works on the mechanism of the knee may not see the knee-bone as connected to the head-bone—and he may not worry about how the patient can find the time or the incentive to do the exercises he prescribes. The orthopedist's attitude is very quickly communicated to the patient, and only increases the distance between them.

Another consequence is that the patient, or the client, looks for ways to match professional skills to his problems. He may rely on a general practitioner within the profession—a family doctor or a family lawyer; he may rely on gossip or on his own research. But however he does it, he cannot escape some feeling of frustration that will in turn reflect on his appreciation of what the professions can do for him.

A further consequence is that the specialist, and particularly the super-specialist, tends to become a professional's professional—a lawyer's lawyer or a doctor's doctor. He gets his clients or patients primarily by referral from other professionals, and he is less in touch with the outside world. His perspective is less likely to be tempered by exposure to different points of view, and his outlook may be a progressively narrowing one. He does not make house calls. There are objective reasons why he does not: the value of his time, and the availability of office-bound technology. But his horizons are still confined within those four walls.

The application of an increasing volume of knowledge in this fragmented fashion depends on a high degree of social organization. And this highly organized, bureaucratized society in turn reduces the distinctiveness of the professional role. If the direct and independent application of knowledge to problems is of the essence of professionalism, then anything that gets in the way between the professional and the problem, or between the solution and the people who benefit from it, only blurs the professional's image.

Before turning to the second challenge to professional status, the challenge of bureaucracy, we need to consider the impact of the knowledge explosion on the trust and confidence that is so essential an element in the professional relationship. It is a paradox of that relationship that although the trust is logically based on the professional's superior knowledge, the greater the area of universal ignorance about the problem being dealt with, the deeper the patient's or client's trust in the professional is likely to be. Judgments based on what is unknowable are inherently more impressive than judgments based merely on what is unknown but can be made clear. When there was relatively little that the physician could do for a sick patient, the patient and the patient's family had to trust the doctor. But to the extent that diagnoses and prescriptions are based on replicable observations and formulated as objective probabilities, trust becomes less of a critical factor. You trust your meter-reader to be honest and careful, but you have no reason to attribute to him superior judgment or wisdom.

Of course there are still essential elements of judgment in the work of all the professions, from the physician to the airplane pilot, and we rely on them, even for our lives. But the medical profession is beginning to develop objective criteria to measure the adequacy of physicians' performance, situation by situation, in admittedly distant analogy to the pilot's preflight checklist. And other professions are developing a concern about objective measures of competence, which was simply not possible in an era of greater ignorance—and greater awe of the professional.

III

In a bureaucratic society, both the professional and the client are likely to be members of organizations, and they must deal with each other through those organizations. The pregnant wife of a corporate employee may enjoy the benefits of health care through a Health Maintenance Organization under a contract between the HMO and the corporation that employs her husband. She is taken care of by a health-care team made up of a number of professionals, and technical and administrative assistants, each of whom deals with a different aspect of her health problems. When her time comes, the obstetrician who delivers her will be the one who happens to be on duty at that time. The law firm that represents even a middle-sized corporation will deal, through a hierarchy of partners and associates, with a corresponding hierarchy of corporation officials, both lawyers and laymen. The social worker who administers a complicated program of government welfare benefits undoubtedly spends more time seeing that the client is complying with government regulations, than seeing that the government meets the client's needs. And even when there is a deliberate attempt to separate the two functions, using different staffs, much of the work of the "helping" staff consists of fitting the clients into the interstices of the bureaucratic system. Similarly, the architect and the engineer spend much of their energies in bringing their clients into line with structural, environmental, and zoning regulations, not always earning their clients' gratitude in the process. The professional in a bureaucratic setting may, and not infrequently will, find himself in a conflict of interest between the concerns of the client organization and the concerns of individuals within the organization.

The growth of bureaucratic institutions has itself created a new professional role, that of the professional manager. But professional managers have difficulty in looking beyond their own bureaucracies to identify their clienteles. For the public manager, is it the interest of his agency's particular set of constituencies, or is it the public interest, however defined? For the private business manager, is it only the shareholders, or is it also the employees, customers, suppliers, neighbors—and how does he or she balance all these interests?

At least in a publicly held corporation, the business manager cannot look to the ownership interest for guidance. He cannot rely entirely on government regulation to set the boundaries for corporate action. The temptation is to focus on means to the exclusion of ends. But to do so is to risk the survival of the corporation itself. Increasingly, this is the central professional dilemma of the private manager.

At the same time, the multiplication of bureaucratic tools also tempts the professional to focus on means rather than ends. A considerable amount of effort goes into computerizing parts of the professional's job. Medical history and diagnosis is assisted by multiphasic diagnostic machines; simple legal research is speeded up by computerizing case materials and statutory references; computers play a larger role in physical design. All these developments, properly employed, can save time and effort. But they also tend to blur the image of the professional as an individual exercising judgment on individual human problems in the light of professional values.

The organization of professionals into peer groups does have a positive effect: it makes it easier to maintain professional standards. When professionals are necessarily looking over each other's shoulders, they are more likely to catch each other's mistakes and bad habits. Uniform standards are more likely to be found in law firms or in group medical practices than among solo practitioners. And mutual support can make life less difficult. Physicians in group practice can fill in for each other on nights and weekends. Lawyers in law firms consistently earn more than lawyers in solo practice, and income increases generally with the size of the firm. This is understandable in economic terms, because a labor-intensive industry is at a continuing disadvantage in an economy where productivity is generally increasing through the application of new capital and new technology. One way to decrease this disadvantage is to delegate tasks, or portions of tasks, to less highly paid associates. Bureaucracy serves the professional as well as the client. But the price may be an even greater distancing between the two.

The multiplication of paraprofessionals, referred to above, further separates the professional from the client. The temptation to delegate tasks to paraprofessionals can be very strong. But what is delegated to a paraprofessional is by definition not a professional task, and if enough pieces are delegated, what remains may not be sufficient to make up a coherent professional relationship.

The difficulties that bureaucracy creates for professionals in serving their clients are matched by the constraints that bureaucracy imposes in managing their own lives. At the Wall Street law firm where I began my professional career, the office manual insisted that there were no fixed office hours, and indeed one lawyer habitually came in at noon and worked until after dinner. The office manual may still make the same brave assertion, but it must present increasing difficulties to the temporal nonconformist. True, there are professionals who use their extraordinary expertise to bargain for an extraordinarily independent life—the international tax expert who lives and works on the North Shore of Massachusetts Bay, commuting only occasionally to the Middle East, or the electronics engineer who sets up his home laboratory in a California exurb—but these individuals are consciously, if defiantly, swimming against the tide.

The proposition that bureaucratic institutions weaken professional relations must be tested against the patterns of two of the three traditional professions—the church and the military—which have been also the most bureaucratized, or, to put it more gently, the most hierarchical. The priest is in fact the archetype of the professional role; in earlier societies, the priest had a virtual monopoly on learning. What preserved the relationship between priest and communicant, despite the massive hierarchy of the church, was that the individual priest was still the direct link; he administered Communion, took confessions, and performed the other pastoral duties himself, without any intermediaries. The self-denying rules of poverty and chastity, even when honored more in the breach than in the observance, helped to preserve the fiduciary principle. The hierarchy served to validate the traditional knowledge base of the priesthood while preserving its essential mystery. With the shift to a congregational polity, the priest or minister in fact loses some of his stature as a professional, and makes up for that loss either by offering new professional services based on individual skills (like family counselling) or by retreating into a bureaucratic role (like managing the church suppers). The traditional church did not present its bureaucratic face to the public, and the democratization of the church structure is rather an aspect of the third kind of societal change, the spread of democratic ideas and ideals, discussed below.

But first we need to examine the impact of the military bureaucracy on the military professional role. The United States military establishment is by far the largest institution in our society, and one of the most highly organized. Even at its lowest stage, between the two world wars, it was large, compared to other organizations either private or public, and it was highly organized. At that time, the military officer was the only kind of professional who did not deal primarily with individual clients or groups of clients. His service was (and still is) to the nation, personified in the civilian political leadership, and specifically in the civilian commander-in-chief. In order to engender the sense of professional responsibility that otherwise derives from the commitment and trust of individual clients, the military developed a complicated and rigid code of behavior, and a highly visible tradition. Military officers were deliberately isolated as much as possible from their civilian counterparts. Great emphasis was placed on the unique aspect of their work—military combat—and the essentially routine nature of most military professional responsibilities was related as closely as possible to (ordinarily hypothetical) demands of combat. Altogether, the system was designed to persuade its members, the professional officer corps, that on appropriate occasions they would have to be more than bureaucrats.

The situation of the U.S. military establishment today has changed drastically. The primary responsibility of the military in connection with the kind of war most likely to threaten the vital interests of the United States—a general nuclear war—is not to fight such a war, but to deter it, because it is not the kind of war that either side can win. The nature of the military job has changed so much that some writers even challenge the definition of the military profession as the "managers of violence," and would substitute a definition that emphasizes the capacity to feed, clothe, and house large numbers of human beings, to move them from place to place, and to train them rapidly for tasks of widely varying complexity—as well as to superintend the development, production, and maintenance of highly complex mechanical and electronic systems.

Particularly as a result of the new emphasis on the development and management of very large systems, there has been a significant change in the dialogue between military professionals on the one hand, and civilian political leaders and their nonmilitary advisers on the other hand. Until recent years the military had complete control of military operations. In fact it was reported that a Secretary of War who asked to see a set of war plans was told they were none of his business.

With the overhanging danger of a general nuclear exchange, however, the civilian managers of the military establishment became involved, perhaps most dramatically in the infinitely detailed White House direction of the military moves in the Cuba missile crisis, and again later in the management of the air war in Vietnam. Although the military professionals are still regarded as the ultimate sources of professional military judgment, they are expected to justify their assessments and their recommendations, rather than to argue from authority and experience alone—in large part because so much of previous military experience is irrelevant to a nuclear-armed world.

There is still a running debate within the Pentagon, and across the Potomac, about the importance of "the smell of the campfire" in military planning and decision making. But more and more the military are seen primarily as expert managers, rather than primarily as professional experts.

In a sense, the military profession has been buffeted first by the knowledge explosion and then by the bureaucracy explosion. So much new knowledge was embodied in the new post-World War II military technology—along with so little experience—that the military professional could not assimilate it all, and had to rely on outside experts to help incorporate it into military planning, so that he is no longer able to maintain the same stance of absolute authority in military matters. Civilians have been and are involved also, as contract employees, in the actual operation of complex systems, serving aboard major Navy ships, at remote missile warning system outposts, and in actual and potential conflict situations throughout the world. The technology they deal with is primarily concerned with nuclear warheads and missilry, but extends also to modern nonnuclear weapons, and to the whole world of sensors and communications and computers as well. Thus the new technology has so complicated the economics and the logistics of military operations that military management appears to be at least as important as military leadership. Taken together, these two developments removed some of the professional aura surrounding the military, even while they tended to make the military establishment bulk even larger as an institution in American society.

Under these circumstances, many of the supports that shore up traditional military professional attitudes have been knocked out, and military officers tend to be as much bureaucrats as professionals, at least until they reach the rank where they are in fact called on for independent professional judgments about the role of military force in American foreign policy, and the structure of the military establishment—and few of them are called upon to make such judgments at any point in their careers.

Even the most hierarchical professions therefore are being deprofessionalized to some extent by the increasing bureaucratization of American society. And they are affected also, as are all the professions, by the spread of democratic ideas and ideals.

IV

Professionals are at a double disadvantage as authority figures in a democratic society. The processes by which they are selected are not essentially democratic. These processes are based not on popular choice but on criteria established within the professions themselves. And professional judgment, unlike the judgment of the salesman or the politician, is not a reflection of popular views. For the professional, the customer is not always right. In any society, the claim to expertise automatically carries some weight, but that claim would seem to have less weight in a society where the political temper is less authoritarian and more egalitarian.

The authority of every profession is increasingly called into question, as individuals and groups assert their right to participate in decisions that affect their future. They want to reach behind professional opinions to examine the underlying facts and arguments, and to make their own judgments. They are suspicious of established authority, whether established by law, by custom, or simply by claim to know better. Where lay persons are included in boards or advisory bodies that have been previously controlled by professionals, they will even arrange to hire their own experts, in order to put themselves on a more nearly equal footing with their expert colleagues.

The hostility of the Indiana constitution makers toward lawyers was a direct expression of resentment toward self-proclaimed experts. Modern democratic societies are wont to proceed more gently. Recognizing that there are areas of genuine professional expertise, they are concerned to protect the public against professionals who set what the public regards as unreasonable conditions on access to their skills, or who attempt to influence public policy under the guise of offering professional opinions.

A special problem area has developed around the role of lawyers, and particularly of judges, in dealing with current social issues. Increasingly since *Brown v. Board of Education*, the courts have been called upon to adjust social policy to constitutional norms. Forced into the fray by the reluctance of executive and legislative branches, the courts find themselves laying out school bus routes, inspecting mental hospitals, and relocating public housing projects.

At the same time, people, individually and in groups, who feel themselves aggrieved by public and quasi-public institutions—or by the slings and arrows of outrageous fortune, acting through those institutions—have been turning to litigation in unprecedented numbers. Even though the statistics cannot be sorted out from the background of general litigation, the indirect evidence is convincing. Public universities, for example, which until recent years relied entirely on outside counsel to defend themselves against occasional lawsuits, have not only hired full-time staff lawyers, but have multiplied their numbers year by year. Malpractice suits, discussed in more detail below, are already a major problem for the medical profession, and are becoming one in other professions—even in education.

Too much can easily be made of the development of public-interest law firms and community legal services. They are still woefully inadequate to the needs of their clients, and several of the instrumentalities they have invented to facilitate their operations—class actions, and legal fees charged off to defendants—have been sharply circumscribed by the courts.

The fact remains, however, that professionals in the law find themselves increasingly involved in challenges to generally accepted (even if specifically unfair) social practices. Although the various establishments that engage in or manage those practices might consider that litigation is preferable to demonstrations, they are more likely to feel that lawyers are exploiting dissatisfactions better handled by informal processes of conflict resolution—or simply overlooked.

V

Professionals can respond to these three limitations on their traditional role—imposed by the proliferation of knowledge, by the growth of bureaucratic institutions, and by the spread of democratic ideas—by retreating behind the walls of established privilege. But those walls are not likely to stand for very long. And there are indications that professionals are accepting, with more or less good grace, changes in their institutional arrangements that should make it possible for them to adapt to the new conditions on the professional role. These changes seem to fall into five broad areas: the ways in which people are selected for professional roles; the ways in which professional services are offered to the public; the governance of the professional corps; the allocation of national resources to the professions; and the content of professional services themselves.

Selection is clearly no longer a matter within the exclusive jurisdiction of those already admitted to the profession. Nor is it enough that everyone have an equal opportunity to demonstrate whether he or she can meet the entrance qualifications set by the profession. Not only must there be room for people whose ability to meet professional standards is hard to recognize at the outset; but there is a public interest in the nature of those professional standards. If medical schools choose their students primarily on the basis of their ability to assimilate organic chemistry, in an extraordinarily competitive field, without a great deal of concern for their (admittedly nonquantifiable) qualities as human beings, it is not surprising that the rising generation of physicians may not demonstrate to a high degree the qualities of compassion and human understanding that are still important in the practice of medicine. And if medical residency positions are established and maintained on the basis of the interests of teaching physicians, rather than the needs of the profession for the various specialties, it is not surprising that there will be a considerable maldistribution of specialties, skewing toward those specialties that have the greatest scientific interest, or that hold the greatest promise of high remuneration. The idea of lay participation in the allocation of medical residencies is just beginning to take hold within the profession. The idea of lay participation in the formulation of the medical-school admissions process is still over the horizon. The idea of lay participation in determining the qualifications for admission to practice has not yet been broached. Resistance to all these ideas, on the basis of "political influence," will undoubtedly continue to be vigorous within the profession. And the concern about political influence is not unjustified. But it cannot long continue to be an excuse to maintain the shaping of the admission processes as an exclusive professional preserve.

The particular problems in other professions add other dimensions to the public interest. How should hospital nurses and nurse practitioners be recruited, and to what extent should there be a professional ladder or lattice within the health professions, so that people can move from one level of skill to a higher and more complex level? How much apprenticeship should be required of architects or engineers before they are licensed, and should the apprenticeship requirement also be applied to lawyers? Where should the lines be drawn between the work of lawyers and paralegals, or between physicians and physicians' assistants? And more specifically, who should be permitted to write prescriptions, or to try cases, and under what kinds of restrictions?

These last questions spill over into the area of how professional services are offered to the public. It has been a convention that professionals do not engage in price competition. Professional advertisements, when they are permitted at all under codes of ethics established by the professions themselves, may not mention prices. Professionals are under no obligation to state their fees in advance, and clients or patients are often reluctant to inquire. Formal qualifications may be advertised, but clients are expected to find out about professionals' competence by discreet inquiry. All this is changing, however, and is likely to change more rapidly. The American Bar Association is revising its rules on advertising, and is under pressure from some of the more enlightened local bar associations to move further and faster. The recent Supreme Court decision removing a judicial ban on lawyer advertising will undoubtedly accelerate the process. Standard fee scales fixed by bar associations have been successfully attacked in court. Group medical and legal practices are actively soliciting business.

It is well within the memory of living people that physicians were denied hospital privileges for joining in a prepaid group practice. It is still grounds for disciplinary action in most jurisdictions for a lawyer to point out publicly that he has special qualifications in, say, antitrust litigation or divorce actions. But the direction of change is clear. The next generation of professionals will be competing openly for their clientele, on the basis of full disclosure of their qualifications and their charges, subject only to requirements perhaps more insistent on complete honesty than those imposed on mere merchants, but imposing few if any more restrictions based on professional ethics or good taste than are applied by Macy's and Gimbels. Indeed, as the doctrine of caveat emptor is gradually replaced by a stricter standard of liability for nonprofessionals, the standards for professionals and nonprofessionals may be tending to converge. Interestingly, however, the letters column of the *ABA Journal* still contains communications arguing that "from a moral standpoint there is only a slight difference of degree between competition by advertising and competition by procuring prostitutes for their clients."[1]

When the first legal services programs were organized in New York, under the aegis of the federal antipoverty program, the courts insisted that the governance of the programs be entirely under the control of members of the bar. But of the 20 board members of Community Action for Legal Services, the legal-service umbrella organization, six to eight are presently laymen. Within the legal profession, the grievance process by which clients' complaints about lawyers are adjudicated has traditionally been in the hands of bar groups. But a recent report of the Association of the Bar of the City of New York concluded that the system for self-discipline should include public participation.

One of the increasingly important ways in which consumers—clients and patients—influence the delivery of professional services is through their grievances as expressed in malpractice suits. Whether the great and growing dollar volume of malpractice judgments is explained as resulting primarily from the increasing complexity of professional problems, the increasing depersonalization of professional-client relationships, or the increasing litigiousness of the public, it is clearly making professional services a good deal more costly, both in malpractice insurance premiums and in "defensive" professional practice, for example, a physician ordering unnecessary X-rays in order to protect himself against a charge that he may have overlooked something. Nor is malpractice litigation confined to medicine and health care. It even extends to claims, in lawsuits by disgruntled students, that educational institutions are not doing their job properly.

The future of malpractice litigation is unsettled. Several study commissions are examining the medical malpractice problem. Proposals in the wind include substituting some kind of no-fault system, comparable to workmen's compensation insurance, but that would be extremely difficult to administer in view of the volume of potentially compensable claims and the difficulties of defining what should be compensable. Another proposal would channel all medical malpractice claims into the hospital or other health-care institution, so as to relieve the individual physician of the burden. In any event, the current flood of litigation is a symptom of real dissatisfaction among the lay public with the way in which professional services are offered, and of increasing effort to bring some judgments to bear on professional performance beyond those of peers within the profession.

By and large, the governance of the professions is still in their own hands, and each profession looks after its own. But the portents are clear. Whether it is called public participation or consumer representation, laymen will have a voice and a vote—perhaps even a majority vote—in how the professions conduct their affairs, not only in how people are admitted to the professions, and how services are offered, but also in the definition and adjudication of unprofessional conduct, and in the maintenance of professional standards. The professional will still be the expert on the state of the art, but not on questions of moral standards or norms of social behavior. On questions of fact, his testimony will be determinative, but he will no longer be entitled to the administrative equivalent of benefit of clergy.

Some groups of professionals have substantially opted out of their professional role by opting for unionization. Collective bargaining for wages and conditions of employment may produce greater material rewards vis-à-vis large employers, like government—as is the case for example with medical residents. But it may also limit both the individual freedom and some of the psychic rewards that go with professional status. At the time when university teachers were debating unionization in a state university system, the student newspaper ran an editorial which referred to the professoriate as "our employees."

Where the professional and the society at large find themselves in direct confrontation is over the allocation of resources. So long as the surgeon required only a scalpel and a basin, he could supply them himself without burdening the community. But when a surgeon needs an operating room equipped for open-heart surgery, and a team of assistants, the burden on community resources can be considerable. And when those needs are replicated throughout the health-care professions, they take a larger share of the gross national product than national defense. It is no wonder that the consumer and the government both have a powerful interest in the allocation of resources to health care. The regional health services planning agencies established under the Health Planning Act of 1974 call for a majority of consumer representation on each local board—a board that has veto power over expansion of medical facilities, even when the expansion is proposed to be financed (in the first instance) by the medical professionals themselves. Of course a good deal of the public interest in the cost of health care arises because a large share of that cost is borne by the taxpayer, either directly by paying hospital and doctor bills for Medicare and Medicaid patients, or indirectly by subsidizing auxiliary health-care activities: education, research, public-health measures, public-hospital deficits, and the like.

Other professions—the military always excepted—make less exigent or less effective demands for supporting resources from the public purse. The public infrastructure that supports the legal profession—the civil courts and the criminal justice system, including courts, corrections, and law-enforcement authorities—is notoriously underfunded. The church is constitutionally separated from the state, although there have been some difficulties in tracing the serpentine wall that separates them, and the church does benefit from tax exemptions. Professional education for substantially all professions is available at public expense, although in varying quantities, at public colleges and universities, but the cost is relatively low.

All the professions, however, are in trouble with their clients over the kinds of resource commitments that are often involved in accepting professional advice, and these conflicts emerge in a variety of ways. Every professional is painfully aware that his client has limited resources. But most are inclined to give priority to their own recommendations in the allocation of those resources, or at least to offer a single solution within (even if at the high end of) the client's price range, whether it is an architect's house design, or a lawyer's estate plan. Clients, on the other hand, are increasingly restive with these arrangements, and are more and more inclined to exercise their traditional prerogative of making their own cost-benefit calculations across professional lines, or even within a single professional formulation. They are asking, "What if I spent 20 percent less (or more) on the problem that you are helping me to resolve; what would I get for it?" or "How might we rearrange the elements of your proposed solution, to devote more resources and reap greater benefits from one part of the plan, and less resources with presumably less benefits from another part?"

Professionals will find themselves more and more obliged to respond to this kind of question, and in doing so, they will be making significant changes in the content of the actual services they render.

In a world where useful knowledge and institutional bureaucracies are both proliferating, the professional is tempted to respond either by narrowing his area of expertise to a manageable subspecialty a good deal smaller than the problems of any client, or by expanding his area of control to an administrable set of human problems a good deal larger than the expertise of any professional. In the first case he runs the danger of becoming a professional's professional, unable to apply his professional skills directly to deal with real-life situations; in the second case he runs the danger of becoming a professional manager, unable to draw directly on substantive professional knowledge. In the first case his knowledge is too limited in scope to be more than partially applicable to human problems; in the second case his knowledge is too limited in depth to bring the full benefits of professionalism to bear on human problems. In the first case the professional is emphasizing his knowledge-gathering faculties, at the expense of his capacity to respond to clients; in the second case he is emphasizing his responsibility to clients, at the expense of his role as a person of learning. In the first case, the professional who deals with individual clients may become callous or indifferent to the client's needs; in the second case he may unjustifiably invade the client's privacy in a manipulative way.

But the professional cannot afford to choose either partial solution. To limit one's professional advice to one's area of expertise is to fail to respond to the client as a whole human being. To limit one's professional role to conveying other people's expertise is to fail to respond to the holistic quality of human knowledge. The physician must apply all the relevant medical knowledge and technique to the problems of the particular patient; but he must have more than an indirect understanding of what medicine has to offer, derived from his own exploration of at least one medical specialty, in order to apply that knowledge effectively. The lawyer must understand the needs of his client; but he must have a feel for the processes of the law, derived both from direct experience and from some historical perspective. The architect must design the building to meet all the needs of its users; but his design must grow out of a direct experience and understanding of the aesthetic and social traditions of architecture. The economist must understand—or try to understand—the impact of the business cycle on unemployment; but he must also understand that the roots of structural unemployment are as much social and cultural as economic.

VI

To meet these competing obligations will be increasingly difficult in a society that is becoming more and more knowledge oriented, more and more bureaucratic, and more and more participatory. But the professional who cannot maintain both capacities will inevitably lose the special place that professionals in American society enjoy today. As a mere technician, or as a mere manager, the future professional will not be accorded the respect that now goes with professional status, because he or she will not be seen as focusing a unique set of skills on the unique problems of a particular individual client, or client group. If individual clients become interchangeable in the eyes of professionals, then individual professionals will become interchangeable in the eyes of clients.

In the end, it is the human qualities of the professional that will determine his future role. To the extent that the aspirations of individual professionals continue to encompass both the accretion of human knowledge, and its application to particular problems, each professional remains a unique resource. The double motivation that leads a person to want to make an individual contribution to the stream of knowledge, and also to apply that knowledge for the benefit of other human beings strikes a responsive chord in the individuals or groups for whose benefit it is applied, so that they can see their professional advisers as whole human beings, relating all their talents to their clients' needs.

For the professionals themselves there will be increasing tensions between the two roles. On the one hand, they will have to learn more and more to apply detailed knowledge from one smaller area by analogy to other areas, to use sophisticated knowledge banks with sophisticated judgment, to apply statistical measures of success and failure to norms of professional performance, to consult fellow experts without giving up their overall responsibility to the client. On the other hand, they will have to learn to work more effectively with groups of clients, and as members of teams of professionals. They will have to learn to listen more attentively and to explain their diagnoses and their strategies more fully to their colleagues (including colleagues on the other side of professional boundaries), to their clients, and to the general public. And they will have to find new ways, not yet dreamed of, to live with their dual roles.

If professionals can continue to maintain that tension between their obligations to their clients, and their obligations to the intellectual tradition of which they are a part, they will continue to be special people in any future American society.

REFERENCE
[1]*ABA Journal* (November 1976): 1390, Letters column, letter from Hyman Diamond.

PAUL STARR

Medicine and the Waning of Professional Sovereignty

IMAGES OF THE FUTURE are usually caricatures of the present. They inflate some recognizable features of contemporary life to extravagant proportions, and out of fear or hope respond to every vagary of historical experience, as if it were a sign of destiny. In America, during the past decade, the future has changed shape altogether. Not long ago Americans generally believed that their society was in an irreversible ascendancy toward greater affluence; then they abruptly rediscovered the problem of scarcity and the insecurities of power and came to imagine themselves at the beginning of a long historical decline. Intellectuals, as much as others, have shared in this reversal of outlook; the more radical generally identify the collapse around the corner as economic and ecological, while the more conservative lament the downfall of civility, self-restraint, and the democratic idea. All this dark pessimism has arisen, remarkably enough, at a time when there has been no commensurate downturn in American society. Despite the commotion of aborted revolts and stalled reactions, politics and culture in America—status relations excepted[1]—are not greatly different from what they were ten or fifteen years ago. Changes in the conditions of material life and in the structure of social institutions have been much slower and less extreme than the oscillations in mood and outlook.

Like the larger society, medicine has suffered a stunning loss of confidence. It used to be the habit on public occasions to celebrate the miracles of medical science and anticipate that new research would bring still more triumphs over dread disease. Then in the last decade the economic and moral problems of medicine displaced scientific progress at the center of public attention. Enormous increases in cost have come to seem ever more certain; corresponding improvements in health ever more doubtful. In intellectual and political circles, a new agnosticism has descended on medical care, as its critics, conservative as well as radical, observe that compared to the influence of environment and behavior, medicine can do little to make people healthy. As the 1960s began, the premise of social policy, as well as popular understanding, was that America needed and would benefit from more medical care—more hospitals, more physicians and other personnel, and more elaborate medical technology. Most of the major federal programs were then devoted to augmenting the country's medical resources. More recently the prevailing assumptions have reversed, as those who shape policy seek ways to reduce the number of hospital beds, slow down the introduction of medical technology, and cut off a potential glut of

175

physicians projected for the 1980s. In a short time, we seem to have gone from too little medical care to too much, from stubborn shortages to irrepressible excess, without ever having passed through happy sufficiency. (In fact, we have long had both shortages and surpluses in medicine—in different places.)

Even some notable medical advances, which would have inspired nothing but grateful wonder twenty years ago, now seem primarily to occasion dour estimates of future expense. Nor do we seem as happy anymore to have the powers that medicine yields. Medicine often raises previously uncontrolled aspects of life to the level of social choice, and instead of giving satisfaction, endows us with some life-and-death powers we might prefer to do without. A genius for technical sophistication may someday, with luck, make it virtually impossible for patients in hospitals to expire, except by someone's (perhaps their own) conscious choice. Professionals already must make more of the "decisions for death," as the pediatrician Raymond Duff calls them, that nature alone once made. So rather than a liberating and life-giving force, medicine now appears to many as a financial onus, to some as a moral burden, and to still others as perhaps the archetypal modern form of domination—of man over nature, and of men over each other.

Most medical care, of course, proceeds unaffected by these shifting perceptions. As in the society, the changes of mood and opinion can be violent while the pace of institutional change is glacial. American medicine today contains a paradox. Outwardly, its institutions, prosperous and authoritative, show imposing strength, yet their social and economic structure is fundamentally unstable, and long-standing assumptions that have governed their operation are in danger of breaking down. A fundamental intellectual reassessment of medicine is taking place; a sense of impending change fills the air. Between 1960 and 1976, the nation's expenditures on medical care rose from $25.9 to $139.3 billion, or from 5.2 to 8.6 percent of the gross national product (GNP). Recent estimates put the comparable 1981 figures at $264.4 billion, or 10.2 percent of GNP.[2] Accelerated growth of this kind, relative to total national wealth, cannot be indefinitely sustained. Controlling costs will mean redrawing the "contract," if you will, between the medical profession and the society, with new terms much less favorable to the doctors. This is already beginning to happen. A variety of forces—political, economic, cultural—are converging to limit the authority of practicing physicians and the autonomy the profession has enjoyed from the discipline of the market and the state. Haltingly, medicine is approaching the end of an era whose signal characteristic has been the sovereignty of the private physician.

I

It is simply not true, as myth might have it, that physicians have always occupied positions of honor, comfort, and authority ever since the first medicine man had the good fortune to recite an incantation immediately before his patient's spontaneous recovery. M. I. Finley notes that in Rome during the Empire physicians were primarily "slaves, freedmen and foreigners" and that medicine was considered a very low-grade occupation. Physicians in eighteenth-century England, while ranking above the lowlier surgeons and

apothecaries, stood only at the margin of the gentry, struggling for the patronage of the upper classes in the hope of acquiring enough wealth to buy an estate
and a title. In nineteenth and early twentieth-century France, as Theodore Zeldin points out, doctors were mostly impecunious, and the successful among
them, conscious that medicine was an inadequate claim to status, pursued an
ideal of general culture rather than mere professional accomplishment. In
America before the twentieth century, medicine long occupied an inferior place
among the professions. "In all of our American colleges," a professional journal
commented bitterly in 1869, "medicine has ever been and is now, the most
despised of all the professions which liberally-educated men are expected to
enter." Although a few eminent doctors made handsome fortunes, the majority
before 1900 could barely scrape together a respectable living. Even today in the
Soviet Union, the average earnings of physicians are less than three-quarters of
the average industrial wage; coincidentally, 70 percent of the doctors are wom-
en.[3]

America today could hardly offer a more striking contrast. Physicians here
now earn the highest average income of any occupation. During this century,
especially for the last generation, medicine has embodied the professional ideal
in American culture. It has commanded faith and ambition, influence and resources. As one of the last enclaves of the self-employed, the medical profession
has until recently held undisputed control over its own work. And as the only
emissaries from the distant world of science that most people ordinarily encounter, doctors hold a singular place in popular belief. In nation-wide opinion polls,
conducted in 1947 and 1963, "physician" ranked as the second most desired job,
next to Justice of the U.S. Supreme Court and ahead of Congressman, member
of the President's cabinet, lawyer, priest, architect, and every other occupational category.

The position of the medical profession in America rests, I would argue, on
its relation to three institutional spheres: the cultural order, the market, and the
state. The cultural authority of medicine—that is, the profession's ability to
define and interpret the nature of reality and human experience—has expanded
as medicine has embraced more aspects of life, and grown more firm as people
have lost confidence in the adequacy of their own senses and understanding and
in their ability to treat their own problems. The profession's authority also
underlies the economic operation of the medical system, as most decisions turn
on the judgment—the authorization—of physicians. What the doctor defines as
medically warranted for the treatment of patients, not only the family but the
society now feels obliged to provide. Insurance companies and government programs will pay for medical services, but only as long as a physician authorizes
them. The habit has been not to question professional judgments. One of the
many anomalies of medical economics is that "demand," normally set by consumers, is in medicine largely determined by the producer, the physician, who
decides whether hospitalization, prescriptions, tests, surgery, referrals, and further visits are needed. Partly because the supply of services, as well as the
demand, has been constrained by the producers—by means of licensing boards,
limits on medical education, and concerted resistance against institutional alternatives to fee-for-service practice—the profession has been in a position to exert
substantial "market power." Rather than being ruled by market forces, Ameri-

can physicians have been able to control them. Roughly since the turn of the century, they have been free of the intense competitiveness that formerly plagued medical practice. "Consumers," ill organized, have achieved almost no countervailing power.

The third bulwark of the profession's position, besides cultural authority and market power, has been its capacity to guide the policies of the state in directions favorable to its interests. In the late nineteenth century, when it was seeking protective licensing laws, the medical profession successfully called for interventionist policies; once having achieved its objectives, it shifted to a principled defense of free enterprise, successfully opposing health insurance as "socialized medicine."

It is symptomatic of the declining political influence of the profession that its old ideological appeals no longer work today. The philippics against socialized medicine have all but disappeared; now rather than debating the principle of health insurance, people debate the mechanics. The American Medical Association (AMA) is a shadow of its former self; since Medicare, it has been unable to stop a long line of federal legislation it considers inimical to physicians' interests. The profession has even lost control of the vocabulary of policy-making. Instead of "compulsory" health insurance, people now speak of "national" health insurance, the compulsory aspect having totally faded from public discussion.

But the AMA's loss of political influence is itself a reflection of the changing structure of the market. The enormous growth of the medical industry over the past two decades has thrown up interests at least as powerful as private physicians. Hospitals, medical school centers, and the insurance industry now count heavily in the medical system; and even though doctors make most of the vital decisions in medical schools and hospitals, and the hospitals virtually control Blue Cross, the interests of the corporate organizations are not the same as those of the profession. To solve their own financial difficulties, the medical schools and hospitals have often invited federal spending, instead of resisting it. The principle of public financing was not imposed on them against their will; it was established partly by their own efforts. But the more the state becomes involved in financing health services, the more pressure it feels to rationalize the system to reduce costs. And so, by an almost irresistible logic, the development of the medical market generates the forces that threaten to transform it.

But even though the medical profession has been losing its domination of the market and government policy, its cultural authority remains fundamentally secure. However irritated Americans may be with their doctors, they are not likely to dispense with them in their need for relief from uncertainty and pain. Yet as the rise in malpractice litigation has made apparent, the public harbors a great deal of unorganized hostility toward the profession. People may even be more generally skeptical of medical authority, although this is hard to confirm. According to a Harris poll, the proportion of the public having a "great deal of confidence" in medicine declined to 42 percent in July 1976, down from 73 percent in 1966.[4] More significantly, the cultural authority of medicine no longer appears to be expanding. In treating compulsions, like drug dependence and alcoholism, or in rehabilitating criminals, the success of medicine has not been notorious. There seems to be a backlash in these areas against the "medical model," encouraged by a desire to reassert the moral character of behavior. And in the middle classes, there is a widely felt urge to "demedicalize" certain aspects of life, on the grounds that medical control has brought with it a cold impersonality. Childbirth, in particular, is being removed from purely medical supervision; there is a parallel urge to make dying more humane. But these are movements that medicine can absorb; they may even help relieve physicians of some difficult responsibilities.

The more serious problems for the profession are those of political economy. If doctors continue to be culturally authoritative, but lose some of their economic and political power, will they be able to retain their high status and income? There is no certainty that they will. The medical profession owes its special position in America to particular historical developments. Its strong position, in relation to the culture, the market, and the state, goes back only to the beginning of this century. And the professional prerogatives established then are now in the process of breaking down, as they did once before.

II

Four critical periods stand out in the development of medical care in America.

The first, beginning in the late colonial era around 1760, saw the formation of the first medical institutions. Out of previously isolated doctors, many of whom pursued other occupations while practicing medicine, a profession took shape as a distinct corporate body, and sought to bring to America the institutional patterns in professional licensing, training, and organization then prevailing in England. The first licensure act calling for the certification of physicians was passed in New York City in 1760, the first medical school was established in Philadelphia in 1765, and the first provincial medical society was organized in New Jersey in 1766. This initial movement toward professionalization was the work of a small medical elite in the larger cities, but the institutions it created gave an emerging profession the capacity to reproduce and enlarge itself, and to reduce its dependence on Europe.

Then in the second quarter of the nineteenth century, during the Jacksonian era, as traditional sources of authority and power were challenged throughout American society, the early efforts to build a strong and exclusive profession broke down. In the 1830s and 1840s, state legislatures repealed the medical licensing laws they had passed in the early years of the republic. While medical schools proliferated, especially in the western states, their standards declined, as nearly all of them became proprietary operations run by their professors for their own profit. The American Medical Association was formed in 1847 in response to the multiplication of medical colleges and the decline of licensing, ʰut for its first half century it remained weak and ineffective, preoccupied with ınternal squabbles.

Medical practitioners split into warring sects—homeopaths, eclectics, hydropaths, and regulars—each denouncing the others' modes of treatment as incompetent and murderous. The profession lost its coherence and its ability to command public deference and respect. Two complementary developments aggravated its situation. A general assault on "privileged monopolies" made the medical profession one of its targets, in the conviction that the arcane knowledge of doctors, like that of lawyers and priests, was no more than mystification. At the same time, within medicine, prominent physicians raised severe doubts as to the validity of known therapies; a current of professional thought maintained that doctors had hardly any remedies of value. This "therapeutic nihilism" within medicine (which was, in fact, entirely justified) echoed the radical doubts abroad in the society, and helped deprive the profession of the authority of self-confidence.

The third critical period, beginning around 1870 and coming to full flower between 1890 and 1920, saw the rise of medicine to its modern status and authority. The achievements of the Progressive era were threefold. Aided by the genuine advances of medical science, the physician's claim on belief was greatly strengthened. By means of licensing laws and restrictions on medical education, the profession secured control over entry into the market. And through the defeat of government health insurance and the restriction of public health activities, it deterred intervention by the state in the financing and control of medical care.

Changes in social structure and the organization of medical practice enabled the transformation to take place. The key developments in medicine were the spread of hospitals and the growth of specialization, which greatly increased interdependence among physicians. Before the late nineteenth century, doctors could practice medicine almost entirely on their own; they had every incentive to distinguish their own brand of practice and to seek public favor by denigrating their colleagues. But as they came to have more need of hospital facilities and patient referrals, their dependence on each other's good will increased. Toward the end of the nineteenth century, the sectarian antagonisms in medicine abated, and the profession began to assert its common interests. The general rise of corporations, trusts, and labor unions encouraged doctors and other groups to develop their own associations and secure legislative protection by licensing.

At the same time, scientific achievements not only improved the efficacy of treatment, particularly of surgery, but also helped restore a sense of the *legitimate complexity* of medicine, which had been lost in the Jacksonian period. In the 1870s and 1880s, after an interlude of a half-century, state legislatures began to restore medical licensing laws, though initially in a weak form. In 1901, the AMA reorganized, turning a hodgepodge of local and state medical societies into a closely knit national federation. Within ten years, its membership grew from 10 to 50 percent of the profession. As state medical societies became more influential, they won stronger licensing statutes, requiring longer and more expensive training to enter the profession. Under the new requirements for laboratories and clinical facilities, medical education became unprofitable and the commercial schools closed. A much-celebrated 1910 report from the Carnegie Foundation, written by the educator Abraham Flexner, reinforced this movement, which was already under way at the time the report appeared.

With the closing of the proprietary colleges, the number of medical graduates dropped sharply, from 5,747 to 2,529 a year between 1904 and 1922. This greatly reduced competition among practitioners. In the same period, two technological developments—the spread of the telephone and of mechanized transportation—drastically reduced the cost of contacts between doctors and patients, and enabled physicians to shift most of their practice from their patients' homes to their own offices, where at regularly scheduled hours they could see many more patients a day than formerly. Medical practice became much more remunerative. Between the turn of the century and the late 1920s, physicians' average incomes appear to have increased sharply, climbing to four times the average income of the gainfully employed, roughly where they have remained ever since.[5]

We are now in the midst of the fourth critical period in the development of medicine. Roughly since 1965, though the main developments have their antecedents earlier, medical care has been in the throes of what editorialists and politicians have endlessly labeled the "health care crisis." The rhetoric of crisis is not innocently descriptive; it is meant to persuade the public—not without reason—that medicine is in trouble and that major changes in its organization must be entertained. Typically, the complaint is that there is no health care "system"; half a century earlier, few would have supposed that such a thing ought to exist. Yesterday's pluralism has become today's disorganization. Implicit in that changed perception is an immense shift in attitudes, brought about by the continuing pressure that the rise in medical costs is putting on government budgets, corporate profits, and the take-home pay of union members. That is why the sense of crisis and the proposals for change have come from corporate and union officials alike, and why conservative political leaders, like Richard Nixon, have taken up the rhetoric of crisis with the same urgency as liberals, like Edward Kennedy. In a sense, the current crisis that the American medical profession faces is that its views and its interests are no longer being defended by the economic and political leadership of the society.

In some respects, contemporary developments resemble the Jacksonian era, in that the threats to the legitimacy of professional authority are intellectual as well as political. Just as serious doubts were raised in the nineteenth century about the value of medicine, so today a revived "therapeutic nihilism" questions the net effectiveness of the medical system as a whole.[6] Now, as then, professional prerogatives established in an earlier period are being challenged by egalitarian demands to democratize medical knowledge and to open up access to the ranks of practitioners. As in the 1830s, the medical profession today is losing its grip on state policy and the structure of the market. But the pattern of events is quite different.

The internal redistribution of power. With the rise of medicine as the second largest industry in the society, there has been a shift in the balance of power from the medical societies to corporate organizations, particularly to the hospitals, medical schools, and insurance and planning bureaucracies. The American Hospital Association, Blue Cross, the American Association of Medical Colleges, and the Health Insurance Association of America are now formidable rivals of the AMA. Even among doctors, the AMA's strength has declined, as physicians identify more with their own specialty than with the profession as a whole.[7]

The extension of citizenship. Entitlement to health care, while not yet universal, has grown, as the idea of citizenship is extended to include entitlements to social welfare as well as to political rights. Whether health care should be treated as a matter of right—in the same sense as, for example, a person's right to counsel when accused of a crime—is a thorny question. At present, no such right legally exists, but the society is gradually coming to act as if it did.

The growing centrality of the state. As a result of both the extention of entitlements and the demands of medical institutions, the government has been drawn into the financing of health services. Public funds now account for more than 40 percent of health expenditures. As its investment has risen, the federal government has assumed an enlarged role in making sure that its money is well spent. The federal budget and federal regulations increasingly become the arena where conflicts in medical care are fought out.

The breakdown of assumptions and the conservative assimilation of reform. Social policy in medicine used to assume not only that more medical care would improve the nation's health, but also that expanded health insurance coverage could be grafted on to the existing fee-for-service system, and that most decisions could be left to individual practitioners. Many who advocated widening access to medical care by national health insurance were especially anxious to reassure physicians that even though the benefits of medicine would be extended, its organization would be preserved. This confidence has been shaken. Even among conservatives in recent years, fiscal prudence has brought an increased willingness to contemplate previously unthinkable changes in the organization of medicine. There have been simultaneous attempts to introduce more regulation and more competition into medicine; so far, the effects have been negligible, and at times at cross purposes, but these measures have yet to run their course.

The growing power of corporate institutions and the federal government, the extension of the idea of citizenship, the discarding of old assumptions and the assimilation of reform—these various developments all have their counterparts in other areas of American society. They are now just lurching forward in American medicine, later and more slowly than elsewhere.

III

Medical care has long seemed to exemplify the ways in which America abstained from the dominant patterns of political development and social policy in the West. For some time the United States has been the only major nation in the advanced industrial world without a national health program. Perhaps the repeated defeat of universal health insurance here was a reflection of an individualistic and heterogeneous society, where the roots of mutual social obligation ran less deep than in Europe; or perhaps only the result of the weakness of socialist parties and labor unions, which were never enough of a threat to the political order for health insurance to be needed as a way to preempt their appeals. Probably the biggest factor, at least the most immediate, was the effective resistance mounted by American doctors, whose political influence, status, and prosperity had risen with the growth of the AMA and the changes in medical education that occurred before the first campaign for health insurance around 1915. Health insurance was the only one of the four major components of European social insurance—workmen's compensation, unemployment insurance, and old-age pensions were the others—that had not been enacted in the United States by the late 1930s. Until quite recently in America, the state played no central part in financing and organizing medical care.

Instead, the government stood at the periphery of the medical system, its role restricted to functions that did not interfere with private interests. In addition to public-health services, the state provided medical care directly to a few groups, which had some special claim on the public interest or no money to pay for treatment on their own. Federal hospitals served merchant seamen, military personnel, and veterans. State governments maintained mental hospitals and tuberculosis sanitariums, providing for patients who had no resources for long-term and custodial care. County and municipal governments maintained hospitals and dispensaries for the poor who were unable to afford private treatment for more acute and episodic problems. These institutions were kept on a short leash. Physicians and upper-class social reformers were anxious to curb what used to be called "hospital and dispensary abuse"—that is, free treatment of patients who really could afford to pay their own way. Similarly, when public health agencies became involved in vaccination campaigns, free treatment of school children, or other efforts that local physicians felt might infringe on their source of livelihood, their representatives fought to make sure that the proper limits to government activity were observed. The state was supposed to plug the gaps in the private sector, not to pay for medical services for the public at large.

Even though the New Deal greatly changed the relationship between state and society in America, it had little impact in medicine. The failure to incorporate medical care in social security proved to be a fateful choice, opening the way for the rise of a private health insurance industry. Insurance financing developed two special features. It emphasized hospital insurance, separate from insurance for other medical care, and it was arranged primarily at the workplace as a fringe benefit of employment. The first Blue Cross hospital insurance plans, beginning in 1929, were organized by the hospitals themselves as they searched for a more stable source of funds than out-of-pocket payments by patients and charitable contributions, which had slumped with the Depression. Opposition from the AMA prevented the plans from offering general medical insurance, which the doctors feared might lead to controls over their fees. Later the medical societies organized Blue Shield plans, under their own control, to cover physicians' services. Commercial insurance companies also entered the field, and by 1951 their share of the market exceeded that of the "Blues."

The federal government indirectly fostered the development of private health insurance plans. During World War II, while wage-and-price controls were in effect, unions turned increasingly to health insurance and other fringe benefits as a way of eluding limits on wage increases. Congress also encouraged private employee health funds by making payments into the plans exempt from income taxes. As inflation and growth in real wages pushed workers into higher marginal tax brackets, their incentive to take income in health-insurance benefits rather than cash increased. Moreover, as medical costs rose, health insurance became virtually a necessity, at least for anyone with an income or assets to protect. The part of the population carrying insurance against hospital expenses grew from 50 to 70 percent between 1950 and the early 1960s, and to

80 percent by the mid-1970s. In recent years, the main growth in health insurance has come from expanded coverage in other areas. Between 1962 and 1974, the proportion of the civilian population covered for prescribed drugs rose from 26 to 67 percent; for X-ray and laboratory examinations, from 35 to 73 percent; for nursing home care, from 3 to 33 percent; for dental care, from 0.5 to 16 percent. With this broadening of coverage, the proportion of total health expenditures paid through health insurance has steadily increased from 12 percent in 1950 to 28 percent ten years later and to 40 percent by 1974. But despite the growth, coverage remains uneven, with numerous exclusions, limitations, and cost-sharing ("coinsurance") provisions. Insurance pays 77 percent of hospital costs, but only half the cost of physicians' services and less than 10 percent of other expenses.[8]

I mention these various statistics because the patterns in the growth of private insurance have had a profound effect on medical care in America. It has given medical institutions, particularly hospitals, immense financial security. Because funds for hospital care are taken out of paychecks before families ever see them, consumers have little opportunity to cut down spending for institutional medical care in a recession. The bulk of funds diverted to the medical system are safe from the vicissitudes of the economy. Furthermore, health insurance increases total spending for medical services by reducing cost-consciousness among both patients and physicians at the time that medical services are provided. If a doctor prefers to be 99 percent sure of a diagnosis by adding a new battery of tests, instead of 98 percent sure, there is little to discourage him from doing so. Neither he nor the patient is likely to pay for it. Unnecessary services, provided simply to recover from the insurance companies, are probably the smaller part of the problem; the greater costs come from paying increasing amounts of money for diminishing improvements in treatment. But so long as hospitals and physicians are paid for individual services, they have an incentive to multiply the number of services and the total cost, without weighing the relationship of costs to benefits. Finally, the insurance system has the additional effect of providing a buffer between the employee groups that purchase medical care and the medical institutions that provide it, preventing any direct bargaining over the quality, cost, and accessibility of services. The general function of insurance for the medical system has been to insulate it from recessions, cost constraints, and public dissatisfaction.

The expansionary tendencies of private insurance have also been reinforced by public policy. After World War II, the federal government entered a new phase in its relation to medical care. While national health insurance was defeated once again under Truman, the government began providing aid for hospital construction (through the Hill-Burton program) and for medical research and training (through the National Institutes of Health and the National Science Foundation). The role of the state in medicine had shifted from peripheral services to *complementary investment*. Over the next two decades, the federal government had as its primary commitment in medicine the development of facilities, scientific innovation, and human capital. In 1950, amendments to the Social Security Act provided that the federal government would share with the states part of the cost of reimbursing private institutions for medical services to recipients of public assistance. This program was the embryo of Medicaid.

The year 1965 was a turning point in the relationship between medicine and government, as it was in so many other areas of foreign and domestic policy. In the wake of Johnson's landslide victory over Goldwater, Congress finally approved government health insurance for the aged (Medicare) as well as expanding federal assistance to the states in financing medical care for the poor (Medicaid). Once again, the major private interests were accommodated. Physicians were promised that no changes would be made in the organization of medical care, hospitals were provided reimbursement on the basis of their individual costs, and Blue Cross and other private insurers were given roles as fiscal intermediaries to process claims and make payments. Far from expanding the state at the expense of the private sector, Medicaid and Medicare proved to be a boon to private physicians, whose incomes increased; to private hospitals, whose bad debts were cut; to profit-making nursing homes, whose business soared; and to Blue Cross, which received a "public service charge" on top of expenses that looked every bit like a profit.

For medical care, the Great Society, unlike the New Deal, was a major break with the past, signaling a turn in federal policy from complementary investment in research and construction to the direct financing of services. But the separate identities of Medicare and Medicaid perpetuated a traditional distinction in American social policy between approved social insurance and disapproved public assistance. As social insurance, Medicare acquired a definite respectability, like social security pensions, while Medicaid, as public assistance, acquired an unmistakable stigma, like "welfare." Nonetheless, Medicaid did eliminate the charity status of many poor patients in hospitals, entitling them to treatment in semiprivate rooms, where they had more privacy than in the large open wards that used to be reserved for the poor. The architecture of hospitals reproduces the history of class relations in a particularly vivid form. When hospitals were strictly for the poor, the open ward, devoid of privacy, predominated. As the rich began to enter hospitals in the late nineteenth century, private rooms increased. The spread of semiprivate rooms was the correlate of the triumph of the middle class, and its extension to the poor has been symptomatic of an improvement in their position.

Medicaid and Medicare resulted in some clear progress toward equal access to medical care. Before their introduction, the poor had lower rates of physician visits and hospital treatment than higher income groups; afterward, the poor actually exceeded other groups in their use of medical services. In 1964, members of poor families averaged 4.3 visits to a doctor, while members of families who were not poor averaged 4.6 visits. By 1973, physician visits by the poor had risen to 5.6 a year, while visits by other persons stood only at 4.9. Yet here one must enter several important qualifications. A great deal of evidence indicates that the poor have more severe health problems than other groups; many people are poor precisely because they are disabled and have been unable to work. Higher rates of utilization are to be expected; some evidence suggests that relative to levels of disability, use of medical services actually remains lower among the poor. Second, despite the aggregate patterns, among two age groups—children and the aged—the poor continue to show lower rates of physicians' services. Third, outside of the states of the north and west, Medicaid programs are often quite limited; the improvements have not been consistent across the country. Rural areas, especially in the South, have been passed by. And finally, the poor receive medical care under less convenient, less pleasant, and less salutary conditions; in urban areas, they depend much more than others on hospital emergency rooms, in part because private physicians are scarce in the neighborhoods where they live. While Medicaid has improved their purchasing power, inequities in the distribution of physicians continue to limit their access to services.

When Congress enacted Medicare, it added Medicaid almost as an afterthought; few people gave the program serious attention. But the costs rapidly burgeoned, rising from $3.45 billion in fiscal year 1968 to $19 billion in 1977. This has occasioned widespread alarm. The increase, as Karen Davis of the Brookings Institution has shown, can be explained almost entirely as a result of the growth in the number of welfare beneficiaries, general medical-care inflation, and rises in the cost of nursing home care. The public image is that Medicaid serves poor families at greatly inflated expense. But when similar populations are compared, Medicaid costs turn out to be no greater than private insurance. Recipients of "welfare" (Aid to Families with Dependent Children) actually receive only a third of Medicaid expenditures, while the elderly in nursing homes receive 40 percent. Medicaid has ended up paying for more than half the cost of nursing homes in the country, primarily for people who have run out of Medicare benefits and exhausted their own savings.[9]

Periodic scandals have beset Medicaid, as duplicate billings, unnecessary services, and other kinds of fraud and inefficiency have come to light. Whether Medicaid is worse than private insurance is unclear; the Medicaid "mills" that have been the targets of exposés may be less able to protect themselves from public embarrassment than respectable nonprofit hospitals that engage in the same practices to balance their budgets. Typically, there is an outcry in the press about Medicaid abuses, a congressional inquiry follows, and perhaps a few indictments are handed down, only to be quietly dismissed after the furor subsides. The attempt to punish miscreants has been unaccompanied by major efforts to provide the poor with superior alternatives to the Medicaid mills and hospital emergency rooms they depend upon. Strapped for funds, the states have responded by cutting back Medicaid benefits. Here the legislature will eliminate hearing aids; there, eyeglasses; in still a third state, the rates for physician reimbursement will be reduced, discouraging doctors from serving Medicaid patients, who are then driven into more expensive hospital outpatient departments. The last few years have seen a continuous retrogression, as medical costs have steadily been thrown back on the poor by state governments unable and unwilling to make savings by reorganizing health services. The aged now pay the same proportion of their income on out-of-pocket medical expenses as they did before Medicare, which covers only 35 percent of their health-care costs.

One of the ironies of Medicaid and Medicare was that while this great expansion in government financing was a windfall for private hospitals and nursing homes, it has not done public institutions much good. In providing services of any kind, the government usually has at least two alternatives. It can produce the services itself through its own agencies, or it can allocate funds (or create tax incentives) for their purchase from the private sector. In medicine, the government has been moving from the first alternative to the second. Increases in the allocative functions of the state have not brought any growth in government "production" of health services. In fact, the movement seems to be in the opposite direction. All the various government-owned hospital systems have fallen on bad times. The old municipal hospitals have been in dire trouble. In cities like New York and Philadelphia, serious conflicts have erupted over whether to close some of them down; in California some county hospitals have already been sold to private investors. Similarly, the hospitals of the Veterans Administration and the U.S. Public Health Services face a doubtful future. For different reasons—the long term drop in the number of tuberculosis and mental patients— state institutions have been in decline. Although vigorous lobbies have kept most of these hospitals open, not one of the government-owned systems is expanding.

These institutions are, in a sense, vestigial; they are left over from an earlier phase in the relationship between medical care and the state. Once the poor qualify for coverage under Medicare or Medicaid, they can receive services from private as well as public hospitals. The more universal the entitlement to health insurance becomes, the less rationale there will be for maintaining a special class of government hospitals limited to particular categories of people. So, paradoxically, the passage of national health insurance may well mean a further shift in institutional ownership from the public to the private sector.

Two principal motives now exist for national health insurance. One is to extend insurance protection to those groups that have been omitted from both public programs and private health insurance. Millions of people in rural families and among the unemployed and those who work in low-paying or temporary jobs still lack any kind of coverage. America has historically restricted social services, except for education, to particularly deserving groups. Income allowances have not been given to the poor generally; they have been given to the disabled, the blind, the aged, and the families of dependent children. To obtain assistance, the poor have had to qualify in some special way. The principle of universal health insurance would announce a major break with that tradition. Yet its practical significance is not as great as it is usually made out to be. The gradual extension of private insurance over more than thirty years means that a national program will add only an incremental amount to insurance protection. Its main effect on medical care is likely to be an increase in demand for ambulatory services, since coverage for hospitalization is already nearly complete. At this point, national health insurance is a midcourse adjustment in a journey long under way.

The main problems arise in regard to the second motive for enacting a federal program—the urge to consolidate the financing of health care in the interests of rationalizing its organization. The politics of health insurance in America today have been greatly complicated by the existence of private insurers. Other industrial nations introduced government health insurance before a substantial commercial sector could develop; America now has the problem of displacing firms that already exist. By the early 1970s most other questions about health insurance had been resolved; the fundamental issue dividing the leading proposals was the role of private insurers. While conservatives have tried to preserve— in fact, increase—the private insurers' market, the liberals want to transfer health insurance to the Social Security Administration, with private firms at most acting as fiscal intermediaries. Because this involves transferring private insurance funds into the federal budget, the general impression is that it would "cost" more. But this may not be so. It depends on how vigorously reorganization is pursued. The continued dispersal of financing among a variety of third-party payers, public and private, makes it difficult to control expenditures. A unified system would permit much greater leverage. The presumption of public debate is that the aim of national health insurance is to increase medical services; its real function may be to constrain their growth, by giving the government the power necessary to limit total expenditures.

What is fundamentally at stake is control over the system. The current "fragmentation" reflects the natural urge of physicians, hospitals, and other institutions to elude checks on their behavior. The call for a coordinated system of health care is, therefore, not merely a desire for bureaucratic rationality, but a challenge to their most deeply felt interests in remaining independent. Oddly enough, the accelerating rise in medical costs is simultaneously paralyzing and driving government policy. Because of growing costs Congress is reluctant to enact a comprehensive insurance program, but to control these costs, it may be pushed to take more radical measures than it would otherwise contemplate. This has already been happening.

IV

In public debate about medical care, national health insurance has usurped attention, overshadowing other developments that may be of equal long-range importance. As the federal government has assumed a rising proportion of the cost of health services, it has appropriated various ideas, such as prepaid group practice, the monitoring of physician performance, and health planning, that were once the proposals of radicals and reformers who were completely outside the regnant political consensus. But a fundamental shift in emphasis has taken place. The same measures that used to be advocated, without much success, as ways to improve medical care are now being adopted as ways to save money.

Prepaid health care. Prepaid health plans offer comprehensive medical services for a fixed amount of money per year (a method of payment commonly known as "capitation").[10] Such programs have met strong resistance from physicians, who see them as a threat to private, fee-for-service practice; in 1943, the AMA was convicted of violations of the Sherman Antitrust Act as a result of its efforts to blacklist doctors participating in a consumer-controlled prepaid plan in the District of Columbia. Many of the early programs had their origins in the cooperative movement; a few were sponsored by physicians. But by far the biggest was the creation of the industrialist Henry Kaiser. Today the Kaiser-Permanente Health Plan has nearly three million subscribers, primarily in California and Oregon. In Seattle, the largest consumer-run program, the Group Health Cooperative of Puget Sound, has more than 200,000 members.

These programs were generally established in the hope of improving the quality of medical care by organizing doctors into groups, coordinating services, and emphasizing preventive care. But during the late 1960s they began to attract wider interest because of the record they established in reducing costs, primarily as a result of low rates of hospitalization. Suddenly, to the chagrin of their old left-wing supporters, they were being touted in *Fortune* as a way to cut rising health expenditures. In the interest of selling the idea to the public, prepaid plans were renamed health maintenance organizations (HMOs), a new term that included not only prepaid group practice, but also the "medical care foundation," a variant more acceptable to doctors. A foundation can simply be a financial entity set up by private practitioners—it need have no actual facilities—to receive annual prepayments from subscribers and to reimburse participating hospitals and physicians by fee for service. In 1971, President Nixon adopted HMOs as a central part of his health policy, but the program was soon scaled down in his own administration and chewed up in Congress. The legislation that emerged in late 1973, supposedly to aid emerging HMOs, required them to offer higher benefits than private insurers under less favorable conditions, and promised to make HMOs the most heavily regulated part of the medical system. By 1975 the program was moribund. Still, the prepaid plans already functioning continue to do well, and amendments to the HMO Act passed in 1976 may help revive the federal program.

Peer review. Since the Progressive era, the United States has relied on licensing to guarantee a minimum standard in medical practice; physicians have strongly opposed any direct monitoring of their actual performance. But in 1972, as part of an effort to cut the costs of Medicare and Medicaid, Congress quietly provided for the establishment of a network of "professional standards review organizations" (PSROs) to monitor physicians' treatment of hospital patients paid for by federal programs. One physician called the measure "the most radical health legislation in this country's history." For the first time, he noted, doctors would be "held publicly accountable for the quality, medical necessity, efficiency, and cost-effectiveness of the health care they provide."[11] Although the principle may be radical, the PSROs are not; they are composed exclusively of physicians. The congressional sponsors of the program hoped to identify doctors who hospitalize too many patients or overprescribe certain drugs and then to deny them reimbursement or impose damages. The hoped-for savings remain to be achieved; some observers think that PSROs may actually increase costs by setting norms for treatment higher than those actually in practice. But they are at least beginning to work out methods for assessing physicians' performance, which may help in determining what standards of medical care can realistically be set. The results may have value even if the program fails to accomplish its original aims.

Health planning. Hospitals and other medical facilities have developed in America in splendid isolation, with no regard to the duplication of services or the overall needs of their communities. In the late sixties, the federal government made some tentative gestures in the direction of planning, without giving planning agencies any effective power. Then in 1974 Congress merged a number of earlier programs into a national network of about two hundred "health systems agencies" (HSAs), to be set up as independent planning organizations outside state and local governments. It also required the states to pass laws obliging hospitals and other institutions to obtain "certificates of need" before undertaking major capital expenditures. (Many states had already done so, at the urging of the hospitals themselves.) Although the AMA fought the legislation, denouncing it as a "dangerous intrusion . . . into the practice of medicine," others have worried that the new agencies will be captured by the dominant "providers" in an area and used by them to prevent the emergence of new competitors like HMOs. Curiously, the federal law imposing this new regulatory structure on the health industry was signed by President Ford while he was calling for a general cutback of government regulation.

Health manpower. Within the last fifteen years, there have been two shifts in federal policy, first to increase the total supply of physicians and then to correct imbalances in their distribution. In the mid-1960s, having accepted the prevailing view that America suffered from a general "doctor shortage," Congress began providing aid to medical schools according to a formula that encouraged them to expand their enrollments. It also revised U.S. immigration laws, abolishing the old national quotas in favor of a system of occupational preferences, which brought about a sharp rise in immigration by foreign physicians, primarily from Asia. The new policies assumed that through the natural workings of the market, doctors would distribute themselves satisfactorily, by region and specialty.

That premise turned out to be wrong. An increased supply of physicians was no guarantee that enough would settle in poorer areas or go into low-status general practice. Instead, they congregated in the suburbs and the high-prestige specialties. By the 1970s, analysts became concerned that a national surplus of surgeons might be driving up rates of surgery and hospitalization and contributing to higher costs. In 1976, Congress decided that there was no longer any general shortage of physicians, and turned its attention instead to encouraging young doctors to enter "primary care" and practice in underserved communities. Recent legislation requires medical schools to offer about half their residencies in "primary care" fields (e.g., general practice, family practice, general pediatrics and internal medicine) and provides scholarships to medical students on the condition that they serve in the National Health Service Corps one year for each year they receive assistance. The Corps, which was created by Congress in 1970 to place volunteer physicians and other health workers in underserved areas, has until now been a small program, but if the scholarships are fully funded, they may increase its size from two hundred doctors to ten or twenty thousand by the late 1980s.

All these measures, from health maintenance organizations to the National Health Service Corps, were anathema to conservatives only a short time ago, yet they passed Congress with important conservative support and were signed into law by Presidents Nixon or Ford. (The PSRO amendment, which was especially reviled by private doctors, was introduced by a Utah Republican, Senator Wallace Bennett, who was originally elected in 1952 with strong AMA support because of his opposition to national health insurance.) By the time these measures were enacted, each had a respectable conservative logic. HMOs were going to bring modern management techniques and an element of competition to health care, while peer review and health planning would cut waste, and the National Health Service Corps would help preserve private medical practice by encouraging doctors to settle in poor areas, thereby making more drastic government programs unnecessary. But whatever justification they had, these were still reforms that a decade earlier would have been rejected out of hand as infringements on free enterprise and the doctor-patient relationship. The political consensus quietly shifted to the left, although the changes have as yet been small in their effects.

It is too early to tell what their ultimate impact will be. In medicine, as in other departments of social policy, many people have been overeager to pronounce the programs of the 1960s a failure. While Medicare and Medicaid did not eliminate inequalities in the distribution of medical care, they have significantly reduced them. While peer review, health planning, health maintenance organizations, the National Health Service Corps, and other initiatives have not yet realized the hopes of their sponsors, they are providing experience that may enable later developments to succeed. Some of the programs are going to begin bearing fruit only in the next several years. For example, the expansion of medical education that began in the late 1960s has doubled the size of medical-school classes, but because of the extended length of training, the full impact of the increase has yet to be felt. Finishing their residencies, many of the young doctors may find it difficult to establish themselves in private practice and may be more readily attracted than their predecessors to alternative ways of providing medical care. A rising supply of physicians could greatly facilitate efforts to change the medical system. But it could also cause further increases in health expenditures by generating a larger volume of services. In either event, it will make it more difficult for fee-for-service medicine to prevail.

V

What are the long-run prospects? The growing urge to control the total resources that medical care absorbs has brought an increased caution about the benefits of medical treatment, especially technologically complex services, and a greater skepticism about turning every form of social distress or personal disquiet into a medical problem. But different lessons are drawn from the limits of medicine. The individualist stresses the responsibility of personal conduct for differences in health and sees voluntary behavior at the heart of the problem. The socialist or environmentalist emphasizes the role of social institutions in creating conditions that are physically dangerous, like carcinogens in the air, or morally unsatisfactory, like oppressive work situations. The unrepentant scientist argues that medicine is still in its infancy and will yield results if sufficient investment is made in research. The unrepentant planner insists that, whatever the state of science, the environment or individual behavior, the system of medical services has to be oriented toward improving health, which means rationally assessing the effectiveness of modes of treatment and investing resources in those programs that count most.

Politically, there is a gathering determination, as yet unrealized, to impose on medical services the rationality of bureaucratic organization, of market competition, or of democratic control. The basic structural issue is in what form these alternatives are combined, and how far they develop. Although no single impulse yet governs, the bureaucratic movement is strongest. One line of development, within the fee-for-service system, is to monitor the decisions of individual practitioners, to do detailed budget review of medical institutions, and to control the supply of manpower and technology at the national level. A second possibility is simply to set a fixed annual budget for medical care, to be allocated by regional authorities, which in all likelihood would be run by the dominant "providers" in an area. Here costs would be controlled by arbitrary ceilings, but the professional and institutional interests would retain their decision-making autonomy within those limits. A third possibility is a system of competing pre-paid health plans, whose internal incentive to control costs would keep expenditures down; here there might also be extensive consumer representation. Finally, if all else fails, there might be a government-run national health service. The future will almost certainly bring an administered medical economy of some kind, not because that is what anyone really wants, but because it is what no one seems to know how to avoid. Whether it will be a more decent and humane system no one yet can tell.

REFERENCES

[1]By status relations I mean primarily relations between men and women and between blacks and whites.

[2]Robert M. Gibson and Marjorie Smith Mueller, "National Health Expenditures, Fiscal Year 1976," Social Security Bulletin, 40 (April 1977): 4; National Health Insurance Modeling Group, Social Security Administration, Office of Research and Statistics.

[3]M. I. Finley, The Ancient Economy (London: Chatto & Windus, 1973), p. 57; N. D. Jewson, "Medical Knowledge and the Patronage System in 18th Century England," Sociology, 8 (1974): 369–385; Theodore Zeldin, France 1848–1945, vol. 1, Ambition, Love, and Politics (Oxford: Clarendon Press, 1973), pp. 23–42; "American versus European Medical Science," Medical Record, 4 (May 15, 1969): 133; David K. Shipler, "Life for Soviet Woman All Work, Little Status," The New York Times (August 9, 1976). Soviet physicians' salaries are, however, supplemented by illegal fees.

[4]"The Troubled Professions," Business Week (August 16, 1976); Richard D. Lyons, "Refusal of Many to Heed Government Health Advice Is Linked to Growing Distrust of Authority," The New York Times (June 12, 1977).

[5]These developments are described more fully in my forthcoming study The Social Transformation of American Medicine, to be published by Basic Books; some of the points are discussed in "Medicine, Economy and Society in Nineteenth-Century America," Journal of Social History, 10 (Summer 1977): 588–607.

[6]See, for example, the articles by John Knowles and Aaron Wildavsky in Daedalus, 106 (Winter 1977); for a more extreme case against medicine, see Ivan Illich, Medical Nemesis: The Expropriation of Health (New York: Pantheon, 1976); for a critique, Paul Starr, "The Politics of Therapeutic Nihilism," The Hastings Center Report, 6 (October 1976): 24–30.

[7]Between 1960 and 1976, the membership of the AMA tumbled from about 75 to 45 percent of American physicians. Even the Journal of the American Medical Association, once the leading medical publication in the United States, has declined considerably in influence. In a recent survey of over one hundred authorities in internal medicine conducted by the American College of Physicians, JAMA rated sixth in quality, even falling behind a regional publication, the New England Journal of Medicine. See Annals of Internal Medicine, 84 (March 1976): 349. The AMA has also had its own "Watergate" scandal, complete with an informer inside the organization whom the newspapers have called "Sore Throat." It seems that the AMA had for several years been lying to the Postal Service about its paid circulation to avoid higher mailing rates for unsolicited copies, which it was sending out to doctors to secure more advertising from drug companies and medical equipment suppliers. The association has had to pay over a million dollars in charges and fines to avoid an indictment.

[8]Marjorie Smith Mueller and Paula A. Piro, "Private Health Insurance in 1974: A Review of Coverage, Enrollment and Financial Experience," Social Security Bulletin, 39 (March 1976): 3–20.

[9]For changes in the rates of physician visits, see U.S. Department of Health, Education, and Welfare, Health: United States, 1975, pp. 289, 409, 569; Lu Ann Aday, "The Impact of Health Policy on Access to Medical Care," Health and Society, 54 (Spring 1976): 215–233; Karen Davis, "Medicaid Payments and Utilization of Medical Services by the Poor," Inquiry, 13 (June 1976): 122–135, and Davis, "Achievements and Problems of Medicaid," Public Health Reports, 91 (July–August 1976): 309–316; Nancy Hicks, "Medicaid and Private Programs Are Similar in Cost, Data Suggest," The New York Times (January 2, 1977); Rosemary and Robert Stevens, Welfare Medicine in America (New York: The Free Press, 1974).

[10]In this section I draw on my article, "The Undelivered Health System," *The Public Interest* (Winter 1976): 66–85.

[11]Jay A. Winsten, "Imposing Controls on Doctors," *Wall Street Journal* (December 6, 1973).

ANTHONY SMITH

"Just a Pleasant Way to Spend an Evening"—The Softening Embrace of American Television

EXERCISES IN PREVISIONING the future may proceed either along the path of extrapolation from the present, or along the path of contradiction of it. In trying to foresee the next stage in the evolution of a society, whether one's own or another, the pessimist is apt to discern merely a more egregious version of what exists, while the optimist recognizes a coming reaction against it. In modern times one is led naturally to the television medium in the search for proofs of almost any predictions made of a society. There one should see both a record and a source of reinforcement of the changing nostrums and moods of a nation. In the case of American television one sees the machinery which fashions the images not only of the American people but of a large part of the rest of the world.

It is more than a fashionable observation, it is a prevailing conviction, that American television, in the last fifteen years, has become a major unelective source of power, the cause of changes in social behavior, in the operations of the Constitution, in the management of the economy, in the ordering, so to speak, of the whole national (and therefore international) agenda. American television is felt to have become a vast broker of social power. In looking at the future of American society, it is impossible to ignore television, but it is impossible also to avoid starting without questioning the prevailing assumption of its power. One thing which will be needed in the new America is a more satisfying definition of where—if anywhere now—the power of television lies. Sometimes one may become totally enthralled by a habit or preoccupation only to throw off its aweful power, after a time, through the easy device of boredom or exhaustion. One may justify a mildly optimistic line towards the medium in seeing in the last part of the 1970s a reaction of a kind occurring in the taste of the audience, and also against the dominance of the television institutions—perhaps mainly, however, in the perceived ability of the society to survive that set of influences which are associated with the phenomenon of television.

Unlike the press and the cinema, in total contrast to the theatre and the musical industry, television has developed towards maturity as a single system—not, in the case of America, embodied in one set of codes and institutions, but certainly as one gigantic response to the supposed requirements of one gigantic audience. It is that central apparatus of organizations and ideas that determines the culture of the medium, and it is in that apparatus that one can now perhaps see a certain set of adjustments being made to regain suzerainty of an audience which, if it has been enthralled by the medium, has been also without the intensity of influence which has been supposed.

It is not that television is rethinking its relationship with the people; it is beginning to wonder whether it has one. Throughout the history of the mass media the audience has bewildered the communicators much more than the reverse. In the era of mass media the terms in which that supposedly inert mass has been apostrophised have constantly shifted. At the turn of the century it was a volatile multitude prone to easy manipulation by master propagandists.[1] By the 1960s, it was the "wad"[2] of the advertising technician, it was "Out There," an undifferentiated, unmoving, automated putty for demographers to mould; it had become the raw material of the "People Machine"[3] of political managers. But it was beginning to demonstrate that it was in possession of many secret selves: it was also "Middle America" and the "silent majority." Behind the television audience, always growing in the ratings, always purchasing what it was programmed to purchase, it became possible to reach out for another manifestation of the people, many of them maturer, more considerate, more aware by some mysterious process of communication of the things which the media had ignored.

What remained inert, gigantic, automated, unmoving was the machinery which served the audience and the assumptions on which it had come to operate in America. Although the abstract phenomenon of "television" has begun to acquire the attention of what are thought at Aspen to be "Thinking People"[4] the machinery of media power has been largely neglected by political and social scientists, also by economists and sociologists. If television is acquiring a new and rather less important place in American society, then it must be *seen* to have done so, for the consequences of that change to have any meaning. Television, together with its regulators, investors, viewers, programmers, and managers must discover what are the new forms of transaction which give this vast structure of social connection and communication its place in American society.

In the 1960s and early 1970s the academic community of America commenced a belated scrutiny of the country's media institutions, which had for forty years, since the start of radio after World War I, been largely ignored by American intellectuals, half through disdain, half through helplessness. The machinery which had sprung up to operate and regulate broadcasting in America *seemed* to have grown out of the colossal power of its vast audiences, the frightful stepchild of democracy. Emerging from the war the American writers of the 1920s found themselves confronting a new audience which was, as it were, out of date in its tastes, as Van Wyck Brooks put it[5] ("half a century behind the times," as Bernard Shaw put it). Shaw and Kipling, Bloomsburyites and Fabians all heavily involved themselves in what England called "wireless" while American intellectuals held aloof from the radio cacophony, wanting no part of it, seldom speaking on or writing for it.

Not until the sudden worldwide quickening of interest in the 1960s did American academics come to admit that something was happening in broadcasting worthy of their attention. Even then they seldom tried to address the new audience themselves, and they were very seldom invited to do so. There was a place reserved for the serious-minded, as a "minority," at the fringe of American television, in educational or public broadcasting, not in the organisations which commanded the great bulk of the audience. Television was for the "majority" and the broadcasters' chief expertise lay in knowing how to monopolise the attention of that still growing audience.

The combination of disdain and social grief with which the American intellectual has traditionally approached the American communications media has, it may be argued, helped to divert attention from the industry itself. The television institutions and their vast financial and political penumbra have been in the main left free of critical analysis. Television as America has developed it (and the world has largely inherited it) has been assumed to be the inevitable result of the nature of the American audience rather than the direct fault of a corporate and regulatory system within arm's reach of reform.

In this respect America finds itself in a different position from all other societies where the institutional machinery of the mass media has been the direct product of social decision-making. Even in societies with a very highly developed preoccupation with media freedom (e.g., Sweden) it has been unquestionably assumed that governments are responsible for guaranteeing an institutional structure though not the informational content. Only in the United States has structure as well as content been left to a combination of free market forces working within a loose system of spectrum regulation. The literature which television developed in its greatest decade of expansion treated the institutions as somehow inexorable; at most they could be subjected to further regulatory procedures, never to fundamental and fresh political choice.

On one side of the Atlantic the new audience created by radio in the 1920s was seen not primarily as a new market but as a new version of the old electorate. In the United States the new medium was balanced upon forces which in the event turned out to be socially unaccountable, dedicated to the honest pursuit of profits, only accidentally acquiring the quasi-political power which is inherent and unavoidable in the practice of broadcasting. America thus found, in the conditions of the 1960s, that an overmighty subject had grown up entwined in constitutional devices and that no apparatus existed by which its stewardship might be publicly examined, and if necessary, reallocated. In the growth period of broadcasting, a series of analogies had been used, analogies with the press, with private business, with local government, with public utilities, each of which, in the light of later experience, came to be judged by many to have been inappropriate. The United States had entrusted a new and different instrument from any which had cropped up previously in the hands of local private owners when the medium by the nature of its audience was national; it had created a regulatory agency at the centre which had no authority over the editorial balance of the content; it had allowed the heartlands of broadcasting, the networks, to emerge in a framework which was completely remote from public scrutiny; it had built up a machinery of cultural patronage within a wholly private and competitive instead of public, coordinating and rationalizing framework; it then had tried to graft a frail public sector onto the side of the emergent monster and to mitigate its power by proliferating new institutions in other parts of the magnetic spectrum, too late to act as real rivals. Finally it had allowed the mechanisms of management to become so powerful, because of the overheated competition at the heart of the medium, that the creative professionals were unable to exercise creative autonomy within the medium.

America remains the only country in the Western world in which a citizen can find it possible in the middle of a national election campaign to switch on his set throughout the whole of prime time without ever seeing a programme dealing with politics, the only country in which broadcasting has been built upon the free choice of viewers interacting with the uncontrolled freewill of broadcasters. America has therefore not been obliged, throughout the great decade of television growth which has just passed, to confront the real paradox of mass media power, viz., that the mass audience though consisting of free citizens in a free society is itself part of the natural environment which has to be protected even against itself. The problem for most countries is how to do this consistently with democratic values. The United States, only in the 1960s, finally began to deal with the problem of whether to do this.

It is strange, at first, to consider the United States as a heresiarch in the world of broadcasting. The content of American television is the principal content of the television systems of scores of other countries. Its broadcasting industry lends its styles and formats to television throughout the world. The investments of American broadcasters are spread through the radio and television stations of several continents. It is in many ways an American medium. But the United States has designed a method for controlling or organising broadcasting which flies in the face of what are the fundamental broadcasting assumptions of most developed societies.

Perhaps the most important of these is the American belief that a society has no right to make policy choices in the mass media through its elected representatives. Elsewhere it is axiomatic that the allocation of spectrum and the establishment of cultural policies in the broadest sense (in particular, to what extent the medium is to be one of entertainment or one of instruction) are part of the same governmental process. The machinery of the mass media, it is generally thought, needs to be rendered socially accountable not only through the choice of citizens as viewers and listeners to switch on their sets and switch them off again, but also through a gubernatorial process by which "society," in some suitable manifestation, instructs those responsible for these all-pervasive media to perform their task along certain lines. Indeed, it is also thought to be axiomatic that the underlying need for diversity can be met only through a process of decision-making at the level of society as a whole; left to the market, broadcasting services always veer away from diversity.

A line has to be drawn between competition and national control which guarantees a suitable range of programme material. Only in the late 1960s, with the refounding of public television as a national service with federal funding, did the United States come to see the point of this argument. For the bulk of the founding era of broadcasting the United States pursued a policy of breeding diversity only indirectly through a regulatory procedure deliberately divested of editorial authority.

The Federal Communications Commission, the regulatory agency constructed in 1927 but reconstructed in 1934, was a very typical product of New Deal thinking; Roosevelt, in explaining the 1934 Communications Act, compared the communications industry with other utilities such as transportation (which was the province of the Interstate Commerce Commission) and electrical power (the province of the Federal Power Commission).[6] The basic task of the

FCC was to preserve competition in a commercial undertaking; it imposed upon the broadcasters to whom it permitted use of the spectrum the obligation "to operate in the public interest and to afford reasonable opportunity for the discussion of conflicting views on issues of public importance."[7]

The 1934 Communications Act imposed no positive broadcasting policy. It went out of its way to deny the FCC "any power of censorship" and prohibited it from taking any step "which shall interfere with the right of free speech by means of radio communications."[8] Simultaneously in the democratic (as well as the non-democratic) countries of Europe, broadcasting institutions were being built in quite different styles. It was obvious to these builders that broadcasting establishments would willy-nilly become something more than instruments of *expression*, they would become concentrations of social power, which rendered the process of *regulation* (which had to be undertaken by the state) inseparable from the duty of imposing forms and structures of social accountability.

Hand in hand with the doctrine of minimum state involvement went the doctrine of localism. Though it was clear from the start that the interests both of broadcasters and advertisers was to reach out towards the great audience of mass society, it was thought both feasible and desirable that broadcasting outlets should spring up in every community and that the process of regulation should be confined to the technical tasks of spreading establishments throughout the land mass of the country. Simultaneously in France and Britain the local stations of the 1920s were closed down when the spectrum problems of concentrated populations made national and regional broadcasting more practical; nationally the medium of radio itself demanded a concentration of intellectual and cultural energy. To build a mass medium out of local outlets would be like trying to construct a great national newspaper upon an organization of newsvendors.

Localism meant inequality of provision throughout the territory of the United States, though it offered an equality of commercial opportunity. It was inevitable that a national machinery, remote from the regulatory mechanism, would develop to provide the essential content. The network, a huge socially unaccountable conglomeration of patronage, capital, and professional employment, emerged as an evasion of an impractical localism and federal regulation. The network imposed the programme formats on the system; it "slotted" radio and television and then filled the slots in commercially saleable series. It competed through an intricate geographical tracery of local stations against other similar networks. It built the culture of the medium of television in particular out of complex corporate needs. It entered into a commercial *situation* created by government regulation rather than a *market*. Out of the strange structure which emerged there arose notions of what the fundamental forms of broadcasting were, and these, because of the sheer size, profusion, and dynamism of the American broadcasting industry, became established as standard forms throughout the globe. In the great era of radio (the 1930s) up to half of the commercial time remained unsold and large amounts of non-sponsored programming were possible. By the end of the 1950s very little commercial time remained unsold in network television, and each minute of time became the object of a relentless competition and a frenzied search for material. The styles and methods of the networks came to be felt to be unavoidable, the true and only destiny of the ineluctable force known as "television" rather than merely the result of the particular machinery which had grown up in the United States.

The market of television, therefore, did not grow analogously with the theatre or the cinema. Television was not a medium of creative professionals but of business managers. It was a medium in which the writer was harnessed as a proletarian to machinery of dissemination. The product of television emerged in series which filled the slots which were created by the kind of scheduling which has been necessitated by the relationship between networks and affiliates. The writer was an individual who worked within a format. The format was everything. The audience was recruited through repetition of familiar forms or familiar performers, and the ratings could be maintained only through the use of large amounts of risk capital.

For a network to mount a new programme format, the investment is similar to that entailed in promoting a new design of motor-car. It is not television by its nature which has created this phenomenon but the American network system. In it the function of publishing crushed the function of authorship. The creative worker became a service industry. Frenetic competition organised within a false market hid from the viewer any sight of the real possibilities of the medium. The suppliers of the medium themselves received a one-sided view of the potential of the audience derived from their own activity. The pursuit of sheer viewing ratings meant that competition took place much further down the market, so to speak, than in any other medium. The relationship between medium and audience was based upon exploitation of emotions rather than upon the exploitation of curiosity. The contrasts between the American and other systems were buried by the overwhelming preponderance of American television products in other countries.

Given the structure in which the radio and television systems grew, the authorities have relied upon the use of commercial regulatory machinery in every attempt to alter the editorial decision-making of the networks. Annual profits of the networks stagnated in the mid-1960s after climbing to $187 million in 1966 from roughly a third of that figure a decade before. Network competition grew more intense in the period of television saturation; violence in programmes visibly increased, and produced a considerable public reaction. The FCC's policy was to use its powers to oblige the networks to divest themselves of their syndication interests and certain other extramural financial interests and to introduce the Prime Time Access Rule (1971), which placed restrictions on the amount of prime-time programming which networks could supply to affiliate stations in the most popular viewing hours. By exempting news, children's programmes, and documentaries from the new ruling, the FCC hoped to bring about an increase in these categories of programmes in peak viewing hours. When this did not work, further plans were made (but never put into practice) for getting the networks to divest themselves of some or all of their wholly owned stations (five per network). The FCC's policy was to try to make the networks produce fewer programmes themselves, to turn them into marketing conduits for programme material, rather than editorial entities.

The FCC thought that by making the networks behave as distributors only and no longer as programme-makers it would force them to behave more evenhandedly with all the other makers of programmes. The networks succeeded in defeating every proposed enactment or rendering it harmless. Almost by accident official broadcasting policy in the United States had created three monsters which were basically beyond public control; all available methods of control were in any case inappropriate to the intended cultural end. The would-be reformers of the system, such as Clifford Durr, Newton Minnow, Nicholas Johnson, and Kenneth Cox within the FCC, or Fred Friendly in the world of programme production, appeared to be asking for the system to make suicidal concessions. All attempts to reform so powerful a structure in the midst of American society carried an aura of puritanical and pecksniffian high-handedness. The reformers were able to add to the system (through cable, public television, the opening up of the UHF band) but not to change it.

The network system allows each strand of programming to be priced and sold separately. Networks realise that news brings in relatively little revenue per dollar of investment. In 1972, for example, the networks as a group spent $300 million on news and sports and earned $400 million on this sector of their output. On the other hand, prime time entertainment brought in $800 million after expenditure of $480 million. Entertainment programmes during the hours of daylight brought in $300 million after expenditure of $105 million.[9] The tension which exists at the heart of the system is between the networks and their affiliates.

No transaction takes place between the editorial suppliers and the actual customers, the viewers. The producers and writers work through a tiny group of seldom-changing entrepreneurs, senior people in the network hierarchies, upon whose judgment arguably rests the major cultural decisions of American society. These, in turn, conduct their business with the managers of television and radio stations who are the direct points of contact with the audience. The local stations make extremely few programmes themselves, since the majority cannot summon up sufficient revenue to do more, at local level, than provide news. The programme makers, therefore, absorb a vision of the American audience derived from people who operate stations but make no programmes mediated by network chiefs who neither operate stations nor make programmes.

Only the unsalted meat of ratings succours this set of relationships. The decisions on the nature of the content fall into natural demarcations of news, entertainment, drama, and so on. The programme makers are trying to raise audiences for someone other than themselves. So many levels of brokerage are built into the system that two main forces involved in the medium, producers and audiences, are kept much farther apart than in other systems and societies.

Repeated efforts have been made to alter the editorial imbalances in America's radio and television through more intensive regulation. One major result was the separation of ABC from NBC to improve competition. As early as 1946, the FCC tried to build upon its slender powers a larger machinery of editorial authority. In the "Blue Book"[10] the FCC argued that would-be license holders often make their applications on the basis of programme policies and promises which are subsequently reneged upon; at the time of renewing their licenses the FCC would henceforth compare their performance in practice with the promises made in their applications. The FCC would add *detailed review* to its range of activities.

In some ways the whole history of the FCC since publication of the Blue Book can be seen as a gradual withdrawal from interventionism on so comprehensive a scale. The 1946 position was rapidly seen to be unworkable; the sheer profusion of stations, the demands of advertisers, the diversity of control, made it impossible for the FCC to conduct an investigatory operation on a scale which could have made stations responsive. Despite sudden eruptions of interventionism during the FCC chairmanship of Newton Minnow, as earlier during that of Clifford Durr, the FCC has necessarily sunk back into a more purely regulatory role, renewing licenses in geographical grouping and issuing rules governing the conduct of business at network level or between networks and stations. The FCC has legislated on the question of fairness, on rights of reply, and on ethical questions in advertising. It has tried to force more local programmes to be made. It has pushed stations and networks into providing more coverage of news, and of better quality. But whenever it summons up the will to take far-reaching action it is defeated either by its adversaries or by the gradual weakening of its will.

The decade of the 1960s began with the firmest declaration in American broadcasting history by an FCC chairman, attacking the failings of the networks and stations. Newton Minnow in his "wasteland" speech described to an audience of shocked members of the National Association of Broadcasters at their 1961 Washington convention what the viewer actually saw on his screen. "You will see a procession of game shows, violence, audience participation shows, formula comedies about totally unbelievable families, blood and thunder, mayhem, violence, sadism, murder, western badmen, western good men, private eyes, gangsters, more violence and cartoons. And endlessly—commercials."[11] It was a patrician denunciation of what was by 1960 an uneradicably commercial popular culture. The system whose heart is the FCC can approach its audience only along such lines. To attack the broadcasters for exercising their full energies within the system provided is merely to perplex them with inexplicable enmity.

It is extremely difficult to try to change the nature of a competitive system by simply demanding self-denial or forebearance. To ask broadcasters within the existing system to provide "less violence" is like asking Shakespeare to reduce the number of murders in *Macbeth*. Systems must follow their own natures. Behaviour within a system can be changed sometimes by massive sanctions, but where the system is not to be changed, and where credible sanctions are not available, exhortation turns out to be useless. Minnow's term of office made no perceptible difference to the powerful constraints which had made the product of American television develop in the way it had, although widespread disappointment with television in America increased during the decade and led to the foundation of a public broadcasting system and to an intense discussion concerning the possibilities of improvement through developing cable television.

In the way that American television has evolved, from the era of the quizzes in the late fifties to the phenomenon of the telefilm and the modern range of prime-time entertainment forms, the viewer has been offered a culture which has grown out of the needs of business, legitimised by reference to audience ratings. It is not a popular culture exploited by business interests, as in other commercial media systems; it is a culture which has been built around the intensifying requirements of advertisers. The regulatory system has attempted

reform through further diversification, through the use of anti-monopoly devices, by trying to open more stations in more places, and this, together with
other restraints upon profits (such as the forced abandonment of tobacco advertising, and pressure against excessive violence) have intensified the competition
taking place within the contrived market of the regulated system.

The techniques of Naderism, borrowed by reformers within the FCC at
various times, are perhaps not appropriate in a medium of culture; consumer
protection is a demand for those responsible to take power—in television, there
is already an excess of power at the center. Broadcasting consists of a privilege
handed out by society; it is in all circumstances an "unfair" privilege the recipients of which can be rendered socially accountable; but without the privilege
there can be no broadcasting. Until the arrival of public television American
broadcasting never tried to face the issues presented by this privilege in a direct
way. It attempted to mitigate the privilege by dividing it, by giving the right to
transmit to people who did not actually make the content and by spreading the
right to transmit into an unpoliceably large number of hands. (In Europe
exactly the opposite dilemma now faces broadcasting policy, and efforts are
being bent in most societies to diversify the privilege from one or two institutions to five or six, but not, however, to several hundreds.) A profusion of
antennae does not make television "free" like the press, nor does it make it a
"mirror of society." The control system arises from society itself, and may be
popular or patrician, democratic or authoritarian, depending on how it is organised.

No pure market transactions take place in any broadcasting system, since
viewers are unable to make choices of specific programmes or kinds of programmes which have direct economic effects on the suppliers (except in the very
rare instance of pay TV). In systems dependent entirely on advertising revenue,
the upper income group pays far more for its programmes (since it spends more
on the goods advertised) than the low income groups. A system which is based
upon official grants paid from income tax, however, would oblige the high income viewer to pay a much higher proportion of the total cost of the service.
According to one study made in 1963 the wealthy American viewer in America's all-advertising system pays two and a half times the amount paid by the less
affluent viewer; if the same revenues had been taken from federal income tax
sources, the difference would have been 10 to 1.

The most usual form of television financing internationally is the licence on
the television receiver; this form of revenue-raising is wholly "regressive," far
more than in an all-advertising system, leaving rich and poor to pay the same
amount for their viewing. However, this last method frees the medium from
demographic constraints and from constraints dependent upon the highly volatile advertising market; with a fixed income, a television channel can operate
according to the demands of sections of the audience which are not necessarily
economically effective when expressed through advertising revenue.

Fears of government intervention in programming for political reasons
where governments control the revenue system have long since abated in the
stable democracies where the peculiarities of television as a market have become
well understood in the last decade. The level of government interference de-

pends not primarily on the method of finance (since a government can, if it wishes, express its editorial desires through the spectrum regulatory system) but on the gubernatorial structure of the broadcasting system itself.

A three-network system serves the interests of a mass market of the kind which sprang up in the growth era of television. It does not serve minorities adequately, and cannot. Increasingly these "minorities" are very large, but not large enough to express themselves as the whole audience of a network. A new network finds it very difficult to break into a three-network system, because while it may attract a large audience for a group of programmes the programme producers, once their popularity is established, are free to move to one of the major networks. The new network requires the sources to bid for a very long run of the successful shows or to bid for a very large spread of attractive programming.

In effect the total market for programmes in America is confined to three networks, and all efforts to increase the number of equally competing stations in the major population centres of America have been frustrated.[13] Each city in the early period of television was provided with four VHF channels, one of which was later set aside for educational purposes; the UHF channels, which were opened up after the Korean war, arrived too late to be absorbed into the networks, which were already very firmly established as the main purchasers and disseminators of prime time programming. If the FCC had decided to allocate signals on a wider geographical basis (regional rather than local) each viewer might have been provided with an available choice of four stations. By maintaining a policy of extreme localism choice was restricted at the local level and, as it transpired, at the national level as well.

The restriction in the number of stations has meant that the minority with an intense interest in an ignored subject has no means to express its will. It is this minority, present in every mass society to a level of, say 15 to 20 per cent, which is the key to the programming of most national television systems. They are politically powerful but weak in numbers; in U.S. television, only numbers count. If there were five channels with equal geographic spread, this minority would claim its share of television by force of numbers. In a three-channel system the minority which wants a given product intensely is unable to bid successfully against a majority which wants a different product less intensively. The only way an all-advertising system can in practice serve its audience's spectrum of interests is through a multiplication of channels, since the redistributive possibilities inherent in a system of publicly financed broadcasting are denied it. In the United States, however, the number of effective channels has been limited to three only, partly as a result of the dextrous pressure of the three, partly as a result of deliberate public policy.

By the middle of the 1950s the highly profitable nature of the new television medium was already clear. The right to transmit, given away by the FCC, became an extremely valuable fixed asset of the fortunate bidder, who could sell his holdings on the market as if the public resource element of the station were a wholly owned investment. Stations rocketed in value by 10 times the actual amount of cash invested in them. A new television station was transformed artificially and overnight into an extremely large block of capital from a small one. The pressure to create from television a really high revenue-generating audience became overwhelming; the only way to create and maintain this audience was through the evolution of a very tight network scheduling policy. The local stations never tried to become powers-that-be; they provided a little local news, sports commentaries, and weather reports, then settled down to taking material from the networks.

The reformers saw the UHF band of frequencies as the only means of inducing change in the behaviour of the broadcasters, and the FCC handed out franchises in the new band in the hope that this new generation of stations would provide competition at a higher level of content. However, the viewers could receive the new stations only after the acquisition of converters or new sets, and manufacturers were loth to add the new equipment to new sets as a matter of course. The new UHF stations could raise revenue only for worse and less diverse programming than their VHF rivals. The FCC thought out a plan for "regulating" the broadcasting system into an enforced diversity, by which certain network affiliates would be obliged, at licence renewal time, to accept UHF frequencies so that the rigid demarcation between VHF frequencies with high audience and network affiliation on the one hand, and UHF low audiences and non-affiliation on the other, would be ended. It was a kind of electronic "bussing" plan, a scheme to "administer" American broadcast culture out of its historic constraints. Deintermixture, as the scheme was called, was a failure. Advertisers and broadcasters blocked it through massive protest and threats to turn in their licenses to the FCC. The ultimate compromise was a new law in 1964 by which manufacturers were obliged to supply the UHF band in all receivers.

By the time that UHF signals spread through American homes, however, a new set of technical opportunities offered themselves which at the same time promised a certain diversity while undermining the long term strategy of pluralising the networks. Cable TV arrived on the scene, or rather, Community Antenna Television (CATV); which brought "distant signals" into one community from another. Homes wired to a CATV system could have up to 20 signals pumped to them without any new stations being constructed; as CATV spread, the whole of the existing mainstream broadcasting industry reached for its lawbooks and found ways to limit its scope just as it curtailed the possibilities of the UHF band a decade before. The programme-makers complained that the CATV operators were in breach of copyright since nothing was paid for the programmes which were lifted from the empty air and given to people for whom they were not originally intended. The owners of local stations complained that their viewers were being filched from them by unlicensed freebooters whose only assets were an aerial and a reel of wire. The networks were the most dismayed of all and complained that the CATV would confuse the neat national system of broadcasting and drive them out of business altogether, leaving the viewer without his prized television services which arrived hitherto at no direct cost to him at all.

The FCC itself did not welcome the cable operators as the long awaited diversifiers for whom they had yearned for so many years but as saboteurs of the UHF stations which the agency had been encouraging for so long and to so little avail. (Even a reforming commissioner like Kenneth Cox earned the reputation of being anti-CATV.) The FCC first established its right to act as the enfranchiser of CATV systems and then proceeded to regulate the new industry into harmlessness. A complex set of rules was drawn up which has made it impossible for the cable operators to distribute distant signals in such a way as to aggregate audiences sufficiently to form a viable revenue base and thus challenge any television network.

At first the FCC's policy was to keep CATV out of the hundred largest cities (in which live 90% of all viewers); in these communities the UHF stations were to exercise the sole privilege of pluralising the content of broadcasting. Later the FCC changed tack and decided that CATV's ability to import signals was to be curtailed because of the copyright infringement entailed. The FCC eventually brought to birth a plan agreed between networks and large CATV operators which effectively prevented powerful rival signals from being imported into the major centres of population. CATV was permitted to grow but not in ways which enabled the powerless minorities of taste, spread across large geographical areas, to exercise major cultural influence or patronage over significant sections of the television medium. The identification of television with the one mass audience was maintained. The removal of this second threat from the networks coincided with a major revival of their collective profits, both as suppliers to affiliates and as owners of stations. For several years (embracing the period in which the pressure against CATV development was at its height), their profits had been stagnating. The total hours of viewing in America increased in the early 1970s, but very little of it was devoted to the new fringe television developments. The profusion of outlets did not materially affect the heartland of American television.

The three networks, having rooted themselves very firmly indeed in the first years of television expansion and them having passed through some years of external threats, lived through the affluence of the 1960s without any serious challenge to their supremacy. Public television emerged, with the help of foundation and federal grants, from being an educational appendage to broadcasting,

TABLE 1.
PROFITS OF THE 3 U.S. NETWORKS AND THEIR WHOLLY OWNED STATIONS

Year	Total ($ millions)	Networks ($ millions)	Wholly Owned Stations ($ millions)
1966	187	79	108
1967	163	56	107
1968	179	56	122
1969	226	93	133
1970	167	50	117
1971	145	54	91
1972	213	111	102
1973	288	184	103
1974	330	225	106
1975	314	209	106

Source: Reprinted with permission from "The TV Networks—a Primer," *Journal of Communication*, 26(4) (Autumn 1976): 59.

albeit with VHF signals, to become at last a serious national presence at the end of the decade. The Nixon administration, however, had so changed the nature of its finance and its governing ordinances that it, too, despite its rapidly growing attractiveness, had hitherto failed to make itself into a permanent and national rival to the commercial networks. It was saddled with localism, in editorial sovereignty and in revenue; to build its teams of programme makers it had perhaps excessive recourse to British and other European imports and models. It has indeed evolved in the direction of becoming a rival programme-making entity in the front line of the television industry, but it is taking its time and has not yet conjured forth out of the mass market that band of consistent upper-middle taste which television requires to achieve its take-off into sustained quality. Public television has nonetheless built up a new professional sector in American television which must be of paramount historical importance. In its five main production centres, each based upon one of the larger local stations, it has acquired the essential fusion of transmission and programme-making in single units.

Public television, in the United States, is confronting one of the great paradoxes of television culture. It has come to rely for almost the whole of its dominant offerings upon British and other foreign material. The British system is built upon an extreme narrowness of outlook, three national channels (two of them owned by one organisation) with very little regional material. The much admired quality of British television, though rooted in the culture as a whole, is channelled into the programmes precisely because of the lack of diversity of outlets; teams of producers may be built up over the course of years like performers in a Japanese opera. The departments of the BBC are in essence workshops where professional techniques and outlook are acquired by an individual over a slow period of years.

The American system has had to look to Hollywood for similar concentrations of trained talent. Public television has provided the structure but not yet the concentration of ability. Recourse to British material has in some ways actually retarded the development of an autochthonous American public television culture, with its own genres and styles. There are signs, however, that in the last four to five years the necessary process of team-building has begun to have its effects, though still betraying its trans-Atlantic borrowing. The *Adams Chronicles* one might cite as one major example, *Nova*, the science series, as another. The regrouping and new recognition of taste requires to go further than the identification of a narrow Anglophilia. No real change may take place in the relationship between audience and medium until television finds a way to attack the central mass of the audience. The siphoning off of a minority or two is not in itself the first step towards conquering the heartland of broadcasting. *Roots* is a token of the fact that there are majorities to be won in America.

The conquering of the ratings by ABC for the first time in many years in 1975 was achieved by the dextrous use of traditional devices, more and better movies, a nightly news which seemed to be brighter than its rivals, skillful choice and scheduling of the mediocre in entertainment, and the willingness to try out certain new formulae in situation comedy. But the restoration in the network fortunes of ABC, which will not be toppled very quickly from its dominance over the other networks—by their own admission—is more than a further round in the endless dograce of the networks. ABC realized that the emergence of "anthology drama," or the dramatization, à l'anglaise, of classic novels of the language, represented a substantial shift in popular taste; the disadvantage of the dramatized novel, in the context of the American television system, is that it provides only an eight- or ten-week run of programmes, when a network requires at least one and preferably two whole seasons to build up and exploit an audience for a new series.

Roots was more than an experiment with a particular genre, it was a scheduling innovation, daring in the extreme by the standards of American television. The successful series brings the inestimable advantages of a high rating regularly once a week, which lifts the average rating for a whole season commensurately. ABC ran *Roots* throughout an entire week, thereby reducing its potential loss should the series become merely a prestige event, but making possible a major leap in its overall rating over a very brief period should the project strike a chord with the audience, which in the event it did. A scheduling experiment is in some ways more meaningful than an experiment with a new programme form or format; a scheduling experiment by its nature is an experiment in a new relationship with the audience.

The utter completeness of the network system's dominance should not lead one to extrapolate very far from one or two remarkable events. What ABC has discovered is something which has always been available for discovery, that the American audience, like any other, can choose only from among what is offered it; an increase in the range of what is available can often pay off handsomely. It entails risk, and the network system in the 1960s and early 1970s has fled from risk-taking simply because there seemed to be more to lose than to win. Today, the financial pressures on the networks have intensified, to the extent that a network may overcome its difficulties by expanding the available choice, by spreading its patronage over a wider range of writers than is normal among television entrepreneurs.

There is, however, another manifestation of a restless audience in America, one that has begun to be recognized and to express itself in financially meaningful terms. An audience has evolved from the generation of the 1960s which is prepared to identify itself across the networks, as it were, and the result is a series of efforts to form "fourth networks" across the United States on an ad hoc basis. *Ten Who Dared*, a BBC import, was turned into one such an ad hoc network when a commercial sponsor (Mobil) assembled a group of stations willing to break ranks with affiliated networks for the purpose of transmitting this single prize-winning semi-documentary series. *Roots* can be cited as another example of an innovation in genre creating an audience for a documentary product which appealed massively at a certain level of the emotions normally unplumbed by network television. The serialisation of the American novel which has now established itself as a new genre within American television is a phenomenon of the new audience. ABC, so long the third of the trio of networks, has had to say something new to American emotions in the course of its successful and sustained assault on the ratings. Ready for the late 1970s these are signs and portents rather than predictive factors gesturing towards a new television culture in an American tradition, which could do more to change the nature of the medium than another ten years of liberal-reformist regulation.

The only test of a television system is whether it attracts the best of the available writers. Whether the system is commercial or public the tangible expression of its cultural purpose lies in the distribution of its patronage, which means in a word from whom it chooses to commission work. The revenue system, however, is itself a reflection of the way in which the audience is being defined and a television based entirely and permanently upon spot advertising and sponsorship, particularly in so segmented and profuse a manner as American television, is very unlikely to provide an audience with whom writers can easily identify. For one thing, it never becomes *their* audience. Out of the profusion, however, there are springing opportunities, perhaps wastefully and prodigally acquired, which American television might seize to take its rightful place as a leader rather than a laggard in the creative use of television.

Perhaps the real key to the imperfections of the American television market has been the fact that the creative worker has been presented in effect with three identical potential employers. No single production firm has ever acquired more than 10 per cent of the series being transmitted at a given moment. Scores of producers have worked in the field. It is the buying side of the market—that which alone represents the audience—which has been distorted. So long as television scheduling depends upon repetitive elongated series this distorted machinery of acquisition imposes its distortions upon the suppliers. A large number of programmes is being offered to a small number of networks; most new series are tried out and then scrapped because they fail, in the few weeks they are tried, to seize the same audience which can be acquired by a more familiar long-running series, based upon a well-established star or popular routine. When a series does indeed break through the structural constraints which operate so harshly against it to begin with, it becomes a kind of monopoly, highly desirable to any one of the three possible buyers, and the producer can command an extraordinarily high price. American television therefore imposes on producers both too near a certainty of failure and excessive rewards for success. It turns creative work into a form of gambling. It imposes upon writers and performers the appalling burden of continuing to produce material according to easily regurgitated formulae. American television is seldom hand-made, therefore, seldom custom-built for an audience chosen by the writer, but mass-produced and assembled by often interchangeable writers or producers. The short series and the single play have been long denied to American viewers and American writers. A tradition going back to the "anthology theatre" of the early 1950s is now being rediscovered. The television seasons of 1975 and 1976 have felt the pressure of a more serious audience. Classic novels have been given a new life in network television. Little has changed in the machinery of the medium: the mass of the audience is still held by the networks collectively. Perhaps the different vision of the audience held by public television has been momentarily communicated to its rivals. It is more important that a different kind of programme has come to be made than that it has come to be watched.

Can it be that the American audience's ardour towards television as a whole has begun to cool? We can compare surveys over the years and argue over the meaning of the data; one can never know whether the audience would have given 1970s answers in the 1950s, if 1970s questions had been asked them. However, in a narrower range of time we can compare Gary Steiner's classic

survey of 1960[14] with Robert Bower's[15] of 1970 and gain the sense that at some
point in the decade television peaked out, even though the answers to many of
the questions remained roughly the same. For instance, half of all viewers on
both occasions said they watched television for no greater purpose than because
it is "such a pleasant way to spend an evening." On the other hand, the number
of people who put television programmes first in importance before automobiles, fashions for women, popular music, and movies dropped from 29 to 16
per cent over the period. Even though the total of television viewing had increased by nearly an hour per day for the average viewer, a higher proportion in
1960 was saying that television "was getting worse all the time"; in fact the
number had doubled. The Lou Harris surveys also have shown a marked dropping in public esteem for the television medium; between the decades the television professional dropped to the bottom-but-one (only labour officials were
below) position in the hierarchy of esteem for different professional groups.

It is not inconsistent with the lowering of television by all the standard questionnaire yardsticks that the viewing of serious programmes has increased. Serious programmes of a kind. The Watergate hearings held a consistently higher
audience than the normal run of daytime viewing, though that is strained evidence to go on. The public affairs programmes of the present time, *Sixty Minutes*
in particular, have shown a far higher survival pattern than their predecessors of
the 1960s, when even the prestige of Murrow was insufficient to keep public
affairs steady in the schedules.

The television of the 1950s, including the "anthology theatre" of
Chayevsky, Mosel, and others and the Murrow-Friendly reports, had perhaps
an easier time. With television reaching 10 per cent of all homes in 1949, and
still at 30–40 percent by 1953–1954, it was easier for such programmes to hold
their place. It was when the medium was present in 88 per cent of all homes at
the dawn of the 1960s that the kind of programme which audiences had deliberately to "select" found it hard to stay in the affections of network management.
By that token the switch, in ratings terms, to more serious forms of television at
the present time tells us something more definite about the average viewer's
attitude towards his programmes. The 1950s, the "Golden Age" of television,
had a much easier time; the whole of television was destined for a "minority."

The gradual loosening of television's grip over the audience, which can be
felt in many societies at the present time, though not necessarily reflected in the
arithmetic of surveys, must have its implications elsewhere, not least in the
revenue calculations of the networks, where advertisers will need to work harder to make viewers respond, or spread their messages across a wider range of
media. Over the last eight years advertisers have had increasing difficulty with
the medium; certain types of appeal to consumers have been less effective,
housewives of this decade do not identify so readily with the houseproud per-
fectionists of the washing ads. On the one hand the networks have fought more
shrilly for their audiences, notably with the widespread development of the
game show format, appealing to the more grasping side of the viewers' nature.
On the other hand, they have made feints at a more mature viewer.

The gentle release from the embrace of television, if that is the right meta-
phor for what is happening, should have some impact upon the image of the
medium itself, upon the range of concerns which society in general visits upon

the medium. The decade of the 1960s generated two separate literatures concerning the media: the former dwelt upon an alleged transformation in perception brought on by the dissemination of increasing amounts of information through pictures while the latter arose fundamentally from a professional sociological concern for the precise effects on mores and attitudes of millions of man-years of television viewing. On the one hand the decade opened with the publication of *The Image* by Daniel Boorstin (which, if any book ever did, left its label attached to a maturing bottle of prevailing ideas), who began his book: ". . . I describe the world of our making, how we have used our wealth, our literature, our technology and our progress, to create the thicket of unreality which stands between us and the facts of life."[16]

In the 1960s we were invited to act upon the assumption that we no longer (could no longer) perceive things as they actually are—the processes of learning were henceforth befuddled by the experience we absorbed from a contraption which stood between all reality and all comprehension. McLuhan and his followers were quick to point out the political implications of the media society; the Jeffersonian voter was decently interred. "Voting in the traditional sense is through," wrote Marshall McLuhan in *Playboy*, "as we leave the age of political parties, political issues and political goals and enter an age where the collective tribal image and the iconic image of the tribal chieftain is the overriding political reality."[17] There was an implicit denial that the viewer could any longer participate in that fuller citizenship which television explicitly offered. The worlds of commerce, education, and political management, among others, were quick to grasp the need to adapt to a new social environment dominated by media messages.

The literature of media effects was of a much older strain. It descended into the universities of the television age partly from advertising research and sprang from the widespread fears generated after World War I concerning the effects of propaganda on the mass mind. A tremendous amount of academic effort had been invested in the search for direct media effects from the birth of television as a mass medium in the 1950s. Effects sociology gradually earned a suspicion amounting to contempt among media professionals and brought about a tension which has survived until the present era when producers and researchers have each come to accept that the other party is there to stay. The effects researchers in the growth period of television thought it might be possible to isolate media from other influences and to decide, in a precise way, which kinds of television content produced which kinds of response through society as a whole. Now that television is inextricable from all other social influences, effects research has developed along other and perhaps more fruitful lines. In the 1960s it lives under the shadow of Joseph Klapper's masterful and devastating summary of all previous research efforts: "Mass communications *ordinarily* does not serve as a necessary and sufficient cause of audience effects, but rather functions among and through a nexus of mediating factors and influences."[18] The research genre grew and fed an increasingly politicised international debate concerning violence in society, but it concentrated more upon its own methodology, allowing itself only the occasional foray directly into the scrutiny of programme-making.

One looks forward, therefore, to an unravelling of the many-sideness of the television relationship with society. The medium is firmly established as a means of commerce, of entertainment, of information of a kind. Rather than concentrating upon its unitary impact on society, its increasing and more subtle uses and potentials should encourage the academic community to see it not so much as a single phenomenon, but as a conduit for a series of influences modified by a single system of governance. An overly crude view of television implies nothing less than an overly crude view of the audience, and that is something from which even the networks are now apparently receding. It is the powerful governing machinery of the media which is the part of the medium most hidden from view, the seven-eighths of the iceberg. So far all that academic observation of the phenomenon has achieved is a distant sighting; what it must now do is to melt it.

If television as such has the power to impose a new cognition upon society, then it has already by now done so; and we are what has resulted; we are what the critics of television warned our parents against. The task in the next period of time—in that new America which must be visible in the screen if anywhere— is to make television the object of the same kind of analysis which is granted to permanent accepted institutions. The media are a kind of surrogate government which should give rise to its own parallel political science. The decline in the intensity of television's relationship with its audience should help it towards a cultural normalcy—just another medium for creative work, for journalism, for political communication. The television of the 1980s might therefore be freer of social magic, but equally in need of internal observation.

REFERENCES

[1] See for example the discussion of the theories of crowd psychology of Gabriel Tarde and Gustave le Bon in Graham Wallas, *The Great Society* (London: Macmillan, 1941), Chap. 80.

[2] See Norman Mailer, *St. George and the Godfather* (New York: New American Library, 1973), and Edwin Diamond, *The Tin Kazoo: Television, Politics and the News* (Cambridge, Mass: M.I.T. Press, 1975), pp. 25–27.

[3] Robert MacNeil, *The People Machine: The Influence of Television upon American Politics* (New York: Harper & Row, 1968).

[4] Douglass Cater, *TV and Thinking People* (Aspen, Colorado: Aspen Institute for Humanistic Studies, policy paper, 1976).

[5] Van Wyck Brooks, *The Confident Years, 1885–1915* (London: Dent, 1953), p. 327.

[6] President Roosevelt's Message to Congress, S. Doc. 144, 73d Congress, 2d Session, February 26, 1934.

[7] The Communications Act, 1934. Public Law 416, 73d Congress Section 315 a (4).

[8] Ibid., Section 326.

[9] Source of figures: FCC reports.

[10] "The Blue Book" is the familiar name given to the FCC's programme policy statement, "Public Service Responsibility of Broadcast Licensees" (March 7, 1946).

[11] See Erik Barnuow, *The Image Empire* (History of Broadcasting in the United States, vol. 3) p. 198.

[12] Francis A. Lees and Charles Y. Yang, "The Redistributional Effect of Television Advertising," *Economic Journal*, 76 (June 1966): 328–336.

[13] See a detailed discussion of this in Roger Noll, Merton J. Peck, and John J. McGowan, *Economic Aspects of Television Regulation* (Washington, D.C.: Brookings Institution, 1973), Chap. 2, "Television and Consumer Welfare."

[14] Gary Steiner, *The People Look at Television* (New York: Knopf, 1963).

[15] Robert T. Bower, *Television and the Public* (New York: Holt, Rinehart & Winston, 1973).

[16] Daniel Boorstin, *The Image* (London: Weidenfeld, 1961), p. 3.

[17] "Playboy Interview: Marshall McLuhan—Candid Conversation," *Playboy* (March 1969): 71–72.

[18] Joseph T. Klapper, *The Effects of Mass Communication* (New York: Free Press, 1960), p. 8.

THOMAS SOWELL

Ethnicity in a Changing America

THE RAPID AND far-reaching changes which swept across the United States in the decades since World War II had especially dramatic impact on racial and ethnic relations. For example, Jews were restricted or excluded from many university faculties before the war,[1] but in the postwar era their representation on such faculties rose far beyond their proportion of the population.[2] Sports which totally excluded black athletes before the war came to be dominated by black athletes after the war; in baseball, for example, there were seven consecutive years in which no white man won the National League's Most Valuable Player award.[3] Anti-Japanese laws, which flourished in California before the war, were resoundingly defeated in a postwar referendum.[4] Attitude surveys showed major reversals of public opinion on race and ethnicity,[5] and rising rates of intermarriage further substantiated these changes. More than 40 percent of all Japanese-American men now marry women who are not Japanese American,[6] and more than half of all Irish-American, German-American, and Polish-American married men are married to women outside their own respective ethnic groups.[7] Ironically, the once popular concept of America as a "melting pot" is now sweepingly dismissed by intellectuals at a time when it is closer to reality than before.

Ethnicity remains a major factor in such objective variables as income, education, fertility, unemployment, and crime, as well as in such subjective variables as general opinions and political preferences. However, ethnicity as an explanation is too general to explain very much. It could conceivably mean anything from genetic determinism to sweeping charges of "racism" as the reason for all intergroup differences. Moreover, American ethnic groups differ in so many demographic, geographic, and other respects that it is necessary to separate out the effects of these other differences in order to determine how much effect ethnicity, as such, has on the behavior of ethnic groups themselves or on the larger society's behavior toward them. For example, American ethnic groups differ substantially in median age—by more than a decade, in some cases[8]—and any two groups (ethnic or otherwise) with differing age distributions would tend to differ in a number of age-related phenomena, including income, fertility, unemployment, and crime, even if there were no other significant differences between the groups, and even if society made no conscious distinctions between them. In short, gross differences among ethnic groups have many sources, some ethnic, and some not; and these various sources of differences have to be considered and weighed individually.

Before attempting to account for the socioeconomic differences among American ethnic groups, it will be necessary to consider the magnitude of such differences, and the trends over time. Then it will be possible to consider such factors as age, discrimination, urbanization, and public policy.

1. Ethnic Characteristics

There is no single, comprehensive source of data on major American ethnic groups, nor any easy or certain way of making the data from various sources completely comparable. However, data for a number of ethnic groups can be obtained from the same sources, so that there is comparability among groups covered by a given source, even if not among groups whose data are derived from different sources. Data for seven of the ethnic groups covered here are from the decennial Census and data for five more ethnic groups are from the occasional *Current Population Reports* of the Bureau of the Census. These data are supplemented by private surveys. Each source will be identified as we consider, in order, income, occupation, fertility, and attitudes.

INCOME

Despite a tendency to think of "minorities" as poorer than the general U.S. population, some ethnic groups are above the national average in income, and some are below it. Those ethnic groups whose incomes are available from the 1970 Census are shown in Table 1. It is noteworthy that both Chinese Americans and Japanese Americans had higher incomes than the U.S. population as a whole, though both groups are visibly, persistently, and genetically different

TABLE 1.
MEAN INCOME (1969) OF EMPLOYED PERSONS

	Personal Income	Family Income
Total U.S. Population[1]	$ 5,817	$ 10,678
American Indians[2]	3,715	6,621
Black Americans[3]	3,680	6,821
Chinese Americans[2]	5,955	12,176
Filipino Americans[2]	5,149	10,395
Japanese Americans[2]	6,330	13,377
Puerto Ricans[2]	4,417	6,728
West Indians[4]	5,057	9,821

Source: 1970 U.S. Census

[1]Data from published 1970 U.S. Census.

[2]Data from 1970 U.S. Census, Public Use Sample.

[3]Data from 1970 U.S. Census, Public Use Sample, excluding black Americans of West Indian ancestry as defined in footnote 4.

[4]Data from 1970 U.S. Census, Public Use Sample; "West Indians" are defined here as black residents of the United States who were either born in the West Indies or whose parent(s) came from the West Indies.

from the general population. It is also noteworthy that black West Indians had higher incomes than Puerto Ricans, most of whom are white. A closer examination of color as an explanatory variable will be made in Section 2.

Some ethnic groups are not directly identifiable from the 1970 Census categories, nor would the decennial Census' "nativity and parentage" data cover them, because these groups immigrated so long ago that many (or most) would now be native born of native-born parents. The data in Table 2 are from special surveys conducted by the Bureau of the Census, but carried out with procedures differing from those of the decennial Census. Because these surveys do not cover 1969, the year whose income is reported in the 1970 Census, data from two surveys for the years 1968 and 1970 are shown in Table 2.

The data in Table 2 are less reliable than those in Table 7, for a number of reasons, but they probably are the best that is available on the groups in question. It is noteworthy that the older European immigrant groups' incomes are not above those of the two Oriental groups, nor dramatically above those of black West Indians.

Finally, there is an important group—Jewish Americans—who are not included in the government's data because of constitutional limitations on religious inquiries by the Bureau of the Census. A private survey by the National Jewish Population Study found a median family income of $19,259 among Jewish Americans in 1969. Even though the exact figure may be questioned (there was a nonresponse rate of about one-third on this question in the survey), the general position of the Jews as first in income among American ethnic groups agrees with the findings of other surveys.[9]

OCCUPATION

Because income and occupation are closely related, it is not surprising to find that those ethnic groups with higher incomes tend also to have higher occupational status. Rather than attempt to enumerate the whole range of occupations, three categories are selected for Table 3. The corresponding data for the descendants of European immigrants in 1969 are shown in Table 4. Because the data for the latter do not include "unemployed," there is some upward bias in the percentages for other occupational groups.

Mexican Americans are missing from Table 4 because their occupational distribution in 1969 was not covered by the *Current Population Reports*. How-

TABLE 2.

MEDIAN FAMILY INCOME

	1968	1970
German Americans	$ 8,607	$10,402
Irish Americans	8,127	9,964
Italian Americans	8,808	11,089
Mexican Americans	5,488	8,946
Polish Americans	8,849	11,619

Source: *Current Population Reports* of the U.S. Bureau of the Census (Series P–20, nos. 213, 221, 224, 249) (Washington, D.C.: Government Printing Office).

TABLE 3.

OCCUPATIONAL DISTRIBUTION, 1969

	Professional, Technical, and Kindred	Operatives	Unemployed
Total U.S. Population[1]	14.0%	17.0%	3.9%
American Indians[2]	9.6	19.5	10.0
Black Americans[2]	7.6	22.4	6.3
Chinese Americans[2]	25.3	14.4	2.7
Filipino Americans[2]	23.1	12.8	4.4
Japanese Americans[2]	18.2	11.9	2.1
Puerto Ricans[2]	5.0	34.4	6.3
West Indians[2]	15.2	12.7	3.7

Source: 1970 U.S. Census
[1]Published Census data.
[2]1970 Census, Public Use Sample.

ever, it is clear from a later survey (for 1971) that their occupational status has been low: only 4.5 percent were professional or technical, and 27.7 percent were operative.[10]

In occupation, as in income, there is no decisive advantage apparent for European minorities as compared to nonwhite ethnic groups as a whole—the differences within the latter being more dramatic than their overall differences from the so-called "white ethnics." The occupational data, like the income data, also demonstrate how misleading it is to compare one group with "the national average," for this average is derived from widely disparate statistical results for different groups. No group is as unusual as comparisons with a mythical "national average" might suggest. All have companion groups in comparable circumstances.

FERTILITY

In general, the respective fertility rates of American ethnic groups in Table 5 are inversely related to their income in Table 1. The lowest-income groups— American Indians and black Americans—have the largest number of children per woman, whereas the higher-income Orientals have among the lowest number of children per woman. This inverse relationship is not perfect, but it is very strong nevertheless.

Although fertility is ultimately a biological function, it has no apparent connection with race. Native black Americans and black West Indians living in the United States have sharply contrasting fertility patterns—the former with one of the highest ratios of children per woman and the latter with the very lowest among any of the ethnic groups shown (see Table 5). These two branches of the same race have greater fertility differences from each other than either has from the U.S. population as a whole. Moreover, the complete reshuffling of the rank order of fertility among American ethnic groups since 1910 also indicates a socioeconomic rather than a biological phenomenon. So too does the fact that some groups have more than halved their fertility rates in two generations—and

	Male		Female	
	Professional, Technical, and Kindred	Operatives	Professional, Technical, and Kindred	Operatives
German Americans	14.8%	18.2%	16.6%	13.0%
Irish Americans	14.1	17.9	14.9	13.1
Italian Americans	13.5	20.0	9.7	25.3
Polish Americans	14.5	19.6	13.1	19.2

Source: Current Population Reports, U.S. Bureau of the Census (Series P–20, no. 221) (Washington, D.C.: Government Printing Office, 1970).

TABLE 5.
FERTILITY

	Children per Woman (1969), 15 years and older[1]	Children per Woman (1969), 15–44 years old[2]	Children per Woman (1969), 35–44 years old[3]	Children per Woman (1910), 35–44 years old[3]
Total U.S. Population	2.1	1.7	3.0	3.4
American Indians	2.8	—	—	—
Black Americans	2.4	2.0	3.6	4.2
Chinese Americans	1.9	—	—	—
Filipino Americans	1.9	—	—	—
German Americans	—	1.8	3.0	4.0
Irish Americans	—	1.9	3.1	3.3
Italian Americans	—	1.5	2.4	5.5
Japanese Americans	2.0	—	—	—
Mexican Americans	—	2.2	4.4	5.3
Polish Americans	—	1.6	2.5	5.9
Puerto Ricans	2.4	2.1	—	—
Russian Americans	—	1.4	2.4	5.3
West Indians	1.8	—	—	—

Source: U.S. Bureau of the Census.
[1] 1970 Census, Public Use Sample.
[2] Current Population Reports, P–20, no. 226, p. 14.
[3] Ibid., p. 28.

that this reduction has been most pronounced among the most rapidly rising group, the Jews (Russian Americans).

The inverse relationship between fertility and socioeconomic status is particularly striking within ethnic groups with a generally low socioeconomic level. The poorest and least educated members of such groups tend to have even more children than equally poor and equally uneducated numbers of the general population, whereas the higher income or better educated members of such ethnic groups tend to have even fewer children than equally high income or equally well-educated members of the general population. For example, Mexican Americans in general have the highest fertility rate among all the ethnic groups shown in Table 5, second column, but Mexican-American wives who have had four years of high school have fewer children than the national average among similarly educated wives, and fewer children than similarly educated wives in the other ethnic groups shown.[11] Many studies of blacks have shown a similar phenomenon: more children than their white counterparts at the low end of the socioeconomic scale and fewer children than their white counterparts at the upper end of the socioeconomic scale.[12] Indeed, upper-level blacks have long had fertility rates too low to reproduce themselves.[13]

Among the grim implications of such fertility patterns in low-income ethnic groups is that much of the hard struggle upward from poverty toward affluence has to be repeated over again from scratch in each new generation, because those who have succeeded do not reproduce themselves and those who remain trapped in poverty supply a disproportionate amount of the next generation. Looked at another way, much hard-won, and extremely valuable, "human capital" (in the form of successful experience) perishes with each generation among low-income minorities, whereas such human capital is progressively accumulated and compounded among groups whose more successful numbers supply a larger proportion of their next generation.

Another grim implication of ethnic fertility patterns is found in a study which showed that three-quarters of all black males who failed the Army mental tests came from families of four or more children, and one-half from families of six or more children.[14] The negative effect of large family size on mental test scores is a phenomenon which extends across racial or socioeconomic lines.[15] It has obvious importance in an era when educational requirements for jobs are rising. Moreover, it may indicate something about the general problems of children raised with an inadequate share of adult attention. Certainly the Army mental test findings undermine the arguments of those who claim that promoting birth control among low-income ethnic groups is a form of "subtle genocide."[16] The behavior of the more successful members of such ethnic groups suggests the opposite. So too does the historical record of sharply declining fertility rates among ethnic groups that have risen and are rising.

ATTITUDES

Although hard data are available on objective variables such as income or education, attitudes must be either inferred from behavior or judged by answers to survey questions—answers which may be biased by such factors as the wording of the question or the respondents' beliefs about the expected or acceptable answer. Nevertheless, attitudes by and about ethnic groups are too important to ignore. When there are major changes in such attitudes indicated by social behavior, survey responses, voting data—or, even more important, by all three indicating the same pattern or trend—then clearly it is a social phenomenon worth noting.

Some indicators of major changes in public opinion on race and ethnicity have already been noted: the breakdown of employment barriers against Jews and Negroes in the post-World War II period, and of intermarriage barriers as regards various ethnic groups, Oriental as well as European. Voting behavior likewise shows similar trends: not only are many more black public officials being elected, but some are being elected by overwhelmingly white constituencies—Senator Brooke in Massachusetts and Mayor Bradley in Los Angeles being the most striking examples. The first Oriental Senator and the first Catholic President were also elected during this period—and both became better known for their personal characteristics than for their ethnic designations. An ethnic slur against the Senator by a minor figure at the Watergate hearings brought instant, outraged mail and forced a public apology. Opinion surveys show similar major changes in the postwar era. As recently as 1958, just over half of the voters said that they would not vote for a "well-qualified" black candidate for President, but by 1971 less than one-fourth of the voters took that position.[17] Similar changes of opinion were apparent in surveys dealing with social contacts: white parents' acceptance of their children's bringing home black playmates grew from 40 percent in 1956 to 81 percent in 1971; a plurality in favor of state laws banning interracial marriage in 1965 changed to a majority against such laws by 1971.[18]

Although the general public's attitudes toward racial and ethnic differences are important, so too are the attitudes of the ethnic groups themselves. These attitudes often differ sharply from the media image of these groups. Almost two-thirds of black Americans found the law "too lenient" with criminals, and 78 percent declared themselves "sick and tired of hearing people attack patriotism, morality and other traditional American values."[19] Even in an era of interethnic rivalries and "white backlash" against policies to advance blacks, Governor Wallace obtained only 7 percent of the Irish votes in New York in 1968, no more than 17 percent of the Slavic vote in any state, only 10 percent of the Italian vote nationwide, and 2 percent of the Jewish vote. At the height of media discussion of "black anti-Semitism," Jewish candidates received overwhelming majorities—over 90 percent of the vote—in black districts in Illinois, Pennsylvania, and Ohio in 1968, and in New York State Arthur Goldberg "won a greater percentage of the black vote than any other similar candidate running for statewide office since Robert F. Kennedy."[20]

The post-World War II era cannot be generalized as the continuation or culmination of historic trends toward racial or ethnic toleration or acceptance, nor are all the current trends promising in that respect. Despite the view that "time" is a key variable tending to produce tolerance, there have been sustained periods of major retrogression in racial and ethnic relationships in the United States. The three decades prior to the Civil War saw ever tighter legal restrictions and ever narrowing economic opportunities for the half-million free blacks in the United States, and the period from about 1890 to World War I saw major political and social retrogression for the black population as a whole, culminating in the Woodrow Wilson administration, which was a disaster for black Americans. Anti-Semitism was stronger in the last quarter of the nineteenth century than it had been before. Mexican Americans likewise suffered growing intolerance around the turn of the twentieth century.[21] The restrictive immigration laws of the 1920s showed an increasing hostility toward ethnic Americans generally, one symptom of which was the spread of the Ku Klux Klan into northern communities on a large scale for the first time.[22] Anti-Japanese prejudice reached a new peak with the mass internment of Japanese Americans during World War II.

Once the post-World War II era is seen as a special period—not absolutely unique, but also not part of a constant or inevitable trend—then questions may be raised about its nature, its sources, and its likelihood of persistence. The racism of the Nazis and its consequences undoubtedly discredited racism in America and elsewhere. The ideals of the war effort, the international cooperation necessary for victory, and the experience of many Americans of serving together in the armed forces with people from other ethnic groups also set the stage for a reevaluation of existing racial and ethnic practices. Judicial and political decisions reinforced and extended these tendencies.

Although there is widespread evidence that American public opinion rejects restrictions based on race, religion, or nationality, there is also growing evidence of impatience with programs providing benefits based on similar ethnic criteria. Quotas or statistical "balance" have been rejected by public opinion and by elected officials, whether in "affirmative action" in employment programs or in school busing.[23] Violence has also polarized the races: after several summers of ghetto rioting, one-third of the American public said that they felt differently about Negroes—and almost all of these had changed to less respect.[24]

2. Causal Factors

Without attempting a definitive disentanglement of multiple causes, it is possible to make some general assessment of various factors in explaining some of the large—and even startling—differences that exist among American ethnic groups. Some of the factors examined here will include such well-recognized variables as discrimination and government policy, as well as the controversial and emotionally charged issue of genetic differences in intelligence. More mundane and more neglected variables, such as age and location, will also be considered. How important any given factor may prove to be in explaining ethnic group differences is ultimately an empirical question which cannot be decided by the amount of support or controversy it generates.

AGE

Age suffers the fate of being a noncontroversial variable, of no political or ideological use to anyone, and therefore it is often overlooked in explaining interethnic differences. But median age differences among American ethnic groups are substantial in themselves, and also substantial in their impact on a wide range of socioeconomic variables. Americans of Irish or Italian ancestry have median ages of about 36 years, whereas Americans of Puerto Rican or Mexican background have median ages of just one-half of that (Table 6). Russian Americans (mostly Jewish) are more than a decade older than Irish or Italian Americans, and are therefore nearly three times as old as the two Hispanic groups. Just over one-half of the Russian Americans are 45 years old or older, whereas only 12 percent of Puerto Ricans are that old. Because younger ethnic groups generally have lower incomes than older ethnic groups, the income differences may reflect age (experience) differences, rather than "ethnic" differences, as such—whether ethnic differences are conceived of in terms of the larger society's discrimination or in terms of the respective groups' "ability." As one striking example, Cuban Americans have higher incomes than Mexican Americans, but Mexican Americans earn more than Cuban Americans in the same age brackets; Americans of Cuban ancestry are simply 10 years older than Americans of Mexican ancestry.[25] Any theory which tried to explain the Cubans' "ethnic" advantage over Chicanos in income would be a theory about a nonexistent phenomenon. More broadly, theories which attempt to explain differences between any two ethnic groups, or between a given ethnic group and the "national average," run the risk of explaining too much if they do not first eliminate those differences due simply to differences in age distribution.

When the personal incomes of 30-year-old males are taken from the 1970 Census (Table 7), the differences among ethnic groups are much less than when gross comparisons are made, as in Table 1. Fertility is also an area where the age distribution of an ethnic group makes a difference (Table 8). If there is a dis-

TABLE 6.

AGE

	Median Age in 1969	% 45 and Older	% under 25
Total U.S. Population	28.0	30.2	46.4
American Indians[1]	20.4	19.5	57.7
Black Americans[2]	22.3	23.6	47.4
Chinese Americans[3]	26.8	—	—
German Americans[4]	35.5	37.0	35.7
Irish Americans[4]	36.7	39.3	35.0
Italian Americans[4]	36.1	38.3	35.3
Japanese Americans[5]	32.3	—	—
Mexican Americans[6]	17.8	15.2	62.4
Polish Americans[4]	39.8	43.4	31.1
Puerto Ricans[7]	18.3	12.1	52.2
Russian Americans[4]	45.8	51.4	26.4

Source: U.S. Bureau of the Census.
[1]U.S. Census of Population, 1970; Subject Reports PC(2)-1F, p. 2.
[2]U.S. Census of Population, 1970; Subject Reports PC(2)-1B, p. 2.
[3]U.S. Census of Population, 1970; Subject Reports PC(2)-1G, p. 61.
[4]Current Population Reports, P-20, no. 221, p. 4.
[5]U.S. Census of Population; Subject Reports PC(2)-1G, p. 2.
[6]Current Population Reports, P-20, no. 213, p. 6.
[7]Ibid., p. 6.

TABLE 7.

MEDIAN PERSONAL INCOME OF 30-YEAR-OLD MALES, 1969

American Indians	$ 5,324
Black Americans	5,838
Chinese Americans	7,638
Filipino Americans	5,795
Japanese Americans	9,528
Puerto Ricans	6,175
West Indians	6,561

Source: 1970 Census, Public Use Sample.

proportionate concentration of women in the prime child-bearing years, then the annual birth rate of a group is biased upward, even if the age-specific annual birth rate is no higher than average. If the total number of children per woman is considered, instead of the annual birth rate, then a disproportionate concentration of older women biases the fertility rate upward, because older women tend to have had more total children than younger women, even though younger women may be having more babies currently.

For example, Table 8 shows Filipino and Japanese Americans to have very similar numbers of children per woman, with the Filipinos having slightly less—1.9 versus 2.0. On an age-specific basis, however, Americans of Philippine ancestry generally have more children per woman than do Americans of Japanese ancestry. The age distributions are simply different—with about 36 percent of Japanese-American women being 45 years old or older, whereas only about 21 percent of Filipino-American women are that old. In the case of native black Americans versus black West Indians in the United States, the gross fertility rate differences understate the actual intergroup differences among women of the same age. In the central 25–44 age brackets, native black Americans of native parentage average more than one full child per woman above the fertility rate of those blacks in the United States who were born in the West Indies, or whose parents were born in the West Indies.

Age is also an important hidden factor in ethnic data in another and a very different sense. The internal age-bracket divisions of a given ethnic group represent cohorts of people whose present careers began and developed in different eras. In a society with the kind of rapidly changing racial-ethnic views and practices already noted, this means that different age cohorts are affected by very different social conditions. In turn this means that gross comparisons of one whole ethnic group and another (or one whole ethnic group versus the "national average") may give a very misleading picture as to the current effects of current conditions and policies. For example, it has been found that the economic rate of return on education is lower for blacks than for whites, but an age-cohort breakdown shows that younger blacks have a slightly higher rate of return than their white counterparts.[26] Older blacks were educated in an earlier period, with far fewer days per school year than their white contemporaries in addition to disparities in the quality of education, and they entered a labor market with far more racial barriers to employment and advancement than today. Their current careers reflect those past conditions, whereas the younger

TABLE 8.

FERTILITY BY AGE

	15–24 Years Old		25–34 Years Old	
	Children per Woman	% all Women	Children per Woman	% all Women
American Indians	0.6	29.5	3.0	20.8
Black Americans	0.7	27.1	2.7	18.7
Chinese Americans	0.2	26.3	1.6	22.5
Filipino Americans	0.4	27.2	1.5	33.5
Japanese Americans	0.2	18.1	1.5	19.1
Puerto Ricans	0.7	31.4	2.6	27.6
West Indians	0.3	18.2	1.6	20.0

	35–44 Years Old		45 and Older		TOTAL	
	Children per Woman	% all Women	Children per Woman	% all Women	Children per Woman	% all Women
A.I.	4.4	17.5	3.9	32.3	2.8	100
Black	3.7	17.0	2.9	37.2	2.4	100
Chinese	2.9	20.0	3.0	31.3	1.9	100
Filipino	3.0	18.7	3.6	20.5	1.9	100
Japanese	2.2	17.0	3.0	35.9	2.0	100
P.R.	3.5	19.1	3.5	22.0	2.4	100
W.I.	2.5	20.2	2.2	41.7	1.8	100

Source: 1970 Census, Public Use Sample.

age cohorts of blacks have income, occupational status, etc., which reflect more of the current effects of current conditions.

The magnitudes of the differences between age cohorts of the same ethnic group may be indicated by the fact that more than 20 percent of all blacks in the 55–64-year-old bracket, and more than 40 percent of all blacks 65 and over, have had less than five years of schooling, whereas less than 2 percent of blacks in the 25–29-year-old bracket had such little education. Among Mexican Americans, more than one-fourth of the 55–64-year-olds, and more than half of those 65 and older, have less than five years of education, whereas only 7 percent of the 25–29-year-old Mexican Americans suffer this much educational disadvantage. Puerto Rican data are quite similar to those for Mexican Americans.[27]

Any evaluation of present conditions or present policies on the basis of gross ethnic data without age distinction runs the risk of considering as failures approaches which have in fact proved successful. It may be decades before most or all of an ethnic group consists of people whose careers have developed completely under the more recent conditions and policies. Yet approaches whose success is visible among the younger age cohorts might be mistakenly discarded as failures during the interim, when the gross statistics are dominated by people whose life patterns were set in an earlier era.

Racial progress in economic terms is especially striking among young college-educated people, where black men have already achieved income parity with white men, and black women slightly more than parity with white women. At higher occupational levels—among doctoral scientists and engineers—blacks under 35 earned slightly more than whites under 35 with the same credentials, even though blacks over 50 earned slightly less than whites over 50 with the same credentials. Among college and university faculties, blacks with top credentials and publications generally earn slightly more than whites in the same fields with top credentials and publications.[28]

A neglect of interethnic age differences sometimes creates an unrealistically optimistic picture as well as an unrealistically pessimistic one. For example, blacks as a group have lower death rates than whites as a group. This might seem to negate the view that blacks live under more unhealthy and stressful conditions than whites. But in fact it is simply an age phenomenon. Younger people generally have lower death rates than older people. On an age-specific basis, whites have lower death rates than blacks, though the differences are narrowing.[29]

Much social pathology is associated with age. More than three-quarters of all serious crime in the United States is committed by young people between the ages of 14 and 25 years—and 90 percent of the violent crimes are committed by males.[30] The explosive rise in crime in the United States during the 1960s occurred when there was an increase in the proportion of such males in the American population, as a result of the postwar "baby boom." Obviously, those ethnic groups with unusually large proportions of their population in the crime-prone years will tend to have higher crime rates, even if there were no other factors at work. A major factor in the large black-white difference in crime rates is the difference in the youth components of the two populations. Although black crime rates are many times as high as white crime rates[31]—and the murder rate more than 10 times as high[32]—the "age-specific crime rates of blacks are only slightly higher than those of whites on the same socioeconomic level."[33] Similar factors influence the crime rates of Puerto Ricans and Mexican Americans: more than half of all Puerto Ricans are under 25 years of age, as are almost two-thirds of all Mexican Americans.

Unemployment rates are also heavily influenced by age. Over the years, young men under 20 have consistently had unemployment rates more than double those of men in the 25–34- or 35–44-year age brackets. Ethnic groups with above-average proportions of young people would therefore tend to have above-average unemployment rates, even if there were no other differences to consider. In some respects, age differences outweigh racial differences: black males in the 25–34- and 35–44-year age brackets have lower unemployment rates than white males under 20—and this has been true, consistently, for decades. The high "average" black unemployment rate reflects a very high black teen-age male unemployment rate—above 30 percent throughout the 1970s—and conceals enormous internal age disparities. By contrast, the unemployment rate among black males in the 35–44-year age bracket has gone as high as 10 percent for only one year in more than a quarter of a century.[34]

Teenage unemployment is quite different from adult unemployment, both in its causes and in its consequences. For teenagers in general, the official unemployment rate is biased upward, because it is based on the noninstitutional population, and teenagers are more often institutionalized than adults—principally in schools, colleges, and the military services. The teenage unemployed are therefore divided by a much smaller denominator than they would be if the same age cohorts were adults, so the unemployment percentage comes out correspondingly higher. This is not the sole reason for high teenage unemployment rates, but it is a statistical bias. Moreover, the nature of teenage unemployment is also different. Among black unemployed teenagers surveyed in 1972, almost half were in school, and 83 percent of those in school were looking for part-time work. Those black teenagers who were both out of work and out of school constituted less than 7 percent of black teenagers.[35] Yet this situation has been statistically—and politically—inflated into a "crisis."

LOCATION

In a vast country with substantial income differences among regions, the socioeconomic condition of any ethnic group depends in part on where its members are located. American ethnic groups are not randomly distributed, either geographically or in terms of rural and urban residence.

The distribution of those European ethnic groups that came to the United States in the era of wind-driven ships was strongly influenced—virtually predetermined—by the respective destinations of cargo vessels leaving from their particular part of Europe, predominately northern and western Europe. When steam-powered ships made mass immigration by passenger vessels economically feasible, a whole new pattern of immigration emerged—dominated now by immigration from eastern and southern Europe.[36] The destinies of immigrants were shaped by conditions in the places where they happened to land. For example, many of the Irish landed in Boston, a city shunned by American working-class groups at that time because of its lack of appropriate job opportunities. But the Irish—fleeing from a devastating famine—had little choice but to make the best of this unpromising situation, which contributed to the relative slowness of their socioeconomic rise.[37]

Those immigrants who arrived virtually penniless—the Irish, the Italians, and the Jews, for example—settled right in the ports of debarkation. Those groups who had enough money left after the voyage to exercise some locational preference—the Germans and Scandinavians, for example—typically settled elsewhere. Today's ethnic settlement patterns still reflect those initial conditions. The subsequent economic history of the United States also affected the location of different ethnic groups differently. Those who arrived during the era of massive railroad building, and who were sufficiently poor to take on this hard and dangerous work, often settled in geographic patterns reflecting the routes of those railroads.[38] Similarly, those groups who arrived during the development of coalmining, steelmaking, etc., also had their geographic distributions influenced by the location of those industries.

Black Americans had their initial locations chosen for them by others during the era of slavery, but again it was not a random choice. They were concentrated in the region whose climate and soil were suited to the kinds of crops that could flourish under the restricted work patterns necessitated by slavery.[39] With the invention of the cotton gin in 1793, slavery in America became overwhelmingly cotton-producing slavery,[40] and the distribution of the black population accordingly moved toward the kinds of land best suited for cotton growing. Beginning with the Census of 1790, the center of distribution of the black population moved southwestward, at an average rate of 49 miles per decade, for most of the nineteenth century. For those blacks who were free before the Civil War—about half a million "free persons of color" in 1850[41]—the movement was in the opposite direction, toward the Northeast and, within both North and South, toward urban areas. The "free persons of color" were more urbanized than the white population,[42] and more urbanized than the general black population would be until almost the middle of the twentieth century.

Oriental ethnic groups have tended to settle in those parts of the United States most geographically accessible to Asia—the West Coast; and Mexican and Cuban Americans have likewise tended to settle in those parts of the United States closest to their countries of origin—the Southwest and Florida, respectively. American Indians are distributed geographically in a pattern reflecting the various tribes' territories in pre-Columbian times and the subsequent locations of reservations chosen for them by white conquerors. The concentration of Puerto Ricans and West Indians in and around New York City reflects the accessibility of air and shipping routes in the twentieth century.

How much difference does location make? Plenty—and it affects not only income but also such variables as education and even fertility. The 1970 Census found the average family income of blacks in New York State to be more than double the average family income of blacks in Mississippi.[43] The average income of American Indians in Chicago, Detroit, or New York City is more than double what it is on most major reservations, and at least $2,000 more than it is on any major reservation.[44] Mexican Americans in the Detroit metropolitan area average more than double the income of Mexican Americans in the Laredo or Brownsville metropolitan areas in Texas.[45]

Location alone is not wholly responsible for all geographic and rural-urban differences, for many other group characteristics vary with location. For example, American Indians living in the urban Northeast are almost a decade older than the American Indians living in the rural Midwest, and the urban northeastern Indians average about three children per married woman (age 35–44), whereas the rural midwestern Indians average about five.[46] Innumerable studies have consistently shown blacks living outside the South to have higher IQs than blacks living in the South,[47] and the IQs of black migrants from the South rise after they leave.[48]

Location in a more narrow sense—within a given metropolitan area—is also associated with significant and even profound intraethnic social differences. In urban ethnic enclaves there has been a tendency for the site of initial ethnic settlements to expand outward, with the more prosperous, more educated, more acculturated portion of the ethnic group leading the expansion into surrounding areas, and away from those members of the group less fortunate in these respects. Such patterns have been common among American ethnic groups, whether black, Jewish, Mexican, or Italian in origin.[49] These simple facts have far-reaching implications for the interpretation of ethnic communities by scholars or journalists at a given time. Life may change very little for people on a given tract of land, even during periods of widespread and rapid upward socioeconomic mobility, because that mobility may take the form of successful individuals' movement outward toward more comfortable neighborhoods, and their replacement by new people struggling through an earlier social-evolutionary phase. In short, the people on a given block may be suffering from the same problems that people on that block suffered from twenty or fifty years ago, even though the particular families who suffered there in an earlier era are now living more prosperous lives elsewhere. Scholarly studies, journalistic news stories, or governmental surveys which focus on the fate of a particular neighborhood (or community or other tract of land) may find a picture of hopeless stagnation even when progress is pervasive.

DISCRIMINATION

Virtually every ethnic group has encountered discrimination in employment, in housing, in the provision of public services, or in all three ways at once. The moral offensiveness of discrimination has distracted attention away from the question of its causal impact on socioeconomic variables—or else has led to the sweeping assumption that interethnic differences can be explained in terms of the degree of discrimination encountered by the various groups.[50] But to test this hypothesis requires considering the results achieved by comparable individuals from different ethnic backgrounds. It has already been apparent that whole ethnic groups are not necessarily comparable—in age distribution, in geographic distribution, or in other respects that influence socioeconomic outcomes. It is not even clear that all relative differences in attributes can be objectively specified and controlled, so that any remaining differences in results could be confidently ascribed to ethnic or racial discrimination. One way to deal with this problem would be to break a given ethnic group down into subgroups who "all look alike" to employers, testers, and other outsiders, even though they may differ for various historical or other reasons. For example, American employers are unlikely to differentiate between those Italian Americans whose ancestors originated in the north of Italy from those whose ancestors originated in the south of Italy. Therefore, if there have been substantial socioeconomic differences between the descendants of northern and southern Italians in the United States—as there have been[51]—then those differences can hardly be ascribed to employer discrimination rather than to attributes of the people themselves. There are problems with both the "comparable individuals" approach and the "internal differences" approach, so that neither can be relied on exclusively.

When age and education are simultaneously held constant, the gross ethnic differences in income narrow but do not disappear. For example, whereas American Indians as a group earned only 57 percent as much income as Japanese Americans, that figure climbs to 85 percent when college-educated members of both groups are compared, and to 89 percent when the comparison is between college-educated males in the 35–44-year age bracket.[52] Because age, sex, and education do not exhaust all sources of income differences, it is clear that even the 11 percent differential remaining in this example cannot all be due to discrimination. Moreover, because Japanese Americans average higher incomes than the U.S. population in general, their incomes can hardly be accounted for by discrimination. Similar comparisons could be made among other ethnic groups, or between given ethnic groups and the "national average."

Successive corrections for age, education, location, etc. sharply reduce income differences among American ethnic groups and between individual ethnic groups and the "national average." Young black married couples located outside the South earned 93 percent of the income of young white married couples located outside the South in 1971—and when both spouses worked in both races, the black couples earned slightly more.[53]

None of this means that prejudice or discrimination have disappeared. It does indicate that the demonstrable magnitude of interethnic income differences among comparable individuals is far less than gross ethnic income differences or popular impressions might suggest. This seriously undermines current employer discrimination as an explanatory variable, though there are other kinds of discrimination—including past employer discrimination and discrimination in schooling—which may still have a major influence on income, especially among older members of various ethnic groups.

Sometimes discrimination is thought to apply particularly to nonwhite ethnic minorities, whose visible and perpetual physical differences make discrimination more easy as well as more likely. The above average incomes of Orientals undermines this hypothesis, though the still substantial black-white income differentials lend some credence to it. However, a very different picture emerges when the incomes and occupations of native black Americans are compared with those of black West Indians living in the United States. It has already been shown (see Tables 1 and 3) that income and occupational differences have been very large as between these two black groups living in the same country. Part of this reflects locational differences, for West Indians are far more concentrated in and around New York City. But even among American Negroes and West Indians living in the New York City standard metropolitan statistical area, the differences do not disappear. Even though the two groups' average years of schooling are the same in New York City SMSA, their median family incomes still differ: $6,881 vs. $8,830 in 1969.

The success of West Indians in the United States has sometimes been attributed to a superior education under the British system in the Islands or to different treatment by white American employers. One way to test these hypotheses would be to isolate second-generation West Indians—those blacks born in the United States of West Indian-born parents, and therefore likely to have been educated in the United States and unlikely to have an accent that would enable a white employer to distinguish them from native blacks.[54] A compilation of 1970 Census data for second-generation West Indians in the New York City area showed them to exceed the socioeconomic status of other West Indians, as well as of native blacks—and of the U.S. population as a whole—in family income ($10,900), education (11.9 years), and proportions in the professions (18.3 percent).

Color alone clearly is not decisive in socioeconomic outcomes, even when that color is black. But from this, it cannot be concluded that "racism" in general is dead or dying. It has already been noted that American racial or ethnic attitudes differ greatly according to the activity involved and the physical or status proximity. In the economic sphere, discrimination can impose onerous costs on the discriminator as well as on those discriminated against.[55] Moreover, the emergence of antidiscrimination laws and changed public opinion in the 1960s added to the costs of discrimination. A sharp rise of black incomes as a percentage of white incomes was one result.[56]

Antidiscrimination laws which prescribe employment, pay, and promotion without regard to race or ethnicity must be distinguished from affirmative-action programs which prescribe employment, pay, and promotion with regard to race or ethnicity in the numerical goals and timetables required of employers. The effects of the two kinds of programs can be separated with respect to time, because affirmative-action mandatory numerical "goals and timetables" are a recent development, since 1971. It is significant that black income as a percentage of white income reached its peak the year before affirmative-action quotas and has declined since. Despite tremendous public controversy, affirmative action in general has produced negligible socioeconomic results for minorities or women. One reason for this may be that although market processes impose certain costs on discriminating employers, affirmative action imposes procedural costs on all employers, whether discriminatory or not, and therefore provides little incentive to reduce discrimination.[57] It may even provide some incentive to intensify discrimination, once employers realize that hiring minority members does not end their legal troubles but only opens up more opportunities for legal penalties and/or costly administrative processes if their pay and promotion patterns do not match the government agencies' conceptions, whether or not there is any actual discrimination. Moreover, a government-approved affirmative-action plan in no way insulates an employer from lawsuits charging "reverse discrimination." In short, affirmative-action programs create no clear incentive to change employment practices in a specified way. This is yet another contrast between such programs and antidiscrimination laws.

Just as substantial interethnic differences in income do not prove discrimination, neither does the absence of substantial differences prove an absence of discrimination. For example, Oriental faculty members earn about the same income as white or black faculty members, but are better qualified than both—in terms of degree level, quality ranking of the department granting their degrees, and individual publication records. When all these variables are held constant, Oriental faculty are typically paid thousands of dollars per year less than either black or white faculty members with the same objective qualifications.[58] In short, discrimination cannot be assessed in terms of gross interethnic differences, without regard to qualifications, for to do so risks both exaggeration and underestimation.

THE GOVERNMENT

Ethnic minorities are affected by government policy not only when these policies are specifically intended to have an ethnic dimension, but also in cases where ethnicity is not an explicit consideration. For example, government regulation of public utilities has usually not involved any concern with ethnic issues, yet by setting up "cost-plus" methods of pricing, the government regulatory agencies have in net effect made employment discrimination virtually costless to the utility, because all additional costs entailed by discrimination are passed on to the public.[59] There has been a history of higher levels of racial and ethnic discrimination in such utilities than in the general economy.[60] Government price fixing in a variety of areas (rent control, minimum wage laws, interest-rate ceilings, etc.) lead to either excess supply or excess demand, depending upon whether the artificial price is set above or below the price that would have existed otherwise. Its net effect is that excess supply allows the demanders to discriminate among suppliers at zero cost to the discriminators, whereas excess demand allows the suppliers to discriminate among the demanders at zero cost to the suppliers.[61] It is therefore not surprising that the minimum wage law, for example, has been found to increase black teenage unemployment.[62]

The direct provision of government services may also be racial or ethnic in its impact, though not explicitly so in its formulation. For example, in the first decade of "urban renewal" three-quarters of the people displaced from their homes or businesses were either black or Puerto Rican.[63] Police protection and public education likewise show a long history of differential quantity and quality, adversely affecting ethnic communities ranging from nineteenth-century immigrant neighborhoods to twentieth-century ghettos and barrios.[64] The government as an employer has a long history of discrimination in both the civilian and military sectors.

It is not that government action necessarily increases discrimination. It simply tends to operate in ways that are less constrained by economic consideration and more determined by political influences. During periods of political concern for antidiscrimination or even affirmative-action policies, those sectors most under government control or influence tend also to react in these directions more quickly and more strongly than do other sectors. The growth of new minority employment in recent years has been especially pronounced in the government itself, in government-regulated industries, and among government contractors.[65] Conversely, during periods of national political reaction, as between World War I and the Great Depression, black federal employees in higher positions declined, and opportunities in military service also retrogressed.

The only general and predictable effect of government control and influence is to free economic decision making from the constraints of the competitive market.

The magnitude of government influence on the fate of ethnic and racial minorities is easily exaggerated, however. It has already been noted that affirmative-action programs have produced no significant gains for blacks. The Irish obviously benefited from patronage jobs in the era of Irish-dominated municipal "machines," but such generally low-level jobs in such politically related occupations have been blamed for the relatively slow rise of the Irish during that era.[66] Certainly such unusually successful ethnic groups as the Jews and the Orientals have not taken the political route. The leadership of the Chinese-American community deliberately decided to avoid politics.[67] "Black power" in political terms was at its peak in the Reconstruction Era after the Civil War—an era of economic retrogression for blacks in many respects.[68] The sharp rise in the black economic position during the 1960s coincided with a period of declining black voter participation outside the South.[69] There is no need to argue for an inverse relationship between political and economic power, but the empirical case for such a position might be easier to make than the empirical case for the opposite view that political power is necessary (and/or sufficient) for economic advancement.

EDUCATION

It has already been noted that education affects income, occupation, and even fertility. One of the difficult problems is to define similar units of education, so as to compare the effect of education on individuals from various ethnic backgrounds. That is, however, virtually impossible, so that what can be done instead is to indicate (1) why and how a given number of years of schooling is a substantially different amount of "education" for different ethnic groups, (2) note the direction and roughly estimate the magnitude of the differences, and (3) consider the gross interethnic differences among individuals from different educational levels against the background of the known statistical biases.

The easiest educational differences to document are black-white differences, especially among older age cohorts. Most black Americans have been raised and educated in the South, even though the percentage has been declining over time, and until the decade of the 1960s most black college students were attending predominantly black colleges. In earlier times, it was not uncommon for the school year for blacks in the South to have one-third fewer days than for whites, so that a black pupil with 9 years of schooling would have been in class the same number of days as a white pupil with only 6 years of schooling. Comparisons of blacks and whites with the "same" education measured in years grossly misstates their respective education in terms of days of schooling. Qualitative differences compounded the disparity. Per-pupil expenditures also varied by race, with black pupils in many parts of the South receiving only a fraction of the expenditures on white pupils.[70] Moreover, black secondary schooling was available at all only quite late in history. The first black public high school in the state of Georgia was built in 1924, and only after bitter political struggles.[71] At the college level, even the best black institutions lag behind white institutions by such objective measures as College Board scores, library resources, departmental rankings, and faculty scholarship record,[72] and evaluations of the intangibles at such schools show at least equal deficiencies.[73] Finally, and perhaps as a consequence of the educational deficiencies mentioned, the fields of specialization selected by black college students are disproportionately the easier and less well-paid fields, notably education and the social sciences.[74]

The trends over time are toward a narrowing of racial differences in education. The end of the dual (segregated) school system in the South has meant the end of differences in days of schooling per year—though not the end of the effect of such disparities on the careers of older blacks educated in an earlier era. Per-pupil expenditure differences have narrowed generally.[75] More black college students now attend predominantly white schools than attend predominantly black institutions,[76] but again the effects differ among age cohorts of blacks, and it remains true that most black college graduates today are graduates of black colleges.

At the opposite end of the spectrum are the Orientals and the Jews. Orientals not only have quantitatively more education than the national average,[77] they are statistically overrepresented in the more difficult and better-paying areas, such as the natural sciences.[78] In general, Oriental faculty members have the Ph.D. more often than either black or white faculty members, and the Orientals' degrees are more often from high-rated departments.[79] Jews are also disproportionately in such demanding fields as law, medicine, and biochemistry, and are educated in the more selective colleges.[80] For Orientals and Jews, statistics on years of schooling understate their real education.

Those ethnic groups attending Catholic colleges and universities are attending institutions which are not included among the top American colleges and universities, either in terms of objective criteria (College Board scores, endowment, library resources, Merit Scholars, faculty publications) or the evaluations of the academic profession. The best of the Catholic institutions rank above the best of the black institutions in these respects, but well below the standards of the Ivy League, of elite colleges such as Amherst and Swarthmore, or of the top state universities. Among those ethnic groups which are predominantly Catholic, only the Irish sent half or more of their college students to Catholic institutions,[81] but Italians, Poles, and Germans also send substantial proportions to such Catholic colleges and universities.

Despite great qualitative differences in schooling, all the ethnic groups for which data are available show a similar pattern of increasing income with increasing years of schooling, and in all cases a college education means an income above the American national average. Moreover, even before the destruction of various racial barriers in recent decades, black college graduates earned more than the average American,[82] despite many individual stories of blacks with degrees working at menial jobs.

3. Summary and Implications

The very concept of ethnic "minorities" is misleading in the United States; and attempts to generalize about minority problems, or to compare one ethnic group to some national average, are still more misleading. Minority is a meaningful designation in countries where there is an ethnic majority, but in the United States the largest specifically identifiable ethnic group—those of British ancestry—constitute only 15 percent of the population, as compared to 13 percent whose ancestry is German, 11 percent Negro, and 8 percent Irish.[83] No small part of the reason why American history has been what it has, is that no one group could achieve overwhelming dominance. Pluralism and toleration were not ideals from which Americans started, but necessities to which they were driven.[84] It was slowest coming in the racial area, where majority-minority lines could be drawn. Nazi racism and its sickening consequences brought racism in general into disrepute in the United States, and set the stage for a series of changes in public opinion and government policy in post-World War II America. The more general and enduring principle of American pluralism was not, however, the result of preachments or "leadership," but of the virtual inescapability of the need to cooperate and the virtual impossibility of achieving the religious, political, or other dominance of any one group—though many tried.[85]

The sheer size of the United States and of American ethnic groups meant that these groups were not mere representatives or appendages of some foreign country or culture. It is a commonplace that there are more people of Italian ancestry in New York than in Rome, more people of Polish ancestry in Detroit than in Cracow, more Jews than in Israel—and so on down the list of American ethnic groups. The distinctive cultures of these ethnic groups are to a large extent creations growing out of their experience on American soil, not mere transplants from other countries. Chow mein, the St. Patrick's Day parade, and the "Afro" hairdo are all American products, some exported back to the homeland from which the groups in question originated. Moreover, the assimilation process has been two-way, with the so-called mainstream American culture incorporating many culinary, vernacular, musical, and other features once specifically and exclusively ethnic. Again, the pluralistic mosaic is more descriptive of American social reality than is a simplistic majority-minority dichotomy.

Rapid changes in the American racial scene are often concealed or muted in gross statistical comparisons which fail to separate out the younger generation reared under the new conditions. The rise and spread of organizations and individuals administering or "representing" racial ethnic groups in various ways (both inside and outside the government) has also created a large constituency with a vested interest in social pathology and even an aversion to consideration of ethnic success, advancement, and development. Ethnic groups are thus constantly presented to the public in terms of "minority problems" to be "solved" by spending large sums of tax money. Whatever the political possibilities—or limitations—of this approach, it has obvious intellectual disadvantages as an approach to understanding reality. The complexities of history, economics, and cultural dynamics cannot be reduced to a simplistic morality play in which the choice is to blame either "society" or to "blame the victim." Variables which do not readily lend themselves to blame—age and geographic location, for example—are simply ignored in this moral, ideological, or political vision. Moreover, the proposed solutions of social problems—the very definitions of such social problems—are similarly constrained within the narrow limits of what is ideologically satisfying or politically palatable. Thus, for example, violent and murderous youth gangs are not dealt with directly as cancerous urgencies but are regarded as social "symptoms" which will go away after some agenda of sociopolitical reform has been carried out. Sometimes there is even a suggestion that, in the interim, "society" needs or deserves such problems as a prod to reform—ignoring the fact that the victims are not some amorphous "society" but the immediate ethnic community itself and that community's aspirations for its children, whose education is easily destroyed by a handful of hoodlums. Aside from the programmatic policy point of view, from an explanatory point of view youth gangs fade into the background as derivative social phenomena, and discussions of education, for example, proceed in terms of teaching methods, racial balance, and other variables which may make far less difference than whether or not there is such sheer turmoil in the schools as to prevent anything from working.

The point here is not simply that a particular policy approach may be wrong, but that the very framework of perception is distorted by moralistic-ideological imperatives. In such a climate of opinion, explanatory variables are acceptable only in the proper sociopolitical attire. Conversely, "explanations" become prominent and even pervasive with no factual support, on the basis of their consonance with the prevailing moral vision. A prime example here is the explanation of the high incidence of "broken homes" and female-headed households among blacks in the middle of the twentieth century as a result of the legacy of similar family instability under slavery. Even though this explanation has been accepted as a matter of course, carrying the imprimatur of such scholars as Myrdal, Frazier, Moynihan, and DuBois, it was not until 1976 that any comprehensive factual research on this point was published—and the facts devastated the vision. The overwhelming majority of black children have been raised in male-headed, two-parent households, under both slavery and freedom, until relatively recent times.[86] Again, the main point is not that a particular view was invalid but that the whole basis for its acceptance for decades was whether it fit in with the prevailing vision.

Age, location, and fertility may never replace "liberty, equality, and fraternity" or other emotionally satisfying slogans, but these neglected variables have major impact on the income, unemployment rates, and even IQs of American ethnic groups. Discrimination and government policy fit the moral-social-political vision better, but the facts are not easily reconciled with the view that these latter are the predominant influences on ethnic economic progress. Age, location, and fertility are functions of complex historical and cultural processes, whereas discrimination and government policy are the direct results of current actions by current people, so that blame, reform, and quick change seem more plausible with the latter. But if "social science" is ever to deserve its name, that cannot be a reason for preferring one set of explanations over another.

Although it is possible to make a general assessment of the relative effects of different variables, it is not necessary to assume that the same variables have the same impact on all ethnic groups. Racially different groups are in a different situation from groups whose differences are of language, nationality, and culture, all of which can be eroded by time; blacks as a group once enslaved are even more of a special case, though there is often a tendency to generalize about ethnicity from the specific history of blacks. Moreover, the relative success of black West Indians—once enslaved under even more brutal conditions than black Americans[87]—suggests that even color differences can be exaggerated in their effects.

What is most clear is that whatever may have determined the past is not inevitably determining the future. There are many objective indications that ethnicity is changing in a changing America. On the whole, and for the present, at least, it is a substantial change for the better.

REFERENCES

The material in this paper owes much to many people besides the designated author. With apologies to many who contributed in a variety of ways, one person must be singled out for her special role: Dr. Lynn D. Collins, without whose skills, insight, and dedication this study simply would not have been possible. Financial support came, at various times and places, from—in alphabetical order—the American Enterprise Institute, the Center for Advanced Study in the Behavioral Sciences, the Ford Foundation, the Hoover Institution, the Liberty Fund, the Office of Economic Opportunity, the Rockefeller Foundation, and the Urban Institute. All conclusions and errors are my responsibility.

[1]Harold J. Laski, *The American Democracy* (New York: Viking, 1948), p. 479.

[2]Everett C. Ladd, Jr., and Seymour Martin Lipset, *The Divided Academy* (New York: McGraw-Hill, 1975), pp. 170–171.

[3]1953 through 1959 inclusive. From the time the first black player entered the National League to the present, more than one-half of all National League MVPs have been black.

[4]Thomas Sowell, *Race and Economics* (New York: McKay, 1975), p. 96.

[5]Martin Kilson, "Whither Integration?" *The American Scholar*, 45 (3) (Summer 1970): 365, 367; Ben J. Wattenberg, *The Real America* (New York: Doubleday, 1974), Chap. 18.

[6]Kilson, "Whither Integration?" p. 369.

[7]Sowell, *Race and Economics*, p. 126.

[8]See Table 6.

[9]For example, Andrew M. Greeley, *Ethnicity, Denomination, and Inequality* (Beverly Hills, Calif.: Sage, 1976), pp. 71, 72.

[10]U.S. Bureau of the Census, *Current Population Reports*, Series P-20, no. 224 (Washington, D.C.: Government Printing Office, 1971).

[11]U.S. Bureau of the Census, *Current Population Reports*, Series P-20, no. 226 (Washington, D.C.: Government Printing Office), p. 20.

[12]Sowell, *Race and Economics*, pp. 135–136.

[13]Ibid., p. 136.

[14]Arthur R. Jensen, "How Much Can We Boost IQ and Scholastic Achievement?" *Harvard Educational Review* (Winter 1969): 5.

[15]See, for example, H. E. G. Sutherland, "The Relationship between IQ and Size of Family," *Journal of Educational Psychology*, 10 (2) (February 1929): 81–90, especially the references cited on p. 81.

[16]For example, Dick Gregory in *Ebony* (October 1971): 66.

[17]Wattenberg, *The Real America*, p. 246.

[18]Ibid., pp. 244, 246.

[19]Ibid., pp. 278, 281.

[20]Mark R. Levy and Michael S. Kramer, *The Ethnic Factor* (New York: Simon and Schuster, 1972), pp. 67, 68, 109n, 128, 172, 207.

[21]Sowell, *Race and Economics*, pp. 38, 39, 52, 70–71, 112–113.

[22]Daniel J. Boorstin, *The Americans* (New York: Random House, 1973), p. 302.

[23]Wattenberg, *The Real America*, pp. 252–253; Lino A. Graglia, *Disaster by Decree* (Ithaca, N.Y.: Cornell University Press, 1976), p. 277; Edward P. Langerton, *The Busing Coverup* (Howard Allen Enterprises, 1975), p. 37; Thomas Sowell, *Affirmative Action Reconsidered* (Washington, D.C.: American Enterprise Institute, 1975), pp. 4–5.

[24]Wattenberg, *The Real America*, p. 251.

[25]U.S. Bureau of the Census, *Current Population Reports*, Series P-20, no. 213, p. 6.

[26]Finis Welch, "Black-White Differences in Returns to Schooling," *American Economic Review*, 63 (5) (December 1973): 893–907.

[27]U.S. Bureau of the Census, *Current Population Reports*, Series P-20, no. 224, p. 12.

[28]Sowell, *Affirmative Action Reconsidered*, pp. 18–20, 22, 41–42.

[29]Wattenberg, *The Real America*, p. 136.

[30]Ibid., p. 120.

[31]Ernest van den Haag, *Punishing Criminals* (New York: Basic Books, 1975), pp. 99–100.

[32]Wattenberg, *The Real America*.

[33]van den Haag, *Punishing Criminals*, p. 100.

[34]*Employment and Training Report of the President, 1976* (Washington, D.C.: Government Printing Office, 1976), pp. 241–243.

[35]Wattenberg, *The Real America*, p. 130.

[36]Sowell, *Race and Economics*, pp. 63–65.

[37]Oscar Handlin, *Boston's Immigrants* (New York: Atheneum, 1970), pp. 25, 26, 36, 37, 53; Chapters 2, 3.

[38]Maldwyn Allen Jones, *American Immigration* (Chicago: University of Chicago Press, 1960), pp. 118–119, 189, 310.

[39]Ulrich B. Phillips, *Life and Labor in the Old South* (Boston: Little, Brown, 1929), Chapter 1.

[40]Robert W. Fogel and Stanley L. Engerman, *Time on the Cross* (Boston: Little, Brown, 1974). p. 95.

[41]Bureau of the Census, *Negro Population, 1790–1915* (Washington, D.C.: Government Printing Office, 1918), pp. 41, 53.

[42]Wilbur Zilensky, "The Population Geography of the Free Negro in Ante-Bellum America," *Population Studies* (March 1950): 387.

[43]*U.S. Census of Population, 1970; Subject Reports* PC(2)–1B (Washington, D.C.: Government Printing Office, 1971), pp. 149, 150.

[44]*U.S. Census of Population, 1970; Subject Reports* PC(2)–1F, pp. 158–163.

[45]*U.S. Census of Population, 1970; Subject Reports* PC(2)–1C, pp. 170, 171.

[46]Ibid., pp. 3, 18, 19.

[47]Audrey M. Shuey, *The Testing of Negro Intelligence*, 2nd edition (Social Science Press, 1966), Chapter 10.

[48]John C. Loehlin, et al., *Race Differences in Intelligence* (San Francisco: Freeman, 1975), p. 154.

[49]E. Franklin Frazier, *The Negro in the United States* (Chicago: University of Chicago Press, 1969), pp. 258–266; Louis Wirth, *The Ghetto* (Chicago: University of Chicago Press, 1956), Chapter 12; Leo Grebler, et al., *The Mexican American People* (New York: The Free Press, 1970), pp. 327–335; Humbert Nelli, *The Italians in Chicago* (New York: Oxford University Press, 1970), pp. 24, 28, 36.

[50]For example, Lester C. Thurow, *Poverty and Discimination* (Washington, D.C.: Brookings Institution, 1969), p. 2.

[51]Sowell, *Race and Economics*, p. 81.

[52]Computations based on data from 1970 Census, Public Use Sample.

[53]Wattenberg, *The Real America*, p. 128.

[54]"The second generation of Negro immigrants . . . have lost most of the social characteristics of their parents . . ." Ira De A. Reid, *The Negro Immigrant* (New York: Columbia University Press, 1939), p. 144.

[55]Sowell, *Race and Economics*, pp. 168–172.

[56]Wattenberg, *The Real America*, p. 125.

[57]Sowell, *Affirmative Action Reconsidered*, pp. 15, 23, 30–31, 38, 42.

[58]Ibid., pp. 17, 21.

[59]Sowell, *Race and Economics*, p. 166.

[60]Loc. cit.

[61]Loc. cit.

[62]Walter E. Williams, *Youth and Minority Unemployment* (U.S. Congress, Joint Economic Committee, Washington, D.C.: Government Printing Office, 1977), pp. 8–13.

[63]Martin Anderson, *The Federal Bulldozer* (Cambridge, Mass.: M.I.T. Press, 1965), pp. 64–65.

[64]Sowell, *Race and Economics*, pp. 182–184, 189–194.

[65]Ibid., pp. 182–184.

[66]Nathan Glazer and Daniel Patrick Moynihan, *Beyond the Melting Pot* (Cambridge, Mass.: M.I.T. Press, 1963), pp. 256, 260.

[67]Ivan H. Light, *Ethnic Enterprise in America* (University of California Press, 1972).

[68]Lorenzo J. Greene and Carter G. Woodson, *The Negro Wage Earner* (AMS Press, 1970), pp. 178–179; Ray Marshall, *The Negro Worker* (New York: Random House, 1967), pp. 8–9; Booker T. Washington, *The Future of the American Negro* (New York: New American Library, 1969), pp. 77–78.

[69]Mark R. Levy and Michael S. Kramer, *The Ethnic Factor* (New York: Simon and Schuster, 1972), p. 61.

[70]E. Franklin Frazier, *The Negro in the United States* (New York: Macmillan, 1971), pp. 425–431.

[71]Thomas Sowell, "Patterns of Black Excellence," *The Public Interest* (Spring 1976): 30-31.

[72]Thomas Sowell, *Black Education: Myths and Tragedies* (New York: McKay, 1972), p. 256.

[73]Christopher Jencks and David Riesman, "The American Negro College," *Harvard Educational Review* (Winter 1967): 3–60; Sowell, *Black Education: Myths and Tragedies*, pp. 250–263.

[74]This is particularly apparent at the doctoral level; see Kent G. Mommsen, "Black Doctorates in American Higher Education: A Cohort Analysis," *Journal of Social and Behavioral Science* (Spring 1974).

[75]Richard Freeman, *Black Elite* (New York: McGraw-Hill, 1976), p. 45.

[76]Ibid., p. 47.

[77]Betty Lee Sung, *The Story of the Chinese in America* (New York: Collier, 1971), p. 125; William Petersen, *Japanese Americans* New York: Random House, 1971), p. 113.

[78]Sowell, *Affirmative Action Reconsidered*, p. 17.

[79]Ibid., pp. 17–21.

[80]Ladd and Lipset, *The Divided Academy*, pp. 88, 150.

[81]See any of the standard college and university reference guides; see also Christopher Jencks and David Riesman, *The Academic Revolution* (New York: Doubleday, 1968), pp. 359–360, 397.

[82]See Charles S. Johnson, *The Negro College Graduate* (Chapel Hill: University of North Carolina Press, 1938), p. 155.

[83]U.S. Bureau of the Census, *Current Population Reports*, P–20, no. 224, p. 3.

[84]John P. Roche, *Shadow and Substance* (New York: Collier, 1969), p. 11.

[85]Sowell, *Race and Economics*, p. 62; J. C. Furnas, *The Americans* (New York: Putnam's, 1969), pp. 522, 527; Jones, *American Immigration*, pp. 150, 151.

[86]Herbert G. Gutman, *The Black Family in Slavery and Freedom, 1750–1925* (New York: Pantheon, 1976), passim.

[87]Sowell, *Race and Economics*, p. 98.

ELLIOT ZASHIN

The Progress of Black Americans in Civil Rights: The Past Two Decades Assessed

In 1954, THE U.S. SUPREME COURT handed down its historic decision in *Brown v. Board of Education*; the Justices unanimously declared unconstitutional the doctrine of "separate but equal" treatment in public education. Segregated public schools were ruled a denial of equal protection to black children. The decision foreshadowed the beginning of a dramatic, intense struggle to make the civil rights of black Americans a reality. Few would deny that blacks have made important gains since that year. However, no consensus about the relative position of black people has emerged, no sure sense of progress. Some Americans, especially blacks, believe that the "dream" is still unfulfilled; others feel that the problems of black people have received a disproportionate amount of attention from government. Thus, there is no agreement about what remains to be done. This has been a disappointment; many citizens wanted to believe that the problem of black inequality had been faced honestly and, if not resolved, then at least sufficiently remedied to enable us to take it off the national agenda in good conscience. Although civil rights is no longer considered an urgent national issue, this is not because Americans feel comfortable with the results of previous efforts. The growing controversy about quotas and preferential selection in higher education and employment reveals that the sensitivities heightened by the civil rights movement are still alive, if less exposed. The issues of black inequality still divide us, and their current complexities have created confusion, compounding the disagreements.

Why, after all the court decisions, demonstrations, legislation, and government programs, has there been no satisfactory resolution? There is no simple explanation, but one crucial reason is that the major successes of the civil rights movement came in the South, and as a "model" for helping blacks achieve "full equality," that experience was terribly inadequate and misleading—as people on all sides of the struggle have learned to their dismay. A brief recapitulation of the major characteristics of the southern situation points up the differences between it and our present situation.

The problem in the South was to eliminate public racism: dual school systems, white-only or segregated public facilities, exclusion of blacks from the ballot box. This did not require much redistribution of material goods. The conflict was primarily over status, a symbolic but paramount consideration. To the extent that whites had to acknowledge black parity in the public realm, their superiority was diminished.

From the perspective of the federal government, the eradication of southern segregation offered several advantages as a civil rights objective. First, because the system was publicly defined, enforced, and supported, it presented a clear target: government activity that maintained segregated facilities and unequal access to public services; and private activity with an obvious public aspect, for example, services and access to goods provided by private businesses to the general public. The system was overt and intentional. Second, segregation was an egregious deviation from democratic norms, and third, it was regionally confined. To say that southern segregation provided an advantageous target is not to suggest that it was easily overcome; as anyone familiar with the civil rights movement is aware, the conflict was intense. Most southern whites did not believe that the elimination of segregation would benefit them in any way, so they resisted change.

The southern situation was easy for Americans to grasp and handle. What we needed to know and to do was, in contrast to our present situation, obvious. This seems evident today, but it was not so then. Southern segregation embodied not only definite attitudes but also practices that flowed directly from these attitudes; each reinforced the other. The activities that constituted segregation were easily indicated and measured: provision of separate and inferior schools, denial of political rights, exclusion from certain occupations and many public facilities, harassment of those blacks who violated the norms. The causal connection between this treatment and the economically deprived and politically powerless condition of southern blacks was painfully obvious. We had few doubts as a nation that southern segregation was wrong in terms of humane and democratic political values, and that southern whites had to make great amends for perpetuating this system to the detriment of blacks.

In the process of change, the government took certain critical actions: President Eisenhower's ordering federal troops to Central High School in Little Rock, Arkansas in 1957; the Justice Department's initiation of and intervention in school desegregation cases; the Department of Health, Education, and Welfare's implementation of school desegregation guidelines; federal court decisions in desegregation and sit-in cases; use of federal registrars to put blacks on the voting rolls in certain Deep South counties; the passage of the 1964 Civil Rights Act and the 1965 Voting Rights Act. Yet the brunt of the conflict was borne by civil rights organizations and the people they mobilized: college students, black and white, organizing in black communities, assisting blacks to register, demonstrating at public facilities; lawyers and law students protecting activists from harassment, gathering depositions for voting rights petitions, serving as counsel in desegregation suits; black citizens asserting rights to vote and to use public. facilities. Without this effort, the federal government's action would have been ineffectual; indeed, much of the federal action would never have been taken because it was the civil rights organizations and their constituencies that created the public demand for federal action.

Tangible results were achieved. The percentages of southern blacks registering and voting increased dramatically; black children began to enter previously all-white schools. Public and commercial facilities open to whites only, for example, restaurants, hotels, motels, parks, and libraries, were desegregated, although for poorer blacks equal access was often largely symbolic; in some instances, local governments closed public facilities rather than permit blacks to use them at the same time as whites.

By the time the focus of civil rights turned to the rest of the nation, the differences within the southern civil-rights movement, for example, between the Congress of Racial Equality and Student Nonviolent Coordinating Committee militants, and the more moderate Southern Christian Leadership Conference, had come into the open and even the appearance of cohesion was dissipating. Nonetheless, within the government, there now were agencies and officials committed to further action to enhance black civil rights. Some of the liberals who had given support to the southern struggle still were sympathetic, although the emergence of black power and ghetto riots diminished their numbers and their effectiveness. There were still activists ready to challenge "racism" in the North, and black communities were being organized to press demands. Yet when the tactics and techniques that had worked in the South were used in the North, they did not have the same impact. In a sense, they were swallowed up in the complexity of the situations and the sheer number of problems that had to be addressed.

The differences between the positions of blacks outside the South and in the South are apparent. Fundamentally, the "evil" in the North was less obvious. Discrimination existed, but less overtly; segregation was not a publicly legitimated way of life. Blacks were neither disenfranchised nor excluded from sharing public facilities. Northern ghettoes with their substandard housing conditions were a product of many factors in addition to discrimination—rapid migration of blacks from the rural South; changing demographic patterns in central cities in the postwar period; the availability of manual, low-skill jobs; low income. The schools of these cities rapidly became racially unbalanced; "white flight" no doubt contributed, but school authorities could appear the passive accountants of demographic change. Racial discrimination seemed obvious in the traditional crafts unions because virtually no blacks were to be found in them, but the concentration of blacks in the lowest-paid occupations and in the lower echelons of professional and technical occupations could be ascribed to fewer job skills and less education. In the 1960s, the federal government had increased its overall percentage of black employees significantly, "proving" that antidiscrimination programs could work; the continued relative absence of blacks from the middle and higher levels could be attributed to the scarcity of qualified candidates. In other words, even though no one doubted that blacks had once been victims of racism and discrimination, many people felt that the economic, educational, and political handicaps which were the legacy of black history were the primary factors currently preventing them from achieving equality.

The shift in attention from the South to the rest of the nation has changed the national orientation toward civil rights. There is greater emphasis on equal opportunity, rather than on equal rights of participation in the public sphere of the community; and the proviso that the opportunities of the white majority not be reduced by efforts to help blacks is increasingly emphasized. To some extent, the very successes of the civil rights movement are responsible for present dilemmas. On the one hand, gains in the areas of education and voting put some blacks in a position to assert claims to equality in other activities and institutions; on the other, the fact that living conditions of many blacks were not basically touched by the civil rights successes forced black leaders to refocus their attention. The disadvantages and inequalities which have come under attack pose more complex issues because the social institutions and practices which maintain them do not purport to be racially invidious or discriminatory. The general inertia of institutions impedes change, but there also appears to be a substantial residue of discriminatory attitudes toward blacks that makes change all the more difficult to achieve.

I will return to the moral and empirical complexities of our present situation at the end of this essay. Now, however, I will review the changes which have occurred in the major areas of civil rights, pointing out new issues and dilemmas that have emerged and what courses of action appear to have the best prospects for producing further change. The areas to be reviewed are (1) Public Education; (2) Voting and Political Power; (3) Occupational Status and Income; and (4) Housing Conditions and Residential Segregation.

Public Education

In the South, the amount of desegregation since 1954 has been very substantial. The dual systems—separate and unequal—that prevailed then have been eliminated. But even though the aggregate changes are impressive,[1] they did not come about as a result of any general willingness to comply with the Supreme Court's decision in *Brown v. Board of Education*. For approximately thirteen years, virtually no desegregation occurred except in the border states. In the Deep South, there was "massive resistance," and it was effective. The federal government and the federal district courts in the South did little to pressure school districts to comply with the mandate of *Brown*. Title VI of the Civil Rights Act of 1964 required federal agencies to cut off funds to programs which involved discrimination, and in 1964, the Office of Education (OE) began developing guidelines to ensure compliance with Title VI. Officials in the Johnson administration did not anticipate the resistance that southern school districts would offer to the guidelines, and virtually no resources were initially available for the implementation program. Gradually learning from their experience, OE officials tightened up the guidelines and used threats of fund cut-offs. Southern school districts began to move beyond nominal compliance to real desegregation. Two developments aided OE's efforts: passage of the Elementary and Secondary Education Act of 1965 substantially increased the amount of federal assistance to public education, thereby making fund cut-offs a more serious threat; and the federal district courts began imposing more stringent desegregation standards. School districts could no longer use compliance with lenient court orders as a substitute for compliance with OE guidelines.[2]

By the early 1970s, the great majority of southern black children no longer attended predominantly black schools, but as Harrell Rogers points out, this achievement depended on several stringent conditions:

> (1) School officials, especially but not exclusively in the South, will normally obey civil rights laws only under coercion. (2) Legal standards for school desegregation must be unambiguous and forceful. (3) Greater progress is achieved if the three

branches of the federal government are reasonably unified and uncompromising in their approach to desegregation. (4) The burden for achieving school desegregation must rest with school officials, not with black citizens and their children. (5) The Administration must be prodded and carefully supervised by the federal courts if significant progress is to be made.[3]

Few of these requirements have been met in the attempt to integrate public schools outside the South. The Nixon administration curtailed the number of desegregation suits in which the Justice Department intervened, and the burden of integration fell upon black plaintiffs and federal judges. Moreover, even in the South, the administration curtailed the use of Title VI enforcement procedures and the threat of fund cut-offs receded. In numerous instances, school districts were found not to be in compliance, and yet the Department of Health, Education, and Welfare (HEW) did not cut off their federal assistance.

At the same time that new problems have developed in southern school districts, for example, segregation within desegregated schools and resegregation caused by changes in residential patterns, the situation outside the South has been worsening. According to the Civil Rights Commission, approximately 70 percent of nonsouthern black children attend predominantly minority schools.[4] The marked division of black and white populations in many metropolitan areas throughout the nation makes racially balanced schools within existing school districts increasingly difficult to achieve. Nearly three-quarters of the black children in the nation's 26 largest cities attend schools with 90 to 100 percent minority enrollments.[5]

The problems encountered in desegregating public schools in central cities indicate as well as any civil rights issue the contrast between the original southern situation which led to the *Brown* decision and the conditions which have been the focus of desegregation efforts since the late 1960s. The *Brown* decision was written in terms of dual school systems: intentional, explicit segregation by race. As cases arising in different contexts—racially imbalanced school districts with no prior dual system, or desegregated dual systems that have become re-segregated—the federal courts have strained to keep them within the mandate of *Brown*. Critics argue that the courts have considered racial imbalance (i.e., de facto segregation) as grounds for invoking the *Brown* mandate, using the guise of dealing with de jure segregation to cover the extension they have made.

In the southern dual systems, all public school segregation was de jure, but now a key issue is the relation between de facto segregation and de jure segregation. Distinguishable in theory, are they distinguishable in practice? Are there situations of racial imbalance in public schools that cannot be traced to instances of "state action" such as city council zoning decisions or school board decisions on attendance boundaries and new school placement? Clearly, this requires a case-by-case examination of factual situations, rather than a priori speculation, but the "facts" are not immediately obvious. How far does one cast the net of "state action"? Beyond school district authorities to state boards of education? Beyond educational administrators and policy makers to government officials who make decisions about zoning, placement of public housing, granting of federally guaranteed mortgages and other housing subsidies? What constitutes a causal connection between culpable[6] state action and racial imbalance? How does one determine the impact of school board decisions made with segregative intent on the composition of other public schools in the same area that were not directly addressed or were in other districts? Who should bear the burden of proof to establish such connections (or lack of them)?

These questions are esoteric to the layperson, but the legal argument is constrained by the constitutional requirement that "state action" must be an element of racial imbalance in order for it to be a violation of the Fourteenth Amendment. This constraint hints at larger issues. Must differential outcomes for blacks and whites be caused by intentionally discriminatory actions in order to be considered morally and politically objectionable? If it can be shown that ostensibly neutral actions produce differential outcomes because of handicaps created in the past by discrimination, can it still be maintained that such actions are not discriminatory? These questions are important because most Americans may be willing to support efforts to root out the effects of an undeniable evil, for example, discrimination or racist attitudes. However, they may not be willing to create integrated situations for the sake of raising black aspirations and educational levels or fostering interracial tolerance and social mixing. Unless white Americans can be shown that practices and institutions which they do not consider racially invidious are in fact causally linked to the inequalities that blacks experience, most whites are unlikely to support remedial efforts, especially in a sensitive area like public education, where their children may have to bear the burdens.

A major determinant of racial imbalance in the public schools of major cities is racial concentration in residential patterns. The inmigration of lower-class blacks to northern and western central cities in recent decades and the outmigration of middle-class whites to fringes and suburbs have played a major role in creating this situation. Thus, some commentators have suggested that residential segregation is the appropriate target for remedial action, not racial imbalance in the schools. However, as we shall see, this, too, is a highly intractable problem, with many of the same issues in dispute, especially the contribution of discrimination, public and private, to its origination and continuation. But advocates of further school integration do not consider the contribution of residential segregation to the worsening racial imbalance in the schools grounds for giving the latter problem a lower priority. Moreover, they contend that the overall pattern of racial separation has been decisively influenced by governmental policies and programs at all levels.

The solutions that federal courts have devised include significant amounts of compulsory busing and, in a few instances, metropolitan desegregation plans, which cross school district boundaries. The Supreme Court apparently has temporized on the latter issue, perhaps fearful that mandating metropolitan integration will create so much social turmoil that racial segregation and inequality will be aggravated instead of ameliorated. In *Milliken v. Bradley* (1974), the Court refused to endorse a metropolitan integration plan ordered by a lower court for the Detroit area; the majority argued that sufficient grounds of discrimination or segregation based on state action had not been established to warrant a plan requiring integration across district boundaries. Under the plan, school districts outside the city would have been compelled to participate. However, the Supreme Court rejected their inclusion in the compulsory integration because there was no finding by lower courts that the school boards of these districts had contributed to the objectionable segregation. The variety of opinions offered by the Justices left the ultimate constitutionality of metropolitan integration unresolved, but *Milliken* still was a blow to advocates of integration, who thought it created "an insulated position for suburbanites" that relieved them of the burdens of integration. Perhaps the majority of the Court was "acting on its perception, circa 1974, of the tolerable limits of judicial meddling with life patterns evolved during the past few decades,"[7] but the decision may have encouraged whites leery of integration to believe that the suburbs would remain a refuge.

The situations the federal courts now confront are not comparable to the southern dual systems, although there is some evidence that school authorities have, at times, acted with intent to maintain segregatory patterns. In effect, the courts have been grappling with the much larger and more complex issue of racial isolation in our major urban centers. The results of their decisions have not been happy. There has been intense resistance to compulsory busing plans in certain cities, most notably Boston, and racial hostility has increased. In the early 1970s, national polls registered increasing percentages of Americans opposed to busing for integration. The rhetoric of politicians made busing an even more salient and highly charged issue. There were popular misconceptions about the incidence and costs of busing for desegregation which made the effects appear much greater than they actually were,[8] but no one can doubt that parents, and not just white parents, had real and justified anxieties about the consequences of such programs. Although it is difficult to believe that fear, dislike, or disapproval of blacks did not underlie some of the white protests, one cannot ignore class differences and educational concerns as factors.

Compulsory busing plans have generated an often impassioned debate on many issues. Opponents of busing have defended the neighborhood school for encouraging parental involvement and community identity, as well as for its convenience, whereas proponents have responded that these are mainly rationalizations for preserving all-white schools. The antibusing position emphasizes cases of substantially increased costs for busing at a time when public education funds are in short supply. The probusing position points to the fact that much busing already occurs and that the increases required for integration are not high in comparison. Apparently, black children are much more likely to ride buses for integration than white children,[9] and black parents have been unhappy about this. Critics of compulsory busing have accused well-known busing advocates of keeping their own children out of integrated city schools, whereas probusing advocates have questioned the motivations of persons opposing busing. A national survey revealed that antibusing opinions were not closely correlated with racist attitudes.[10]

The learning achievements of black and white children in integrated schools have been studied intensively. Advocates of integration point to the gains that black children have made; opponents note the increase in black-white differentials caused by greater white gains.[11] Generally the black gains—the social benefit usually offered as the major purpose of integration—have been modest at best. Opponents of compulsory integration cite studies indicating that students, white and black, who were involved in busing programs were less supportive of such efforts than students who were not[12]; they also note racial disturbances occurring at the onset of integration programs. Proponents of further integration point to studies which show positive changes in racial attitudes and interracial relations in integrated schools. They caution that we should not be too hasty in our evaluation of integrated education; can we be certain that the situations being evaluated are truly integrated?

White flight has also been the focus of considerable attention; some sociologists see integration of public schools as a major cause. Other commentators emphasize different factors. A recent study, using data from 86 northern school districts, concluded: "White flight, if it occurs at all, occurs not from the problems experienced during the first year of desegregation but from the fear of problems. In other words, if whites leave, it is typically not because they participated in the plan and did not like it, but because they refused to participate at all. Apparently, whites who did participate in the first year of the plan did not leave after that."[13] Critics of busing contend that the federal courts have pushed aside the 1964 Civil Rights Act prohibition on busing to achieve racial balance; more important, they claim that the plans are producing results directly contrary to the courts' ostensible aims of integration and racial harmony. Proponents contend that further efforts, particularly metropolitan integration, are constitutionally required to give black children equal opportunity in education and are feasible in terms of achieving racial balance with reasonable costs. Some commentators, seeking a middle ground, have proposed that black students be guaranteed the right to attend predominantly white schools with busing provided to make the choice of school a genuine one.

In this debate, consensus has been a scarce commodity and it does not seem likely to increase. Although one cannot be optimistic about the short-run consequences of compulsory integration, it seems highly improbable that racial integration of the schools will come in the foreseeable future if it must wait upon residential integration. A society in which blacks and whites are physically divided is undesirable. Young white people grow up in almost complete isolation from members of other races, and in this environment, existing racial stereotypes and fears are transmitted from one generation to the next; the same phenomenon occurs in the black community. Severe racial imbalance in the public schools is likely to be both invidious and detrimental to black children. Generally it does not represent a choice by black parents to send their children to predominantly black or minority schools. Furthermore, in many instances, the public resources devoted to such schools are fewer than those devoted to predominantly white schools, especially considering the obstacles to learning which characterize the former. Integrated schools provide the only chance to modify these consequences in the near future. The dangers are real; integration without careful preparation, skillful matching, and continued sensitive supervision may serve only to reinforce the attitudes and fears which do much to maintain the separation of the races.

Metropolitan integration, the most ambitious option proposed by advocates of integration, may offer the best prospects of achieving stable racial balance with moderate increases in busing, limited class mixing, and high majority-to-minority school population ratios. In some instances, pairing schools across metropolitan boundaries may even reduce the amount of busing. It also has the best prospects for succeeding in educational terms because schools with a predominance of middle-class white children seem to have the clearest impact on the achievement of black children. In addition, lower- and lower-middle-class whites in central cities may feel that the burdens of integration—which have fallen disproportionately upon them—are distributed more fairly under metropolitan desegregation than under intracity plans.

This is not to suggest that voluntary approaches to busing and metropolitan desegregation should be ignored or that metropolitan integration plans should necessarily take precedence over intracity plans. Federal funds could be used as incentives for school districts undertaking such efforts, as well as for planning. On the other hand, voluntarism did not work except on the periphery of the South, and there is no reason to suppose that many northern school officials are going to undertake large-scale integration voluntarily. In the early 1970s, certain politicians were suggesting that militant opposition might even block court-ordered integration. Evidence that the federal government will not be firm in implementing the rights of minority-group schoolchildren is likely to increase opposition and conflict. The availability of court-ordered integration seems a necessary spur to action. Without it, voluntary integration initiatives probably will decline.

Many persons may have resented the very considerable authority that federal judges arrogated to themselves in desegregation cases; it may be that the responsibility is too great and the consequences too serious to let individual judges, although supervised by higher courts, determine final plans. In some instances, federal judges may have felt that the lack of cooperation and good will of school boards required them to increase their intervention. There is a positive role here for the federal executive: to provide assistance in the development and implementation of metropolitan integration plans and to assist in the mediation of conflicts. Recently, the Carter administration reversed a Ford administration policy not to withhold federal funds from school districts that refused to pair schools to facilitate desegregation. This change may indicate that the Carter administration will take a more active role in the area of school desegregation.

Voting and Political Power

Voter registration and voting is the second major area of civil rights in which significant progress was achieved in the South. Prior to the passage of the 1965 Civil Rights Act, only about 29 percent of the eligible blacks were registered to vote in the seven states covered (wholly or in part[14]) by the act. By 1972, over 1 million additional blacks had registered, raising the percentage to more than 56. Before passage of the act, the gap between white and black registration rates in the affected states averaged 44 percent; by 1972, the gap had dropped to nearly 11 percent. As with school desegregation, these gains were the result primarily of organization and pressure, not the acquiescence of southern officials. Voter registration campaigns mounted by civil rights organizations and the use of federally appointed registrars in a limited number of especially recalcitrant areas overcame the atmosphere of intimidation and the often blatantly biased tactics of southern officials, especially in the Deep South.

It is generally assumed that increased black voter registration led to increased black voting, but this is difficult to prove because most states do not keep records of voting by race. Presidential election statistics in the states covered by the 1965 act provide, by inference, some basis for this conclusion, although it appears that there is still a gap between the levels of white and black voting.[15] Other evidence of increased black political participation is to be found in the growing number of blacks running for public office and, in some instances, winning. Some southern white politicians are showing concern about the impact of their public positions upon potential black support, for it appears that the black vote is influencing outcomes where white candidates only are competing.

Outside the South, the civil rights and subsequent black power movements apparently contributed to black cohesion at the polls. The first notable results came in the 1967 victories of black mayoral candidates Richard Hatcher in Gary, Indiana, and Carl Stokes in Cleveland, Ohio. Blacks also voted cohesively for recent Democratic presidential candidates, reaching a peak in the 1976 election; surveys completed immediately afterward indicated that over 90 percent of the blacks who voted cast their ballots for Carter. This support was considered crucial for his electoral victory.

Despite substantial increases in the number of blacks holding office in the last few years, they constitute only a very small fraction of the total: as of 1974, less than 1 percent of the 79,000 public officials in the South and 0.6 percent of elected officials in the nation as a whole.[16] In the early 1970s, it appeared that black candidates needed an electorate with a majority or near majority (2/5) of blacks to win an election. People seemed to be voting strongly along racial lines. However, the data on medium and large cities with black mayors suggests that this is not necessarily the case. Of 26 such cities, blacks were a definite minority in 17 in 1974.[17] On the other hand, in the South, "Most blacks holding municipal or county offices who are elected at-large serve predominantly black communities. This is especially true of black mayors, 93 percent of whom are in majority black municipalities."[18] White resistance to voting for black candidates obviously limits the potential gains, but in those southern counties where blacks are a majority, it would appear that they can translate their votes into black office holding. At present, blacks are still rather underrepresented among office holders in those counties. One important factor may be increased white voting in response to greater black political participation. A study of black voting in the 29 Mississippi black majority counties during the late 1960s and 1970 suggests that economic vulnerability was a major factor inhibiting black voting. The authors believe that political organization could be a critical factor for blacks in overcoming fear of economic reprisals.[19]

Even when blacks obtain office in the South, their ability to influence policy appears to be limited. A 1970 study found that in the 125 southern city councils with black representation, only 25 had more than one. Thus black council representatives usually were not in a position to form caucuses or voting blocs. The political influence of black officeholders may also be substantially restricted by the fact that many run as token representatives on tickets supported by white-dominated party organizations. In general, at-large jurisdictions probably serve to limit black representation.[20]

In other parts of the country and in larger constituencies, for example, congressional districts, the prospects of significantly increasing black office holding depend crucially on the willingness of whites to choose a black candidate in

preference to a white one. Except in those large cities where the black population is rapidly nearing a majority, an increase in black registration and voting
can at best affect outcomes marginally because the great gains have already been
made. In addition, the remaining gap between black and white registration and
voting rates may not be closed because the young, the poor, and the poorly
educated tend to participate less in politics than their opposite numbers, and
blacks tend to fall disproportionately in the former categories.

Continued black involvement and white support for black candidates probably will be determined largely by the performance of black office holders, especially black mayors, who may be in the best relative position to meet the needs
of constituents. Unfortunately, the obstacles that black mayors face are very
formidable. The Joint Center for Political Studies found in 1974 that the southern communities with black mayors (generally quite small, i.e., populations of
1,000) were characterized by low per-capita income, poor housing, high
unemployment or underemployment, poor health and sewage facilities, minimal administrative staffs, and difficulties in obtaining federal aid. In the 23 of 26
medium and large cities with black mayors studied by the Center, 16 ranked in
the top third of all American cities based on rates of poverty; nearly one-half
had sharp population declines in the last decade (prior to the election of the
black mayors), and 15 ranked in the bottom half of all cities based on per capita
income. In many, housing was old relative to other cities. Generally, "the structural characteristics of city politics . . . by nature are painfully restrictive and
often unresponsive."[21] But the situations in which black mayors must work are
especially unpromising, and at the same time, the expectations of black constituents are high.

Because black mayors in the larger cities depend on white support to win,
they cannot develop programs which ignore their white constituents, whose
needs often are rather different from those of black constituents. Moreover,
many of these mayors lack the resources which seem to be necessary for leadership in large cities. Most of the black mayors are independent of political
machines or established political elites; they have little party support. In addition, they usually have no influence on the selection of state and congressional
candidates or over county machines which impinge on city administration. In
13 of the 23 cities studied by the Center, black mayors lacked significant authority over appointments and budget control, and they had no veto over council
resolutions and ordinances. In general, black officials have avoided championing
militant black causes, at least in part because of their weak positions. They have
even sacrificed reform goals in order to work out compromises which have
gained white support for distributions of existing public services and benefits
that would be more equitable vis-à-vis the black community. As a result, it
appears that they have been ineffectual in achieving systemic changes in power
relationships.

Black mayors must use what authority they have over appointments and
their influence on personnel policies to recruit competent blacks and to develop
their administrative skills and political expertise. When Richard Hatcher made
his first appointments, 90 percent of the persons in key staff positions had no
previous governmental experience. To supplement the limited power of black
mayors, black organizations must expand and develop political resources. Black

officeholders need broad and cohesive support from black constituents; divisions within the black community can negate initial electoral gains. Black constituents are particularly vulnerable to disillusionment and consequent withdrawal from active political involvement. Thus, black political leaders face a formidable challenge in maintaining high levels of black political participation and translating it into political influence.[22]

The increasing urban-suburban division of whites and blacks also threatens to limit the impact of newly attained political representation for black constituents. Although this division makes it more likely that blacks will become a political majority (or near majority) in central cities, thereby increasing the number of black officials, another result may be some polarization along racial lines between state governments and city governments on revenue allocation and tax matters. At the same time, the problems of central cities seem less and less tractable within their own boundaries and unless there is some form of metropolitanization (formation of political units that encompass central cities and suburbs), central cities probably will suffer continued and perhaps worsening financial, employment, school segregation, pollution, and mass-transit conditions. Yet the prospect of metropolitanization means the dilution of black representation as the "threshold" problem reemerges for blacks in larger political units.

Occupational Status and Income

Eliminating discrimination in employment—public and private—was a major objective of federal civil-rights legislation and executive orders in the 1960s. The underlying assumption was that racial discrimination played a major role in creating the income and occupational differentials that existed between whites and blacks. In 1965, the median annual income of all black families was 55 percent of the white median figure; it had hovered near that point since the early 1950s. Occupationally, blacks were disproportionately concentrated in the low-skilled, low-paying categories of employment. For example, in 1965, the percentage of white males in the professional and technical category was 12.8; for nonwhite males (of whom blacks constitute about 90 percent), the figure was 5.7.[23] In other major categories, the percentages were as listed in Table 1.

TABLE 1

PERCENTAGES IN OCCUPATIONAL CATEGORIES

	White Male	Nonwhite Male		White Male	Nonwhite Male
Managers and administrators	10.2%	4.0%	Craft and kindred workers	20.2%	11.1%
				White Female	Nonwhite Female
Nonfarm laborers	6.3	21.0	Private household workers	4.4	30.1

Source: Bureau of Labor Statistics, Department of Labor, Handbook of Labor Statistics 1975 (Washington, D.C., 1975), Table 19.

John F. Kennedy was the first President since World War II to initiate concerted action against employment discrimination. In 1961, he established a committee on equal employment opportunity to recommend affirmative steps to implement the federal policy of nondiscrimination. Blacks began to enter high-level agency positions in significant numbers. Title VI of the 1964 Civil Rights Act prohibited discrimination by employers with more than a certain number of employees; however, the federal government was not brought under the purview of this prohibition. In 1965, President Johnson transferred responsibility for federal equal-employment opportunity enforcement to the Civil Service Commission. In 1969, President Nixon issued an executive order emphasizing the responsibility of each federal agency to develop an affirmative action program.

None of these initiatives significantly increased the percentages of black employees at the middle and upper levels of the federal service. In 1965, the percentage of black employees in the GS 9–11, 12–15, and 16–18 levels was 3.4, 1.3, and 1.0, respectively. Five years later, the comparable percentages were 5.3, 2.6, and 1.6.[24] By this time blacks constituted 11.1 percent of all employees on General Schedule and similar pay plans, and 15.2 percent of all federal employees. Thus, the problem was not to open up federal employment in general to blacks but to promote those hired into more responsible positions and to find others qualified to enter at the higher levels. A congressional study in 1971 found defects in Civil Service Commission (CSC) procedures and as a result of this finding, Congress legislated amendments to Title VII of the 1964 Civil Rights Act, bringing protections already afforded to private-sector employees to federal employees. Previously, complaints filed against a federal agency were investigated and judged by the agency itself, and this procedure undermined confidence in the complaint process. Now the CSC was directed to review and approve affirmative action plans annually and to evaluate agency programs. Until 1972, the CSC apparently regarded itself as a consultant on affirmative action, not as an enforcer.

In 1974, the Civil Rights Commission (CRC) issued a massive study of federal civil-rights enforcement[25]; it was severely critical of the federal effort, citing such deficiencies as inadequate staffs, loose guidelines which often lacked a basis for evaluating improvement, inadequate monitoring, overreliance on voluntary compliance, and the build-up of large caseloads of complaints with resultant delays in processing. In that year, the percentages of black federal employees in the GS 9–11, 12–15, and 16–18 grades were 7.2, 3.6, and 2.8. Civil rights supporters evaluated these figures from a number of baselines, for example, percentage of blacks in the federal work force, percentage of blacks in the total work force, and percentage of blacks in the total population, and found them disappointing.

A similar picture appeared in the work forces of state and local governments, where data on minority group employment was not collected by the federal government until 1973. The percentages of high-status positions filled by blacks that year were as listed in Table 2. Serious efforts to increase minority employment in state and local government have begun only in the last few years, so it is too soon to judge their impact, even if the data were available.[26]

TABLE 2

BLACKS IN HIGH-STATUS POSITIONS

	State Government	County Government	City Government	Township Government
Officials and administrators	3.9	4.4	5.2	1.0
Professionals	5.9	5.9	11.9	1.2

Population parity for blacks was 11.0% nationally.

Source: From Harry Kranz, *The Participatory Bureaucracy* (Lexington Mass.: D. C. Heath, 1976), Tables 5–14, 5–24, 5–32, and 5–37. The original data came from the EEOC.

It is difficult to compare the experience in the private sector with public employment except in gross terms. In 1974, the proportion of nonfarm managers and administrators who were black was 6 percent; of professional and technical workers, 6 percent; of crafts and kindred workers, 7 percent. Again, judged against the baselines that civil rights activists were using, these figures were thought to represent a continuing failure to overcome discrimination. On the other hand, improvements had occurred: "the proportion [of blacks] employed as managers and administrators, professional and technical workers, and craftsmen and kindred workers—the three highest paying occupations—almost doubled between 1958 and 1973, while the proportion employed in service work, nonfarm, and farm labor—the three lowest paying occupations—fell by one-third."[27] The changes for the period 1960–1970 can be observed from the percentages, listed in Table 3, of major occupational categories filled by non-whites:[28]

TABLE 3

NONWHITE MAJOR OCCUPATIONAL CATEGORIES

	1960	1970		1960	1970
Private household workers	50	42	Clerical	5	8
Nonfarm laborers	27	23	Craftsmen and foremen	5	7
Farmers and farm workers	16	11	Managers and officials	3	4
Operatives	12	14	Sales	2	4
			Professional and technological	4	7

Source: Bureau of Labor Statistics, Department of Labor, *Handbook of Labor Statistics 1975* (Washington, D.C., 1975), Table 19.

Whereas blacks made a significant movement out of the most menial, poorest paid jobs, their gains in the higher status positions were modest. What impressed those critical of the antidiscrimination effort was the slowness of the changes in occupational status. Economists have pointed out that the major impact, if any, of antidiscrimination programs such as that conducted by the Office of Federal Contract Compliance must be in narrowing the differentials in pay to members of different racial groups with similar "endowments." However, much of the pay differential apparently is instead a function of intergroup differences in "endowments" (i.e., differences in education, skills, etc.), and antidiscrimination programs can have, at best, only a limited effect there.

The government did not neglect the skill side of the employment problems of blacks in the 1960s. During the height of the War on Poverty, several programs were established to upgrade vocational skills and provide employment for members of disadvantaged groups.[29] At first, blacks were enrolled in these programs in large numbers and thereby gained income from their employment. However, possible long-term effects of these programs were negated, at least in part, by the decision of the Nixon administration to cut back on them. At the same time, there was a marked decline in black participation beginning in the late 1960s. Apparently program priorities were shifted in some instances to other minorities and veterans; in the case of the JOBS program, the recession seems to have been a contributing factor, with black participants down from 74 percent of the total in fiscal year 1970 to 41 percent in fiscal year 1973. New employment gains seem to be tenuously held. On balance the long-term effects of such manpower programs seem to have been limited, in part because they could reach only a fraction of all those who might have benefited from them.

The occupational changes recorded here have been reflected in income gains by certain groups of blacks. For example, the annual incomes of black males with some college education reached 80 percent of white counterparts' annual income in the early 1970s. The median annual income of young black couples when both work has matched that of their white counterparts. What has apparently depressed the annual median income of all black families relative to white family income is "the rapid increase of female-headed families from 23.7% of all black families in 1965 to 34.0% in 1974."[30] This group is a particularly vulnerable one, and neither antidiscrimination nor manpower programs may help them.

In the last two or three years, the affirmative-action stance of the federal government has come under increasing criticism, with goals and timetables the focus of attention. Critics of affirmative action contend that the whole federal antidiscrimination program has been perverted by the imposition of statistical parity (between blacks and whites) goals. Federal agencies have pressured employers, public and private, to hire and promote increasing percentages of minorities, and strenuous efforts to recruit qualified minority group members are not considered satisfactory unless they produce results. The implication is that blacks are being hired whether or not they are qualified. Critics also contend that blacks were making significant gains in employment without additional federal pressure for measurable progress. Whereas instances of overzealous enforcement can be cited, and goals and timetables have been required in some instances, we do not have the data necessary to evaluate these criticisms. With regard to the federal agencies as employers, we are not in a position to say what results have been achieved when goals and timetables have actually been employed. With regard to employment under federal contract, there have been specific plans employing goals and timetables (in which the burden of proof of good-faith efforts has been placed on the employers and unions), for example, the Philadelphia Plan, but employment gains have been modest, and institutional changes few.

With respect to general employment in the private sector, it is hard to evaluate the impact of the Equal Employment Opportunity Commission (EEOC), for its primary role is to deal with individual complaints. The fact that complaints have increased year by year probably is a function of the agency's greater visibility and enlarged responsibilities (state and local government coverage was added in 1972), but according to the CRC, the EEOC has no monitoring capability to determine the effectiveness of its entire compliance process in terms of results. Black employment gains in the high-status occupational categories of the total work force in the 1970–1974 period were virtually nil. Because this was a recessionary period, such a result suggests that equal employment opportunity efforts are quite vulnerable to economic conditions. It is often hard to separate program impact from the effects of economic conditions on labor markets.

The key problem with federal equal employment opportunity agencies is not the aggressiveness of their public posture—which seems to disturb critics of affirmative action—but whether they can effectively implement and monitor a coherent set of guidelines. Before deciding that federal agencies should restrict their efforts to requiring nondiscrimination, we need to know more about the actual practices of federal agencies and federal contractors in implementing the "basic ingredients" of their affirmative action programs, for example, their efforts to find qualified minority-group members, to upgrade minorities already on their staffs, and to make employment attractive to such persons.

The equity of goals (or quotas, as critics refer to them) and of preferential selection is becoming a highly salient issue,[31] yet we are not in a position to say that whites have suffered from the use of such devices. Because we do not have a clear picture of when and how these devices have been used, we cannot talk about overall impact knowledgably. Of course, one can point to a few highly publicized instances of white students being passed over for less qualified black students in admission to professional schools, but it seems to be this kind of situation to which the public is reacting, not firm information about consequences. Are white candidates for jobs actually being passed over for less qualified blacks, and if so, how extensive is the practice?

The equity issues involved in preferential higher-education admissions policies should not obscure two important unanswered questions in the employment area: Are the qualifications imposed by employers job relevant? Do employers, public and private, have enough information about the presence of presumably qualified blacks in the relevant work force to determine whether or not sufficient numbers are available to meet the goals set by federal agencies? In most instances, we probably do not know what qualifications really are necessary for successful performance of specific jobs. This has been a major issue of contention between supporters of affirmative action and the Civil Service Commission. The former point out that most job selection tests and devices have not been validated as performance relevant. Critics of affirmative action respond that meeting federal guidelines on test validation is difficult because the requirements are very stringent and validation research is expensive. At the same time, it appears that federal agencies are not making the efforts necessary to develop adequate information about the availability of minorities in the general work force. Supporters of affirmative action will question the "good faith" of antidiscrimination programs until employers develop validated job-related selection criteria and devote greater efforts to gathering information about potential minority employees.

Recently, Joseph Califano, Secretary of HEW, said that "employment quotas can and do work in reversing patterns of job discrimination." Two weeks later, he admitted that he had made a mistake in advocating quotas.[32] Califano's quick retraction suggests how sensitive the issue has become in political terms, but his statements point to the symbolic aspect of the federal government's public posture. If federal agencies were to communicate to their constituencies that they will not require goals, timetables, and the data collecting necessary to evaluate progress, the result, I suspect, would be a definite decline in affirmative action as a priority for private and public employers. At the same time, agencies enforcing equal employment opportunity compliance must recognize that "good faith" efforts may not produce significant increases in the number of blacks hired and promoted. Even though it is unfair to equate "good faith" with hiring results, employers should be able to show that their affirmative action activities—information gathering on the availability of qualified minority persons, recruiting, skill inventories on black employees, in-service training, and promotion reviews—are indeed being pursued energetically.

Housing Conditions and Residential Segregation

For blacks, inadequate housing and residential segregation are closely related problems. To a large extent, residential segregation has meant that blacks are confined to areas with poor housing; of course, many black families could not afford decent housing even if it were available. Recently, the connection between improving the quality of housing available to blacks and increasing the opportunities of blacks to live in integrated neighborhoods has tightened because (1) the federal courts have begun to insist that federally supported housing not maintain or foster racial segregation and (2) the housing needs of the growing class of middle-income blacks apparently could be met to a much greater extent if these blacks could compete on an equal basis for housing available in predominantly white areas of central cities and in the suburbs.

In general, the housing of blacks has been no more than minimally adequate. For example, in 1970, 23 percent of all nonwhites lived in housing rated as substandard by the Census Bureau. Although this was a major improvement from 1950, when the figure was 73 percent, most of this housing is modest in value and limited in amenities. In 1970, the median value of black homes was $10,800. Only 8 percent of black-owned-and-occupied homes were worth $15,000 or more and were built after 1960. Nearly one-half of black homes lacked a clothes washer; 82 percent lacked an air conditioner. A considerable gap remains between housing conditions for blacks and for whites. In 1970, blacks were still four times more likely than whites to live in substandard units, and three times more likely to be overcrowded.[33]

Residential concentration and segregation of blacks in central cities is intense throughout the nation, although commentators disagree about trends and causes. In recent years, central cities and urban fringes have generally gained blacks, while nonurban areas have lost them. A study using 1970 data found that blacks at all value levels of housing (owned and rented) were overrepresented in central cities and underrepresented in suburbs.[34] Glazer points out that a substantial increase in black population in the suburbs between 1950 and 1970 (from 2.2 to 3.7 million) tends to be concealed by the rapid white migration to the suburbs, so that blacks constituted a slightly smaller percentage of the total suburban population in 1970. He also notes that the number of central cities in which the segregation index decreased between 1960 and 1970 was much greater than the number in the period from 1950 and 1960.[35] He acknowledges that the figures are high; for example, the median housing segregation index for 53 northern cities was 81; for 10 western cities, 81; for 12 border cities, 87; and for 34 southern cities, 91. Pettigrew estimates that "it would require at the 1960 to 1970 rate of change four to five centuries to eliminate" these racial concentrations.[36]

The federal effort to make good on its commitment to provide decent housing for low-income families has been a failure; urban renewal in particular has an especially poor reputation because many such projects demolished more low-income housing than they replaced, and blacks were especially vulnerable to these consequences. During President Nixon's first term, there was a great increase in subsidized housing programs (rent and purchase subsidies), and by the end of 1972, blacks occupied more than one-third of all such subsidized housing. However, near the end of that year, the Nixon administration placed a freeze on new commitments. According to Levitan, the subsidized housing was not much more than minimally adequate; outside central cities, racial integration and dispersal of subsidized projects did not occur on a large scale. The record of the federal government in providing blacks with equal opportunity in housing has generally been unimpressive. Two major federal mortgage-insuring agencies, the Federal Housing Administration and the Veterans Administration, did not make a concerted effort to help blacks obtain mortgages until the late 1960s. During the Nixon administration, blacks began to receive a proportion of federally guaranteed housing mortgages that was commensurable with their numbers. At the same time, neither agency used its lending power to encourage the development of integrated housing projects.

Although the number of whites who agree, in response to survey questions, that blacks are entitled to equal opportunity in housing has increased substantially in the last two decades, many whites apparently still do not want to have blacks for neighbors. Whereas many blacks may also prefer to live in homogeneous neighborhoods, polls taken in the late 1960s indicated that a very considerable number preferred racially mixed neighborhoods. The problem seems to be that neighborhoods which blacks would regard as desirable, that is, racially mixed near 50:50, whites would regard as undesirable. Of white respondents to a 1971 survey, 70 percent said they would move if blacks entered their neighborhood in "great numbers"; the "tipping point" may be as low as 15–20 percent black.[37] Fear that a neighborhood into which blacks are moving in substantial numbers will become virtually 100 percent black may motivate whites to leave, but this result can, of course, be a self-fulfilling prophecy. Only collective measures such as some communities have taken—action against blockbusters, prohibitions on "for sale" signs[38] and on canvassing and solicitations by realtors—can prevent that outcome.

For blacks with low and moderate incomes, the only possibility for improved housing lies in public housing or subsidized private housing. Public housing has a troubled history. The large-scale high-rise projects constructed after World War II often created conditions conducive to a variety of social pathologies. Public-housing income requirements tended to prevent socioeconomic mixing and to exclude the more successful members of a community. One response has been to plan smaller clusters on scattered sites and another to combine low- and moderate-income families within the subsidized projects. These changes in concept have not been so easy to implement. Federal subsidies have been available for such housing on an integrated basis, but there has been considerable resistance from white middle-income neighborhoods within central cities and in the suburbs.

Two recent Supreme Court decisions have been viewed as supporting this opposition. In June 1976, the Supreme Court ruled 6–3 "that it is constitutional for a city to require property owners who want their land rezoned to first get approval of the city's voters in a referendum."[39] As a result, residents can block attempts to introduce into their communities low-income housing projects that would be available to minorities. Another recently decided case, *Arlington Heights v. Metropolitan Housing Development Corp.*, arose from the refusal of a village board to rezone acreage for multiple family units of low and moderate income housing. A private, nonprofit development corporation was chartered to develop integrated housing in suburban areas, subsidized by federal funds for low and moderate income residents. It signed a 90-year lease (and option to buy 15 acres) with a religious order. The village board and plan commission rejected the corporation's request for the required rezoning, and the corporation sued the village in federal district court, contending that the village violated the Constitution by discriminating against the rights of blacks and other minorities to equal access in housing. The case was appealed up to the Supreme Court, which ruled that the refusal to rezone was not unconstitutional merely because it had a "racially disproportionate impact." Intent to discriminate also had to be proved, and the Court decided that this element had not been demonstrated.

A similar issue has been posed in suits against public-housing authorities which charge them with violating the constitutional rights of racial minorities by locating federally funded public housing in nonwhite areas of their cities. Although federal district courts have found discrimination in such cases, effective remedies are difficult to devise. Mandating that housing authorities build public projects in predominantly white areas does not ensure that units will be built, only that they will not be built in predominantly minority areas. Resistance by middle-income whites to low- and moderate-income public housing has slowed such developments within central cities and in suburbs.

Because the Supreme Court upheld the zoning authority of suburban communities against the charge of racial discrimination based on racially disproportionate impact, the likelihood that blacks will achieve significant improvements in either housing conditions or residential integration apparently is reduced. There is federal legislation—Title VIII of the 1968 Civil Rights Act—and a Supreme Court decision—*Jones v. Mayer*—which together prohibit discrimination in all housing. However, the burden of action falls largely on the individual who thinks he or she has been the victim of discrimination. The Department of Housing and Urban Development can take enforcement action under the 1968 law, but it lacks sanctions. More can be done in this area, especially against large rental corporations, developers, and real estate agencies. But it will take concerted action by civil rights organizations to make the legal remedies available to individuals effective on a significant scale. An attack on the institutionalized discrimination of the private housing market would help middle-class blacks able and willing to move to the suburbs.

Whatever can be accomplished by such challenges to discrimination, the greatest opportunities to improve black living conditions may not lie in the suburbs. Although some analysts have suggested that blacks must get out of central cities to find employment because jobs are moving to the suburbs, others claim that central cities may still be economically viable for blacks. Studies of black income and occupational status comparing city, periphery, and suburbs indicate that blacks in the suburbs are not distinctively better off than their city counterparts. There are still large numbers of jobs in central cities for which blacks can compete, although it appears that job training, job counseling, and placement services on a large scale, as well as improved urban transportation systems, are required to make these job opportunities real options. One cannot be optimistic about the possibilities of rebuilding the ghetto economy; nonetheless, the suburbs are no panacea for black needs in housing and employment. As Glazer notes, there is more housing being built in central cities than in the suburbs relative to population growth.[40] Moreover, dispersion in the suburbs would undermine recently achieved political gains and the possibility of community-controlled institutions that many blacks appear to want. In the short run at least, it will be extremely difficult to make significant improvements in the housing available to blacks while simultaneously reducing the level of residential segregation.

Conclusion

In the early 1960s, black inequality suddenly became a national issue. For approximately a decade, there was intense activity to narrow the various socioeconomic and political gaps between blacks and whites; then, not long after the shock of ghetto riots and armed black militants, it subsided rapidly. By the early 1970s, the civil rights movement had passed into American history.

The movement represented the first broad effort to eliminate black inequality since Reconstruction. For nearly ninety years, we had, as a nation, largely ignored the plight of the black population. Major changes in American society occurred in this period, and the problem of black inequality also changed. It was no longer only the reverse side of southern racism and southern poverty[41]; blacks had migrated to urban areas throughout the nation, taking with them the legacy of slavery and segregation. In the institutions and mores of our increasingly urban society, black inequality was taken for granted; school systems, residential patterns, labor markets, and commercial practices developed in ways that accepted and exploited the various forms of black inequality. Taking black inequality for granted did not seem racist or even discriminatory to most Americans; northern whites did not see themselves as culpable for the poverty, poor education, ill health, and crowded living conditions that most blacks had to endure. These were the legacy of the South's treatment of blacks.

In a sense, the civil rights movement had to begin in the South, but unlike Emancipation and Reconstruction, it could not stop there. The southern civil-rights movement raised the group consciousness and the expectations of blacks throughout the nation, and it made many whites uneasy—for the first time—about the forms of black inequality in their own areas. It set in motion individuals, organizations, and federal programs that began to attack these problems, but as I have already argued, it could not provide an adequate model for achieving the elimination of black inequality in the complex, interrelated forms it now encompassed. The nature of southern segregation, with its direct connection of racist attitudes and discriminatory actions and institutions, was not suited for the primary educational task outside the South: to make whites see that many actions and practices in which they engaged without invidious intentions reinforced the handicaps blacks already suffered as a result of their experience under slavery and segregation.

In a sense, much of the controversy about black inequality arises because the links between differential intergroup outcomes and discriminatory attitudes and actions are not apparent. The questions underlying opposed points of view revolve around that indeterminacy. Are the differential outcomes themselves—the forms that inequality takes—objectionable whether or not discriminatory attitudes and intentions can be shown to be proximate causes? Some Americans say that these differences are not invidious in themselves and thus do not call for remedial action unless a causal connection to discrimination can be shown. Others argue that seemingly neutral decisions can perpetuate the differentials between races by accepting as givens situations that were created by discrimination. Is this kind of connection sufficient to make those "neutral" decisions objectionable?

We need to see more clearly the links between racially discriminatory attitudes and differential outcomes for racial minorities, but a judgment will still have to be made whether ostensibly nondiscriminatory decisions must also be changed. If differential treatment is used as a prima facie or surrogate measure of discrimination, then who should be compared to whom and how different must the treatment be to qualify as objectionable? What should be the basis for comparison in determining whether and how much discrimination in employment and segregation in housing exists? For example, is the appropriate baseline for judging discrimination in employment the percentage of blacks in the total population? Is a random distribution of blacks and whites the proper standard for determining the amount of segregation in housing? What role should minority group preferences play in determining such baselines?

These questions lead inevitably to more explicitly value-laden ones. What is the ultimate goal of our efforts in the civil rights area? What situations are we trying to approximate with the measures taken and proposed? Equality of opportunity is much too vague a concept to be regarded as an answer to such questions, yet it is the one most commonly offered. Another abstraction is "full participation as equal citizens." A third proposal is the goal of a fully integrated society. Even if defined, such concepts still pose difficult problems of application. How does one determine when equality of opportunity has been achieved, for example, in employment or admission to professional training? If our goal is full integration, how much concentration by race is probable, given "reasonably" free choice? Does choosing to "segregate" oneself represent a manifestation of democratic freedom or a failure of democratic socialization? If we can answer these kinds of questions, we still have to consider what rate of change is desirable? tolerable? feasible? Finally, we have to ask ourselves how much these goals are worth to us. What burdens are we willing to shoulder to achieve them? How much should we be willing to sacrifice? How are the burdens likely to be distributed in light of what we know about the distribution of power in our society? How should the burdens be distributed—if we are guided by democratic principles?

These questions are not intended to numb or bewilder the reader. They may suggest that consensus is hopelessly unobtainable. Perhaps. Nonetheless, we must try to formulate explicit answers; then, at least, the substance and extent of our disagreements will be clear and the chances of reasoned debate between partisans, public, and government officials increased. Muting differences in order to avoid conflict may seem expedient, but in the long run, it will not improve the basic situation. Decisions affecting black inequality will continue to be made, and if these questions are ignored, the decisions are likely to be piecemeal and ex parte—not conducive to a measure of progress even as large as that already achieved.

The gains of the past two decades have placed blacks in general much closer to equality—however defined—than ever before in our history. We cannot return to the conditions which prevailed before the 1960s; blacks are too conscious, civil rights legislation barring overt discrimination is too much a part of our practice, and blacks have achieved enough of a political foothold to prevent a return to a not terribly benign neglect. But I do not think that one can say objectively that black inequality is no longer a major problem in American society, nor can one say with confidence that the forces set in motion by the developments of the last two decades will—say, in two or three more decades—eliminate virtually all the handicaps that have been the legacy of racism and discrimination. We must confront the issues posed by continued black inequality, or the effects of past racism and discrimination will persist many decades into the future. Apparently, most whites are not inclined to think that black Americans are victims of discrimination any longer; this climate of opinion bodes ill for the educational and remedial tasks that remain.

REFERENCES

I found the following works especially valuable in preparing this paper: Sar Levitan, William Johnston, and Robbert Taggart, *Still A Dream: The Changing Status of Blacks Since 1960* (Cambridge: Harvard University Press, 1975); Nathan Glazer, *Affirmative Discrimination* (New York: Basic Books, 1975); Harrell R. Rogers, Jr. (ed.), *Racism and Inequality: The Policy Alternatives* (San Francisco: W. H. Freeman, 1975); and U.S. Commission on Civil Rights, *The Federal Civil Rights Enforcement Effort—1974* (Washington, D.C., 1974, 1975). A number of essays by Thomas F. Pettigrew also were quite useful.

[1] By 1972, only 31.6% of black students in the South attended schools that were 80–100% black. Harrell R. Rogers, Jr., "On Integrating the Public Schools: An Empirical and Legal Assessment," in Rogers (ed.), *Racism and Inequality*, p. 126.

[2]The story is well told by Gary Orfield in *The Reconstruction of Southern Education* (New York: Wiley-InterScience, 1969).

[3]Rogers, *Racism and Inequality*, p. 131.

[4]U.S. Commission on Civil Rights, *Twenty Years After Brown: Equality of Educational Opportunity* (Washington, D.C., 1975), p. 80.

[5]U.S. Civil Rights Commission, *Statement on Metropolitan School Desegregation* (February 1977): 6

[6]Not all state action may be culpable; it might have to be action with foreseeable and avoidable consequences, such as assigning pupils to schools using geographic criteria.

[7]Norman C. Amaker, "Milliken v. Bradley: The Meaning of the Constitution in School Desegregation Cases," in *Milliken v. Bradley: The Implications for Metropolitan Desegregation*, Conference before the U.S. Commission on Civil Rights, Washington, D.C., November 9, 1974, p. 4.

[8]James Bolner and Robert Shanley, *Busing: The Political and Judicial Process* (New York: Praeger, 1974), pp. 242–243, cite a study commissioned by the Civil Rights Commission in late 1972.

[9]John McAdams, "Strategies for Integration: Can Open Enrollment Work?" *Public Interest*, no. 37 (Fall 1974): 85–86.

[10]Jonathan Kelley, "The Politics of School Busing," *Public Opinion Quarterly*, 38 (Spring 1974): 23–39.

[11]See the essays by David Armor and Thomas Pettigrew and associates in *The Public Interest*, no. 28 (Summer 1972) for a review of the evidence and the points in contention.

[12]Lino Graglia, *Disaster by Decree: The Supreme Court Decisions on Race and the Schools* (Ithaca: Cornell University Press, 1976), p. 276 cites the above-mentioned essay by Armor ("The Evidence on Busing") in *Public Interest* for this finding. I have taken many of the criticisms made of the probusing position from Graglia's book.

[13]Christine H. Rossell, "School Desegregation and White Flight," *Political Science Quarterly*, 90 (Winter 1975–1976): 683–684.

[14]Alabama, Georgia, Louisiana, Mississippi, North Carolina, South Carolina, and Virginia.

[15]A survey of voting in the 1972 presidential election reported that the black turnout in the whole South was 9.2% lower than the white turnout. Bureau of the Census, "Voting and Registration in the Election of November, 1972," Series P–20, no. 253 (October 1973).

[16]Michael Preston, "Limitations of Black Urban Power: The Case of Black Mayors," in Louis Masotti and Robert Lineberry, *The New Urban Politics* (Cambridge, Mass.: Ballinger, 1976), p. 112.

[17]Herrington J. Bryce, "Problems of Governing American Cities: The Case of Medium and Large Cities with Black Mayors," Joint Center for Political Studies, 1974, cited in Preston, "Limitations of Black Urban Power."

[18]Charles S. Bullock, III, "The Election of Blacks in the South: Preconditions and Consequences," *American Journal of Political Science*, 19 (November 1975): 728. Bullock notes that black "councilmen, county commissioners, and school board members are more often elected in white communities," but he thinks it likely that these offices are chosen by districts and that the black officials have predominantly black constituents.

[19]Lester M. Salamon and Stephen Van Evera, "Fear, Apathy, and Discrimination: A Test of Three Explanations of Political Participation," *American Political Science Review*, 67 (December 1973): 1288–1306. See also the Comment by Sam Kernell and the Rejoinder by Salamon and Van Evera.

[20]William Nelson, Jr., and Winston Van Horne, "Black Elected Administrators: The Trials of Office," *Public Administration Review*, 34 (November 1974): 528–529.

[21]Preston, "Limitations of Black Urban Power," p. 128.

[22]The above cited essays by Preston and by Nelson and Van Horne were useful in gaining an overview of the problems faced by black officials.

[23]Bureau of Labor Statistics, Department of Labor, *Handbook of Labor Statistics 1975* (Washington, D.C.: 1975), pp. 70–72, Table 19.

[24]U.S. Bureau of the Census, Current Population Reports, Special Studies, Series P–23, "The Social and Economic Status of the Black Population in the United States," (1971), p. 73, Table 57; (1973), p. 58, Table 42.

[25]U.S. Commission on Civil Rights, *The Federal Civil Rights Enforcement Effort—1974*; the study ran to several volumes, some of which were issued in 1975.

[26]Harry Kranz, *The Participatory Bureaucracy* (Lexington, Mass.: D. C. Heath, 1976), p. 160–189, Tables 5–14, 5–24, 5–32, and 5–37. The original data came from the EEOC.

[27]Levitan, Johnston, and Taggart, *Still a Dream*, p. 44.

[28]Bureau of Labor Statistics, *Handbook of Labor Statistics 1975*, pp. 70–72, Table 19.

[29]JOBS—Job Opportunities in the Business Sector; businesses provide jobs for disadvantaged persons, government subsidizes the extra costs of hiring and training. MDTA—Manpower Development and Training Act; provides institutional training to aid those with socioeconomic handicaps (vocational and basic education plus financial allowance). CEP—Concentrated Employment Program; funds channeled by government to local groups (e.g., community action agencies) which can

provide manpower services to clients primarily in central city ghettoes. WIN—Work Incentive Program; preemployment services and training (basic education, vocational training, child care and counseling) provided to persons on welfare, who are allowed to keep a portion of their earnings. See Levitan, Johnson, and Taggart, *Still a Dream*, pp. 252–262.

[30]Glazer, *Affirmative Discrimination*, p. 41.

[31]Even more so in higher education than in employment.

[32]*New York Times* (March 18, 1977): 1; (April 1, 1977): 1.

[33]Levitan, Johnston, and Taggart, *Still a Dream*, pp. 114, 146.

[34]Albert Hermalin and Reynolds Farley, "The Potential for Residential Integration in Cities and Suburbs: Implications for the Busing Controversy,"*American Sociological Review*, 38 (October 1973): 595–610.

[35]Nathan Glazer, "On 'Opening Up' the Suburbs," *Public Interest*, no. 37 (Fall 1974): 94, 97. The segregation index indicates the percentage of nonwhites who would have to move in order for each block to have a proportion of whites to nonwhites equal to the city as a whole.

[36]Thomas F. Pettigrew, "A Sociological View of the Post-Milliken Era," in *Milliken v. Bradley*, pp. 61, 66.

[37]Levitan, Johnston, and Taggart, *Still a Dream*, p. 160. See Thomas F. Pettigrew, "Attitudes on Race and Housing: A Social-Psychological View," in Amos H. Hawely and Vincent P. Rock, *Segregation in Residential Areas* (Washington, D.C.: National Academy of Sciences, 1973).

[38]On May 2, 1977, the Supreme Court ruled that ordinances prohibiting such signs violated constitutional guarantees of free speech.

[39]"The Court's ruling, involving a referendum provision adopted in 1971 by the voters of the city of Eastlake, Ohio, appears limited to localities where there is a provision—as in Ohio's State Constitution—reserving the referendum power for the voters on local and municipal matters," *New York Times* (June 22, 1976): 22 ("Voters' Approval in Zoning Upheld"); *Eastlake, Ohio v. Forest City Enterprises*.

[40]Glazer, "On 'Opening Up' the Suburbs," p. 91.

[41]I do not mean here to imply that racism and black inequality were only southern phenomena until a relatively recent period in our nation's history.

DANIEL YERGIN

Order and Survival

I

To ask the question if there is "a new America?" in the context of foreign affairs is to pose another question—is there "a new world?" For the character of a nation's foreign policy cannot be judged apart from the challenges it faces in the world, and from the shifts in the distribution of power in the international system. Thus, we are pressed to identify the elements of change and of continuity. In so doing, three critical problems come into clear view—involving order, security, and the conceptual basis of U.S. foreign policy.

The two decades between 1940 and 1960 witnessed a transformation in international politics. The European-centered state system, solidified after the Napoleonic Wars, collapsed in 1939. It could not be repaired after 1945. Its place was taken by a new system, characterized by a confrontation between two hostile alliance systems, one led by the United States and the other by the Soviet Union. This was the bipolar international system. Yet, even though both were called superpowers, the disparity between the United States and the Soviet Union was considerable. By every index, the United States was far and away the most powerful nation in the world, the preponderant nation in the international system, the "freest" in the choices it could make. It was truly a global power, the hegemonic leader of the coalition of industrial democracies, possessing worldwide capabilities and networks of interest. On its side of the confrontation with the Soviet Union, the United States shaped and managed almost single-handedly the political and economic rules, norms, and procedures that constituted the "order" in which interacted the Western industrial nations, as well as most of what became known as the Third World. Thus, it is fully appropriate to describe the postwar years as the "American era of international relations."[1]

In the 1960s, however, a process of erosion began, at first visible only to those with a professional interest in such matters as the balance of payments, but by now, revealed to all. Indeed, by the end of the 1970s, the American-shaped and -dominated order had been subjected to four severe challenges; the attainment of "near economic parity" by Western Europe and Japan; the rapid rise of the Organization of Petroleum Exporting Countries (OPEC); the call by the Third World for a radical transformation of the entire order; and the prospect of nuclear proliferation.

263

These challenges to the order are, ipso facto, challenges to America's preponderant position in that order. They represent conscious or structural constraints and checks on the exercise of American power, that is, of America's ability to determine outcomes. They also mean a change in the foreign policy agenda. Formerly, the items at the top were composed of the relatively well-defined primary security questions. But now the more confusing and obscure questions that are an admixture of politics and economics have been added. With these latter questions, absolute measures of power do not necessarily mean that a country can decide the outcome in one issue area or another.[2]

Here—coping with the issues of order—is the first of the three critical problems for American foreign policy. It is one that arises, then, from a shift from American hegemony to American interdependence. Yet care must be taken in such an analysis, for there is a real danger of seeing a sharper change than has been the case. America is not an "ordinary country," and shows no immediate prospect of becoming such.[3] Even though its relative power has declined, America is still the most powerful country in the world, the dominant country in the world, and this first problem before it is to decide how it can and should most effectively wield that power. For, when a country is as powerful as is the United States, to not exert its power also constitutes a form of action.

While the issues of order represent the new problem for U.S. foreign policy, no less pressing, despite its familiarity, is the enduring issue of survival and the balance of power, the problem posed by the confrontation with the Soviet Union.

The third problem derives from the preceding two. It is a conceptual problem—to find a way to think about America's role and goals in a world in which issues of order and issues of survival both claim centrality, a world in which America, although no longer preponderant, remains the dominant power.

II

Even before the 1970s, the first significant challenge to this order had been lodged—as a response to its success, a fruit of the liberal international economy created in the immediate postwar years. The order had depended upon America's power being so much greater than that of its allies. By the late 1960s, the gap had dramatically narrowed, at least in the economic sphere.

American economic policymaking during and immediately after World War II drew its inspiration from the experience and perceptions of the interwar years, not as a model to follow, but as a fate to avoid. U.S. leaders feared a return to the chaotic international economic conditions of the 1920s and 1930s—trade barriers, protectionism, competitive devaluations, inflation, and slump. They believed that a barricaded international economy made bad economic sense; they also believed that the disrupted world economy had contributed to the political developments that culminated in war. Thus, they labored to establish a new regime for the international economy—an open, multilateral trading and payments system that harked back to the Pax Britannica of the nineteenth century.

The Bretton Woods arrangements provided for fixed exchange rates, and a monetary system resting on a dollar-gold base. The General Agreement on Tariffs and Trade set the basis for a reduction in trade barriers. U.S. leaders aimed, at least at the beginning, not at the imposition of an order, but rather at a negotiated settlement, especially with the sterling bloc.[4]

In 1947 the character of the enterprise changed, on the one hand somewhat reducing the openness, on the other, actually augmenting American power. In late 1946 and early 1947, it became apparent that the wounds of war ran far deeper than had been perceived, and that the return to a normal economic life was going to be much more difficult than expected. Britain's retreat from economic leadership proved precipitous, not gentlemanly; Britain simply could not bear those burdens. At the same time, the confrontation with the Soviet Union intensified, and the basic bipolarity of the international system was clearly etched. In these circumstances, the Western Europeans (including the British) and the Japanese became less partners in negotiations than dependents, to be protected and nurtured. The United States quickly assumed the role of stabilizer—of organizer and leader, willing to bear the extra costs—that it had not played in the late 1920s and 1930s.[5]

Within the context of the overall order, American policies now were much more explicitly geared to promoting the revival of the Western European and Japanese economies. The goals were several: the economic recovery of Western Europe and Japan; the maintenance of an international economic environment hospitable to democracy and capitalism; the shoring up of a balance of power; and the containment of the Soviet Union and communism. Particular emphasis was placed on integrating West Germany and Japan into the international economic order.[6] The United States postponed elements of a pure multilateral program. Instead, it encouraged Western Europe to form itself into an economic bloc that would discriminate to a certain degree against U.S. exports. It also encouraged Japanese exports to the United States while acceding to Japan's own restrictions on imports and foreign investment. Security concerns, a view of the overall economic environment, and America's own favored and bountiful position—these were enough to justify the considerable exceptions to the free trade system.

The order so constructed was markedly successful in achieving its several goals in the 1950s and the 1960s, a period of unprecedented economic growth. In the late 1950s and into the 1960s, world trade grew at 7 percent a year. Trade within the Western system more than doubled between 1960 and 1969.[7] Three characteristics of the period bear noting. First, Europe and Japan largely completed the process of recovery and modernization. Second, with sterling shoved aside, the dollar itself became the basis of the international payments system. Third, there was an awesome growth in the export of American know-how and capital, especially as measured in the spread of American multinational corporations. The book value of American multinational investment overseas rose from $7.2 billion in 1946 to $100 billion in 1973, accounting in the last instance for an output of $200 billion.[8] A number of factors encouraged this development: the establishment of the European Community drew American businessmen with a vision of another continental market to conquer, and at the same time made them fear the competitive consequences if they were excluded by trade barriers. Lower costs abroad, an overvalued dollar, and American technological levels all provided incentives for foreign investment, which was facilitated by the U.S. tax code. The American business community, as it surveyed the world, shared in the general self-confidence of postwar America. The shrinkage of international space, in terms of communications and travel, made control a much more reasonable undertaking for a firm. But, undoubtedly, a most important factor was the American hegemony over the entire order.[9]

In 1967, J. J. Servan-Schreiber published his influential book, *The American Challenge*. But, as is so often the case, the owl of Minerva was cleared for takeoff only at midnight. Indeed, by this point, the American challenge was in fact beginning to ebb. The period of recovery in Western Europe and Japan had ended. Both areas had, in David Landes' phrase, achieved "economic parity" (or "near parity") with the United States.[10] These economies were now asserting themselves as innovators.[11] Non-American multinational corporations were observed to be growing faster than American ones.[12] The indicators of recovery were most dramatic in the Japanese case. Japanese productivity doubled between 1965 and 1970; Japan sold 1.5 million television sets in the United States in 1967 and 3.1 million sets a mere two years later; its gross national product had grown almost five times over between 1962 and 1972. The annual Japanese growth rate was 13 percent in the 1960s; Europe's, 7 percent; the United States', between 3 and 4 percent.[13]

The consequence of all this was that America's political partners had become its economic rivals. Trade policy and monetary affairs became major arenas for conflict. There was a widespread fear of American loss of competitiveness abroad, and Washington began to attack a number of the European Community's practices on trade. The French, hostile to American investment in Europe, overtly led the challenge on monetary affairs, with de Gaulle criticizing what he described as the "monumentally overprivileged position that the rest of the world has conceded to the American currency."[14] But it was neither ideology nor visions of grandeur, but real economic conflicts that generated the tension. The United States was now finding the costs of hegemony too great. It no longer felt inclined to "allow" the Europeans and the Japanese the dispensations that it denied itself. The dollar-based monetary system was proving inadequate to the growth of world trade, the effects of inflation, and the costs of the Vietnam War, and was increasingly ill adapted to the new parity among Western nations. The United States had depended upon its trade surplus to balance off the costs of maintaining troops abroad and the export of capital. In the 1960s, that trade surplus disappeared. In 1970, the United States ran a deficit on the official reserves transaction balance of $10 billion; in 1971, it reached $30 billion.[15]

These developments worked together to create a situation of tension and contradiction. After all, the United States, Western Europe, and Japan remained political partners in a security system in which America played the dominant role and bore the main burden of the costs. Yet, these countries were more and more conscious that, with recovery and modernization complete, they were economic rivals. At the same time, their economies were increasingly interdependent. What happened in one economy affected the others; even that of the United States was becoming less insulated. Droughts elsewhere did affect the cost of bread in the supermarket. The postwar international order had facilitated dramatic increases in output, productivity, and living standards throughout the Western world. But this also meant an increased vulnerability to disturbances outside the nation's borders as well as constraints on the ability of national governments to wield effectively the instruments of domestic power. Balanced against this was the widespread acceptance of the welfare state, with a considerable enlargement of the responsibility of governments for such matters as growth, employment, and inflation. Such developments created, in the words of Marina v. N. Whitman, "tension between international integration at the market level and the sovereignty of the nation state at the policy level."[16] Add to that another tension—this between common security interests and economic interests that, at one and the same time, were common and in conflict. Factor in as well the United States in turmoil about the nature of its leadership role in the world, and an administration somewhat more nationalist than predecessors, perhaps even Gaullist manqué.

All of this called into question the bargain, the "agreement," on which the postwar order was based—that the United States would occupy a "special position," a hegemonic place. The United States had in effect agreed to foreswear short-term interests for the sake of maintaining a system from which it, along with the others, certainly benefited. The others had allowed the United States this special role because of the overall importance of maintaining the system. The balance of payments deficits of 1970 and 1971 tolled for the end of that bargain.

Between 1971 and 1973, in response to these tensions, the old order—if it did not quite collapse—was substantially transformed. On August 15, 1971 Richard Nixon abruptly announced a "new economic policy" which ended the convertibility of dollars into gold, and which placed a 10 percent surcharge on most imports. In December of that year, under the Smithsonian agreements, the dollar was devalued, and was again devalued in February 1973. (These devaluations certainly increased the competitiveness of American exports, and along with political uncertainty and fear of American barriers became one of the important reasons for increased foreign investment in the United States.[17]) In March 1973, fixed exchange rates were abandoned, and the dollar now floated with other currencies. All of this, aggravated by inflation and by the somewhat bellicose manner in which changes were executed, created great uncertainty in the Western world. The perception of basic conflicts among allies was growing. August 15, 1971, became a slogan for a certain disengagement from dependence on the United States. That a need was felt to call for a "Year of Europe" in 1973 (whatever that was to be) was in itself a recognition of the difficulties.

Yet the adaptation to the challenge in the first half decade has proved less difficult than might have been expected. First, the challenge was aimed at reforming the order, adapting to "economic parity," without radically changing it. In other words, the challenge was not aimed at the fundamental premises. Moreover, the continuing common security interests helped to assuage some of the tensions that many had expected, and, at least for the time being, the monetary system that emerged in 1971–1973 stands legitimated and accepted by the Jamaica agreements of January 1976.[18]

Second, the rapid and unexpected rise of OPEC at the end of 1973 presented a far more basic challenge to all the industrial democracies. It underlined their community of interests, and made clear that their destinies were linked, that basic political stability was more important than sectoral pains. Third, while the effects of the "oil revolution" have hurt the economies of all the industrialized countries, the Europeans and Japanese were more vulnerable than the United States and suffered more. Thus, OPEC widened the gap again between the United States and the other advanced industrial countries, and, now from America's point of view, the problem is not the strength of the European and Japanese economies, but their weakness.

Matters have worked out better over the last several years than one would have expected when, on August 15, 1971, Richard Nixon's "new economic policy" seemed to suggest that the "creator" of the postwar international order had in a fit of frustration and rage consigned the work to the pyre. But all these changes have not been enough to restore the old order. The United States cannot unilaterally set out the rules, although it can dominate all proceedings. Instead, there has been a movement toward what the years of 1945–1947 had prefigured—toward a "negotiated system," a collective management (albeit with hierarchy) of interdependence.[19] Strenuous efforts have been made on the official and private levels to work out a common agenda and frame of reference.[20] The series of summits of Western leaders at Rambouillet, Puerto Rico, and London have expressed the drive to find ways to coordinate and manage interdependence. Such meetings can be of real help, but they may turn out to be of more help in reducing suspicion on such matters as the control of nuclear proliferation than at conquering the current international economic dilemma (in contradistinction to "beggar thy neighbor") or "wait for thy neighbor" to begin his economic expansion first.

There is reason to fear that the disintegration predicted for 1973 or 1974 has only been postponed, not avoided, that the cumulative economic problems may succeed in preventing the Western nations from negotiating a new order among themselves. How long can politicians, responsive to domestic pressures and elections, continue to resist protectionism and short-term nationalist solutions? The single greatest problem comes from outside the triangle of the United States, Japan, and Western Europe, and is not very responsive to the interests of those nations—and that is the pricing policies of OPEC. The second constraint is internal, the highest unemployment rates in the postwar era. Other related factors include faint recovery, low confidence, and unwillingness to invest because of uncertainty about political trends and the future shape of the international economic order.[21] These pressures circumscribe the ability of politicians to cooperate in shaping and maintaining a negotiated system for managing interdependence, and suggest that we may observe, if these trends continue for a few more years, not the modification of the postwar order but rather a discomforting process of disintegration.

III

The second and third challenges, together far more fundamental, to the established order rose in the 1970s. They were expressed in the actions of the nonindustrial oil-producing countries and by the claims of the Third World less developed countries (LDCs) for a global redistribution of wealth and power. Of course, the Third World was not a recent discovery; on the contrary, it had engaged the attention of the Kennedy administration. But what has changed dramatically are the role and perception of the Third World nations and the stakes involved in relations with them. Putting it simply, they have gone from being objects of international politics to actors.

The Soviet-American confrontation had begun as a contest over the political orientation of Europe in the late 1940s. This competition came to focus on Germany. Berlin provided the setting for a crisis a decade later, at the time when John Kennedy became President. Yet Europe had already been stabilized by then, the unanswered questions about its political geography, mostly resolved. By this point, decolonization was in full swing; the Western European countries were divesting themselves of their overseas colonies. By 1960, this process had already shifted the Soviet-American competition to the peripheries, outside Europe, to what was becoming known as the Third World. What was of concern were the new unanswered questions—the political orientation of the successor states to the old colonial empires. The United States and the Soviet Union entered into a competition for influence and allies among these new nations.

The Third World nations were also beginning an effort to assert themselves as an independent bloc in the world. The first obvious attempt was at the first meeting of the United Nations Conference on Trade and Development in Geneva in 1964. The "Group of 77," as these nations described themselves, called for major changes in relations between North and South. And yet as independent actors—rather than as chess pieces in a bipolar game—they were not taken very seriously, for what appeared to be going on, in the words of one observer, was "a demand for everything by those who have nothing."[22] They continued to make their demands through the next decade. Among the most consistent themes were calls for preferential access to markets of the rich countries, greater foreign-aid development assistance, limitations on the activities of multinational corporations, stabilization of commodity earnings, shifts in the international terms of trade in their favor. These demands were reiterated yet again in September 1973, at the fourth summit of the nonaligned nations in Algiers. There did not seem that much more likelihood that they would get their way than had been the case a decade earlier at Geneva.

Certain underlying changes had taken place. These nations had become more powerful. Broadly speaking, one could say that the Third World had passed through one stage. The process of self-determination had been assured. The new entities had taken considerable steps toward organizing themselves as nations, delimiting their borders, asserting sway over rebellious minorities, building up their armies. Now, they were more prepared to try to assert themselves as an independent force in world politics.

Yet they were still far short of commanding the careful attention of the industrialized world. That all changed a month later. On October 6, Arab armies attacked Israel. Two weeks later, in retaliation for Western and particularly American support for Israel, the Organization of Arab Petroleum Exporting Countries announced an embargo on the delivery of oil to Western countries. A similar attempt during the 1967 Arab-Israeli War had failed. But now key conditions had changed. The dependence of the Western world on Middle Eastern oil had grown. There was not much spare capacity in oil-producing regions. Since the late 1960s, power had been shifting from the international oil companies to the producing countries. The situation was enough to set off panic buying of oil at prices ten times what had been the market rate—which was enough to lead to the sensible idea, from the point of view of the producing countries, that they really ought to raise the price of oil.[23] And so within the 15 months following October, the price of petroleum quintupled.

With the passage of more than four years, there can be no question but that achievement by the OPEC bloc is as important a development as the Sino-Soviet split was in the previous decade, in terms of changing the basic character and alignments of international politics. It may well even be more important, for OPEC has had direct and measurable impact on the way people live throughout the world. It has brought about a vast shift in economic power. In 1977, the OPEC countries earned $130 billion in revenues, more than ten times what they earned five years earlier. Since 1974, they have built up surplus accounts of over $150 billion. This wealth—combined with their control over supply—has given them considerable political power. In particular, Saudi Arabia, as the cartel's regulator and residual supplier, has gained enormous political power, perhaps much more than it would like to be responsible for.

While the shift in economic tilt has proved a great bounty for the producers, it has imposed heavy costs on the rest of the world, as measured in inflation and oil-induced recession.[24] There has been a significant withdrawal of income that otherwise would have gone into investment and spending. Many of the industrial countries find it difficult to apply their tools of economic management in an environment where OPEC can, at any moment, raise its tax. The international monetary system lumbers under the strain of recycling, and the non-oil-developing countries now stagger under an enormously increased debt load. OPEC, thus, has gone much further than ever did America's allies in changing the international economic order—not by questioning the rules, but rather by transforming that order so thoroughly.

These oil costs have directly weakened Western society. There are also other problems. Energy is now linked firmly into the Middle East conflict, one of the world's most intractable and unstable political problems.[25] The growth of OPEC power has certainly diminished American power. The United States is now much more dependent on decisions made in Tehran or Riyadh. It has encountered considerable difficulty in finding a constructive role to play on energy, and instead has been drawn along rather passively by events.

OPEC's success also provided the power and inspiration for a more far-reaching challenge to the order, an occasion for what has been portrayed as mobilization in an international class war. This challenge has been laid down in the call for a new international economic (and political) order, vividly expressed in a Third World resolution adopted by the Sixth Special Session of the U.N. General Assembly in the spring of 1974 in the aftermath of the demonstration of oil power:

> The present international economic order is in direct conflict with current developments in international political and economic relations. . . . The developing world has become a powerful factor that makes its influence felt in all fields of international activity. These irreversible changes in the relationship of forces in the world necessitates the active, full and equal participation of the developing countries in the formulation and application of all decisions that concern the international community.[26]

In a multitude of forums since, the Third World has left no doubt that what is at the heart of the North-South dialogue (or confrontation) is a struggle over the classic and basic issues of international order—the distribution of power, prestige, position, and wealth. No less clear is the South's determination and confidence that it can achieve what it desires.

The initial response of the United States, the organizer of the present order, was to reject the general claim, as well as many of the specific instrumentalities. Then, at the Seventh Special Session of the United Nations, in September 1975, Secretary of State Kissinger announced a major shift, at least a verbal commitment to take such reform seriously.[27] The Carter administration has gone further in its general endorsement. Emphasis is placed here on the declaratory as opposed to the operational character of the new American commitment. For no real consensus has formed on what the United States should do out of obligation and self-interest. Should the United States pursue an accommodationist strategy or a rejectionist strategy?[28]

This question must be faced at two levels—one practical, one more abstract. A number of issues might be grouped under the heading of practical. First, how vulnerable is the First World to the Third? Initially, there was an expectation that a host of other cartels, from bauxite to bananas, impended, and that the Third World would be able to coercively apply commodity power to the West. This, it has become clear since, is not likely. For the next few years, the OPEC cartel will surely retain its power. The political and economic benefits from its members remaining together provide ample incentive to avoid a break-up. However, oil is the exception. Substitution in the Western world in the case of oil is proving very difficult; it would be much easier for other commodities. In addition, the supply and consumption patterns for other raw materials and commodities—for instance, Australia is one of the major bauxite producers—would tend to rule out First World-Third World confrontations over other products.[29]

Second, the Third World is vulnerable to the First. There is some evidence that direct foreign investment in Third World countries provides the most dynamic element in their growth, and an assault on trading links with the North could place heavy costs on economic development in the South.[30] The dangers for the South become clearer when one considers that over 60 percent of the industrial countries' foreign trade moves among themselves.

Moreover, the very term "Third World" papers over many differences. Even though the Group of 77 has grown to over 100 nations, there is much that divides this group. Some of its members see themselves as of the revolutionary left; others do not. Some are theocratic; some, atheist. Some are rather advanced in development; some, rising fast; others, still stagnating in underdevelopment. Per capita income on the Indian subcontinent and in many parts of Africa and the Caribbean, for instance, is less than $100 a year, while many nations in Latin America, and some in Asia and Africa, range between $400 and $1,000 a year.[31] Moreover, the nonoil-producing LDCs are the nations that have suffered the most from OPEC's price increases, not only in terms of the actual costs of oil, but also in the dampening of demand for their exports in the advanced countries because of the postembargo downturn. "The OPEC knows no mercy," in the words of one Caribbean leader, yet most Third World countries are not willing to phrase the problem that way. Indeed what is surprising is the degree of unity that has been maintained by the Third World in the face of these very obvious differences and clash of interests. They see their longer-term interests being better met by continuing association with OPEC. Their hopes, ambitions, and resentments have become bound up with OPEC's success. Groups often define themselves in opposition to other groups, and the Third World countries had chosen to define themselves as an entity as victims of the First World. Thus, the Western world should count on a continuing coherence of the Third World.

Finally, there is an important question about the effects of a new international order on the world economy and on the developing countries themselves. We have already noted the deleterious effects of the OPEC quintupling on the world economy and other LDCs. A wholesale transformation could impede trade and cripple international economy. The LDCs would suffer in such a situation. [32]

At the same time, the Third World's challenge has been based on certain moral assertions. What type of "obligation" do the United States and the other First World countries bear to the Third? For some of the other Western countries there are special ties that have persisted out of the former empire imperial connections, but those are specific. The general basis for obligation seems to be twofold. The first is the assertion that the First World is in some way "guilty" for the condition of Third World countries, that the First World has systematically "exploited" the Third and thus owes reparation on a large scale. If this question is explored in terms of economic analysis rather than emotion, then such evidence as exists does not necessarily support that charge. [33] But it will be said that the First World has "robbed" the Third World of precious raw materials and commodities. Yet such charges depend on odd notions of value. Middle Eastern oil had no value, for instance, until Western nations and oil companies discovered and developed the fields. In further reply, it will be said "Yes, but look at how Western Europe's postwar growth depended upon cheap oil." Unhappily, there is no way to determine a just price for petroleum, to decide whether it was cheap or expensive. But, taking a longer-term view, we can see that the increasing European dependence on petroleum—and the shift away from coal—increased the value of the Middle Eastern oil, and indeed of oil worldwide.

The second basis is one of "shared humanity." Few would deny a concern with suffering and poverty worldwide. But the issue is how responsible are we for it, and how much can we do to solve it? For this concept has become very expansive in recent years. Global redistribution is discussed not on the basis of person-to-person, but rather state-to-state, but many of the claims tend to attribute to states the character of individuals. There seem to be real limits to how high a priority "shared humanity" can be given as an operational foreign policy interest of the United States. [34]

The challenge of the other Western nations to the international order was not directed at basic assumptions and principles. What was really sought was an adjustment within a given system. This is not true of the Third World challenge. Its demands are far-reaching, and the West would obviously be mistaken if it did not recognize the reality of those demands.

This reality, however, does not mean that the West should immediately accede on either practical or moral grounds. There may be "time consuming monster meetings," in the words of Harry Johnson,[35] but that does not mean that the First World is economically vulnerable in any gross way. The bargaining power of the Third is more limited than the relative population figures would suggest. For instance, if the assault on multinational corporations is too strenuous, then one will see, as is happening today, a drawing back of these international companies, in many cases to the greater detriment of the host countries than to the firms.

But this does not mean that the Third World lacks power to pursue its goals. The strength of OPEC provides the force for its demands, insofar as the oil cartel wants to bankroll the overall Third World effort and link oil to the larger demands. While the cartel could not be accused of being overly generous in its aid, the cartel countries will generally go along with the effort, at least up to a point, out of ideology and as an insurance policy—better the other Third World countries be arraigned against the First than against the oil producers. In addition, the multitude of developing countries can assert themselves politically on such matters as the creation of a new international regime for the seabeds. In sum, the Third World does have growing power, and will assert it, though not to the extent that rhetoric and conventional wisdom suggest.

How should the United States respond? In answering this question, we need to keep in mind one important constraint. Although the idea of accommodation may have captured much of elite opinion with what Robert W. Tucker has called its "new political sensibility," there is little reason to believe that it has captured the public's imagination. It is very unlikely that the public in the United States (or in other Western nations) will endorse a major transfer of wealth. Indeed, as the Third World has defined itself by its common opposition to the West, so one observes a further twist in the dialectic today—a hardening of public attitudes in the United States against compromise and concessions to the Third World.

A sensible policy might be to look for special areas and instrumentalities of cooperation. Nothing is accomplished by polarization for the sake of polarization. But the United States would do well to avoid too vocal a championing of a new order, for it will only increase expectations that are unlikely to be fulfilled.

Of course, we need to keep in mind that change is an inevitable feature of world politics, and little good will come from trying to reject the very force of industrialization as it spreads around the world. After all, once Britain was the world's only industrial power. The difficulties encountered in trying to accommodate other emerging industrial powers, most notably Germany, helped precipitate the two world wars. Change will occur. We would be wise to try to encourage its course in such a way as to suit our own more enduring interests.

IV

The fourth challenge to the international order takes the form of a changing distribution of force capabilities. Of course, the Soviet Union and the United States preside over awesome and growing arsenals. Yet a startling diffusion of conventional armaments is in progress outside the traditional alliances systems. Military expenditures by African countries in 1976 were almost twice what they were in 1972 in constant dollars. In the Middle East, such expenditures doubled between 1973 and 1976, again in constant dollars.[36] In the fiscal period 1975–1976 global arms transfers reached $10 billion, having doubled over the decade.[37] The character of these transfers is changing as well, with increasing emphasis on high technology, with some sophisticated weapons going into Third World arsenals before they go into American arsenals.

This comes at a time when the utility and disutility in the use of force by the United States is being much debated. For instance, the United States did not give serious consideration to the use of force during the oil embargo, despite the hostile character of that act. Similarly, the developed states have been unwilling to retaliate against those states that equip and organize terrorists who attack international commerce. The further diffusion of advanced weapons would seem likely to encourage states outside the alliance systems to take arbitrary and dangerous actions with a sense of impunity, thus contributing to a breakdown in international order.

An even more fundamental aspect of this challenge is posed by nuclear proliferation. A key element in such stability and restraint as the international system has known has been a hierarchic distinction between nuclear and non-nuclear states. This is now threatened by the spread of nuclear weapons and nuclear weapons capability, especially in the Third World. Today, there are six nuclear weapon states—the United States, the Soviet Union, Britain, France, China, and India. India's accession with a test on May 18, 1974 signaled the arrival of what might be called the Second Nuclear Age. In the First, a country desiring such weapons had to mount an expensive, complex program directed toward that end. In the Second, a country can acquire the capability to produce nuclear weapons with relative ease, as the by-product of developing atomic power. In other words, such nations will acquire nuclear competence without making any firm decisions to do so. One route is through the acquisition of uranium enrichment facilities; the other, by amassing plutonium in the nuclear waste, and then separating it. A standard reactor can produce 200 kilograms of plutonium a year, while a crude implosion device requires only 10 kilograms. According to current plans, about 40 nations will have nuclear energy programs by 1985, producing enough nuclear material for 3 or more bombs. Most will have enough material for 30 or more. By 1990, Third World countries could be generating enough plutonium to make 3000 Hiroshima-sized bombs a year.[38]

We can identify several effects of proliferation, first, the undermining of the Soviet-American balance. Defense thinking is based on the notion that, in order to have nuclear stability, there must be parity and balance between the two superpowers, so that no intelligent person will make a mistake. "There cannot be a balance where there are many different parties with many different objectives, and with entirely different levels of technology," observed Herbert York. "So if there is—and there does seem to have been—a stability in the nuclear relationship between the United States and the Soviet Union, the stability will be wiped out by proliferation. Even its theoretical underpinnings will be wiped out."[39]

Second, proliferation increases the chances of a chain reaction, leading to a superpower confrontation. Iran and Iraq could become nuclear weapons states. A border clash between them could escalate into a nuclear exchange between them, one of them a key American ally, the other tied by treaty to the Soviet Union, thus possibly setting off a general exchange.

Third, the nuclear taboo could lessen. The world, as it observes "local" nuclear wars, could become accustomed to the idea that nuclear weapons are not merely for deterrence, but are actually of considerable value in a war. Or a "crazy state" might seek to use such weapons as a bargaining chip to achieve some demand. Fourth, there is an increased danger from microproliferation, that terrorists or criminals will seek weapons or nuclear weapons material. Finally, the spread of such weapons will in itself change perceptions of the international order in a way detrimental to stability.

A host of factors have contributed to the coming of this Second Nuclear Age. After OPEC, there was a new emphasis on and drive for nuclear energy technology throughout the world. Some nations, like South Korea and Taiwan, have reason to question the security guarantees of the United States; nuclear weapons would afford a more autonomous security policy. For others, such as Israel, nuclear weapons acquisition may be regarded as essential for survival. Regional rivalries, as those between Pakistan and India, can be an important motive force. Two key factors can be put in the context of North-South relations. One is a drive for national self-assertion by Third World countries. The other is the resentment of the status afforded to First World countries by the possession of nuclear weapons. A leading Indian spokesman dismissed, for instance, Western expressions of concern about nuclear spread as merely "modern versions of the doctrine of the white man's burden."[40]

Until 1974, the United States pursued a "two atoms" policy—premised on the view that the routes to nuclear power and nuclear weapons were different. Thus, the development and export of nuclear technology was encouraged. On the other hand, the United States was a major force between the strengthening of the International Atomic Energy Agency founded in 1957, and the Nonproliferation Treaty, which went into force in 1970. Yet this "system" was primarily oriented to the First World, in particular to reassure both Germany and Germany's neighbors.

The system has proved inadequate in the Second Nuclear Age. It took congressional pressure and the entrance of arms controllers into what had been a restricted world of nuclear policymaking to shift American policy in the aftermath of the Indian explosion. The Ford and Carter administrations have sought to extend nuclear safeguards; to pressure other suppliers (particularly Germany and France) not to export dangerous technology; to step back from a commitment to a "plutonium economy"; and to renegotiate a host of our own supplier agreements. The entire process is very difficult, for American dominance in the nuclear energy field has eroded. Extremely sensitive interests are involved in other countries, where OPEC and the perturbations in the world economy in the 1970s have led to a strong drive to decrease energy dependence. Many conflicting interests are involved in the United States as well, and an effective antiproliferation policy—if one is possible at all—will require trade-offs (do we wish to keep troops in Korea or do we want to risk Korea's going nuclear?), as well as greater integration of our domestic energy programs with our foreign policy objectives.

V

Although the issues of order have risen to the top of the agenda, we would be mistaken if we failed to recognize that communism and the Soviet Union continue to pose the single most pressing problem for American foreign relations.

International politics is, after all, about the competition and cooperation of states. Competition, and rivalry, and the issues of survival are most starkly drawn in the relationship between the United States and the Soviet Union. In the last two decades, the military power concentrated in the competition has grown dramatically in both scale and sophistication. This is not new; it is a continuation of a long trend.

What has changed is the arrival, however bedraggled, of the policy of detente, the conscious pursuit of a lessening of tension. Detente was a fact before it was a policy. The Cold War—the armed truce between two nations never actually at war—began in the first instance as a confrontation over the political orientation of Europe. The dangers were reduced in 1948 and 1949, with the division of Europe into two blocs. The German question found an answer of sorts with the permanent division of the country. At the same time, there emerged a mostly unspoken rule regarding containment—not containment in the fashion normally thought, but an unstated agreement between the United States and the Soviet Union to cooperate in containing crises to prevent their explosion into direct superpower confrontations. This "rule" was summarized by Walter Bedell Smith, the American ambassador to Moscow, in September 1948, three months after the beginning of the Berlin blockade: "My opinion is [that the] Kremlin discounted completely the possibility that we might actually force the issue to the point of hostilities, just as we estimated no similar intention on their part."[41] In addition, after the death of Stalin, the Soviet Union became a more modern and more rational political system, one with which diplomacy was potentially more reliable.

Yet, even though detente was a fact, it was not perceived as such. Certainly, Washington was unwilling to take its existence as a working premise. Indeed, the Kennedy administration came to power at a time when the rivalry was in one of its most intense phases. John Kennedy's inaugural address was a summons to the confrontation, a new generation called to an old battle.

Neither before nor since has the rivalry been so dangerous as in November 1962 during the Cuban missile crisis. Here the superpowers came very close to breaking the "containment" rule. Leaders learned from it how diverse factors—political calculations, domestic pressures, prestige, the awesome military might at hand—can almost inadvertently come close to locking the countries into a fatal march to war.

The Cuban missile crisis provided the impetus to seek consciously to reduce tension. As Schlesinger observed, thereafter Kennedy "was rather more impressed by the risks of war than by the risks of detente."[42] Certain features of what could be said to be a detente policy were quickly visible—the test ban treaty, some increase in trade. There was a definite change of attitudes within the government as well, best expressed in John Kennedy's speech at American University in 1963, which really introduced the detente era. It reflected a major attitudinal change among Kennedy and his advisors and called for one among the public. The Soviet leaders needed a more enlightened view, Kennedy said, but so did the Americans. "I also believe," he explained, "that we must re-examine our own attitude—as individuals and as a Nation—for our attitude is as essential as theirs."[43] Under other circumstances, this speech might have been heard as a historic turning point.

As it was, the policy of detente was postponed for a decade, partly because of the death of Kennedy and the removal of Khrushchev by more conservative leaders. The primary reason was that the War in Indochina became the focus for American foreign policy. Military conflict with communism in Asia reduced both the desire and possibilities for American leaders to pursue a detente policy, especially in the earlier part of the conflict, when the American involvement was seen as containment, in its traditionally understood form, of Soviet communism. The Soviet invasion of Czechoslovakia also stalled detente.

But, by the late 1960s, both sides had important reasons for pressing ahead. Obviously, the developments in weaponry provided an impetus to investigate arms control as an alternative form of security to arms development and deployment. The character of the military balance had changed by the middle 1960s when with a major push, the Soviet Union attained strategic "parity" with the United States. This did not mean an exact numerical or even technological balance. What it did mean was that each side "has an assured destructive capability and neither has a potential for destroying by a first strike enough of the other's offensive forces seriously to restrict its choices of response."[44] On the Soviet side, its rivalry with China, so intense that it broke out into military conflict in 1969, made the Russians more interested in further stabilizing relations with the West. The economic problems of the Soviet Union, particularly those involving innovation and productivity, provided incentives for the Soviets to seek to participate on a broader basis in international economics and technological scientific life, to benefit from Western technological strengths.[45] As U.S. leaders saw that the war in Vietnam was not with Moscow or Peking's surrogates, but with a powerful national communism, they became interested in finding a way to use Moscow to end the war. At the same time, the experience of the Indochina War had given rise to a more differentiated view of communism. The United States was also concerned that, if it did not go ahead, certain of its allies, notably Japan and Germany, would move far ahead in both political and economic relations with the Soviet Union, thus threatening the Western alliance. Finally, after 1968, the United States had in Richard Nixon a President with the impeccable anticommunist credentials required for the public acceptance of such a policy.

American leaders would have found it difficult to proceed on a detente policy without certain changes in basic assumptions about the Soviet Union and Soviet communism. For decades, American policy toward the Soviet Union has been faced by two questions: What is the relationship between Marxist-Leninist ideology and Soviet foreign policy? And, What is the relationship between the Soviet domestic system, which is totalitarian and repressive, and Soviet foreign policy? Until the late 1960s, the answer went something like this: Marxist-Leninist ideology is the primary driving force of Soviet foreign policy, and the imperatives of statehood, secondary. A totalitarian system at home drives the Soviet Union toward a totalitarian foreign policy—that is, one which seeks to overturn the international system in order to completely dominate it. The series of premises that lead to this answer I have called the Riga axioms.[46] According to these premises, the Soviet Union is a monolithic, world-revolutionary state, systematically geared to expansionism, to a totalitarian foreign policy. Soviet policies are seen as well worked out, consciously coordinated.

There is thought to be little confusion in the Kremlin about goals, which are preponderance and hegemony over the entire international system. The view derived from these axioms tends to emphasize Soviet strengths and capabilities, not difficulties and weaknesses. Thus, the Soviet Union is seen as a permanent and fundamental adversary of the United States, one with which mutual interests cannot be pursued.

Such views are obviously inconsistent with a detente policy, which has depended upon a different set of assumptions, the change of attitude Kennedy called for in 1963, what I have called the Yalta axioms.[47] These axioms posit the Soviet Union less as a world revolutionary state than as a more traditional imperialist power. While obviously possessing vast military strength, and hardly lacking in expansionist drives, it is still relatively cautious, concerned to protect what it has, and with much to gain from stability. Internally, its ideology has lost its force and is primarily a technique of control and regimentation, although it can have a powerful appeal abroad, to those seeking change in their own societies. The Soviet leaders are motivated not so much by clearly defined objectives as by the need to reconcile many competing interests and demands, to cope with internal problems, to balance risk against opportunity. The Soviet Union is not genetically programmed to move in one direction. Its leaders can make choices that would move it in different directions. The United States can provide incentives in military, political, and economic spheres that at least pose interesting choices for the Russian leaderships.

Such a view constituted a less ideological view of the world, a more traditional view of international politics—that is, that nations are moved by their interests. Two factors gave special force to this shift in assumptions. The first was that Richard Nixon's special assistant for national security, subsequently his Secretary of State, Henry Kissinger, tended to see the world in these terms, and was powerful enough and skillful enough to impose such a view on the American policy process. Yet it is still difficult to imagine this change without the Sino-Soviet split. The intracommunist rivalry dramatized the truism about nations' interests, to some degree reduced the overall sense of "threat" that "communism" had seemed to pose for the Western world, and established the conditions for pursuing a "national interest" rather than "national security" policy toward the Soviet Union and China.

The split also provided the basis for another very significant change—a limited detente with China. For two decades, Sino-American relations had been even more bitter and hostile, more estranged, than relations with the Soviet Union. Relations today are still far from "normalized." But certainly the American sense of concern about a "China threat" has been considerably reduced.[48] Once again, attitudes toward communism have undergone some modification. Where formerly Peking's ideological fervor was seen as operational, today it is thought to have been, at least to some degree, compensation for a very weak economy and military establishment. How significant is the change in Sino-American relations? It has certainly made for new power relationships in East Asia. It has stimulated truly dramatic shifts in public perceptions of China in the United States, far more so than occurred with the Soviet Union, but on the basis of strikingly little information from the world's most populous country. The Sino-American detente has helped to push Soviet-American detente. But, further steps toward a detente with China are blocked by two specific questions—what to do about Taiwan, and the instability on the Korean peninsula.

Yet the steps toward normalization have, with the exception of Taiwan, excited far less controversy than detente with the Soviet Union. The reason may well be that, Taiwan aside and with the Indochina War over, less is at stake. For the present and immediate future, and into the 1980s at least, the issues of survival are, insofar as they are clear, cast in terms of the Soviet-American relationship.

Detente was a highly significant development, yet still its meaning was exaggerated. After all, it suggested only a lessening of tension, not the disappearance of tension. There has been no way the superpower competition could be eliminated. What constitutes detente can be expressed thus: a somewhat more explicit agreement on the rules of the competition; a certain number of cooperative efforts; increasing communications and contacts on many levels; and a reduction in the state of permanent alarm on both sides. Of course, the United States and the Soviet Union have not been the only actors in this process. West Germany took important initiatives with the Soviets to defuse somewhat the German problem.

Of the cooperative projects, arms control has been the most important. The major steps have been the treaty limiting each side to two antiballistic missile sites and an interim Strategic Arms Limitation Agreement, putting a ceiling on the number of fixed land-based intercontinental ballistic missiles that each side can have. This process has hardly ended the arms race. The constant intrusion of new systems and technologies, the asymmetries in the force structures, doubts about parity, multiple suspicions, the very magnitude of the stakes— these are some of the key factors that have made more substantial arms control very difficult.

The other major cooperative venture has been in trade. Starting from a very low level ("trivial," Aleksei Kosygin called it in 1971), commerce between the two nations has grown at a very rapid rate. The total trade turnover between the two countries was almost four times greater in 1972–1974 than in 1969–1971. U.S. exports to the Soviet Union reached $2,300 million in 1976.[49]

Although hardly fulfilling the more expansive promises, important changes thus have taken place in Soviet-American relations. Prior to this decade, relations were characterized primarily by their absence. Mutual deterrence, the military balance, and the unstated rule to cooperate in containing crises—this is what existed. There was little communication between the two superpowers, and very little comprehension of how the other's system worked. The network of relations is much denser today than it was seven years ago. A whole host of exchanges, involving such different groups as doctors, water pollution engineers, scientists and other academics, have become much more extensive, frequent, and productive. The civil bureaucracies of the two governments have some involvement with each other. Arms control negotiations have proved, to some degree at least, to be a mutually educative process for the military bureaucracies of both nations. The man-in-space programs of the two countries, born of cold war rivalry, turned in 1975 into a joint production for a worldwide television audience. But the most intense of all relations is that which now exists between American businessmen and their counterparts in the Soviet Ministry

of Foreign Trade, the foreign trade organizations and banks, and increasingly,
in ministries and enterprises as well.

What is even more striking is the interpenetration of the two political processes. The U.S. Congress and American public opinion have had an impact on
the Soviet treatment of political dissidents and minorities. In turn, there was the
spectacle in 1974 of Soviet officials lobbying on the trade bill on Capitol Hill,
suggestive almost more of a platoon of out-of-town shoe manufacturers worried
about tariff protection than of emissaries from America's most deadly rival.

The entire process has been unsteady, characterized by many disputes and
problems, and many, many doubts. Still, much of what has happened would
have seemed altogether beyond the realm of political possibility prior to 1970.
As Secretary of State Henry Kissinger assessed the matter, detente involves
areas of both competition and cooperation. The thrust of the effort has been to
expand the range of mutual interests. Detente has offered no guarantee that the
Soviets will behave in ways that we desire, but it does enable us to pose choices
for the Soviet leadership where it did not face choices before.

In its early stages, the acceptance of the detente policy was surprisingly
broad. It quickly, however, became the target of criticism because of the way in
which Richard Nixon had so thoroughly personalized it. As Nixon's political
fortunes waned, so suspicion grew that detente was a double trick—by Nixon,
to improve his position in domestic politics; by the Russians, to improve their
position vis-à-vis the United States. The effects of the great grain deal of 1972
and 1973 provided a reason to articulate those suspicions, as did the Yom Kippur War, and then the Soviet adventure in southern Africa.[50] The critics of
detente quickly moved beyond the person of Nixon to the substance of detente,
at least to what they see as the substance of detente. The result has been a
vigorous, at times ill-tempered, debate about strategies for survival. The debate
may well give way to a new consensus. There certainly is no consensus today,
which makes it difficult for the United States to pursue a consistent policy in its
relations with the Soviet Union.

The critics are moved by a mixture of various considerations. Some are
worried that defense expenditures in real terms are growing insufficiently to
maintain what they regard as necessary strength. Some are institutionally interested in the development of particular weapons systems, and, in order to ensure
appropriations, must find particular Soviet threats to "master." Some are deeply
suspicious and resentful of anything touched by Henry Kissinger. Some are
worried by Soviet adventurism. Some believe that detente is primarily a Soviet
smokescreen, meant to lull us into complacency while the Russians take unilat-
eral advantage. Some are deeply concerned about disorganization and a lack of
will in Western society, and fear that detente is appeasement.

In its entirety, the attack of these critics represents an effort to reassert the
Riga axioms. The critics present a particularly ominous view of Soviet intentions, drawn from a deep distaste for the regime and a heavy emphasis on
Marxist-Leninist ideology. They tend to eschew the less dramatic but more
interesting point that capabilities can shape intentions, for such a view has less
to do with Marxism-Leninism than with more traditional ways of understanding state behavior in the international system. The critics also interpret in a
categoric way what is deeply ambiguous evidence. But then they are deeply

skeptical of the arms control process. Indeed, here is a fundamental point of contention in the debate—whether American security is better assured by the ever ongoing development and deployment of ever more sophisticated arms or by a process of arms control. Risks, as one looks ahead a decade or two, are to be found on both sides.[51] But the fact of the matter is that the Soviet Union exists. The question is how to seek to structure relations with the Soviet Union in our own interests, even as such steps might also be in Soviet interests. This will remain the single most important problem in American foreign policy, for survival is the basis of order. As we consider the alternatives, we might bear in mind an observation Walter Lippmann made three decades ago, when the nature of Soviet-American relations was also very much a subject of debate:

> The history of diplomacy is the history of relations among rival powers, which did not enjoy political intimacy, and did not respond to appeals to common purposes. Nevertheless, there have been settlements. Some of them did not last long. Some of them did.
>
> For a diplomat to think that rival and unfriendly powers cannot be brought to a settlement is to forget what diplomacy is about. There would be little for diplomats to do if the world consisted of partners, enjoying political intimacy, and responding to common appeals.[52]

VI

All the preceding questions have summoned up in one form or another a basic problem—how to think about the world, the issues that the world poses for the United States, and America's place in that world. In 1968 Henry Kissinger wrote: "In the years ahead, the most profound challenge to American policy will be philosophical: to develop some concept of order in a world which is bipolar militarily but multipolar politically. . . . Wherever we turn then, the central task of American foreign policy is to analyze anew the current international environment and to develop some concepts which will enable us to contribute to the emergence of a stable order."[53]

A decade later, such remains the central task. Perhaps the very fact that this always seems to be the central task is a testament to at least one aspect of American exceptionalism—that, as a nation, we are constantly faced with the problem of defining and then defining again the purpose and goals of U.S. foreign policy. These are not givens. Several reasons can be suggested: the nature of American ideology; the openness of foreign policymaking to domestic debate; the consequent need for a domestic consensus; geography; and experience. Add to the above two other data: first, the world is complex, change does occur with rapidity, and there is nothing simple about being powerful. Second, because the United States is so powerful, it is not constrained in the way other nations are. Its possibilities are still, even after Vietnam and changes in the world economy, to a considerable degree what it chooses them to be.

Until the twentieth century, a world view in a literal sense was not very important. American foreign policy primarily involved continental and then regional expansion, sufficiently motivated by doctrines of manifest destiny and commercial interest.[54] The basic issues of international politics—survival and the balance of power—were hardly posed. The international hegemon was Britain, and America's geography and dynamism guaranteed it, in Walter Lippmann's phrase, "unearned security."[55]

At last the world caught up with the United States. World War I drew the United States into the mainstream of international politics and the struggle over what was then the key issue, the balance of power in Europe. In the course of this involvement, Woodrow Wilson articulated an ideology of liberal internationalism that has, since, been at the heart of twentieth-century U.S. foreign policy. "Wilsonianism" is a powerful and attractive vision of how the world might be organized, and of America's role in it. This vision has sought to project American values into world politics, the values being those of a liberal society united in a broad Lockean consensus. Wilson, like many subsequent American leaders, hoped and/or believed that the often brutal anarchy of the international system and the balance of power could be superseded by a juridical international community, committed to due process and common values. The United States would work within the old system in order to reform. The United States saw itself as a disinterested, innocent power, whose own desires and aims were thought to express the yearnings of all people, and whose responsibilities were to become inescapable and worldwide. As it sought to remove conflict and anarchy from international relations, Wilsonianism was truly seeking to abolish the very substance of world politics—balance of power, spheres of influence, power politics. These are the ineluctable features of the "anarchical society," to use Hedley Bull's phrase,[56] of an international system composed of sovereign states. Two impulses are associated with this outlook. One is an optimism about the possibilities for resolution and harmony, an "invisible hand," if you like, for the political affairs of the world. But there is a contrary impulse as well—a belief that the world as constructed is not merely harsh, but also evil, and that the inability to attain the first goal is not a consequence of the character of the enterprise but of moral failing and danger.

That latter impulse led to the retreat from the first great burst of Wilsonianism, which did not outlast the post-World War I disillusionment. In the interwar years, the United States, though still involved economically, eschewed a political role. Despite the desires of some leaders, there was a consensus not for involvement, but for withdrawal. Franklin Roosevelt's complaint in 1935—that "no European capital in the present confusion gives a continental damn about what the United States thinks or does"[57]—was the result of the fact that America had evidently decided to stand aside.

World War II brought a profound reassertion of Wilsonianism. The conditions were more right this time—the old international system had collapsed— and the United States, by design and circumstances, found itself the linchpin of the new system. The acquisition of a hegemonic role happened even more quickly than those who had directed America's global war had expected. "We are in the thing all over the world to an extent that few people realize," James Byrnes, the first postwar Secretary of State, told his colleagues in the Cabinet in April 1946.[58]

Wilsonianism remained the basic ideological framework. But it was not enough. Two key sets of ideas gained quick expression—what might be called "commanding ideas"—that is, concepts that explain America's relation to the rest of the world, integrate contradictory information, suggest and rationalize courses of action, and, as almost a court of last resort, provide a resolution for debates and disputes.

One, already alluded to, was anticommunism as expressed in the Riga axioms. The question about Russia was posed at the war's end by James Forrestal, shortly to become the first Secretary of Defense: "Are we dealing with a nation solely as a national entity or are we dealing with such a national entity plus a philosophy which amounts to a fervent religion?"[59] The answer was generally thought to be the latter, and the United States did indeed embark on a crusade to contain communism. The second commanding idea was a "doctrine of national security," a very expansive definition of security, a tendency to push the subjective boundaries of security outward to more and more areas, to encompass more and more geography and more and more problems. Here was Wilsonianism made into realpolitik.[60]

Of course, there were other important ideas, such as those we have already discussed relating to an open international economy. But these were part of the Wilsonian program, and were additionally validated as they were subordinated to the two commanding ideas.

These ideas and formulations held powerful sway well into the 1960s, providing the real impulse for the American role in Vietnam, a war, at least until we have more of a perspective, that can probably be better understood as a conflict over ideology and theories than for treasure and gain. But in Vietnam, these ideas were stretched almost to their breaking point—for a time, it seemed, even beyond their breaking point. Certainly the anticommunist consensus, which had been generated from these two commanding ideas, collapsed.

Anticommunism proved too undifferentiated a concept, at least as balanced against the other evident costs. It tended to obscure the local character of the contest. National security also proved too undifferentiated a concept, for, when the idea was challenged, it could not be established, whatever else was at stake, that American national security was in question. Indeed, the enterprise damaged America's overall world position. Obviously, as well, Vietnam raised basic questions about power and the utility of force.

What then was to guide American foreign policy? Here perhaps Henry Kissinger made his most lasting contribution—to set out a different conception of foreign policy, one that might well be described as "European," that is, that international politics is less about ideology than about the cooperation and competition of states for power, prestige, position, and wealth, and that nations pursue these as their interests. When the competition becomes very severe, then the most basic of all values, survival, is at stake. "We are immersed in an unending process, not in a quest for a final destination," Kissinger wrote in 1968.[61] Such a view does not accord with the traditional American vision, for it says that there are no final solutions, no resolutions, no ultimate harmony, only that endless process. The basic problem of international politics remains as expressed by Rousseau:

> The state, being an artificial body, is not limited in any way. . . . It can always increase; it always feels itself weak if there is another that is stronger. Its security and preservation demand that it make itself more powerful than its neighbors. It can increase, nourish and exercise its power only at their expense. . . . While the inequality of man has natural limits, that between societies can grow without cease, until one absorbs all the others. . . . The formation of the first society necessarily led to the formation of all the others. It was necessary to join it or unite in

order to resist it. It was necessary to imitate it or be engulfed by it. . . . Because
the grandeur of the state is purely relative, it is forced to compare itself with that of
the others. . . . It is in vain that it wishes to keep itself to itself; it becomes small or
great, weak or strong, according to whether its neighbour expands or contracts,
becomes stronger or declines.[62]

It cannot be otherwise.

Such a vision clashed sharply with the Wilsonian ideology. It seemed im-
moral and inconsistent, lacking in purpose. How, critics asked, could the
United States at the same time both pursue detente with the Soviet Union and
yet do political battle with the Soviet Union in southern Africa?[63] How could
both enterprises be "valid" at the same time? The unpalatable response was that
detente was in our interest—not a favor we bestow, in Kissinger's words—while
not to act in southern Africa was also a form of action. The choice in southern
Africa was not about the estimates of Soviet intentions, but rather a balance
between the effects of a predominant Soviet role in a tense situation against the
risks of sliding into a deeper form of military intervention.

Such realpolitik was too uncomfortable, too cynical, for many Americans.
Much of what the Carter administration did in its first year appeared to be for
the purpose of establishing that Kissingerism was banished from the realm of
policy, so that Americans might "feel good" about their foreign policy again.
This is a very helpful step for rebuilding a domestic consensus, but it is an
inadequate basis for a foreign policy. "Human rights" cannot by itself provide
an effective commanding idea for foreign policy in an anarchic world.

Can we find a new intellectual basis for a post-postwar foreign policy? We
can look toward certain elements. The first is to attempt to define problems in
terms of American interests. There are no absolute tests. Rather, it involves a
process of choice and balancing—between accommodating ourselves to change,
pursuing change that is just and desirable, and yet seeking to maintain an international environment hospitable to our values and institutions. Second, it involves a continuing recognition of the role of power, and no pretense about its
abolishment. It involves a staking out of positions between those governed by
ideological shibboleths of the past and deceptive romanticism about a new international order. And, third, it still involves the endless need to come to
grips with the fact that we do live in a world in which communism, Marxist-
Leninism, continues to be a mode for capturing control of and organizing states.
"Being confident of our own future," President Carter said at Notre Dame on
May 22, 1977, "we are now free of that inordinate fear of communism which
once led us to embrace any dictator who joined us in that fear."[64] But we would
be deluding ourselves if we dispensed with the "ordinate fear," not so much on
ideological grounds per se, but that in the name of ideology, shifts in the international balance can occur that are detrimental to our interests.

Fourth, in an increasingly multipolar world, we would do well to maintain
the perspective of the First World, to cooperate and collaborate as much as
possible with the other industrial democracies, the other nations that share our
values and institutions. This should be the basic building block of American
foreign policy.[65]

All this does not point to a conclusion, to a clear end goal for foreign policy.
It does suggest modification, but not the abandonment, of the postwar command-

ing ideas. It emphasizes, in addition, the range of uncertainty and risk, the constant need for choice; and it requires an endless process of analysis, of questioning, of differentiation, and of honesty with ourselves as well as toward others. All this does not call up crusades, and it may not sit well with the requirements of the American domestic polity. But such is the task before the nation that remains the dominant power in the world, a nation that as such must cope simultaneously with the critical issues of order and the fundamental issues of survival.

REFERENCES

[1]Robert Gilpin, *U.S. Power and the Multinational Corporation* (New York: Basic Books, 1975), p. 5.

[2]Robert Keohane and Joseph Nye, *Power and Interdependence* (Boston: Little, Brown, 1977), pp. 49–54, 221–242.

[3]Richard Rosencrance (ed.), *American as an Ordinary Country* (Ithaca: Cornell University Press, 1976).

[4]See Richard Gardner's classic, *Sterling-Dollar Diplomacy* (London: Oxford University Press, 1955; new ed., 1969).

[5]Charles Kindleberger, *The World in Depression* (London: Allan Lane, The Penguin Press, 1973), Chap. 14.

[6]See Daniel Yergin, *Shattered Peace: The Origins of the Cold War and the National Security State* (Boston: Houghton Mifflin, 1977), pp. 303–309, 396–397.

[7]Keohane and Nye, *Power and Interdependence*, p. 30; Joan Spero, *The Politics of International Economic Relations* (New York: St. Martin's Press, 1977), p. 72.

[8]Gilpin, *U.S. Power and the Multinational Corporation*, pp. 12–13, 17.

[9]Raymond Vernon, *Storm over the Multinationals: The Real Issues* (Cambridge, Mass.: Harvard University Press, 1977), Chap. 1; Gilpin argues the last point strongly in *U.S. Power and the Multinational Corporation*, pp. 12–13, 17.

[10]David Landes (ed.), *Western Europe: The Trials of Partnership* (Lexington, Mass.: D.C. Heath, Lexington Books, 1977), p. 7.

[11]Vernon, *Storm over the Multinationals*, pp. 47–48.

[12]Stephen Hymer and Robert Rowthorn, "Multinational Corporations and International Oligopoly," in Charles Kindleberger (ed.), *The International Corporation* (Cambridge, Mass.: M.I.T. Press, 1970). See also Robert Stobaugh, "Competition Encountered by U.S. Companies That Manufacture Abroad," *Journal of International Business Studies* (Spring–Summer 1977): 33–43.

[13]Alaistair Buchan, *The End of the Post-War Era* (New York: Saturday Review Press, 1974), pp. 36, 81–82; Gilpin, *U.S. Power and the Multinational Corporation*, p. 189.

[14]Richard Cooper, "Trade and Monetary Relations Between the United States and Western Europe," in Landes (ed.), *Western Europe: The Trials of Partnership*, pp. 338–339.

[15]*Survey of Current Business* (March 1971): 31; (March 1972): 34.

[16]Marina v.N. Whitman, "Leadership Without Hegemony," *Foreign Policy* 20 (Fall 1975): 159.

[17]M. Y. Yoshino, *Japan's Multinational Enterprises* (Cambridge: Harvard University Press, 1976), pp. 20–21.

[18]Brian Tew, *The Evolution of the International Monetary System* (London: Hutchinson, 1977), pp. 194–198; Tom deVries, "Jamaica—or the Non-Reform of the International Monetary System," *Foreign Affairs* (April 1976).

[19]Gilpin, *U.S. Power and the Multinational Corporation*, pp. 260–262. The Smithsonian negotiations in December 1971 were "the first ever conducted to adjust exchange rates on a multilateral basis," writes Brian Tew in the *Evolution of the International Monetary System*, p. 172. See Miriam Camps, *The Management of Interdependence: A Preliminary View*, and Charles Kindleberger, "Systems of International Economic Organization," in David Calleo (ed.), *Money and the Changing World Order* (New York: New York University Press, 1970), pp. 32–37.

[20]This was the essential purpose of that new favorite of advocates of conspiracy theories, the Trilateral Commission. See Zbigniew Brzezinski, "U.S. Foreign Policy: The Search for Focus," *Foreign Affairs* (July 1973): 708–727.

[21]For a good cross-section of constructive gloom, see Lawrence Veit, "Troubled World Economy," *Foreign Affairs* (January 1977); Paul Lewis, "Protectionism Plagues Free Trade Talks," *New York Times* (October 2, 1977), Section 3; International Monetary Fund, *Annual Report 1977*; "Floating Exchange Rates: The Calm before an Economic Storm," *Business Week* (October 3, 1977):

68–80; Senate Foreign Relations Committee, Subcommittee on Multinationals, *International Debt, the Banks, and United States Foreign Policy*, 95th Congress, 1st session.

[22]Cited in Fred Hirsch, "A New International Economic Order?" *International Organization* (Summer 1976): 524.

[23]Edith Penrose, "The Development of the Crisis," in Raymond Vernon (ed.), *The Oil Crisis* (New York: Norton, 1976), pp. 39–57.

[24]Lawrence Veit, "Troubled World Economy," *Foreign Affairs* (January 1977): 264–269; Robert Rasche and John Tatom, "The Effects of the New Energy Regime on Economic Capacity, Production, and Prices," *Federal Reserve Bank of St. Louis Review* (May 1977): 2–12; Robert Rasche and John Tatom, "Energy Resources and Potential GNP," *Federal Reserve Bank of St. Louis Review* (June 1977): 10–24.

[25]The linkage, however, probably runs in only one direction. While the Arab-Israeli conflict can obviously accentuate tensions over energy, it is not at all clear that a settlement of the conflict would do much to diminish OPEC's new power or its will to use it.

[26]Cited in Guy F. Erb and Valeriana Kallab, *Beyond Dependency: The Developing World Speaks Out* (Washington, D.C.: Overseas Development Council, 1975), p. 186.

[27]In Henry Kissinger, *American Foreign Policy*, 3rd ed. (New York: Norton, 1977), pp. 237–276.

[28]An accommodationist case is outlined by Tom Farer, "The United States and the Third World: A Basis for Accommodation," *Foreign Affairs* (October 1975): 79–97. Also see Jan Tinbergen (ed.), *Reshaping the International Order. A Report to the Club of Rome* (New York: Dutton, 1976). The most penetrating and powerfully argued rejectionist case is to be found in Robert W. Tucker, *The Inequality of Nations* (New York: Basic Books, 1977).

[29]See Fred Bergsten, "The Threat from the Third World," *Foreign Policy*, 11 (Summer 1973); Stephen Krasner, "Oil Is the Exception," *Foreign Policy*, 14 (Spring 1974); Michael Mazur, "The Developing Countries in the World Economy," in David Baldwin (ed.), *America in an Interdependent World* (Hanover, N.H.: University Press of New England, 1976).

[30]Tony Smith, "Changing Configurations of Power in North-South Relations since 1945," *International Organization*, 31(3) (Winter 1977):14–18. Smith observes: "Ironically, then, the greatest threat posed by the South in its demands for a new world economic system may be to itself. Not international but *internal* crisis would be the most likely result of a paralyzing Southern attack on the world economic order."

[31]Arthur S. Banks (ed.), *Political Handbook of the World: 1977* (New York: McGraw-Hill, 1977).

[32]See Nathaniel Leff, "The New Economic Order—Bad Economics, Worse Politics," *Foreign Policy*, 24 (Fall 1976): 202–317.

[33]Richard Cooper, "A New International Economic Order for Mutual Gain," *Foreign Policy* 26 (Spring 1977): 75–93.

[34]Robert W. Tucker writes in *Inequality of Nations*, p. 142: "What is novel is the insistence that men now act upon this assumption [of shared humanity] in a manner they have not acted in the past, that they draw positive duties of distributive justice from it that they had not heretofore drawn, and that they give a scope to those duties they have never before been willing to give. The simple, though decisive, claim of the new political sensibility is that we no longer differentiate, for *certain purposes*, between fellow citizens and mankind."

[35]Quoted in J. E. S. Fawcett, "Unctad IV: Another Bill of Rights," *The World Today* (April 1976): 158.

[36]Stockholm International Peace Research Institute, *Yearbook: 1977*, pp. 229, 237.

[37]International Institute for Strategic Studies, *Annual Survey: 1976*, p. 19.

[38]Albert Wohlstetter, "How to Spread the Bomb Without Really Breaking the Rules," *Foreign Policy*, 25 (Winter 1976–1977): 152–154.

[39]Herbert York: *In Export Reorganization Act of 1976: Hearings before the Senate Government Operations Committee:* 94th Congress, 2nd Session, p. 58.

[40]Quote in Hedley Bull, "Rethinking Nonproliferation," *International Affairs* (April 1975): 178. See Michael Nacht, "The United States in a World of Nuclear Powers," *Annals of the American Academy*, 430 (March 1977): 162–174; John Maddox, "Prospects for Nuclear Proliferation," Adelphi Paper, no. 113.

[41]*Foreign Relations of the United States: 1948*, vol. II, p. 1161.

[42]Arthur M. Schlesinger, Jr., *A Thousand Days: John F. Kennedy in the White House* (Boston: Houghton Mifflin, 1965), pp. 893, 889.

[43]John F. Kennedy, *Public Papers: 1963*, p. 460.

[44]Walter Slocombe, "The Political Implications of Strategic Parity," Adelphi Paper, no. 77, p. 7. He writes: "Since some time in the 1960s—perhaps as early as 1962, perhaps as late as 1966—the USSR has had a strategic nuclear striking force with an 'assured-destruction' capability. That is, its force has had a size and survivability sufficient after absorbing the heaviest first strike the United States could launch against Soviet nuclear forces effectively to destroy the U.S. as an organized modern society" (p. 1). And vice versa, of course. Despite his calls for "superiority" during the 1968

presidential campaign, Richard Nixon, shortly after the election, adopted the notion of "sufficiency," that is, the premise of parity. Jerome Kahan suggests three reasons: economic costs; unattainability of a meaningful superiority; and the possibility of heating up further the arms competition. Jerome Kahan, *Security in the Nuclear Age* (Washington, D.C.: Brookings Institution, 1975), pp. 113–117, 143–145.

[45]Abram Bergson, "Soviet Economic Perspectives: Toward a New Growth Model," *Problems of Communism* (March–April 1973): 1–9; Joseph Berliner, *The Innovation Decision in Soviet Industry* (Cambridge, Mass.: The M.I.T. Press, 1976).

[46]Yergin, *Shattered Peace: The Origins of the Cold War and the National Security State*, Chap. 1.

[47]Ibid., Chap. 2.

[48]See A. Doak Barnett, *China Policy* (Washington, D.C.: Brookings Institution, 1977).

[49]Daniel Yergin, "Politics and Soviet-American Trade: The Three Questions," *Foreign Affairs* (April 1977): 517, 519–520.

[50]Theodore Draper, "Appeasement and Detente," *Commentary* (February 1976).

[51]See George W. Rathjens, "Changing Perspectives on Arms Control," in Franklin Long and George Rathjens (eds.), *Arms, Defense Policy and Arms Control* (New York: Norton, 1976), pp. 210–211.

[52]Walter Lippmann, *The Cold War* (New York: Harper & Row, 1972, reprint edition), p. 50.

[53]Kissinger, *American Foreign Policy*, pp. 79, 91.

[54]See, for instance, Walter LaFeber, *The New Empire* (New York: Wiley, 1967).

[55]Walter Lippmann, *U.S. Foreign Policy: Shield of the Republic* (New York: Pocket Books, 1943), pp. 35–36, 106.

[56]Hedley Bull, *The Anarchical Society* (New York: Columbia University Press, 1977).

[57]Orville Bullitt (ed.), *For the President: Personal and Secret* (Boston: Houghton Mifflin, 1972), p. 113.

[58]Quoted in Tom Paterson, "If Europe, Why Not China: Defining the Containment Doctrine," unpublished paper.

[59]Quoted in Yergin, *Shattered Peace: The Origins of the Cold War and the National Security State*, p. 164.

[60]See Robert W. Tucker, *The Radical Left and American Foreign Policy* (Baltimore: Johns Hopkins University Press, 1971), pp. 105–106. Such an expansive doctrine was also a sign of the extent of American power. As Arnold Wolfers once observed: "Probably national efforts to achieve greater security would also prove, in part at least, to be a function of the power and opportunity that nations possess to reduce danger through their own efforts." In *Discord and Collaboration* (Baltimore: Johns Hopkins University Press, 1962), pp. 151–152.

[61]Kissinger, *American Foreign Policy*, p. 79.

[62]Quoted in F. H. Hinsley, *Power and the Pursuit of Peace* (Cambridge: Cambridge University Press, 1967), pp. 50–51.

[63]In 1968, Kissinger wrote: "Nothing has been more difficult for Americans to assess in the nuclear age than the fact that even enmity is complex. In the Soviet Union they confront an opponent whose public pronouncements are insistently hostile. Yet the nuclear age imposes a degree of cooperation and an absolute limit to conflicts." (Kissinger, *American Foreign Policy*, p. 85).

[64]Department of State News Release, May 22, 1977.

[65]Some would cast "interdependence" in the role of a commanding idea. Insofar as it would remind us of the reality and importance of our close links and identification with the other industrial democracies, it is useful. But it is doubtful that it can perform the role of a commanding idea, for it does not clearly set out a goal, but rather describes a condition, a situation, and one in which conflict coexists with cooperation.

MCGEORGE BUNDY

The Americans and the World

ANYONE ATTEMPTING to consider what Americans now understand about their relations with the world must begin with modesty, both in looking forward and in looking back. To ask what will happen to us on the world scene in the next twenty years is to ask a question that can have no answer. A world as complex as ours has now become, with interconnecting forces of astonishing variety and power, forbids such prophecy.

To assert that our past experience gives us clear guides to action is no less dubious. The twentieth century is already full of grim examples of experience wrongly interpreted. For us the lessons of each decade since 1945 have generally been overlearned in the decade that followed—among the major powers from total war to cold war to detente, and in the Third World from independence to development to disillusion and then to something, so far short of concrete meaning, called a new dialogue. Almost the only general rule that seems sure to fit both past and future is that what happens beyond our borders can be decisive for our own society. The proposition is not one we like, and alone it is no guide to action. The effective use of our limited strength and energy to cope with indeterminate and unpredictable reality is hard indeed.

But if we dare not ask for answers, at any level of prophecy, we can still consider in a more general way what we may have learned about the relation between the American polity and the dangerous and uncertain world. Our experience of great responsibility in the world is brief but intense, and if it offers no answers to the special or general dangers of the future, it may tell us something about our own strength and weakness as we confront them. That would help, or so we must believe. And to tell the end at the beginning, what I find in the record is this: that the Americans are, first, a world power with no national taste for world politics, nonetheless drawn deeply into it by general dangers, special interests, and a considerable national pride; second, a society of extraordinary tensile strength which can survive great internal stress and perform with great effectiveness when united; and third, a people ordinarily tolerant of special concerns, including those of Presidents and foreign policy "experts," but deeply resistant to demanding political action in situations not clear and compelling. From this triple reality I draw the conclusion that in the absence of shared consensus about complex issues we are likely to have a series of bruising contests between hope and reality, supportable because the society is strong internally, but raising repeatedly the question whether we can learn fast enough to pluck the flowers of safety from the nettles of danger all around us. Our future seems open to both triumph and tragedy.

In this paper I test these notions briefly against two relatively visible and still unresolved crises, both centered in the Middle East. In choosing these examples I make the assumption that if we find it hard to confront such relatively obvious issues, we may find it even harder to deal with others that are more obscure or less evidently demanding.

The prospect that emerges is at once disturbing and challenging, and the moral of the analysis, for both political leaders and students of policy, is to do their work better—and to do it in ways that their country can understand, ways that relate seriously and believably to what citizens want for themselves. It is not a new conclusion, and I think I would mistrust it if it were.

The American society puts private before public purposes. The politics of our country still begin with the individual, not the state. Our tests of ourselves, as a good or not so good society, relate to the human conditions of our citizens. Our political principles begin with the rights of man, and it was not manifest destiny or imperial ambition, or any accepted priority for the interest of the state, that brought us as far into the world as we have come. It was rather a combination of perceived danger and an exuberant nongovernmental expansion of particular interests. Both have had enormous impact on our behavior and on the level of our engagement; neither has changed the fundamental political priorities of our people.

Thus it is an elemental fact of our political life that most of our national elections—and 1976 was surely no exception—do not turn on issues of foreign policy. Such issues are always present and often hotly debated, but they are rarely decisive. An unpopular war can work strongly against the party in power, as in 1952 and 1968. A candidate who is perceived as dangerously hard (Goldwater) or soft (McGovern) can lose heavily from that perception. But most voters, most of the time, are moved by issues that are closer to home.

Even on domestic issues what the voter has most on his or her mind, most of the time, is a private interest, or at most a group concern—what will these politicians do for me and my family, or for us: the farmers, or the working men, or business and commercial forces, that in our view "really make the country run." The surprisingly large groups that are still dominantly Democratic or Republican, in a nation where David Broder tells us that "The Party is Over," reflect no systematic political commitment of an ideological sort, but rather a persistent perception that Democrats, or Republicans, are good for "us."

In this society of private concerns, even domestic public policy is of derivative importance. The services, the tax breaks, and the transfer payments of the government, expanding decade by decade for forty years, are now deeply imbedded in our social expectations. But what the public opinion analysts report confirms our common-sense awareness of the way we are: we want the services, tax breaks, and transfer payments that help *us*, but these practical requirements do not give rise to any general approval of big government. In Europe—even in England—the kingdom, and with it the state, came before the rights of man, and statecraft has been a national calling for centuries. But here the state as such is a concept of interest only to scholars, and only interest, never principle, has supported the reality of growing government.

This ambivalence is shared by Americans of all sorts, and by men of great distinction as well as ordinary citizens. John Quincy Adams did study state-craft, but he said he did it so that his grandson might study the arts, and Saul Bellow, speaking through his hero Herzog, before Vietnam or Watergate, re-minds us that "In every community there is a class of people professionally dangerous to the rest. . . . I mean the leaders." Wildly different in so much else, the nineteenth-century public man and the twentieth-century novelist are both, in these attitudes, profoundly American. Yet neither an Adams nor a Bellow has believed that in fact we could do without the state, or put an end to politics. Americans are quite realistic about such necessities—what they do not have to do is enjoy them. And it has been so since the Constitution was framed.

A people for whom politics is thus in principle a secondary matter is not likely to take naturally to the pursuit of weltpolitik. Even where the state has more standing than it does with us, the intricacies of international politics have seldom engaged the ordinary citizen. Always excepting the astonishing and un-predictable force of nationalism—admittedly a big exception—we may note that in most societies, and especially in undemocratic ones, international politics is a game for leaders. There is much of that among us too, but not when the game closely affects our private interests. Thus it remains remarkable that in fact this society of private concerns has sustained an active foreign policy, a heavy bur-den of national defense, and engagements of all sorts in all continents, ever since 1940. With the extraordinary exception of Vietnam, moreover, these manifold activities have been relatively successful. By the grim standards of international catastrophe set in the century's two World Wars, the last thirty years have been good ones, and the part played by the United States has been critical in that record.

What has enabled a society so naturally and strongly inclined away from such a role to do all this, or at least to allow it to be done? The answer I have already put in one phrase needs consideration: "a combination of perceived dan-ger and an exuberant nongovernmental expansion of particular interests." Take "perceived danger" first—it has not been easy to keep in mind the enduring strength of this element in our affairs across the trauma of Vietnam, where so many perceptions were so wrong. Nonetheless the point must be insisted on: what has sustained the international role of the United States as an active world power has been the general public understanding that without major American engagement both the balance of power and the prospect for human freedom would be affected in ways that would in fact be a grievous threat to our own hopes for ourselves.

The perception that the world is like this became a part of our permanent politics only with the fall of France in 1940. That grim summer (which only those over the age of forty can now remember) marks the decisive turning point in the national understanding of our relation to the world beyond the Atlantic and the Pacific. Since that summer we have been continuously aware that, in our most traditional language, the life, liberty, and pursuit of happiness of the individual American *require* a world role for his country.

Most historians would probably agree that in reality this proposition became true a generation earlier, as a consequence of World War I. But our people did not see it that way, and so we played no large role on the international political scene between the two wars. But since 1940, and overwhelmingly since the emergence of nuclear weapons, we have been an active world power, and the right of our government to play that role has rested squarely on the consent, indeed the insistence, of the governed.

In thirty-five years we have had time for many blunders, the worst of them in Southeast Asia. The public has not liked the blunders or wanted them repeated. Moreover it has recently been shocked by particular cold-war excesses like those of the CIA or the FBI, just as earlier it was shocked by the "loss" of China and Cuba. But the general perception that the world is dangerous, that we must be strong, and that American power and diplomacy must be active has been constant. In understandable anguish over Vietnam a large number of Americans reached the conclusion that the notion of an international threat to the hope of freedom was unreal—or still more frantically, that the threat was us. They never persuaded the American public. The proofs are many: the heavy defeat of George McGovern (beaten by his own words, not by Watergate tricks), the suspicion of one-sided detente from all quarters beginning in 1974, and perhaps most strikingly the care with which all serious candidates in 1976 protected themselves against charges of weakness or softness on national defense—all of these attest to the continuing reality of the fundamental American acceptance of the proposition that if we are to be free to do our own things, we must do what we must in the world.

Thus no amount of revisionism, whether dogmatic or pragmatic, has changed the dominant national judgment, shaped far more by Joseph Stalin than by any other one individual, that there is a Soviet danger. Nor have the Americans, as a people, been unable to hold in mind the double proposition that there is both a Soviet danger and a requirement for coexistence. Indeed there is some evidence that the oscillations of opinion, between exaggerated hope (Yalta, or certainly Teheran) and exaggerated fear (over China or Castro), have become more moderate and also closer to reality as our collective experience of Soviet strength and weakness has increased. Seen in the perspective of thirty years, what is remarkable about our current arguments over policy toward the Soviet Union is how moderate most of them are. Hardliners tend to be less hard, and softliners less soft, than they were when all this was new to us. Henry Wallace was, after all, a presidential candidate created in considerable measure by Communists and party-liners, and James Forrestal, as Secretary of Defense, was driven to despair by his conviction that not enough was being done by a feckless democracy to defend freedom against Communism. We have not had anything quite like either of them lately. Mr. McGovern and Mr. Goldwater were rejected for kinds of "extremism" more moderate than those. There are a few real extremists, perhaps, at both ends of the spectrum of the debate on strategic weaponry—but they have deservedly little support.

The case of Vietnam, in this context, with all its excesses, may have been a force for enlightenment. There we learned, in a very hard way, that it was not enough to be right about the purpose of an opponent; we had to understand also our own limitations and those of our friends, and above all we had to distinguish more sharply an interest that was real but limited from an interest that was "vital." This adjective, used in the Tonkin Gulf Resolution, came to represent the crucial difference between what Lyndon Johnson honestly believed and what the country would support. If not earlier, then at least from the time of the anti-Communist revolution in Indonesia, late in 1965, that adjective was excessive, and so also was our effort.

But if one lesson is more clear than another now, it is that we learned that much about Vietnam. And we also know that the internal divisions which seemed so shocking at the time turned out to be endurable. Even at the most painful moments—in 1968 between Tet and the Conventions, in 1970 after Cambodia, and in 1972–1973 between the primaries and the false peace—the general opinion of the country rejected extreme courses. It can be argued that this persistently centrist reaction helped to prolong the agony, because it provided a partial but inconclusive reinforcement to the attitudes and techniques of the two Presidents most concerned. Nonetheless the existence of a strong center must be counted on the larger scale as a most important national asset. If Vietnam is a demonstration of our capacity for many kinds of error, it is also, even more than Watergate, a demonstration of our internal tensile strength.

Vietnam and Watergate, together with other events of the last few years, have also led to a healthy decline in the autonomous power of certain special interests. The national reaction to perceived danger had given great strength to many interests in the forties and fifties, and especially to the set of forces described by President Eisenhower as the military-industrial complex. As in all other merely human activities, the military services and their industrial and technological suppliers inevitably came to serve not only the general interest in effective national defense, but their own special interest in playing a large role in that process. The danger created by such forces is real, but it can be exaggerated; it is well to remember that in noting their power President Eisenhower was careful also to note that they were indispensable.

What is most interesting about this particular "complex" in 1977 is that on the whole its strength seems lower than it has been at any time since President Eisenhower discussed it in 1961. The most striking example is the change in the position and influence of three of the great national security bureaucracies, the CIA, the FBI, and the Joint Chiefs of Staff. In 1960 the first action of a relatively untested President-elect was to announce that Allen Dulles and J. Edgar Hoover would be continued in office. This declaration of confidence in effect confirmed them in a high degree of autonomous power, and there was a close parallel in the wary relation that existed throughout the Kennedy-Johnson years between the White House and the Joint Chiefs. In 1977 the President has easily chosen his own man to head the CIA (the oddly assorted coalition that opposed his otherwise excellent first choice, Theodore Sorensen, had special and essentially personal origins), and he has had at least equal freedom, constrained by a similar need for a defensibly "safe" selection, in his distinguished choice of a new Director of the FBI.

But perhaps the most dramatic example of the new relation between these special interests and the Presidency is the ease with which Mr. Carter has had his way in deciding the fate of the B–1 bomber. The case is particularly interesting because here the President confronted a partnership of industry, labor, and bureaucracy of almost classic form. There has seldom been a more intense lobbying effort than that put on by Rockwell International for the B–1, and seldom a weapons system dearer to a major military service. Yet when the President reached his decision, it was no contest. One need not unravel all the strands of cause and effect here to know that they are bound up somehow with the events of the preceding decade.

This general reinforcement of the White House as against the national security bureaucracy does not of itself mean that the strength of the Presidency is in a healthy balance with its responsibilities or with those of others, most notably the Congress and the general public. We do not even know whether in fact the Presidency of the past has been too strong or too weak; the true answer may be a bit of both. The lessons of Vietnam and even Watergate are deeply ambiguous on the question whether we ever had much more than the appearance of an "imperial Presidency." I myself find it instructive that the dominant mental mode of Richard Nixon toward his "enemies" (like that of Lyndon Johnson toward "his" war) was one of frustration; it was a mode which certainly led to presidential abuse, but it is at some distance from the general attitude of a Caesar or an Augustus. Neither President was ever nearly as imperial in his own mind as he seemed to his critics.

It is equally far from clear that either Vietnam or Watergate has led to any permanent weakening of the Presidency. Temporary decline in readiness for commitment abroad certainly occurred, along with a dramatic immobilization of the Presidency as an institution in much of 1973 and 1974. This particular moment of weakness, combined with a massive earlier neglect of public and congressional opinion in the shaping of the false peace in Vietnam, was the proximate cause of the administration's impotence in the face of a North Vietnamese aggression more flagrant than any before it in 1975. But the Spenglerian gloom that seems to have comforted Henry Kissinger in the face of this ugly denouement was somewhat misplaced. The country was not going to hell.

There remains a question whether we have learned too much from Vietnam. For example, many think that if it was wrong to fight in Vietnam, it was also wrong to fight in Korea, and the nonsequitur makes it harder to keep a steady course in our behavior toward that other divided country where the real balance of both opinion and strength is quite different. The recovery from our internal divisions has been rapid, but the price of comity may be a dangerously low readiness to act in the situation that is not "another Vietnam" but that does arouse that fear.

So quite possibly the tendency in the immediate future will be to attempt too little, not too much. There may have been some of this in the congressional view of Angola in 1976, although here again it is hard to separate the reaction to Angola itself from the reaction to renewed evidence of secretiveness and inattention to public accountability in the Executive Branch. But we have almost never had a serious and generally understood policy toward Africa. We have seldom agreed among ourselves how far we would act, or whether open force would ever be justified, or even, in many cases, what side we should be on. Thus the wise inaction of our government in the Nigerian civil war was bitterly, if ineffectually, criticized by many people who could not have located Biafra on the map. The degree to which, more recently, the eloquence of Andrew Young, or the latter-day attentiveness of Henry Kissinger, is matched by any serious national commitment is far from clear, if only because so little effort has been given to the analysis and explanation of what we could, should, or would do in this or that eventual crisis. Our policy toward Africa may, for this reason, turn out to be almost as empty as it was before we began to pay attention.

But this is a general difficulty for us, and not a new one. Given the private and even individualistic starting point of our politics, it is indeed a long way to Angola, and even to Rhodesia. The shared sense of perceived danger may serve well enough in shaping a consensus for avoiding World War III or reacting to Soviet arms policy, but it does not give the same guidance on Africa, or even on policy toward the internal politics of Western Europe.

The consequence of this lack of guidance is paradoxical. In one sense it liberates the government. At levels of behavior short of heavy commitment, the President and his associates have considerable freedom of action. The average man could not care less whether Mr. Nixon tilts toward Pakistan or Mr. Carter toward black Africa when the actions involved are small and their consequences intangible. Thus an election which turns on quite different and usually domestic issues, like that of 1976, can have considerable consequences in the policy of the United States at this secondary level. Mr. Carter's foreign policy team had no electoral mandate for such enterprises as its new effort in human rights, but neither was there a mandate against it. On this issue the serious difference between Mr. George Kennan (skeptical) and Senator Moynihan (passionate) is one which leaves most voters cold, or at least uncertain, and the President and Mr. Vance have been free to make their own choices (which, perhaps predictably, have pleased neither Moynihan nor Kennan). The willingness of the citizen to leave such relatively difficult issues to the government does not constitute a choice between President and Congress, and congressmen also have been attracted to the action here, both by their own convictions and by the surface popularity of human rights.

There are hazards in this kind of freedom, as the early stages of our engagement in Vietnam quite plainly demonstrate. It is dangerous to begin things that one cannot finish without a level of support that one has not somehow ensured in advance. It is also dangerous to suppose that what led oneself into a candidate's corner is what led the American public there. There was a bitter little struggle, in early 1977, between Democrats of very different world views on exactly this question. Those who favored and those who opposed Mr. Paul Warnke were equally fervent, and I think equally wrong, in their conviction that the election gave entitlement to their opinions. All it did was to entitle Mr. Carter to choose. This is not a trivial entitlement, and it accounts in part for his ability to decide with ease such issues as the fate of the B-1.

Yet the other side of the paradox is that the absence of a mandate can be constricting as well as liberating. It keeps policy on a fairly short rein, in that there is no authorization for large-scale commitment beyond the area directly and visibly involving the Soviet danger. In situations of this sort authority can easily pass to strong groups and even strong individuals in Congress.

Where there is need for sustained appropriations or for explicit commitments of military strength, outside the area of direct U.S.-Soviet relations, the United States government has to rely either upon the existence of strong particular interests supporting such commitments, or else upon an effective (and often very difficult) demonstration that the course of action involved does indeed relate persuasively to the general safety and welfare of our own citizens. When the reliance is more on particular interests than on a national consensus, there is a continuous danger that at some point the general and the particular interest may collide. Or there may be a general interest unsustained by an adequately lively sense of danger, and in such a case the inertial forces of private preference may lead to a later and more intense crisis. A consideration of two present cases may serve to clarify the suggestion that problems of these kinds are likely to be troublesome.

There is a deep irony in the fact that the two gravest problems facing Mr. Carter as he entered the Presidency (the general relationship with the Soviet Union always excepted) had their center in the Middle East. The Middle East is not where Americans as a whole have wanted problems. In the board rooms of large corporations and the halls of great universities the area has been one to conjure with for a long time, and the constituency with a particular interest in the safety of Israel is both strong and devoted—and not limited to American Jews. Yet even those with these kinds of sophisticated and long-standing concern in the area were startled by the double crisis set off in 1973 by the Yom Kippur War and the use of the oil weapon. Their surprise was shared by both the federal government and the public as a whole—and even after almost four years there persists a widespread feeling that these crises are problems only for those who have their particular reasons for worrying about them. Nothing could be plainer to students of the international scene than the fact that the prospect of a reasonable and peaceful settlement of the double crisis depends heavily on the American government and the public that sustains or restrains its actions. But there is no clarity at all about the readiness of either government or people to do what might be required for such a settlement. What we have here, in each case, is a deep involvement created by private and particular interests and capable of resolution only by an overriding concern for the wider interest of our society as a whole.

To say that the American engagement in Israel has been fueled mainly by particular American interests is not at all to say that there is no general American interest, today, in Israel's survival. The opposite is the case. Even at the beginning, when men like Marshall and Acheson feared the consequences of setting a small Jewish state in a subcontinent of enemies, there was a constituency of considerable breadth that sustained Mr. Truman in his firm and prompt support of Israel—his opponent, Thomas Dewey, could do no more than say "me too." And today, after thirty years, the sheer injustice of an end to Israel would be so great, and the level of our own engagement is so deep, that an abandonment of Israel by the United States would be a national shame quite unacceptable to our people as a whole. There can be argument about how we got to this point, but none about where we are now.

But we must distinguish sharply between this general commitment and the extensions of it which are preferred, and have very often been obtained, by Israel and its backers in the United States: that there should be no American position on the shape of a settlement which is not agreed between Jerusalem and Washington, and also that the United States should be the residual supplier of Israel's economic and military needs as defined in Jerusalem.

Even though obviously there has been energetic bargaining as to what Israel really needs, and frequent differences of emphasis, still it is fair to say that with the single and instructive exception of Suez in 1956, successive administrations have made it a policy to do nothing that was violently opposed by the American backers of Israel, and those supporters in turn have taken their cue, on most issues, from existing governments in Israel. In consequence of this policy, and of the real needs of Israel, every stage of the 30-year contest has deepened our engagement. Even the small concessions wrung from a reluctant Israel by Secretary Kissinger in 1974 and 1975 had big price tags. So did the concessions of Egypt, for that matter, and in consequence the American government is now helping both sides to pay for their armed truce. But it is Israel whose survival remains at issue, and the American stake in that survival is currently costing our government about $600 a year for every one of Israel's 3 million people.

We have now reached a stage where that past policy is almost sure to be inadequate. It is too soon to say that we are facing any breakdown of confidence between the two countries, or even any unavoidable diplomatic "crunch"—that depends as much on the Israelis as on us. But there is a dangerously widening gap between what Israel wants and what our public as a whole can support.

The root of the difficulty here is territorial. Throughout the ten years since the Six-Day War there has been a persistent and substantial difference between every Israeli cabinet and every American administration over the basic shape of a workable settlement on the ground. In the beginning, and especially in the negotiation of the controlling Resolution 242 of the Security Council, this difference was papered over, and the Johnson administration allowed differences of interpretation even among its own members as to exactly what was meant by that resolution's call for "withdrawal from territories occupied in the recent conflict." But as time has passed, the difference between the two governments has become more and more visible, and its existence has been publicly acknowledged by Israeli leaders as different as Itzak Rabin in 1976 and Moshe Dayan in 1977. There is no reason to doubt the depth of the Begin government's conviction that most if not all of the West Bank is liberated land that belongs to Israel by right, and no way to square this conviction with any American interpretation of the meaning of Resolution 242. Still less does the Israeli government's view of the matter command support among other members of the Security Council—indeed only the American veto stands between Israel and a much less favorable interpretation or reframing of its obligation to withdraw in return for peace.

A difference that was latent for ten years has become obvious in 1977. What is much less clear is when or how it will be resolved. Both governments still correctly tie withdrawal to peace, and there is room for plenty of doubt that the neighboring states are ready for anything that will mean peace either to Washington or to Jerusalem. Moreover diplomacy in the area has usually been slower than observers have expected, and predictions of a crisis have been rather like Paul Samuelson's description of the stock market as a prophet of recession—the doomsayers have predicted at least ten of the last four wars.

Nonetheless there have been four wars, and one use of oil as a weapon. To suppose that all this is over seems fanciful, and on the record of the last ten years the policy of delay does appear to have had high costs for both Israel and the

United States. So at some stage the American government will have to decide what to do about its serious difference with Israel.

For the purpose of this paper the only point that matters is that this is a decision so large that it must be made with a readiness to accept real war-and-peace consequences. It will therefore have to rest on an informed public support with a base much broader than the particular groups most interested in Israel. I believe that such broad and general support can be found in a form that meets our basic interest in Israel, but what I underline here is simply that an indispensable test for the United States government, when the time of testing comes, will have to be its sense of what can be defended and supported as fair by the public opinion of our country as a whole. Those friends of Israel who think that it is enough for the United States to follow the Israeli lead are wrong—almost as badly wrong as the larger (but less concerned) number of Americans who suppose that it is only the organized influence of American Jews which makes support for the survival of Israel a necessary cardinal point in American foreign policy.

The record of the last generation shows only one force that can undermine basic American support of Israel: Israeli excess. It is only when the United States has been asked to support a posture which even good American friends of Israel find excessive that there has been real trouble. That is what happened in a big way at Suez, and in a much more personal and ambiguous way with Kissinger in 1975.

What is excessive and what is essential to survival are not absolutes determinable in advance. Between democratic allies there will always be differences at least at the edges, and differences also inside each country. All that I need for my present purpose is the proposition that in this matter no American government can rightly or safely go beyond what will be acceptable to the American people as a whole. The particular interests of Israel will be pressed by its particular American friends; that is how this democracy works, and should work, and it is foolish to be disturbed by it, as so many "experts" are. Moreover, the quality and sensitivity of American support for Israel can be much affected by the skill and energy with which particular Israeli interests are argued, and there is nothing wrong with that either. But as and when Americans are asked by their own government to go on the line for any further settlement, it will be no service to Israel, or to peace, to ask the people of our country to go against the best American judgment of what is fair; nothing else will sustain any policy at all when there is a real test. Our public opinion as a whole, and not the concern of any one group, has been decisive at the most crucial moments in our thirty-year relation to this conflict, and it will be so again.

We must hope that it will prove possible to reconcile differences with Israel in ways that serve the true interests of both countries. No sensible politician in either country can think it desirable to have any open rift. We must try to maintain our partnership with Israel even while insisting on our right and obligation to base our policy on our own best judgment of what our people as a whole can be asked to support. In all this it is essential to remember that Israeli leaders live in a democracy too.

We know from the calculated inaction of 1976 and the jerky beginnings of 1977 that such a course is not easily set and maintained. In this respect the example of Suez is, perhaps fortunately, misleading. When President Eisenhower parted from Israel over that campaign and the ensuing occupation of the Sinai, he did so first in the context of a sudden crisis which, as such crises will, strongly intensified the President's authority. In addition the Israelis were seen to be in bad company; they were tarred by the brush of British and French folly, and in any case there was no immediate or plausible threat to their survival. It is obviously much harder to part from the Israelis in a situation well short of open war, and one in which no one can deny that there is danger to Israel. The nature of any authority that would replace the Israeli administration of the West Bank is indeed a matter crucial to Israeli security, and while the idea that Israeli sovereignty is there for good may be (I think must be) rejected, the shaping of arrangements that could be acceptable to all concerned will be enormously difficult.

I leave it there. All I want is to illustrate my general point; here is a case where the stakes are so high that the support of our public as a whole is essential, and where the legitimate particular interests are so strong that the temptation to put off hard choices has governed three Presidents already since 1967. Can we expect Mr. Carter to seek and find a course that will command effective general support without a destructive undermining of our relations with Israel? Can he make this course clear and compelling in time to prevent the next round of fighting or the next twist of the oil weapon? Or will particular interests outweigh the general interest of both countries until it is too late?

The oil weapon came into existence through the play of essentially nongovernmental, even nonpolitical forces. It was not governments or politics which so ordered events so as to make a single voice, that of the King of Saudi Arabia, decisive in the supply and pricing of oil in the international market. And politics was never the prime mover in the ascendancy of oil as a source of energy. Especially in the United States the age of oil was the product of other forces that could seem larger or smaller than government, depending on whether one looked from the perspective of the macroeconomist or from that of the individuals who wanted clean heat for homes and convenient fuel for cars and boats.

Serving these very large and very small interests were the oil companies, and to understand their part in all this one must have a happy tolerance of paradox. In all sorts of ways they have had great power; they could usually defend their tax privileges; they could complicate the lives of their smaller competitors; they could, for a time, keep the international price of oil very low; they could and did supply the demands of Americans, and of many others too. They could even operate, in quiet cooperation with a few foreign sisters, to restrict the effect of the oil weapon when it was used in a limited way against only a few.

But the oil companies were never more than private and particular forces; they were not governments, and in the United States they were not only constrained to keep a safe distance from the Executive Branch (it was different on Capitol Hill) but deeply on the outs with the average citizen, who never saw his interest and theirs as one, to put it mildly. They were rich and efficient in their way, and they were certainly necessary and often skillful middlemen. But neither the government nor the public ever thought of them as partners. As in the Middle East, so in the United States, their wealth and their economic strength were tolerated only in return for their acceptance of ultimate political weakness, and even subservience. There is no one more timid than an oil mogul at the White House, except perhaps his colleague in Riyadh.

Once we understand the derivative nature of the role of the oil companies, we are better placed to see that the enormous American stake in Middle Eastern oil is itself derivative. It becomes a state interest because so many particular interests are so heavily engaged—and not the other way around. The degree of dependency which has developed, and which has increased steadily in the very years in which politicians have talked emptily of nonsense like Project Independence, is the product of no plan, and there is no plan because not planning such things is truly the American tradition.

At the extreme of this tradition some spokesmen for the American government have allowed themselves to talk as if the stars in their courses made it needless to plan a response to OPEC. Because OPEC's denial of ordinary market process was unnatural, it must collapse, and to admit its temporary success would merely delay its inevitable failure. Anyone who finds this dim religious view astonishing in 1977 is invited to examine the public record of the American Secretary of the Treasury in 1974. And Mr. William Simon is well known as a hardheaded man.

In 1977, for the first time, the Executive Branch has put forward a general plan for dealing with the general energy crisis, and it is no pleasure to have to say that this plan too is inadequate. As it came from the White House it was already too small, and when the Congress is through with it, the inadequacy will be still greater. There is no present prospect that there will be any early reversal of the remorseless trend to an increasing dependence on foreign oil. Even among those who believe the crisis is real there has been an essentially destructive squabble among those whose preference for conservation or for production makes them hostile to any emphasis on the other. And in between is the general opinion of the country, for which there is no crisis that calls for pain to "us."

So it appears that before there is an adequate policy there will have to be a wider and deeper understanding, in the country as a whole, that nothing less will do. And this understanding will have to be based clearly and persuasively on what matters to us—to us all. The general crisis of supply which threatens us threatens our friends in Europe still more gravely. There is a double gap here: between what is needed and what Mr. Carter proposed and between what he proposed and what the country will accept. More particularly, we are a long way from coming sharply to terms with the proposition that it will be impossible to sustain an effective Middle Eastern policy without an effective energy policy. It is a disturbing fact that one can find more understanding of this point among moderate Arabs than in American public opinion as a whole.

The root of the matter is that while our citizens did not will our dependency on foreign oil, it is their wants that have produced it, and their unawareness of the danger involved that allows it to grow and discourages effective countermeasures. The simplest and most important protective device—an ample emergency reserve—could easily have been in place by now if the national interest had been our guide since 1973.

This separation between the public will and the national need can be narrowed in many ways, and while those who believe in narrowing it have their own duty to speak and work to that end, a special opportunity and responsibility fall to the President. Mr. Carter has shown his awareness of that role, but his experience in 1977 shows the limits of the President's power to make distant danger seem near enough to support efforts that have real costs. It can be argued that Mr. Carter explained himself badly, and also that he did a feeble job of enlisting support among other leaders of opinion. Certainly he did not succeed in lifting the discussion beyond interest-group concerns, and in part the relative narrowness of the advice he received may be responsible. Still it is hard to avoid the conclusion that what most weakened his message was the absence of any shortage or other crisis that people could recognize as real and urgent. No matter what investors and planners may say, a shortage predicted for 1985 seems very far away if the gas pumps are full in 1978.

This experience suggests that while the President can dramatically heighten a national perception of danger, he cannot create it alone. In all our great political crises, over slavery, over the world wars, and over the Soviet threat, it has been events, not exhortations, that have been decisive. That is at once the most fundamental consequence, and the plainest demonstration, of the essentially private nature of our polity.

To wait upon events is not all wrong; it was Lincoln himself who refused to force the war that history required and who freely confessed how far events had shaped him. The fog that hides the future is frustrating to the analyst but salutary insofar as it induces caution at the center. We have already seen that even in the volatile case of the Arab-Israeli conflict there is often more time than the experts predict. When two crises intersect, as energy and this conflict do, the value of prudence is multiplied. It would be very easy indeed to do the wrong thing in the Middle East, and even though it is right to recognize the high price we have paid in buying time since 1973, it is another matter altogether to conclude that the price has been too high, or that we should not go on paying, and perhaps even seek to buy time again.

But time is bought to be used, and the use which is the subject of this essay is public understanding. What these two cases underline is what our history tells us too, that because we are the kind of people we are, we cannot rise to great tests unless we rise together, knowing why we must. We have often been awakened and unified by calamity, or what we join in understanding that way, as by those who attacked Fort Sumter and Pearl Harbor. Less often we have met a rising challenge by adequate early understanding. The textbook case may be the Marshall Plan, but in that bipartisan national decision the most important influence of all was that of Stalin, not any American. There was danger as well as help in this personification of real evil. The issues of the rest of the century are not likely to be so simply clarified. There are few easy villains, from the American standpoint, in the Middle East, let alone in the oceans or the upper atmosphere.

Even easy villains can be badly misread, as Hitler was by the French and British governments until Czechoslovakia was taken. Good old Joe was not that

good in 1944. It seems wildly unlikely that the China of Mao was ever as terrifying as we thought in 1950 or as wonderful as travelers said in the early
1970s. The most puzzling case of all may be one of the most important: what
kinds of parties must not become dominant in Western Europe, from our standpoint—and how much, if anything, can we do about it?

What this last example suggests strongly to me is how easy it is to be wrong
about such matters. What becomes of Western Europe matters most profoundly
to us, as our behavior since 1940 shows. But that fact does not of itself tell us
what to think of left or right in any country. There are hazards in believing too
much about either the virtue or the vice of European Communism, and in any
case it is not clear that our government knows how to take a role in these matters
that will in fact serve whatever interest we have. It is easy to say and do the
wrong things about other people's elections.

There may also be a special danger for us in the persistence of our considerable national pride. A relatively simple test presents itself in Panama, where
there may be a stronger bipartisan consensus of leaders in favor of the new
treaties than we have had on any large issue in this decade. Yet what four
administrations have sought may not be what the people want, and even if the
treaties are approved in the Senate we cannot be sure that the life of the Canal
will really be serene from here to the end of the century. Our strong national
feelings on a matter like this can be aroused by accident; if they are not to
become explosive, they too must be respected. Even for our own leaders this is a
complex counsel—and for foreign politicians, the temptation to pull Uncle
Sam's beard is likely to be both severe and destructive. If it was so for Charles
de Gaulle, why not for lesser men?

Our national pride is of course intimately related to our national strength;
few indeed are the great societies which have been unfailingly moderate. Yet the
very size and variety of our involvement in the world ensures that we shall have
disappointments. If the capacity to live with such trouble has been demonstrated in our ability to put Vietnam behind us, that experience itself also tells
us the cost of proud persistence in increasingly evident error.

Yet there is magnanimity among us too—perhaps as much as in any leading
power ever. Can we learn to connect this national largeness of spirit with a
largeness of national understanding not only in small but telltale cases like Panama, not only in large matters like energy and the Middle East, but also more
generally, in accepting the proposition that what is safe and fair for us must
somehow be consistent with what is safe and fair for others? The notion that the
American interest can meet the test of consistency with the interests of all men
is as old as the Republic. It is a test we have often failed, but one that we
have never rejected.

Although the choices will be hard, and errors many, although our private
concerns will still make us slow to recognize both foreign danger and foreign
responsibility, and although a nation can be magnanimous while its agents are
mean, none of all this is predestined—and indeed what may be most important
about the Nixon years is precisely that such meanness in the White House is
atypical.

The moral and intellectual imperative, then, is understanding. And even
though we may not have the help of a clear-cut challenge like Stalinism, we do

have, today, the advantage of a considerable collective memory. Moreover, it is some comfort to remember that the persuasive brutality of Stalin, in 1947 and 1948, was worth nothing without a prior understanding in Washington, both of the general need for action and of the ways to begin. That is where thought can help, both in and out of government, even when it may be too soon for the unifying strength of danger truly perceived.

That is the challenge, in the calm before the storm, to both analysts and actors. The fallow years can be put behind us—years of meanness and manipulation in government, and of division and anger in the academy. The pain of Vietnam recedes, and perhaps also the lassitude that followed it. There is no reason why we cannot meet the test of educating ourselves to the necessary levels of new understanding—both in what students learn and say and in what statesmen preach and perform. But what all concerned must always remember is that in the end the policies they propose can be effective only if the country will support them. I believe the test is fair; I know it is necessary.

RONALD I. MCKINNON

America's Role in Stabilizing the World's Monetary System

SINCE 1945, THE UNITED STATES dollar, and American financial policies toward foreigners, have been the central elements in the international monetary system. Despite events that would seem to point to the contrary, the evolving key-currency role of the dollar has shown surprising robustness. The articles of the International Monetary Fund (IMF) and other international agreements, however, treat all nations as equals and somewhat disguise this underlying reality. And American authorities themselves often fail to appreciate the singular economic position of the United States in keeping the world's money machine going.

Signed at Bretton Woods, New Hampshire, in July 1944,[1] the IMF articles remain the principal legal basis of the world's monetary system, even though they have been substantially amended since then. They have been ratified by almost all noncommunist countries. Nations were anxious to avoid returning to the chaotic exchange-rate practices of the 1930s that severely attenuated international commerce. Thus each participating country committed itself to maintain free currency convertibility (under Article VIII) as well as a stable par value for its currency (Article IV). A parity once fixed was to be changed only when threatened by a "fundamental disequilibrium" in the exchange market, and only then with the mutual agreement of the IMF. In a formal sense, these rules applied symmetrically to all countries—including the United States.

Fixed exchange rates among convertible currencies of the major industrial countries[2] were, on balance, well maintained into the late 1960s. Together with the General Agreement on Tariffs and Trade (GATT), this international economic order was associated with unprecedented growth in world commerce that was essential to the postwar prosperity enjoyed by Europe and Japan, and enjoyed by a few developing countries—such as Taiwan, Korea, and Israel—which did not unduly restrict their own participation in international trade.

How worried then should we be about the disintegration of the fixed exchange-rate system in the late 1960s? Strenuous efforts to enforce a new legal basis for fixed exchange rates, which was agreed to at the Smithsonian Institution in December 1971, collapsed completely in February 1973. The present regime of "free floating" is subject to only the loosest kind of supervision by the IMF.[3] The recent marked divergences of exchange rates (against the U.S. dollar) of major industrial economies are portrayed in Figure 1. Important monetary values such as the deutsche mark-dollar exchange rate now seem to

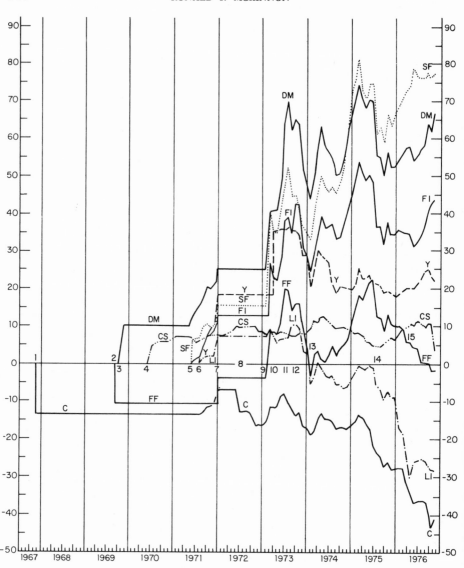

Figure 1. Foreign Exchange Rates of Major Currencies (percentage deviations with respect to dollar parities of October 1967; end of month figures)

Key to figures: 1: £ devalued (18 11 67). 2: French franc devalued (10 8 69). 3: DM floated (30 9 69) and revalued (26 10 69). 4: Canadian dollar floated (1 6 70). 5: DM and Dutch guilder floated; Swiss franc revalued (9 5 71). 6: Dollar-gold convertibility suspended (15 8 71); major currencies de facto floated. 7: Smithsonian realignment dollar formally devalued; yen, DM, and other currencies revalued (18 12 71). 8: £ floated (23 6 72). 9: Swiss franc floated (23 1 73); dollar devalued; yen and Italian lira floated (13 2 73). 10: Markets closed (2 3 73); DM revalued; "joint float" (19 3 73). 11: DM revalued (29 6 73). 12: Dutch guilder revalued (17 9 73). 13: French franc left the "joint float" (19 1 74). 14: French franc returned to the "joint float" (10 7 75). 15: French franc left the "joint float" (15 3 76).

Source: Reprinted with permission from *OECD Observer* (November-December 1976): 101.

fluctuate about 15 to 20 percent in the course of a year, whereas under the old system the rate fluctuated within a 2 percent margin.

Fortunately, a regime of common law in international monetary affairs continues to operate vigorously even if some of the important statutes of the 1944 Bretton Woods agreement have been suspended. But the present (apparently disordered) system is viable only if the rules of the game are understood by all the players, particularly the American government. The markedly asymmetrical but central role of the United States can best be understood by tracing its evolution through four distinct phases: the Marshall Plan and European recovery (1948–1958), realization of the Bretton Woods agreement and fixed exchange rates under the dollar–gold standard (1959–1968), uncertainly pegged exchange rates and international inflation (1968–1973), and finally the present regime of uninhibited floating of the freely convertible currencies of major industrial economies.[4]

Because somewhat differing American obligations and policies have been appropriate (and not always followed) in each of the four phases of the evolving world dollar standard, let us distinguish among them by discussing each in turn.

The Marshall Plan and the Remonetization of European Trade (1948–1959)

In the recovery of Western Europe trade from the paralysis with which it was afflicted in 1946–1947, the International Monetary Fund was not operational. None of the previously belligerent countries had multilaterally convertible currencies in the sense of Article VIII, and none would make payments in terms of gold or dollars (which they did not have) to support an officially fixed parity in the sense of Article IV. All made use of various "escape" clauses in the fund's charter. Moreover, the fund's bylaws would not permit lending gold or dollars in substantial amounts to build up European reserve positions when prospects for repayment were dubious. Instead, in its early years, the fund specialized in helping a few less developed countries with better than average repayment prospects and less massive borrowing needs.

But the European trade and payments mechanism was sunk in a mire. The absence of owned reserves of gold or internationally convertible foreign exchange, coupled with their voracious appetite to absorb industrial goods and primary products, meant that European countries quickly spent dollar earnings from their limited exports. They then rationed in great detail—by means of exchange controls and quota restrictions—the potentially huge excess demand for further imports available only from hard-currency countries such as the United States and Canada. This was indeed the era of the "world" dollar shortage that many people projected to be chronic.

Discriminatory trade restrictions against the importation of American goods were only part of the problem, however. Europeans had potentially strong reciprocal demands for each other's goods, but each of their currencies was inconvertible. Nonresidents, unlucky enough to acquire balances of inconvertible European currencies, could freely buy neither commodities nor convertible currencies without going through a complex licensing process. Therefore, any one European country would try to avoid acquiring inconvertible monetary claims on any European trading partner. This froze multilateral trade within Europe: Country A could not effectively use credits from a trade surplus garnered from country B to offset a trade deficit with country C.[5]

> By 1947 . . . the system was in deadlock. Debtors were not prepared to make payments in gold or dollars, and creditors were not prepared to extend credit beyond existing limits. Thus there was an incentive to discriminate in trade, debtors discriminating against imports from their creditors in favour of imports from those countries with whom they had a bilateral surplus, hoping that this would prevent a drain on reserves and encourage a repayment of previously extended credit. The consequences of such trade restrictions and discrimination was a stagnation in the growth of intra-European trade in 1947. Europe . . . was being choked by the self-imposed collar of bilateralism.[6]

The resulting bilaterally balanced trade diverted both production and consumption from the most efficient sources and uses by country. Moreover, decision making was largely taken out of the hands of individual firms and households in Europe and placed with the foreign-exchange licensing authorities in national central banks, which then negotiated the bilateral exchange of exports for imports with their counterparts in other national central banks.

The United States European Recovery Program in its most general form, commonly known as the Marshall Plan, was not enacted by the U.S. Congress until April 1948. Previously, some piecemeal bilateral aid had been extended in 1946 and 1947 for famine relief to particular countries, and to support a premature and abortive effort to restore nonresident convertibility for the pound sterling in 1947. But whatever its initial institutional shortcomings, the 1948 Marshall Plan funneled aid in the form of generally usable dollar credits to Europe as a whole. Indeed, the Organization of European Economic Cooperation (OEEC), consisting of 17 European countries, was formed in 1948 to help the Economic Cooperation Administration of the United States distribute American aid on a multilateral basis.[7]

In retrospect, why was the Marshall Plan so successful?

The quantitative magnitude of American balance of payments support for Europe (mainly official credits supplemented by some private investment) was very large in absolute terms by the standards of the time: $4 to $5 billion annually from 1948 to 1951. Yet conceived of as simply making possible additional consumption plus investment in Europe, the magnitudes were not large relative to the total size of Europe's own gross income:

> The total supply of goods and services available to Western Europe is estimated at $145 billion in the year 1948–49, of which Western Europe's gross national product accounts for $140 billion and net imports of goods and services from the outside world for the remainder. Thus, the external deficit has recently been providing only 4 percent of the goods and services available to Western Europe, the remaining 96 percent coming from Europe's own production.[8]

Even though they were only about 4 percent of Europe's collective GNP, American capital transfers did amount to about 40 percent of Europe's total receipts of "hard" foreign exchange—that which could be spent freely anywhere in the world. Yet, subsequently, similar amounts of aid directed toward less developed countries such as India had nothing like the enormous payoff in augmented growth that seemed to characterize the Marshall transfer to Europe.

To explain the apparently high leverage from Marshall Plan aid, one has to look for a lever. The first temptation is to consider specific shortages or materials bottlenecks in Europe. Basic food grains (wage goods) for consumption might come to mind. But the dominant image is the restocking of war-torn European factories with American machines, spare parts, and perhaps even industrial raw materials from third countries financed by dollar credits. To take a hoary example, the want of specialized ball bearings, whose European output sources were flattened during the war, might keep a complete European factory closed save for a trickle of ball-bearing imports from America that, in monetary value, need be only a trivial proportion of the factor's gross output. And Marshall financial industrial procurement by Europeans in America was undoubtedly one important reason for the remarkable European recovery.

However, to base the leverage argument solely on the transfer of key physical commodities—those in accidentally short supply in Europe—implies that the system would have worked equally well even if American aid had been bilaterally given, with separate arrangements for each European country. In an economic sense, the multilateral character of OEEC would have been largely redundant, and the financial deadlock in intra-European trade described above would not have been important in "real" terms. Moreover, Europe's limited exports to hard-currency countries still amounted to about 6 percent of European GNP from 1948 to 1952—more than enough by themselves to overcome many highly specific shortages such as that of ball bearings.

To supplement this standard argument, I would emphasize the financial leverage achieved by Marshall Plan aid, with the flow of finance from America (inclusive of unutilized precautionary credit lines) being ultimately successful in eliminating the money muddle that was repressing intra-European trade. Hence, the relatively slender American financial resources directed toward this particular end sharply increased real output—once multilateral trade revived and resources in Europe came to be more efficiently allocated.

But how was this financial lever applied? After only partial success in 1948 and 1949,[9] the European Payments Union (EPU) was formed in 1950 under the auspices of the OEEC. The United States provided the initial capital fund of $350 million; and the American dollar was formally set up as a unit of account in which intra-European receipts and payments would be denominated as claims against the clearing union (EPU) itself. Each European currency was then pegged at a fixed dollar parity.[10]

At monthly settlement dates, national central banks would submit a record of receipts from, and payments to, all other members of the union. For country A, the EPU secretariat would then offset the sum of bilateral deficits with countries B, C, and D with the sum of bilateral surpluses with E, F, and G. Thus, every month, the multilateral net debtor-creditor position of each national central bank vis-à-vis the union was established, and settlements were made. The means of settlement was initially 40 percent gold or dollar payments by debtors, and 60 percent net credit extension to the EPU by creditor countries. With the American financial backing, the EPU itself would make gold-dollar settlements if any debtor country should default. Similarly, guidelines for maximum credits from the EPU were imposed on debtor countries. Thus, creditor countries within Europe could be assured of eventual payment in truly hard money; and they no longer had to strive for bilateral balance with each trading partner in order to avoid acquiring unusable soft currency claims. Moreover, the clearing mechanism within the union—and the credit lines provided—greatly economized on the scarce gold- and dollar-exchange reserves held by each European country.

Multilateral trade within Europe was no longer inhibited for monetary reasons; and, after 1950, the European countries moved vigorously to remove tariffs and quantitative restrictions on particular commodities imported from European trading partners. The surge in trade was dramatic. With 1949 as 100, the volume of intra-European imports rose to 141 in 1950, and by 1956 had climbed to 226.[11]

Throughout this period of European recovery, the United States tolerated the maintenance of discriminatory tariff and quota restrictions on many potential American exports to Europe—thus allowing the individual European countries to build up their dollar and gold reserves more rapidly and so set the stage for the return to full currency convertibility in 1959, when such restrictions were removed. Afterward, it became appropriate for the United States to lobby hard to have payments restrictions removed whenever possible, as with the achievement of full convertibility by Japan in 1964. Unlike the industrial economies, however, less developed countries have not been similarly pressured by either the United States or the International Monetary Fund to eliminate financial or other restraints on their foreign trade.

Realization of the Bretton Woods Agreement and the Dollar-Gold Exchange Standard (1959–1968)

With all its great advantages in reestablishing a monetary basis for intra-European trade, the EPU in its initial "pure" form had certain economic limitations. (1) Intra-European payments were placed on a substantially different basis from trade with non-European countries; the latter had to be financed by open-market purchases and sales of foreign exchange. The clearing machinery of the EPU permitted discrimination against purchases or sales of commodities outside of the union. (2) The EPU relied heavily on national central banks for recording all settlements, and indeed this funneling of transactions through central banks facilitated the maintenance of exchange controls and payments restrictions. Hence, on December 24, 1958, the European Payments Union was officially disbanded and exchange restrictions against dollar-area imports were removed. Fourteen Western European countries—including all the industrial ones—made their currencies fully externally convertible for current transactions, and finally made fully operational the par-value obligation under Article IV of the 1944 Bretton Woods agreements:

> 1. The par value of the currency of each member shall be expressed in terms of gold as a common denominator or in terms of the United States dollar of the weight and fineness in effect on July 1st, 1944.
> 2. The maximum and minimum rates . . . shall not differ from parity, in the case of spot transactions by more than one percent. . . .[12]

As a practical matter, it was awkward to buy and sell gold directly for national currencies in the open market in order to maintain exchange margins. Gold is costly to store and transport, and the world gold supply was still asymmetrically concentrated in the United States in the late 1950s. Moreover, European countries had already been maintaining exact dollar parities as part of EPU agreement. Thus, in 1959, Article IV was interpreted such that member countries of the IMF all pegged their currencies to the U.S. dollar within a 1 percent margin on either side of "parity." Each national central bank kept reserves to buy or sell dollars for the domestic currency in the open-market foreign exchange in order to maintain the 2-percent margin for all who wished to trade with the country in question. Thus the dollar became the official intervention currency used by European and other central banks the world over.[13]

What were the reciprocal American obligations in the brave new monetary order? The formal obligation, under Article IV, was to fix the dollar's parity in terms of gold. Although all other countries pegged to the dollar, the American authorities agreed to sell (or buy) gold to foreign central banks upon demand in exchange for dollars at a fixed parity of $35.00 per ounce with no band of variation. Such government-to-government transfers took place outside the open market for foreign exchange. Thus, the world was put on a full-fledged dollar-gold exchange standard.

The second important American obligation under the dollar-gold exchange standard was implicit. Because all foreign central banks were intervening with their own currencies against the dollar to maintain parities that were occasionally changed,[14] the American government essentially stayed out of the open foreign-exchange markets in order to avoid conflict. The Bank of England, for example, would buy or sell dollars for sterling to maintain the exchange rate between $2.78 and $2.82, but the Federal Reserve System would stay out of the dollar-sterling market—and also stay out of 100 or so other markets in foreign currencies. Indeed, the U.S. did not hold reserves of other currencies with which to intervene. And this American passivity in allowing other countries to choose their exchange rates against the dollar was, and still is, an essential element in the harmonious working of the global monetary system.

An important consequence, however, was that the U.S. government did not have direct control over the state of its balance of payments in the 1960s—nor should it have. As long as other countries succeeded in setting their exchange parities as "equilibrium" levels vis-à-vis the dollar so as to have a payments surplus that allowed them to accumulate reserves (U.S. dollars) as they wanted, the state of the American balance of payments was residually determined. But American authorities responded with alarm to the resulting "accounting deficits" in American foreign payments, even when America was running large trade surpluses in the early 1960s. Instead of welcoming the voluntary build-up of dollar reserves by foreigners in a period of world-wide price stability (Table 1), in the 1960s the American authorities made the mistake of restricting some kinds of capital outflows from the United States (as discussed below).

As a partial quid pro quo, however, the United States could use its own dollars to cover payments deficits as they developed, whereas other countries had to use scarce foreign exchange. This asymmetry in the dollar standard was called by Charles de Gaulle an "exorbitant privilege of the United States"— indicating that official misinterpretations of international monetary phenomena were not confined to the American side of the Atlantic Ocean.

Before discussing the reasons for the inevitable collapse of the pure dollar-gold exchange standard, let us describe its rather remarkable accomplishments.

TABLE 1
THE WORLD'S DOLLAR PRICE LEVEL
(U.S. WHOLESALE PRICE INDICES)

Year	Price Level	
1951	82.5	
52	80.3	
53	79.2	
54	79.3	
55	79.5	
1956	82.2	
57	84.5	
58	85.7	
59	85.9	Dollar price stability and internationally
60	86.0	fixed exchange rates
1961	85.7	
62	85.9	
63	85.6	
64	85.8	
65	87.5	
1966	90.4	
67	90.6	
68	92.8	
69	96.5	
70	100.0	Accelerating world inflation and the
1971	103.3	breakdown of fixed exchange rates
72	107.9	
73	122.0	
74	145.0	
75	158.4	High world inflation and freely floating rates
1976	165.7	

Source: IMF, International Financial Statistics and Data Fund.

For the industrial economies, it allowed free multilateral exchange of their convertible currencies among private commercial banks and trading firms without having to channel foreign payments through central banks. Within the 1-percent margins on either side of parity, exchange rates were very stable and payments restrictions absent so that domestic monies in the industrial economies were virtually as good as international money. Meanwhile, under GATT, tariff and quota restrictions on commodity trade with industrial countries were progressively reduced. In addition, foreign trade grew even more rapidly than national incomes in the 1960s, so that all the industrial economies became more open to foreign trade, as output per capita rose impressively by any historical standard.

(It should be noted that most LDCs maintained inconvertible currencies in the late 1950s and 1960s, and also intensified payments restrictions as well as tariff and quota barriers to their own external trade. This "import-substitution" strategy of economic development meant, effectively, that they did not participate in the world trade boom and their economies became more closed. Indeed, we have a paradox. U.S. aid in the late 1950s and 1960s to less developed countries was often associated with more centralized planning (India, Latin America) and the imposition of restraints on foreign trade, whereas the earlier more successful Marshall Plan aid to Europe was associated with the removal of trade restrictions! Quite possibly, AID administrators in the 1950s and 1960s failed to recognize the monetary reasons for the Marshall Plan's success.)

Stability in a macroeconomic sense was also achieved. Those countries that effectively fixed their exchange parities to the U.S. dollar and kept convertible currencies as well, had their price levels (in terms of tradable goods) pegged to that in the United States[15]—the latter being quite stable from 1951 to the mid-1960s, as indicated in Table 1. Their domestic monetary policies had to be passively adjusted to maintain this fixed exchange rate while accommodating quite high rates of growth in real output. Indeed, a convincing peg to the U.S. dollar allowed Germany and Japan, which had experienced traumatic monetary upheavals in the late 1940s, to restore confidence in the deutsche mark and yen faster than would otherwise be the case. Inflationary expectations were also dampened elsewhere in Europe if citizens came to believe that their government was committed to a fixed-dollar parity. (This earlier favorable experience induced many countries to continue their dollar parities into the early 1970s, well past the point that it was desirable to do so.)

A truly international capital market was an outgrowth of the dollar-gold exchange standard, and essential to its smooth functioning. Countries and individuals who were net savers (surplus units in a financial sense) could deposit in New York banks or buy bonds in New York; whereas countries that had a need for investment resources (deficit units in a financial sense) could borrow in New York, both creditors and debtors using the dollar as a vehicle currency to finance this net international transfer of capital. And in the late 1950s and early 1960s, New York was the dominant entrepot center for international capital, although not on the grand scale that London had been prior to 1914 under the old gold standard.

Besides bringing net savers and investors together, financial intermediation through New York had another important aspect. Governments abroad had a continuous need to tailor their "owned" reserves of freely usable dollars for intervention or precautionary purposes; and commercial banks also had a demand for dollar checking accounts and term deposits because of the dollar's role as a vehicle currency. Either group was then free to borrow at "long" term— say, by issuing bonds—in New York, and use the proceeds to build up their short-term "liquidity": freely usable deposits in New York.[16] Although this freedom to borrow long and lend back (deposit) short in dollars did not result in any net international transfer of capital, foreigners could acquire international liquidity when they needed it, and hence more easily preserve currency convertibility with fixed exchange rates.

In discussing the collapse of the dollar-gold standard and fixed exchange rates, I shall first look at the proximate reasons for virtually ending in 1968

American gold sales to foreigners, and then discuss the deeper reasons rooted in the increasing instability of the American economy in the late 1960s. Gold could have been phased out of the system—and indeed some kind of gold crisis was inevitable—without causing the collapse of the fixed exchange-rate regime.

After the European recovery, the world's stock of monetary gold changed little because the official price was fixed at $35.00 per ounce until 1971, and the net flow of newly mined gold relative to industrial usage was—and remains—small relative to existing stocks (Table 2). In 1951, the total official gold reserves of IMF members amounted to $33.5 billion and was $38.7 billion in 1968. Of this, official American holdings amounted to $22.9 billion in 1951, but fell to $10.9 billion by 1968. As rapidly growing European economies allowed their reserve positions to grow commensurately to purchasing dollars in the open markets for foreign exchange, some chose to convert their dollars into gold that the American Treasury was obligated to supply.

More impressive to American authorities was the rapidly rising stock of dollar claims on the United States held by foreign banks (commercial and central) that had not yet been converted. These rose from about $8.95 billion in 1951 to $38.5 billion in 1968 (see Table 2). Thus claims potentially convertible into gold in 1968 amounted to over three and a half times the remaining American gold! Concern with protecting the last American gold reserves and avoiding the inevitable run on the bank prompted the American authorities in the mid-1960s and afterward to pressure "friendly" governments not to convert existing dollar holdings, as was their right under Article IV. Finally, on March 15,

TABLE 2

OFFICIAL GOLD HOLDINGS AND EXTERNAL DOLLAR LIABILITIES
OF THE UNITED STATES (IN $U.S. BILLIONS)

Year	Official World Gold Holdings[1],	U.S. Official Gold Stocks[1]	Outstanding Dollar Claims on U.S. held by Foreign Banks
1951	$33.5	$22.9	$ 8.9
1956	35.7	22.1	15.3
1960	37.7	17.8	21.0
1964	40.5	15.5	29.4
1968	38.7	10.9	38.5
Closing of the American Gold Window			
1972	$38.7	$10.5	$ 82.9
1974	43.5	11.8	119.1
1976	41.1	11.2	151.3

Source: IMF, International Financial Statistics and Data Fund.

[1]Gold is valued throughout at SDR 35 per ounce, equivalent to U.S. $38 per ounce from December 1971 through January 1973, to U.S. $42.22 per ounce from February 1973 through June 1974, to the U.S./SDR value as measured by the "basket" valuation of the SDR beginning with July 1974. After 1968 the open-market price for gold was two or three times this official price. Nevertheless, no major country could sell all of its official gold in the open market without driving the price down quite drastically. Therefore, choosing a "correct" price for evaluation is difficult.

1968, official sales of gold by a consortium of central banks (including the United States Federal Reserve System) on the open private gold market in London were terminated, thus segmenting the official price of gold from the free market price. And subsequently the free-market price has fluctuated well above the official price of $35.00 per ounce, which was raised to $42.00 in 1971. Even though the American gold window was not closed officially by President Nixon until August 1971, negligible American sales of gold to foreign central banks took place after 1968.

Worse than simply "leaning on" foreign central banks not to convert dollars into gold, was the spate of balance-of-payments restrictions on capital outflows imposed by Presidents Kennedy and Johnson: (1) the interest-equalization tax on foreign securities sold in the United States in 1963, (2) the restrictions on bank lending to foreigners in 1965, and (3) attempts to force multinational corporations in 1968 to finance their foreign operations overseas. These were concrete responses to accounting balance-of-payments "deficits"—the overseas build-up of dollar claims on the United States (see Table 2)—that in turn augmented official fears of losing gold. If effective, such restraints would have seriously impeded the key role of the New York capital market in providing dollar liquidity to the rest of the world. Fortunately, these regulatory efforts were undercut by the development of the Eurodollar market centered in London outside the web of American capital controls.[17] Hence, an international capital market continued to provide dollar liquidity as well as to bring net savers and investors together. And the American balance-of-payments restrictions themselves were eventually terminated in 1974.

From Table 2, it is clear that the build-up of dollar claims on the American gold stock as the world economy grew would sooner or later force termination of the American Treasury's unlimited obligation to convert extant dollars into gold,[18] and that balance-of-payments restrictions that contributed to the market's nervousness would be ultimately self-defeating. America's principal international monetary obligation was not the pro forma link to gold but rather the maintenance of stable dollar prices of internationally tradable goods as well as an open capital market. This it did successfully throughout the 1950s and early 1960s (see Table 1). However, severe inflationary pressure developed in the United States in the middle and late 1960s that ultimately cracked the system of fixed exchange rates, and ended the international harmonization of stable monetary policies across the world's major industrial economies.

Uncertainly Pegged Exchange Rates and the International Transmission of Inflation (1968–1973)

There has never been a great inflation that has not been preceded or accompanied by large increases in the nominal supply of money. Nevertheless, plenty of observers, including government authorities, are always available to point out special "nonmonetary" circumstances associated with high or rising prices. In the great German hyperinflation of 1922–1923, where both prices and cash balances increased by several thousand-fold, people could blame the unfair burdens imposed on Germany by the Treaty of Versailles and the French occupation of the Ruhr as somehow directly pushing prices up.[19] Similarly, in the great world inflation that began in the late 1960s but broke with full force in 1973–1975 (Table 3), "special" circumstances abounded: crop failures in Russia and India, the disappearance of anchovies off the coast of Peru, the formation of the OPEC oil cartel in 1973–1974, and so on. Into 1976, one could note the freezing of Brazilian coffee trees and the general feeling of the Club of Rome that we are running out of natural resources.

Some of these special circumstances may have had indirect monetary consequences. However, I shall stress the remarkable loss of monetary control among the major industrial economies concurrently in the last years of the fixed exchange-rate regime. The aggregate money supply of the 10 industrial countries cited in Tables 3 and 4 grew about 12 percent per annum in the 1971–1973 period as compared to a little over 7 percent in the preceding 10 years (Table 4). What lay behind this unfortunate orchestration of international monetary events?

For countries other than the United States, incipient or actual balance of payments surpluses or deficits—measured according to the "official settlements"[20] definition—have the immediate impact of increasing or reducing the domestic money supply. For example, if the German Bundesbank actively enters the foreign-exchange market to buy dollars with deutsche marks to prevent the DM from appreciating, then the DM reserves of German commercial banks—an important component in the nation's monetary base—are increased directly. Unless the German government takes direct countervailing action (which is difficult to do successfully), the stock of deutsche marks available to individual households and firms in Germany will expand. This increased monetary liquidity then induces people to increase their demand for both tradable and nontradable goods and services, and thus bids up their prices measured in DM. From the end of 1970 to the end of 1973, the Bundesbank purchased about $U.S.14 billion in the open market for foreign exchange, with the extraordinary impact on the German monetary base indicated in Figure 2.[21]

In the pegged exchange-rate system, therefore, inflationary pressure originating in the "center" country, that is, the United States, took two complementary channels for inflating prices in the rest of the world. (1) The direct increase in the dollar prices of tradable goods (see Table 1) automatically raised tradable goods prices in deutsche marks, kronor, sterling, and so on unless these countries took discretionary action to appreciate their currencies in terms of dollars. (2) The heavy pressure on aggregate demand in the United States also sharply deteriorated the American trade balance. This deterioration helped to precipitate capital flight from the United States as people speculated that the dollar would eventually be devalued. These current-account and capital-account movements together caused inherently stable countries like Germany to run large balance-of-payments surpluses—the foreign counterpart of the American deficits. This led to unwanted increases in the domestic money supplies in Germany, Japan, Sweden, and so on that added further pressure to increase the world price level, perhaps with a lag of one or two years.

Although this international mechanism for the transmission of inflation is largely monetary in nature, one need not be a pure "monetarist" in explaining the origins of the inflation in the United States. With the inauguration of Presi-

TABLE 3

INFLATION (CONSUMER PRICE INDEX): ANNUAL OR ANNUALIZED PERCENTAGE
CHANGES OF PERIOD AVERAGES FOR SELECT COUNTRIES

From Prior Year in Percent	U.S.	Canada	Japan	U.K.	Germany	France	Italy	Netherlds	Belgium	Switzld	10 Countries Combined
Weights	.4705	.0518	.1257	.0630	.1108	.0830	.0481	.0192	.0150	.0130	
Actual 1960	1.5	1.3	3.7	1.0	1.5	4.1	2.3	2.7	0.3	1.4	2.0
1961	1.1	0.9	5.2	3.5	2.3	2.4	2.1	1.2	1.0	1.9	2.0
1962	1.2	1.2	6.8	4.1	3.0	5.2	4.7	2.4	1.4	4.3	2.8
1963	1.2	1.7	6.3	2.1	3.0	5.0	7.4	3.2	2.1	3.4	2.8
1964	1.3	1.8	3.8	3.2	2.3	3.2	5.9	5.9	4.2	3.1	2.4
1965	1.6	2.4	6.7	4.8	3.3	2.7	4.5	4.8	4.1	3.4	3.0
1966	3.0	3.8	5.0	3.8	3.5	2.6	2.4	5.7	4.2	4.7	3.4
1967	2.8	3.6	4.0	2.6	1.7	2.8	3.2	3.5	2.9	4.0	2.9
1968	4.2	4.1	5.3	4.7	1.7	4.5	1.3	3.7	2.7	2.4	3.9
1969	5.4	4.5	5.3	5.4	3.1	6.0	2.7	7.4	3.7	2.5	5.0
1970	5.9	3.4	7.6	6.4	3.3	5.8	4.9	3.6	4.0	3.6	5.6
1971	4.3	2.8	6.1	9.4	5.3	5.4	5.0	7.5	4.3	6.6	5.1
1972	3.3	4.8	4.5	7.1	5.5	9.2	5.6	7.8	5.5	6.7	4.8
1973	6.2	7.6	11.8	9.2	6.9	7.4	10.8	8.0	6.9	8.7	7.7
1974	11.0	10.9	24.4	16.0	7.0	13.5	19.2	9.6	12.7	9.8	13.2
1975	9.2	10.7	11.9	24.3	5.9	11.8	17.0	10.2	12.8	6.7	10.8

Source: Reprinted with permission from Harold van B. Cleveland and W. H. Bruce Brittain, The Great Inflation: A Monetarist View (Washington, D.C.: National Planning Association, Committee on Changing International Realities, 1976), p. 54.

TABLE 4

MONEY SUPPLY FOR NARROWLY DEFINED PERIOD AVERAGES: ANNUAL OR ANNUALIZED
PERCENTAGE CHANGES OF PERIOD AVERAGES FOR SELECT COUNTRIES

From Prior Year in Percent	U.S.	Canada	Japan	U.K.	Germany	France	Italy	Netherlds	Belgium	Switzld	10 Countries Combined
Weights	.4705	.0518	.1257	.0630	.1108	.0830	.0481	.0192	.0150	.0130	
Actual 1960	−0.1	1.3	19.9	3.3	9.3	11.2	13.0	5.2	2.1	7.3	5.5
1961	2.1	5.2	25.1	0.7	9.3	16.4	14.1	7.8	5.2	14.7	8.0
1962	2.2	3.3	16.0	−0.0	11.0	16.9	17.8	5.7	7.0	10.4	7.0
1963	2.9	5.9	26.4	6.2	7.3	16.7	17.1	9.7	9.9	8.0	8.8
1964	4.0	5.1	16.8	5.4	8.4	10.1	7.3	8.5	5.6	5.5	7.0
1965	4.3	6.3	16.8	3.1	8.9	9.1	12.7	10.9	7.8	4.5	7.4
1966	4.6	6.9	16.3	3.1	4.3	8.9	15.1	7.2	6.7	2.6	7.0
1967	4.0	9.7	13.4	3.8	3.4	7.1	13.1	7.0	4.3	3.0	6.1
1968	7.1	4.3	14.6	4.6	7.5	5.7	13.3	8.8	6.6	9.5	8.0
1969	6.0	7.5	18.4	5.2	8.2	4.3	15.1	9.5	4.8	5.4	8.2
1970	3.9	2.2	18.3	6.7	6.5	0.2	21.7	10.6	5.6	4.9	6.8
1971	6.7	12.8	25.5	12.9	11.7	13.5	22.8	16.7	9.9	16.5	12.0
1972	7.1	13.9	22.0	14.7	13.8	12.9	17.9	17.8	12.7	17.5	12.0
1973	7.5	14.5	26.2	8.6	5.9	10.8	21.1	7.4	12.7	2.2	11.0
1974	5.5	9.8	13.2	5.5	6.0	10.8	17.1	3.1	8.6	0.1	7.6
1975	4.2	13.7	10.4	16.3	14.1	11.8	7.7	18.6	11.7	4.6	8.5

Source: Reprinted with permission from Harold van B. Cleveland and W. H. Bruce Brittain, *The Great Inflation: A Monetarist View* (Washington, D.C.: National Planning Association, Committee on Changing International Realities, 1976), p. 56.

billions of dollars

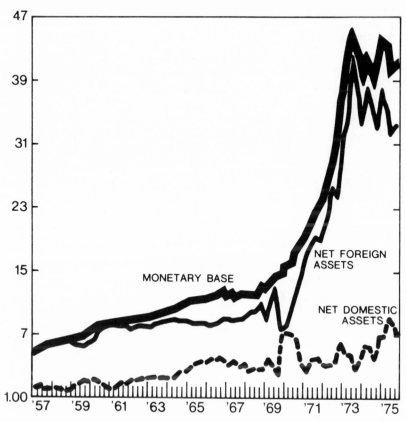

Figure 2. Sources of the German Monetary Base

Source: Reprinted with permission from Harold van B. Cleveland and W. H. Bruce Brittain, *The Great Inflation: A Monetarist View* (Washington, D.C.: National Planning Association, Committee on Changing International Realities, 1976), p. 36.

dent Kennedy in 1961, fiscal policy became increasingly expansionist in the United States, leading to the major policy error under Lyndon Johnson of spending to fight a substantial war in Vietnam while simultaneously introducing costly new social programs that were inadequately financed by duly legislated taxation, and which were beyond the fiscal control of succeeding administrations. Alternatively, one can make a case that the United States' money supply expanded after 1961 more rapidly than it had in the 1950s.[22] However, American money supply growth in 1971–1973, although significant, was not as great as that induced in many trading partners (see Table 4). Perhaps lags are important. In any event, I take the more eclectic view that expansionary macroeconomic policy with fiscal and monetary origins in the center country touched off the great world inflation that is with us yet.

Although only a moderate increase in the statistics on indigenous growth in the American money supply is apparent in the early 1970s, one can make a somewhat more definite statement. The asymmetrical exchange-rate position of the United States vis-à-vis other countries acted to prevent American balance-of-payments deficits from automatically contracting the monetary base of the United States. Even though European and Japanese balance-of-payments surpluses induced substantial monetary expansion as described above, the monetary impact in the United States of the corresponding American payments deficits was fully sterilized. To oversimplify somewhat, when foreign central banks buy "dollars" in the open markets for foreign exchange they do not withdraw those dollars from monetary circulation in the United States. Instead, dollar checking accounts on the Federal Reserve System or on American commercial banks are used immediately to buy U.S. Treasury bills or longer-term Treasury bonds. Hence, no monetary contraction within the United States automatically occurs.[23] In summary, in the world economy the expansionary monetary effect of European and Japanese balance-of-payments surpluses in the 1969–1973 period was not offset by any monetary contraction caused by the equivalent American deficits.[24]

Automatic sterilization of the center country's payments deficits becomes a defect in the world's monetary system only when that country itself is unstable—as the United States has been from the late 1960s. If not abused, however, this unique monetary independence given to the center country in a world of fixed exchange rates can work well. American dollar prices were very stable from 1951 to the mid-1960s (see Table 1), making it much easier for other countries to maintain their own macroeconomic stability. Therefore, allowing the accumulation of dollar claims by Europeans, in, say, the 1950s to force a monetary contraction in the United States would have been entirely inappropriate. Thus it need not be desirable to force American monetary policy to respond mechanically to the state of American foreign payments, unless such monetary rules are carefully hedged.

Even though it was not playing by the mechanical rules of the classical gold standard, the United States still had the important international responsibility to maintain price stability in dollar terms. The abrogation of this obligation after 1968 (1966?) was finally enough to drive other industrial countries away from fixed exchange-rate parities[25] by 1973 in a crisis atmosphere. The new regime of floating exchange rates then allowed other industrial economies to establish independent control over their domestic money supplies. Most LDCs, however, continue to peg their exchange rates in one way or another—largely to the U.S. dollar.

Freely Floating Exchange Rates (1973–Present)

After such a debacle in the foreign exchange markets, and with the residue of high world price inflation that is not yet under control, the world dollar standard—which had been with us in one form or another since 1945—would seem to be finished. Yet, even though the forms have changed, I suggest that much of the substance remains.

Although traumatic at times, the transition to floating exchange rates among the currencies of the major industrial economies allowed the preservation of currency convertibility for both residents and nonresidents of these countries.

Thus, the socialist economies of Eastern Europe, the hundred or more less developed countries, and the residents of the industrial economies can continue to use twenty or so "Western" currencies to invoice their exports and make payments for imports. In contrast, the inconvertible currencies of these socialist economies and LDCs still are unusable as monetary vehicles for international trade.[26] Fortunately, we have been spared the proliferation of exchange controls among industrial countries that characterized the floating exchange-rate system of the 1930s. Private individuals or firms or communist-state trading monopolies can freely buy or sell goods in international markets by using one of the convertible currencies as a unit of account and means of payment. Poland may invoice many of its exports in deutsche marks, whereas Argentina invoices most of its exports in U.S. dollars. The demonetization of international trade and relapse to bilateral barter that characterized the 1930s have been avoided. Indeed, world trade has continued to grow relative to national outputs since 1973.

But among the twenty or so effectively convertible currencies, an asymmetrical two-tier system still exists. Nonbank enterprises may invoice or make payments in any of the twenty convertible currencies as described above. However, banking systems everywhere continue to rely heavily on the U.S. dollar as the prime vehicle currency for commercial banks and intervention currency for central banks. The American dollar is still interbank money internationally, even when nonbank firms and enterprises do not use it directly.

Suppose that a commercial bank is asked to sell Australian dollars in order to buy French francs to facilitate the importation of French automobiles into Australia. The commercial bank will first sell the Australian dollars for U.S. dollars, and then use the U.S. dollars to acquire French francs for its Australian customer. The U.S. dollar is similarly used as an intermediary currency for forward-exchange market transactions, in which foreign currency is contracted for at a stipulated price and is payable at the future date when delivery occurs. The reason for so using the U.S. dollar is to greatly reduce the number of foreign-exchange markets[27]—and rates quoted in those markets by private foreign-exchange dealers.

Even with the ending of their fixed-parity obligation in 1973, central banks continue to intervene heavily in the foreign exchange markets to smooth the surprisingly large exchange-rate movements (see Table 1) among the convertible currencies. For the most part, the U.S. dollar is still the prime intervention currency, and foreign official reserves are mainly held in U.S. dollars. And for this system to work without conflict, the U.S. Federal Reserve System must still remain passive. When the Bank of Canada intervenes to buy Canadian dollars with American dollars to keep the Canadian dollar from falling below, say, U.S. $0.95, the Federal Reserve System simply smiles and does not set any exchange-rate target of its own.

Any international monetary "reform" that attempts to terminate the key-currency role of the United States dollar simply to make the system more symmetrical among nations in a pro forma sense would be quite dangerous; it would mistakenly encourage the American government to undertake an independent exchange-rate policy without regard for its effect on other nations.

For example, in the early months of 1977, high American officials expressed unhappiness about the alleged "undervaluation" of the Japanese yen in terms of dollars.[28] Whatever the advantages of publically chastizing the Japanese, it would be entirely inappropriate for the Federal Reserve System to enter the foreign-exchange market directly and purchase yen with dollars. To avoid international conflict, the Japanese government should be discreetly persuaded of the merits of the American case. Then the Bank of Japan can take the appropriate action in the foreign-exchange markets. Germany and Japan are probably the only two countries large enough to warrant even this limited pressure from the United States—and then only in unusual circumstances.

Thus benign passivity by the United States in its official exchange-rate targets, and its willingness to let the dollar be used on a worldwide basis as interbank money, remain key elements in maintaining currency convertibility under fluctuating exchange rates. And having an open capital market in dollars, where foreigners can enter freely as depositors or borrowers, is an essential source of "international" finance for the rest of the world: a source that cannot easily be replicated by any other country or institution, such as the International Monetary Fund. Today what the United States does still determines whether or not international trade will be effectively monetized and multilateral.

In the breakdown of fixed exchange rates, what has been lost, for better or for worse, is the direct and pervasive influence that the United States once had on the domestic monetary policies of other industrial countries. Flexible exchange rates better allow other countries to insulate their money supplies not only from American policies, but from each others' policies as well. Instead of having the more or less common international price level for tradable goods of the 1950s and 1960s, in the mid-1970s Germany and Switzerland are selecting lower rates of price inflation than the United States, whereas the United Kingdom, Italy, and France are selecting markedly higher rates (see Table 3). Unfortunately, continuing uncertainty about these differing relative rates of inflation is the prime cause of substantial day-to-day and month-to-month fluctuations in foreign exchange rates (see Figure 1). Hence, the international values of national monies are not as stable as before, and international commerce—on both the production and the consumption sides—is somewhat less efficient.

Of course, a return to monetary stability in the United States can induce other industrial countries to voluntarily fix their exchange rates vis-à-vis the U.S. dollar again, resulting in greater international monetary harmony.

Even under flexible exchange rates, however, the dollar-based convertible currency system can still be undermined. Suppose that monetary instability of the kind generated in the later 1960s in the United States was to escalate, making the dollar unacceptable either as a reserve asset or as a vehicle currency. Attempts to unload existing dollar reserves could then cause wild exchange-rate fluctuations and payments restrictions among Western convertible currencies that would send us back to bilateral barter and uninhibited protectionism.

Hence, the United States' own role in stabilizing the world's monetary system should be, first, to avoid further debasement of the U.S. dollar—i.e., to avoid domestic price inflation—and second, to maintain a passively open foreign trade and payments mechanism. Neither policy conflicts with any reasonably posed domestic economic goals for "a new America."

REFERENCES

[1] They were the product of purely British-American negotiations. Canada acted as an umpire or "honest broker" between the British delegation, headed by John Maynard Keynes, and the American delegation, headed by Harry Dexter White. The White Plan eventually became the principal basis of the IMF charter.

[2] From the outset of the Bretton Woods agreements, many countries in Latin America, Asia, and Africa continually adjusted (devalued) their largely inconvertible currencies mainly to compensate for high and unstable internal rates of inflation.

[3] "The significance of the [IMF] agreements reached in Jamaica in January 1976 is that they make· provision for legalizing the existing nonsystem governing international monetary relations. . . ." John Williamson, "The Benefits and Cost of an International Monetary System," in E. M. Bernstein et al., *Reflections on Jamaica*, Essays in International Finance, no. 115 (April 1976): 54.

[4] It is interesting to note that only 11 currencies are independently floating, 7 are floating jointly (the European Snake), and the 105 remaining members of the IMF (mainly less developed countries, or LDCs), peg to a convertible currency of a major industrial economy. IMF *Annual Report*, 1975. Most of the 105 currencies are inconvertible for international commerce and make use of waivers in the IMF's charter.

[5] The same problem afflicts multilateral trade among Eastern European countries—none of which has convertible currencies—to the present day. See Chapter III of my *Money in International Exchange: The Convertible-Currency System* (New York: Oxford University Press, 1978).

[6] Peter Coffey and John R. Presley, *European Monetary Integration* (London: Macmillan, 1971), p. 5.

[7] Substantial effort being made to ensure that each European country received a fair share.

[8] See G. M. Meier (ed.), *International Economic Reform—Collected Papers of Emile Despres* (New York: Oxford University Press, 1973), pp. 30–31.

[9] The first Intra-European Payments Scheme in 1948 was still mainly bilateral in character. Certain bilateral deficits between any pair of European countries were financed by Marshall dollar credits, thus avoiding the need for strict bilateral balance in trading transactions. The second Intra-European Payments Scheme in 1949 took some small steps toward multilateralism, but intra-European trade was still negotiated through formal bilateral agreements. For a more detailed account of these early schemes, see Coffey and Presley, *European Monetary Integration*, and Robert Triffin, *Europe and the Money Muddle* (New Haven: Yale Univeristy Press, 1957).

[10] Without even a small margin or band of exchange-rate variation of the kind that was permitted under the Bretton-Woods agreements, which was later to characterize the "fixed" exchange-rate system of the 1960s. This avoided ambiguity in ascertaining the exact dollar value of monetary claims within the union at the end of each month.

[11] Randall Hinshaw, "Toward European Convertibility," in *Princeton Essays in International Finance*, no. 31 (November 1958): 16. Hinshaw also demonstrates how a more normal "open market" in foreign exchange transacting developed after 1953. Within Europe, traders began to exchange one currency for another by the media of commercial banks. The proportion of transactions channeled through, and approved by, central banks to be cleared by the EPU progressively diminished.

[12] *The International Monetary Fund 1945–65*, Volume III: Documents (Washington D.C., 1969), p. 189.

[13] An ever increasing number of ex-British colonies continued to fix their exchange rates in terms of sterling; and a similar overseas franc area was maintained in Africa among ex-French colonies. Canada floated without an official par value from 1950 to 1962. Otherwise, virtually all other members of the IMF did define their exchange parities in dollars.

[14] Among LDCs these parities were frequently changed. Note that it is sufficient to establish all the cross rates of exchange in the system if each country intervenes against a common intervention currency, e.g., the U.S. dollar.

[15] Of course, countries suffering from often massive internal inflations—such as Argentina, Brazil, and Chile—could maintain neither fixed parities nor convertible currencies.

[16] This process is described in more analytical depth by C. P. Kindleberger in "Balance of Payments Deficits and the International Market for Liquidity," in *Princeton Essays in International Finance*, no. 46 (May 1965).

[17] A more complete description of the fascinating financial phenomena of Eurocurrency trading can be found in Chapter 9 in my *Money in International Exchange: The Convertible-Currency System*.

[18] Britain managed the pre-1914 gold standard with even more slender gold reserves behind extant sterling claims. But everyone realized that the Bank of England would undertake a contractionary monetary policy to defend itself against gold losses, unlike the Federal Reserve System in the 1960s.

[19] It would, of course, be legitimate to go one step further and ask the additional question of

whether these external imposed burdens made it inevitable that the Wiemar authorities would lose monetary control.

[20]Roughly speaking, the cumulative volume of official purchases of foreign exchange (U.S. dollars) in the course of a year needed to maintain an official exchange-rate peg.

[21]See *International Financial Statistics* as of May 1976. Whereas such overt balance-of-payments surpluses in 1969–1973 best explain monetary expansion in countries such as Germany, Japan, and Scandinavia, incipient balance-of-payments surplus still contributed to monetary inflation in countries such as Britain, Italy, and France. Incipient surpluses in these latter countries allowed faster monetary expansion by domestic means without incurring unmanageable foreign payments deficits. For a nice description of these various monetary transmission mechanisms, see Harold van B. Cleveland and W. H. Bruce Brittain, *The Great Inflation: A Monetarist View* (Washington, D.C.: National Planning Association, 1976).

[22]As has been done very impressively by Jurg Niehans in "How to Fill an Empty Shell," *American Economic Review* (May 1976): 177–183.

[23]This system is in contrast to the workings of the classical gold standard prior to 1914, when gold losses would have induced an "automatic" American monetary contraction.

[24]A description of the technical details associated with this automatic sterilization, and what might be done to change it, can be found in R. McKinnon, "A New Tripartite Monetary Agreement or a Limping Dollar Standard?" *Princeton Essays in International Finance*, no. 106 (October 1974).

[25]An exception is some very loose arrangements among a small group of European countries with a nonpermanent membership—the European Snake.

[26]For example, the Swedish economist Sven Grassman has demonstrated that all of Swedish trade with Eastern Europe or less developed countries is invoiced either in Swedish kronor or in the currency of some third industrial country—mainly dollars or deutsche marks. S. Grassman, *Exchange Reserves and the Financial Structure of Foreign Trade* (Saxon House, Lexington Books, 1973).

[27]In a world of N national currencies, where all possible exchange rates are quoted symmetrically, there will be $N(N - 1)/2$ rates to quote! However, if all rates are quoted only against a single vehicle currency—the U.S. dollar—the number of exchange markets is then reduced to $N - 1$.

[28]The large Japanese trade surplus in 1977 need not reflect undervaluation of the yen. American and Japanese price levels do not appear to be disaligned. Rather, the surplus more likely reflects the high propensity to save in Japan relative to the current flow of investment opportunities.

PIERRE NORA

America and the French Intellectuals

JIMMY CARTER AND Alexander Solzhenitsyn may one day enjoy the unexpected privilege of having their names associated with a chapter of French cultural history: namely, that curious moment when the negative remodeling of the image of socialism in the latter's work seems to have favored a rehabilitation of the image of America, as symbolized by the former's election. Such a turnaround would not be unthinkable if the freeze between the two cultures only came from the cold, that is to say, from the fascination exerted on France, at least since the war, by the country which, for sympathizers and opponents alike, is supposed to embody "the fatherland of socialism." But the roots of the issue go deeper. For reasons which neither psychoanalysis[1] nor politics[2] can explain, a strange impermeability has always separated the two cultures. Despite a handful of brilliant exceptions who remain relatively unrecognized in their own country,[3] despite a small, permanent group of advocates whose reasonable arguments have never seemed to have had much of an impact on the debate,[4] the United States has never occupied the central position in the mental geography of French intellectuals which England held in the eighteenth century, Germany in the nineteenth, or the Soviet Union and the Third World in the twentieth. A reflection, an offshoot of Europe: that is how America is always seen; the intelligentsia of the Old World has not yet discovered the New World.

If one wishes to investigate this mystery, the past thirty years would certainly provide an excellent starting point. It is not just that they describe a major cycle during which the United States moved from the lowest of mythological reputations to a less uninformed and more realistic appraisal—for this curve is limited to the level of public opinion. It is also that in this period one can decipher the clearly legible and conveniently concentrated reasons for a constant: namely, the fact that, despite the richness of its historical repertoire and the vastness of its territorial expanse, America has never constituted a positive pole of attraction within the European system of reference.

Indeed, as France, already after World War I and especially since World War II, gradually lost the reality of great power status to become a small hexagonal country, and even as the United States was acceding nolens volens to the responsibilities of a leading world power, French culture as a whole seems to have reacted with a compensatory self-defense reflex—a sort of reconquest on the cultural level of the "leadership" it had lost on the political level. Inclined to be garbed in folklore or Parisian faddishness, it was a rivalry that had no importance or real weight in the balance of international power. It was doubtless irritating and disconcerting. Yet this paltry, decisive stance is perhaps the key to a profound disagreement: a conflict of universality.[5] Which of the two countries, all questions of power aside, still seems to be the locus of exportable values? Culturally speaking, which is the province of the other, America or France?

The Europeanization of America

Remember, it was not so long ago: America was never more absent from Europe than during the years of its military and economic presence, after the Liberation. The cold war had its counterpart in America in the cold ideology,[6] against which France reacted with a mixture of political aggressivity and intellectual ignorance, doubtless aggravated by a profound sense of guilt toward the country that had come to save Europe from disaster for the second time in half a century: the trauma of the Liberation was settled by a major excommunication of the liberators. At no other moment would an inventory of stereotypes disclose anti-American reactions as convulsive and as deeply felt as those one saw in the France of 1947, impoverished by the war, ill equipped to regain its "rank,"[7] reduced to the role of a thankless beggar of the Marshall Plan.[8] The United States was not a country, but a sin. The execution of the Rosenbergs and witch-hunts were the real America.

In this sense, the 1950s merely continued the thrust of the war; the fight against fascism had only changed labels. And yet, one wonders whether such a visceral reaction does not suggest an implicit, jealous recognition of the exceptional nature of the American adventure that was unfolding safely out of range of the old continental maledictions. However isolated the intellectuals may have been politically, their anti-Americanism expressed a deep popular sentiment, an injured nationalism. One can find proof of this a contrario in the pro-American arguments of the advocates of "atlantisme." Take for example that major text of the cold war, the "Appel aux intellectuels,"[9] in which the Malraux of the "Rassemblement du Peuple Français" (R.P.F.) attempts to deny the United States' "claim to the cultural heritage of the world":

> First point: there is no culture in America that claims to be specifically American; that is an invention of Europeans. . . . Once Europe is eliminated, American culture becomes a field of technical knowledge rather than a domain of organic culture. . . . It is Europe which still defends the highest intellectual values of the world. . . . What is the fate of Europe within the Soviet structure? The Atlantic civilization appeals to, and basically still respects, Europe as a culture; the Soviet structure disdains its past, detests its present and will only accept a future in which absolutely nothing will remain of what Europe was. . . . Only to the precise extent that Europe resigns from it can there be a hypothesis of a specifically American culture opposed to ours.

The text speaks for itself: America exists only in its mass arts—the movies, the detective story[10]—and in the novels of William Faulkner[11]—that is, in folklore, lowlife, and the South. Meanwhile, Hegel and Heidegger are being discovered, Marx is being published in French[12]: none of which encourages a serious consideration of the American reality. The border that is being disputed is the one that passed, at that time, between orthodox Marxist-Leninism in its Stalinist version illustrated by Aragon,[13] and Sartre's humanist existentialism.[14] The Atlantic frontier, however, remained intellectually closed.

The rebuff came all the more readily that the two types of Americans who had an intellectual interest in France were themselves prejudiced. There were those who overestimated France and underrated America because they felt marginal at home; like Edmund Wilson, for example, they would profess a slightly old-fashioned admiration for the French "art de vivre" and cuisine, while generally ignoring the changing political and social realities of France. Others—the majority—saw only a Europe that was stricken in its vital energies, that was politically unstable and cloistered in the narcissistic contemplation of its past glory. Each type accused the other of provincialism.

Ethical condemnation led to cultural blindness. France loftily dismissed American sociology, history, psychology, and economics, for it seemed as if the American intellectuals of the late forties and fifties were exclusively bent on erecting a rational and scientific framework for the American conscience that would make of Truman's, Eisenhower's, and even Kennedy's United States "The First New Nation" (to borrow Lipset's term): a kind of historical "monad" unlike any other national endeavor, which could be explained only by original concepts and was answerable only to its own history. A country comparable to others only inasmuch as they would all have to pass through "the stages of growth."[15] In history, there was the so-called school of consensus which "reconstructed"[16] American history by means of the concepts of continuity, conservatism, liberalism, and individualism—concepts which, for the first time since Puritan providentialism, owed nothing to the old dialectics of the European type. In sociology, Talcott Parsons and his school seemed to be raising a monument to American self-justification, a theory of social harmony, a closed system of social and national integration. The notion of "the end of ideology,"[17] which Raymond Aron popularized in France, as well as that of the "affluent society,"[18] met with success only among the candidates to the École Nationale d'Administration. On that score, American culture has borne the brunt of a long-standing debate which continues to divide French intellectuals. All of postwar French thought developed precisely out of a reaction to positivism—which, in fact, America, the inheritor of a certain scientific and analytically-minded nineteenth century, carried on. And the very fact that during these same years, psychoanalytic practice, which was perceived in Europe as a last stronghold of dissidence, was being used as a technique of social integration in the United States, only tended to fuel French mistrust for a model of society which applied it as a means of "functionalizing" all forms of negativity. For the intelligensia, the American social sciences—with their assumptions of rationalization and efficiency, and the correlation they apparently made between economic growth, democratic progress, and the decline of ideological fervor—all seemed too manifestly intended to cement the American consensus to be seen as anything else than diabolical, insidious tools of Yankee imperialism.

In America, this block of certainties was slowly dissolved by the crisis of the sixties, from which the United States emerged less sure of its exceptional destiny, but more certain of its vocation. For paradoxically, the groundswell that threw the whole country into upheaval, from the civil rights movement on through Vietnam, Watergate, and the election of Jimmy Carter, led to a seemingly contradictory result: it put America's claim to exceptionality into question, yet at the same time reconfirmed it. Was the United States now a quasi-Europe or a super-Europe? In either case, it seemed back in the Old World.

The myth of American infallibility came to an end, and with it died a tradition which had been consciously entertained since the end of the Civil War. The bankruptcy of the ruling classes, the revolt of the disadvantaged and of the various ethnic groups in effect desacralized the hegemonic social model of the WASP elite, as well as the model of growth which equated happiness with wealth, individual fulfillment with the expansion of capitalism—the "democratic contract" that Tocqueville saw as the core of American success. The universalism which narrowly associated idealism with imperialism was also desacralized, even as, at the height of the Vietnam War, it still clung to something like Theodore Roosevelt's article of faith during the Spanish-American War: "Charity demands we impose American institutions on the entire world." Finally, the political and institutional system crowned by the office of the Presidency itself no longer seemed sacred after it had been profaned by Watergate. In short, all the principles which underlay the supposed exceptionalness of the American system were called into question.

Suddenly, the same historical schema, the same type of analysis of the destiny of men, societies, and nations, could be applied at home and abroad. In politics, the diplomacy of Henry Kissinger, that old Bismarckian practitioner of Realpolitik, symbolized the change. France dropped its policy of cultural arrogance and hastened to jump onto the revisionist American bandwagon; it was all the more inclined to overestimate European influence on America that the latter appeared eager to burn what it had once revered and to revere what it had burned in the past. Indeed, a whole range of intellectual phenomena seemed to attest to this: the outbreak of historical radicalism, the debate over slavery, the decline of the "melting-pot" ideal, the dissemination of a certain brand of Marxism (mainly via the Frankfurt School), the abandonment of optimistic models of growth and the entirely new attention given to all aspects of economic lag, the limited but definite influence of historiography as practiced by the *Annales* group, the appearance of the Freudian Left and of antipsychiatry. Though France immediately mistook the part for the whole, the peripheral for the central, intellectual decolonization had nevertheless been achieved. America had rejoined the ranks of the mortal nations.

But at the same time, a European looking on from the outside is struck by the typically American nature of this crisis and the way in which it was reabsorbed solely by the virtues of the American system. For what was it that gave force to the different forms of protest—whether political, ethnic, or ecological—if not a desire to return to the ideal of America's original promise, to the founding message? What did the utopian trend express, if not a desire to adapt to the late twentieth century the ideals of justice and equality whose failure and perversion were apparent everywhere? Thus, although American democracy had undoubtedly passed through a crisis, it was far from finished. The United States has never ceased being an ideological nation in the sense that the Soviet

Union is an ideological state. It has merely traded one consensus for another,[19] egalitarian legitimacy based on the group[20] for egalitarian legitimacy based on the individual, in order to continue as a nation "puzzled and prospering beyond example in the history of man," to use one of Jefferson's favorite phrases. Thus, too, there was no break but rather a continuity between the crisis of the sixties and the new America of Carter—who appears as the institutional translation of revolutionary protest. Not that the former governor of Georgia has anything of a revolutionary about him. But in this land without roots, his election has taken the proportions of a pilgrimage back to sources: the land, the Bible, the faith in basic American values. It confirms once again the American habit of making every innovation pay tribute to tradition (New Liberty, New Freedom, New Nationalism, New Frontier), the need to root the present in the most distant past, to invoke the promises of the Founding Fathers, the fruits of an eternal future, in moments of crisis. In America, as Paul Valéry once said, one backs into the future.[21] Within the last thirty years, the United States has evolved in the eyes of Europe from something intolerable into something familiar, from the twenty-first century back to the eighteenth, from something Europe could never be into something it will never be again.

The Turning Point

In this major reassessment of the American image, the years 1956–1958 played a determining role in France. Destalinization, Gaullism, economic growth, the Algerian War: this was the turning point. During those two years there appeared almost simultaneously the phenomena which affected, each in its own indirect and ambiguous way, the image of America.

The most decisive of these events was of course Khrushchev's report to the Twentieth Party Congress, soon followed by the Budapest uprising. The great diaspora of Communist intellectuals had begun. Up until then, ever since the war and the Resistance, morality and reason, truth and justice had appeared to be on the same side. Now the revolutionary pattern had to be reinvested elsewhere: Cuba, China, Algeria—most did just that. But all the same, for some—for many—the liberation from Marxist-Leninist orthodoxy resulted in a more attentive curiosity about America, which was no longer looked on as our future, but as our present. In the land of Voltaire, there will always be Candides who are mainly interested in tending their own gardens first.

Another factor was crucial in determining the direction of this evolution: Gaullism, both in its political and its economic aspects. Politically, there was General de Gaulle's anti-Americanism. The electoral equilibrium of the Fifth Republic rested on a foreign policy of friendly relations with the Soviet Union and an aggressive independance vis-à-vis the United States—for this policy, with its "system of reciprocal and controlled aggression" which Annie Kriegel has described,[22] neutralized the domestic Communists. But, because General de Gaulle had personally decided to conduct the anti-American campaign, the intellectual Left, out of anti-Gaullism, found itself in a position to reconsider its anti-Americanism. All things considered, though, this was less important than the second aspect of Gaullism: the economic boom which experts had predicted as early as 1954 and which public opinion began registering in 1956. The intelligentsia, still reeling from the Twentieth Party Congress, could no longer ignore, and even the French Communist Party had to face, the incontrovertible evidence and abandon its obsolete dogma of the "absolute pauperization of the working class." The rise in the standard of living obliged one to think in terms of reform, to try to secure a status for gradual change in a society which, it was still agreed, must not remain quiescent. Whereas Americans mainly noticed the nationalistic rhetoric of Gaullism, the French took note primarily of the profound industrial transformation that was shortly to acquire such importance under the aegis of Georges Pompidou.

It was during this period that the Club Jean Moulin, the most renowned of the many intellectual circles then flourishing, assembled top civil servants and intellectuals, ideologists and technocrats, economists and philosophers, around the newly found persuasion that the French reality required analyses free of any dogmatism whatsoever. During these years, too, an unobtrusive administrator, François Bloch-Lainé, suddenly entered the limelight with his successful book, *La Réforme de l'Entreprise;* Michel Crozier, and his fellow sociologists trained in the techniques of the American social sciences, launched the concept of the "stagnant society" (*société bloquée*) that was soon to become a byword; the former Communist, Serge Mallet, elaborated the notion of a "new working class" and published articles, even in Sartre's *Les Temps Modernes*, about computers; Raymond Aron was appointed to the Sorbonne and delivered his *Eighteen Lectures on Industrial Society*, which became the first bestseller in France's first paperback series of topical essays. Inevitably these studies of the various problems encountered by industrialized societies referred one back to America, even though the latter had lost some of its exotic appeal. "The New World has ceased to be *another* world," wrote Edgar Morin in the preface to a significant translation[23]:

> Our Americanization has led us to reject the worst aspects of that European contempt for America, that crude deprecation which supposedly expressed our own refinement. . . . American society has ceased to be an "impossible" society for us, a society without political parties with structured ideologies, without any revolutionary protest, containing only technocrats in "human relations" and "public relations." . . . We sense that, from the point of view of civilization, America not only preserves the present of Western civilization, but also the future of the human race. . . .

And what about the Algerian War? François Furet has shown by what subtle detours the perception of the war in France was linked to the success of structuralism, which was the intellectual badge of the period.[24] A historian attentive to the possibly symbolic coincidence of dates cannot but notice that 1955, on the eve of destalinization and the inception of the Algerian War, was precisely the year in which Raymond Aron's *L'Opium des Intellectuels* appeared simultaneously with Lévi-Strauss's *Tristes Tropiques*—the latter work marking the moment when structuralism emerged from the laboratory and suddenly went public to become a fashion, a philosophy, even an ideology. "Lévi-Straussism" shared its hour of glory with "Aronism." As concerns America, however, structuralism is a double-edged phenomenon.

In contrast to existentialism with its debauchery of the philosophy of freedom and its phenomenological analyses of experience, structuralism introduced itself with the modesty of social research, detailed field observations, the respect for facts, monographic scrupulousness and the cult of mathematical models. Above all, structuralism posited itself as a scientist discipline, as a series of procedures that would make it possible, independently of any ideological a priori and beginning with the simplest social and mental mechanisms, to establish certain truths of a scientific order. At the same time, structuralism also illustrated a much more sweeping and decisive turn in French culture—the moment when ideological supremacy began to shift from literature to exact knowledge, from novelistic and philosophic expression to history, economics, ethnology, and linguistics; in short, when it transferred to the so-called human sciences. Now the very language of those human sciences had the effect of drawing cultural life in France both closer to and further away from America. Had not Lévi-Strauss himself spent the long war years in the United States? And even though he had returned with a rather lukewarm taste for the "American way of life" and a confirmed aversion for modern civilization, was he not indebted to the United States, whose museums, libraries, scientific collections, and universities he had admired, for a not inconsiderable part of his intellectual training?

But on the other hand, one cannot silently pass over the fact that whereas structuralism in America has remained an analytical technique by and large restricted to its original field of linguistics, in France it developed out of ethnology during the Algerian War. The Algerian War involved something far different from what those unfamiliar with the intricacies of French politics might have supposed. The ideological tension it created was not based on the traditional opposition between an old nationalistic and colonialist Right and an old internationalist and anticolonialist Left. The gravity of the crisis came from the fact that the integrationist Left, which had believed that Algeria should reap the full benefits of French nationality, now had to convert to the entirely novel idea of Algerian independence. This conversion, which took place very slowly, involved a painful revision of all the mental habits acquired since elementary school, a break with the entire republican tradition concerning the Empire and its colonies[25]; in short, it entailed the birth of a new awareness, the awareness of the Third World—the very term was coined during these years. The Algerian War would not have affected the French conscience so deeply or caused such profound ideological upheavals, had it merely brought traditional currents of thought into conflict. Far more concretely than the lyricism of the Cuban revolution or China's schism, the Algerian War provided an ephemeral but powerful impetus to a new constellation of revolutionary extremism. There is little doubt that the structuralist vessel, well launched on its way by *Tristes Tropiques*, was sped by a wind that blew out of the Algerian War, which contributed largely to the specifically French ideological connotation of this new language of the social sciences.

It is, in fact, highly significant that what Americans call "social sciences" are termed "human sciences" in France. The difference in expressions indicates two different cultural contexts, two national traditions, perhaps even two distinct roles. Whether abstract or empirical, the social sciences in America are an integral part of social development itself. They are included in the social institutions and practices. And that is the reason why they have long been suspected by the French of being docile in principle to their political utilizers. In France, a country with strong humanistic and literary traditions, the human sciences are less attentive to the patient study of facts, and are more interested in theoretical constructs and in their own prophetic role; as such, they constitute a definite political and social stake. They may, as a result, quite rightly be suspected by Americans of tending constantly to deviate toward ideology, like Marxism which participates in both models, the analytic and the prophetic. That is why the recent arrival of these sciences on the French cultural scene has made dialogue between the two countries at once easier and more difficult. France and the United States have begun to be separated merely by a common language, as George Bernard Shaw once said of the Americans and the British. But what does this separation consist of?

The Revolutionary Mortgage

For a long time it was thought that it was the influence of Marxism that constituted the main barrier between the two cultures. This illusion is now losing its force, given the way that current avant-garde thinkers are brutally and boisterously liquidating Marx, without America's position having noticeably changed as a result.

For that matter, the influence of Marxism on intellectuals has gone through several very different phases. After France had haughtily ignored Marx for almost a century[26] (just as it has been particularly unreceptive to Freud), it was the Communist Party which imposed Marxism on it after the war, proclaiming the Soviet Union as its unassailable—and unassailed—seat. Marxism was used less as an instrument for analysis than as an authoritarian argument. From the affirmation of class struggle as the driving force of history to the dictatorship of the proletariat, from the dictatorship of the proletariat to the Soviet Revolution, from the Soviet Union to the Party, and from the Party to the Politburo, the equation drawn by Jdanov once and for all left intellectuals no other role but that of valet, traitor, or aggressor. As for America, it had no place at all. Krushchev's speech at the Twentieth Party Congress put an end to this dogmatism, but at the same time it inaugurated a dissemination of Marxism which was no doubt all the more massive in that it favored a reprieve, a slow-down as it were, to the serious historical analysis of the ever problematic identification of Marxism with the Stalinist adventure. The granite-hard version of Marxism was thus succeeded by a soft, elastic, mealy Marxism—the "impassable horizon of our time," according to Sartre's famous phrase. There was an "existentialist" Marx, a "structuralist" Marx, a "Freudian" Marx, a "Catholic" Marx, and, in reaction to this vulgate, a Marx whom Althusser returned to the diamond purity of Science and Theory.[27]

May 1968 exploded this quiet, steady drone and ushered in a totally new way of looking at America. In their holiday exuberance, the leftists suddenly discovered that most of their themes, born, they believed, from a typically French ménage-à-trois of anarchism, surrealism, and situationism, had in fact been invented on the campuses of America years before. Take their wall slogans: "Objet cache-toi!" "Faites l'amour et pas la guerre!" "Le droit à la paresse!" Reacting with light-hearted anarchism to bureaucratic Stalinism, verbally hostile to the consumer society yet solidly entrenched in it, iconoclastic and utopian, an entire segment of France marvelled at the retrospective discovery of its complicity with the hippies, Zen, Jerry Rubin, the Black Panthers, the underground America of subversion.[28] The rejection of traditional political forms, the acute awareness of the impasses and contradictions of the affluent society, the astute exploitation of the loopholes of the capitalist system and the conversion of its apparent strengths into weaknesses, the decolonialization of the nation's oppressed minorities and underprivileged ethnic groups, the generation gap, the crises of authority, of belief, of civilization: all of this made the United States appear to them as an inexhaustible laboratory of auguries and surprises.[29] The entire post-1968 generation in France experienced a fascination with America, and used it, after it had rid itself of its Maoist straightjacket, as a means of self-discovery.[30] The Internationale of protest seemed far more exciting than the elusive Internationale of workers. Revolutionary Atlanticism passed through an extreme phase of sentimental Americanophilia, which paved the way for deeper upheavals.

Actually what we are witnessing today is a libertarian Left execrating the Marxism which the totalitarian Left had striven so jealously to monopolize. It is to the Gulag and to Alexander Solzhenitsyn that we owe this extraordinary expiatory ceremony taking place under our eyes. Not that there was ever a lack of voices, even leftist ones, ready to denounce, from Trotskyist or other vantage points, the bureaucracy and atrocities of Stalin.[31] But even in the wake of 1956, these voices were immediately discounted by orthodox communist intellectuals, intent on preserving the identification of Marxism with the Soviet Union. Despite the dialectical casuistry which they turned into a fine art, despite the intellectual acrobatics, the hairsplitting and the factual manipulations they increasingly resorted to, it became more and more difficult to deny what Jean Kanapa cautiously labeled at the fourteenth French Party Congress in 1956 "certain violations of socialist legality"—and which finally had to be called "the crimes of Stalin." Furthermore, these crimes had to be explained.[32] But even as the various excuses were dredged up—the famous Russian "lag," Russia's economic backwardness, the traditional barbarity of its customs—the "positive achievements" of Stalinism appeared less and less convincing as an argument for the Marxist identity of the Soviet Union.

Now, ironically, it was this identification which Solzhenitsyn so spectacularly reconfirmed in the grand accusatory style. Triply unimpeachable in that he speaks from the triple depths of the people, the camps, and exile, Solzhenitsyn is the reincarnation of the great intellectual—Voltaire, Victor Hugo, Zola—who denounces the powers that be and shows how they can be resisted. Has he really opened people's eyes; has he really been a lever? At any rate, far from bringing about a critical and rational reassessment of Marx stripped of Soviet or Chinese dogma, Solzhenitsyn has encouraged a new libertarianism, of which André Glucksmann is a good representative,[33] to enclose Marx entirely within the Soviet socialist experiment, the better to consign both to flames. For good measure, and in order to reassure those who might feel guilty about such apostasy, the entire tradition of western rationalism from Plato and Descartes to Marx is also tossed into the fire. With the result that, on this interminable pre-electoral eve during which intellectuals have ample opportunity to air their views, the Left is split between those who believe that the Soviet Union is not the homeland of socialism (which has yet to be invented) and those who are persuaded that the Soviet Union is, alas, the model of socialism, and that the Union de la Gauche will lead us directly to it. As always, though, this new extremism leaves out America, eternally absent.

Thus it is neither the Soviet phenomenon nor the phenomenon of Marxism which constitutes the line of demarcation between France and the United States; it is rather, within each culture, the idea of Revolution itself,[34] the *mater et magistra* of the European intelligentsia. It seems to me that the major difference lies in the fact that in France the revolution occurred in a country which had already had a long history, a powerful collective conscience, and a strong tradition of centralized state power. The revolutionary upheaval never became an accepted fact; it only provided the pattern of Right vs. Left inside which all subsequent history was acted out. The revolution had barely begun to seep into the depths of society with the victory of the secular Republic in the late nineteenth and early twentieth centuries, when the Russian revolution (first and foremost) arrived on the scene, followed by those of China and the Third World; thus providing ancient France, whose revolution had never really been completed, with a series of messianic relays whose high points were the Popular Front, the Resistance, and the Algerian War. In no other country has the Communist Party acquired such a universal legitimacy and put down such deep roots—nor such disproportionate ones compared to its actual strength—in the national culture and memory. The extent to which the Party has used and abused this credit involves a great deal of history, for which it is now paying a heavy price among intellectuals. One wonders whether it will not also pay a price among tomorrow's electorate. Still, the fact is that the Party has carried on, right up to the present, the revolutionary idea whose simultaneous death and resurrection we are witnessing today. This is not to say that there have been only leftist intellectuals in France, or only a leftist intellectual tradition. But the Left has directed the intellectual traffic and, in opposition to the established power, it has constituted a counterpower which has given the intelligentsia its prestige. Now the revolutionary idea lies in the heart of a left which is itself located at the heart of the national culture.

The opposite is true of the United States, where leftist extremism has remained marginal, no doubt because the revolution coincided with the founding of the nation. Incorporated from the outset into a heritage that was questioned but nevertheless remained intact, the American revolution established rather than destroyed the consensus. The national ideal absorbed the revolutionary ideal and, rightly or wrongly, claimed to be its realization. America has presented itself, both as a history and as a nation, as the incarnation of a set of values, as the fulfillment of an original promise. Its historical mission was not to have an ideology, but to be one. In other words, whereas in France, Revolution is the eternal future of a country with a long memory, in America it is the eternal past of a nation which has no memory. It is this symmetry which makes for the incommunicability of the two cultures and sets the terms of the impossible dialogue.

The pro- or anti-Americanism of French intellectuals is therefore merely a secondary phenomenon, a mere surface effect linked to the particular vicissitudes of the moment, as compared to a deeper structural reality which is not so much cultural in nature as sociological and historical. The crucial role of circulating cultural values which the intellectuals of the Old World have held since the Age of Enlightenment does not have an equivalent in America, where it has never been necessary. American intellectuals are invested with a function, not a ministry; they exercise a trade not a stewardship. In America the intelligentsia is diffused throughout the political and social body, it is geographically dispersed, culturally scattered, or else confined to the oases of university campuses. The intelligentsia of France, on the other hand, is concentrated in a narrow, isolated social stratum which possesses its own history, its own traditions, its own network of communications, its own conditioned reflexes.

An American intellectual will always have trouble understanding why for twenty years so many young people in France preferred being wrong with Sartre than right with Raymond Aron; and why this youth immediately turned Michel Foucault's historicophilosophical investigations of madness, penology, and sexuality into concrete everyday political issues. He will always have difficulty in understanding why the entire field of French intellectual research is so dominated by political considerations. Inversely, the French will always find it hard to accept the fact that an American can tolerate such a wide gap between his intellectual interests and his specific political commitments. A case in point: the lack of French enthusiasm for Noam Chomsky, a Cartesian in logic and an anarchist in politics. Perhaps the difference is a small one, but it expresses the fact that, since the eighteenth century, France has had a secularized heritage of several hundreds of years of Christian transcendence and the Catholic Church; whereas the United States has not. And that makes it so difficult for us, locked as we are in our intellectual Gallocentrism, to understand the dynamics of a history that is an indissoluble weave of realism and dreams—we who no longer see any choice except conservatism and revolution.

Translated by Michael Taylor

The author and the translator wish to express their thanks to Maria Jolas, who very kindly read the translation and made valuable suggestions for improving it.

REFERENCES

[1]Cf. in particular, in the wake of American cultural anthoropology, the intelligent essay of Louis Dermigny, *USA, essai de mythologie américaine* (Paris: PUF, 1956), Chap. 1, "La mort du père."

[2]The last overview to date: J. B. Duroselle, *La France et les États-Unis, des origines à nos jours* (Paris: Le Seuil, 1976).

[3]For Tocqueville, cf. René Rémond, *Les États-Unis devant l'opinion française, 1815–1852*, 2 vols. (Paris: A Colin, 1962). But one should also mention that excellent observer of Civil War America, Duvergier de Hauranne. An abridged edition of his work is available in France, *Les Etas-Unis pendant la guerre de Sécession, vus par un journaliste français, Ernest Duvergier de Hauranne*, presentée par A. Krebs (1966). The Americans, on the other hand, have published a complete translation of the work, *A Frenchman in Lincoln's America*, translated and edited by R. H. Bowen (Chicago: Donneley, 1974–1975), 2 vols.

[4]I am of course thinking of Raymond Aron and, more recently, of J. F. Revel.

[5]This initial idea as well as some of its ramifications in this article were suggested by Diana Orvieto Pinto, both in pleasant conversations at Harvard and in her unpublished Ph.D. thesis, *Sociology as a Cultural Phenomenon in France and Italy, 1950–1972* (Harvard University, 1977). I take the opportunity to thank her here.

[6]This complements what K. Papalïoannou described in *L'Idéologie froide, essai sur le déperissment du marxisme* (Paris: Pauvert, 1967).

[7]A Gaullist term which provides the title for the second chapter of the final volume of his *Memoires de Guerre* (Paris: Plon, 1959).

[8]One can find a very clear echo of this in the highest governmental circles in those various passages devoted to America in my complete edition of *Vincent Auriol, Journal du Septennat* (vol. 1, 1947), (Paris: A. Colin, 1970).

[9]Speech given on March 5, 1948 at the Salle Pleyel in Paris and published as an appendix to the Pléiade edition of *Les Conquerants* (Paris: Gallimard, 1976).

[10]It was around this time that Marcel Duhamel started Gallimard's incredibly successful "Série Noire," which introduced Chester Himes, Dashiell Hammett, Raymond Chandler, etc. to France.

[11]Does one have to be reminded that Faulkner's reputation rebounded back to the United States from France, and that André Malraux himself wrote a famous preface to *Sanctuary?*

[12]Either in the edition of A. Costes, or in the edition brought out by Editions Sociales, the publishing house of the Communist Party, which was then in the process of accelerating the pace of its official publications.

[13]Cf. David Caute, *Communism and the French Intellectuals, 1914–1966*, translated as *Le Communisme et les Intellectuels français* (Paris: Gallimard, 1967).

[14]Cf. M. A. Burnier, *Les Existentialistes et la Politique* (Paris: Gallimard, "Collection Idées," 1966).

[15]The expression became classic after W. W. Rostow's book, *Stages of Economic Growth*, translated as *Les Etapes de la croissance economique* (Paris: Le Seuil, 1962).

[16]Cf. John Higham (ed.), *The Reconstruction of American History* (London: Hutchins, 1962).

[17]Daniel Bell's celebrated work, *The End of Ideology* (1960) was naturally never translated into French. Later, when it might have been translated, its cultural moment had already passed.

[18]It should be noted that the readership of John K. Galbraith's *The Affluent Society*, published in 1961 in a series edited by Raymond Aron for Calmann-Lévy, which had also published Vance Packard's works, was infinitely smaller than the readership of *The New Industrial State* (1967), translated by Gallimard in the year of its original publication.

[19]Cf. the most recent analysis by an excellent British observer, Godfrey Hudgson, *America in Our Time* (New York: Doubleday, 1977), Chap. 4, "The Ideology of the Liberal Consensus," and Chap. 24, "Ideology and Consensus."

[20]François Furet has argued this point very convincingly as it relates to the black problem in an "analysis" published by the *Nouvel Observateur* entitled "Jimmy Carter, une revolution a l'américaine" (January 24, 1977).

[21]Cf. an attempt to analyze this phenomenon by Elisa Marienstras, *Les mythes fondateurs de la nation américaine* (Paris: Maspero, 1976), and my article "Le fardeau de l'histoire aux Etats-Unis," *Etudes d'Histoire des Relations internationales* (Paris: PUF, 1966), pp. 50–75.

[22]Cf. Annie Kriegel, "Le Parti Communiste Français et la Vème République," published in *Contrepoint* (1973) and included in *Communismes au miroir français* (Paris: Gallimard, 1974), Chap. 11.

[23]David Riesman, *The Lonely Crowd*, translated as *La Foule Solitaire* (Paris: Arthaud, 1964). Together with the translations of Rostow and Galbraith already mentioned, the first and most significant translation of this period was that of W. Whyte Jr.'s *The Organization Man*, *L'Homme de l'Organisation* (Paris: Plon, 1958). It should be remembered that it was Léon Blum who introduced the French to James Burnham's *The Managerial Revolution*, translated just after the war as *L'Ère des Managers* (Paris: Calmann-Lévy, 1947). This was part of that old tradition of attempting to rationalize the management of modern industry which dates back to the thirties and to André Tardieu and the neosocialists. It was, however, soon monopolized by the so-called "synarchic," Vichyist technocratic Right. As a result, it came to incarnate that kind of power against which the intellectuals had never stopped fighting.

[24]F. Furet, "Les intellectuels et le structuralisme," *Preuves* (February 1977).

[25]This is what I had tried to express in an essay of this period entitled *Les Français d'Algérie* (Paris: Julliard, 1961), Chap. 1, "Qu'est-ce qu'un libéral?"

[26]Cf. the interesting line of research suggested on this score by D. Lindenberg, *Le Marxisme introuvable* (Paris: Calmann-Lévy, 1976).

[27]Cf. Althusser's canonical work, *Lire le Capital* (Paris: Maspero, 1965), as well as his "retractions," *Autocritique* (Paris: Maspero, 1975).

[28]Cf. Annie Kriegel, "Communisme et gauchisme d'Europe dans le miroir américain des années 60," Chap. 12 of her *Communismes au miroir français* (Paris: Gallimard, 1974), originally published in English in *Daedalus* under the title "Consistent Misapprehension: European Views of America and Their Logic," *Daedalus*, 101 (4) (Fall 1972). I refer the American reader also to the most complete selection of texts on the 1968 student revolt: Alain Schnapp and Pierre Vidal-Naquet, *The French Student Uprising, November 1967–June 1968* (Boston: Beacon Press, 1971) translated by Maria Jolas.

The introduction relates the French student movement to the international and particularly the American context.

[29]To the extent that Jean-François Revel in *Ni Marx, Ni Jésus* (Paris: Laffont, 1970) considers it the site of "the second world revolution."

[30]Cf. of course Edgar Morin, *Journal de Californie* (Paris: Le Seuil, 1970). It would be interesting to chronicle the ever-growing fascination with America among a fraction of the intellectual "avant-garde" which, since 1968, has never ceased to proclaim its allegiance to the extreme communists, later to the Maoists, and now to the "New Philosophers." Philippe Sollers declares in the last issue (Fall 1977) of his review, *Tel quel*, which is devoted to the United States, that in working on his next book, entitled *Paradise*, "he felt at home in the U.S. . . . ."

[31]One thinks notably of B. Souvarine's *Staline*, which orginally appeared in 1935, and has been very recently republished by Editions Champ Libre (Paris), as well as of the collective mole-like labors of the group assembled around C. Castoriadis in the fifties in the magazine *Socialisme ou Barbarie*—their articles were recently republished in *L'Institution imaginaire de la Société* (Paris: Le Seuil, 1976). Claude Lefort has republished his articles in *Eléments d'une critique de la bureaucratie* (Geneva: Droz, 1971).

[32]The most recent explanations of this are Jean Ellenstein's *Histoire du phénomène stalinien* (Paris: Grasset, 1975) and *Histoire de l'Union Soviétique*, 4 vols. (Paris: Editions Sociales, 1972–1975). The official commentaries of the Socialist Party are in accordance with these.

[33]André Glucksmann, *La cuisinière et le mangeur d'homme, essai sur les camps de concentration* (Paris: Le Seuil, 1975), and more recently, his *Les Maîtres penseurs* (Paris: Grasset, 1977). In an interview recently published in the far-left Italian daily, *Lotta continua*, Simone de Beauvoir more or less excepted André Glucksmann from the excommunication which she and J. P. Sartre have pronounced against the "New Philosophers," who are guilty in their eyes of the worst sin: "They have all been coopted by the Americans" (quoted by *Le Monde*, September 24, 1977).

[34]After all the historiography of the revolutionary period occasioned by the Bicentennial, one returns to Hannah Arendt's *On Revolution* (1963). It was translated in France as *Essai sur la révolution* (Paris: Gallimard, 1967) and met with no success whatsoever.

338

Notes on Contributors

SYDNEY E. AHLSTROM, born in 1919 in Cokato, Minnesota, is Professor of American History and Modern Religious History at Yale University. His publications include *Theology in America: The Major Protestant Voices from Puritanism to Neo-Orthodoxy* (1967) and *A Religious History of the American People* (1972, National Book Award 1973) together with many articles.

McGEORGE BUNDY was born in Boston in 1919. President of The Ford Foundation, he is the coauthor, with Henry L. Stimson, of *On Active Service in Peace and War* (1948), editor of *Pattern of Responsibility* (1952), and author of *The Strength of Government* (1968).

JOHN T. DUNLOP was born in 1914 in Placerville, California. Now Lamont University Professor, Harvard University, he was United States Secretary of Labor from March 1975 to January 1976. His publications include *Wage Determination under Trade Unions* (1944, 1950); with Derek Bok, *Labor and the American Community* (1970); and, as editor, *The Lessons of Wage and Price Controls—The Food Sector* (1977).

EDWARD K. HAMILTON was born in 1939 in Minneapolis, Minnesota. He is President of Hamilton-Rabinovitz, Inc., and Adjunct Professor of Public Management at the University of California at Los Angeles. Coauthor of *Setting National Priorities, The 1971 Budget* (1970), he was director of the commissions that produced *Partners in Development*, Report of the Commission on International Development (the Pearson Commission) (1969) and *To Serve Seven Million*, Report of the Public Commission on Los Angeles County Government (1976).

ELIZABETH HARDWICK was born in Lexington, Kentucky in 1916. A writer, critic, and advisory editor of the *New York Review of Books*, she has published two novels and a book of essays. Her latest book, *Seduction and Betrayal: Women in Literature* (1974), was a nominee for a National Book Award.

ROSABETH MOSS KANTER was born in 1943 in Cleveland, Ohio. Associate Professor of Sociology at Yale University, her publications include *Commitment and Community* (1972), *Another Voice: Feminist Perspectives on Social Life and Social Science* (1975), and *Work and Family in the United States: A Critical Review and Agenda for Research and Policy* (1977).

RONALD I. McKINNON, born in 1935 in Canada, is Professor of Economics at Stanford University. He is the author of *Money and Capital in Economic Development* (1973), *Money in International Exchange: The Convertible Currency System* (to appear in 1978), and numerous articles on international trade and finance.

STEVEN MULLER was born in 1927 in Hamburg, Germany. He is President of The Johns Hopkins University and The Johns Hopkins Hospital. Author of articles in *Foreign Affairs, World Politics, American Political Science Review*, and *Bulletin of the Atomic Sciences*, he also has written *Documents on European Government* (1963).

PIERRE NORA, born in 1931 in Paris, France, is Directeur d'Études at the École des Hautes Études en Sciences Sociales, Paris. Author of *Les Français d'Algérie* (1961), he is also editor of *Vincent Auriol, Journal du Septennat, 1947* (1970) and, in collaboration with Jacques de Goff, of *Faire de l'Histoire* (3 vol., 1974).

ANTHONY SMITH, born in 1938 in London, is a television producer who writes on media affairs and who contributed to the recent national inquiry into the future of broadcasting in the United Kingdom. His publications include *The Shadow in the Cave: The Broadcaster, the Audience, and the State* (1975) and *The Politics of Information: Problems in Communications* (forthcoming).

THOMAS SOWELL was born in 1930 in Gastonia, North Carolina. Now Visiting Professor of Economics at Amherst College, he wrote this paper while a Fellow at the Center for Advanced Study in the Behavioral Sciences, Stanford, California. His publications include *Economics: Analysis and Issues* (1971), *Black Education* (1972); *Classical Economics Reconsidered* (1974), and, as editor, *American Ethnic Groups* (forthcoming).

PAUL STARR, born in 1949 in New York City, is a Junior Fellow, Society of Fellows, Harvard University. He is author of *The Discarded Army: Veterans after Vietnam* (1973).

NANCY NEEDHAM WARDELL was born in 1941 in Chicago. At present a consultant on strategic planning and antitrust litigation at the Cambridge Research Institute and part-time lecturer at the Boston University School of Management in business and public policy, she has served on the faculty of the Harvard Business School, where she developed numerous case studies.

LOUISE WEINBERG, born in 1932 in New York City, is Associate Professor of Law at Suffolk University Law School. Her publications include articles on federal courts and the federal system, the conflict of laws, and the remedial power of courts. This article was written while she was visiting Associate Professor of Law at Stanford Law School, on leave from Suffolk University 1976–1977.

MARVIN E. WOLFGANG was born in 1924 in Millersburg, Pennsylvania. He is Professor of Sociology and Law and Director, Center for Studies in Criminology and Criminal Law, University of Pennsylvania. His publications include *Patterns in Criminal Homicide* (1958), *Subcultures of Violence* (1967), and *Delinquency in a Birth Cohort* (1972) as well as numerous articles and edited books.

ADAM YARMOLINSKY, born in 1922 in New York City, is Ralph Waldo Emerson University Professor at the University of Massachusetts. He is the author of *Recognition of Excellence* (1961), *The Military Establishment* (1971), and many journal articles.

DANIEL YERGIN, born in 1947 in Los Angeles, is lecturer at the Harvard Business School and in the Department of Government at Harvard University. He is the author of *Shattered Peace: The Origins of the Cold War and the National Security State* (1977).

ELLIOT ZASHIN was born in 1940 in New York City. Associate Professor of Public Management, Graduate School of Management, Northwestern University, he is the author of *Civil Disobedience and Democracy* (1972).

Index